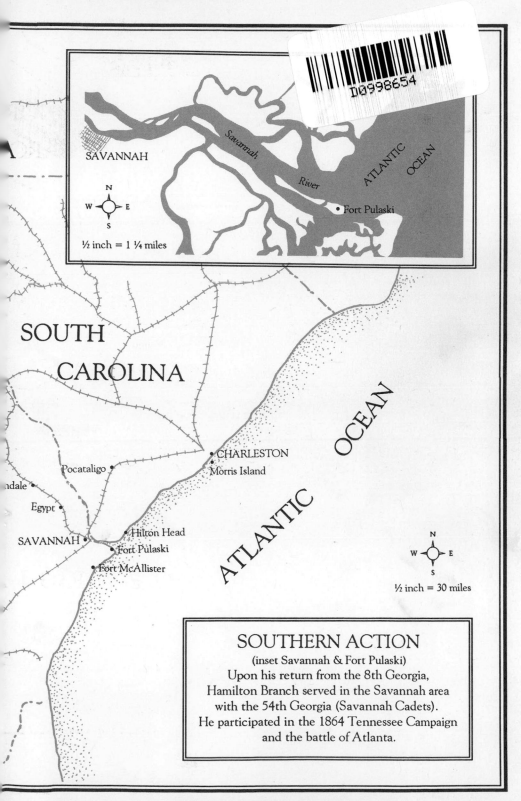

SAVANNAH

Savannah River

ATLANTIC OCEAN

N
W E
S

½ inch = 1 ¼ miles

Fort Pulaski

SOUTH

CAROLINA

Pocataligo

ndale

Egypt

SAVANNAH

Hilton Head

Fort Pulaski

Fort McAllister

CHARLESTON

Morris Island

OCEAN

ATLANTIC

N
W E
S

½ inch = 30 miles

SOUTHERN ACTION
(inset Savannah & Fort Pulaski)
Upon his return from the 8th Georgia,
Hamilton Branch served in the Savannah area
with the 54th Georgia (Savannah Cadets).
He participated in the 1864 Tennessee Campaign
and the battle of Atlanta.

CHARLOTTE'S BOYS

Civil War Letters of the

Branch Family of Savannah

Mauriel Phillips Joslyn

CHARLOTTE'S BOYS
Civil War Letters of the
Branch Family of Savannah

Mauriel Phillips Joslyn

Rockbridge Publishing Company
Berryville, Virginia

Published by

Rockbridge Publishing Company
Post Office Box 351
Berryville, VA 22611
(540) 955-3980

ISBN 1-883522-12-9
Library of Congress Number 96-68733

10 9 8 7 6 5 4 3 2 1
First Edition

Contents

PREFACE

Letters are a tapestry, their words threads that weave the image of an individual whose existence is otherwise lost to time. They carry us through the lives of their writers, compressing lifetimes into a matter of pages and hours. Loved ones are introduced, then disappear; new names replace those deleted by death or superseded by new acquaintances. So it was with the Branch family of Savannah.

They were typical of their class: Charlotte, the widowed mother, and her three sons, John, Sanford and Hamilton, called Hammie. They were typically tragic in the battering they sustained, caught up in the whirlwind of war.

I discovered their letters in a manuscript collection at the Hargrett Library at the University of Georgia in Athens while researching a book about 600 Confederate officers. It was a long shot, but I checked the library's holdings for any of the sixty Georgians on my list, one of whom was Sanford W. Branch. Amazingly, his name was in the card catalog. The Branch family and I met over a large mahogany table in a quiet reading room one winter's day in 1992. I was the only one there, yet the spirit of the participants in the letters surrounded me. What I found was a remarkable story of survival, courage, and love, with a cast of characters as diverse as a novel.

Sanford, the middle of three brothers, was the main focus of my work, due to his direct involvement in my book at the time. He held his dying elder brother in his arms at 1st Manassas, then later he himself was severely wounded and listed as dead at Gettysburg. He survived only to begin a new role as a prisoner of war, an extraordinary role that he played for eighteen months.

I worked on the book all that spring and summer. Sanford was only a minor player in the action, but I never forgot his family. "Perhaps another project one day," I said to myself, and let it go at that.

In October 1993 I visited an exhibit at the Atlanta History Center. "Gone for a Soldier" contained well displayed and documented artifacts and military items of Civil War soldiers. I strolled from one glass case to another, but my heart bounded when I found myself staring at a handsome uniform of the Oglethorpe Light Infantry, the uniform of Lt. John L. Branch of Savannah—Sanford's elder brother.

Through that exciting chance encounter on that brisk fall day I met Gordon Jones, curator and designer of the exhibit. He showed me the part of the collection not on display—photographs of Sanford and his brothers and many more items that had belonged to them: uniforms, swords and personal treasures. My fate was sealed. I knew I had to see their story told. I had to publish their letters, and so began the task of transcribing all 312 of them.

I had "known" Sanford for three years at that point, yet his brothers and mother were virtual strangers. Soon I could recognize their handwriting at a glance and quickly caught on to Hammie's peculiar habit of not crossing his t's and Charlotte's phonetic spellings, while the vernacular of their speech reminded me of my own grandparents' voices. They became like members of my own family.

The boys' personality characteristics were reflected in their writings. John was serious, responsible and ambitious, mature at an early age. Sanford was the dutiful son, reticent but dependable, with a sensitivity toward others. Hammie, the baby, whose youthful innocence contrasted starkly with the grisly horror of his battlefield surroundings, grew to manhood through the years of war.

The secondary correspondents are themselves noteworthy, and are useful in filling in information. Because so few of John's letters have survived, we come to know him largely through the observations and impressions of others. Tallulah Hansell imparts to us the portrait of a sensitive young man, whom she judged through the intimacy of love, a classic tragic hero whose destiny is inexorable.

I looked forward to the time spent with them, hearing their story unfold through laughter, tears and sometimes anger. To keep those feelings fresh, I transcribed the letters with no grammatical or spelling corrections and added only minimal punctuation.

Initially, the letters sometimes raised more questions than they answered, and I had to look for answers from the secondary correspondents and identify the friends they mention. I was immediately misled by the endearing terms of "cousin" and "aunt and uncle" used for apparently everybody the family knew. Orlando and Laura Lufburrow figure prominently in the boys' affections. I was fortunate enough to meet Mr. Albert Lufburrow, Orlando's great nephew, who has thoroughly researched his family history. But the Branches were not blood relations, despite John's middle name—Lufburrow.

Another mystery I hoped to solve was the whereabouts of the items I knew Tallulah had owned—photographs of the family, a locket with John's hair and a spoon engraved with their names. Lula, as she was called, had married John Pelham's brother William. Through the John Pelham Historical Society I contacted Peggy Vogtsberger, who gave me the name of Dan Sullivan, Lula's grandson. Alas, they had none of the hoped-for artifacts, yet I did learn the circumstances of Lula's later life. One letter from Charlotte, written after the war, revealed where she was living in 1868.

Other occasional correspondents remain beyond any firm identity. But it was the family themselves who painted a vivid picture for me. Woven throughout the letters from the warfront are the human stories, the friendships and beating hearts whose names comprised the Oglethorpe Light Infantry and the Savannah Cadets.

When I first met the Branch family, it was as if a wall separated us. From my side of the wall, in the present, I could touch only its surface and know little of the family beyond it. Through the words of others and their faces in photographs, I could glimpse their personalities. But it was by reading their letters that I came to know them intimately. I put my ear to the wall, and although it was 130 years wide, their lives were revealed to me as vividly as if I had stepped into their presence. Their soft Savannah accents whispered from the pages. This is the story I heard. It is as much a tribute to a mother's devotion and faith as it is to the courage and sacrifice of her soldier sons.

ACKNOWLEDGEMENTS

Bringing the Branch family's story to print required a hefty amount of research and was a personally rewarding experience for me. But it would not have been possible without the help of many individuals. When an author undertakes the study and quest for details necessary for a project like this, she is given a rare opportunity—one that puts her in touch with otherwise unknown and dedicated people whose names are not yet household words, but which I think should be. I consider myself fortunate to have made their acquaintance, and my thanks are extended to the following:

Gordon Jones, Curator of Military Artifacts at the Atlanta History Center, gave of his valuable time to allow me to see all the Branch brothers' personal belongings and worked with me on speculation and details to solve mysteries. His assistant, Kirk Henderson, also deserves a thank you. Both were patient, and I appreciate their dedication and respect for the family treasures.

Mary Ellen Brooks, Director of Special Collections at Hargrett Library, University of Georgia, was invaluable. She gave permission for the use of the letters, and without her they would still be buried in folders waiting to speak. Her cooperation while the 312 letters were transcribed and double-checked to ensure that none were missed is very much appreciated. Melissa Bush, also at Hargrett, was patient with special copying requests and arrangements, carefully assuring that every copy was legible. She greatly aided my task.

Of course, Savannah held the key to a large part of the research. The staff at the Georgia Historical Society came to recognize my face on visits there as I sought clues about the history of the Oglethorpe Light Infantry and Savannah Cadets. Norman Turner of the Georgia National Guard deserves a thank you for his searches to find the flag of the O.L.I. at the armory in Savannah.

Mr. Albert Lufburrow of Savannah helped to clarify family relationships, intrigued at the Branches's closeness to his ancestors. Reese and Carol Shellman, also of Savannah, provided information on his great-great-uncle, William Shellman, who succeeded John Branch as adjutant of the 8th Georgia. Paul Blatner graciously allowed me to photograph Lt. Fred Bliss's uniform and presented me with the gift of a whiskey bottle embossed "S.W. Branch Grocery." It is a prize I treasure.

At Fort Pulaski Superintendent John Breen and Ranger Tally Kirkland, with whom I have worked on other projects, were, as usual, helpful and a pleasure to visit.

Since the Branches have no descendants, the only "family" I found was that of Tallulah Hansell. Her grandson, Mr. Dan Sullivan of Marietta, was a gem to discover. He provided details of Lula's life before and after the letters, and I reciprocated with her letters, revealing a facet of his grandmother's life of which the family had previously known nothing—her first love, John Branch.

The military history of the war was so intertwined with the lives of the writers, especially Hamilton, that I sought expertise in that field for my narrative. This led me to Thomas Cartwright, Curator of the Carter House Museum in Franklin, Tennessee, one of the most dedicated people I have ever met to preserving this special place associated with the war. He gave generously of his time, and I am indebted to him. Also, Tim Burgess of White House, Tennessee, helped me find Lula's friend, Lt. William Spencer, who was killed at Franklin. Tim continues his research to tell the story of all the Confederate soldiers who, like Lt. Spencer, sacrificed their lives at Franklin; he has my best wishes for his project.

For the Atlanta Campaign, Dennis Kelly at Kennesaw Mountain Battlefield Park amazed me. He critiqued my narrative and made many valuable suggestions which I gratefully incorporated. William Scaife must be the most noted map maker of the war since Jedediah Hotchkiss, and I was thrilled at his consent to use his maps for the military locations described by Hamilton.

Mr. Scott Sheads at Fort McHenry is a scholar on the prisoners confined there. He confirmed my details on Sanford's prison time there and is doing commendable work in an area of the war largely neglected.

Last of all, I thank my family—my husband Rick and sons Nick and Alex—who have lived with John, Santy and Hammie for over a year and who with me have come to adopt them as our own.

INTRODUCTION

Savannah, Georgia, was founded in 1733 by a visionary and idealist, Gen. James Edward Oglethorpe. He asked the native Creek Indians for the use of their land to establish a town to be built on the fundamental premise of equality in all areas, with a portion of land of the same quality reserved for the use of the tribe outside the town limits. Tomachichi, their chief, and Oglethorpe were good friends, and the natives and colonists, called Free-holders, lived in harmony and peace.

Savannah's first citizens each were given a lot of 60x90 feet for a dwelling house. Farms were strictly limited to fifty acres per family to insure that no one had more land than they could tend. Inheriting and uniting the lots by marriage was forbidden to prevent the rich from monopolizing the country.[1]

The city was designed with wards of forty houses each that were supervised by a constable and four tithing men. Squares were set aside between wards for the use of outlying farmers in case war or another emergency brought them inside the town fortifications. They could camp on the squares and use them to graze their stock.[2]

Oglethorpe was concerned that the free labor enjoyed by slaveholders would reduce the need for the services of skilled craftsmen in town, so slavery was forbidden.[3] This decree was eventually lifted as the interior became largely rice plantations, yet even in 1860 only 8% of the residents of surrounding Chatham County were slaveholders.

Despite her British heritage, Savannah was an American city, and she joined with the fight for independence in 1775. Her militia, the Liberty Boys, fought with distinction, yet the British captured the city in 1778 and practiced many cruelties and atrocities upon her residents.

Savannah blossomed after the Revolution only to be engulfed by a disastrous fire in 1796. In four hours an estimated 300 houses burned; two-thirds of the city was in ruin. Four hundred families were destitute, and most of its colonial heritage was reduced to charred rubble.[4] The destruction of the fire necessitated new building, and many well-known architects and builders from the North left their mark on the graceful buildings that line her streets today.

Savannah was generous in her prosperity. A poorhouse and hospital established in 1811 cared for indigents, both white and black. The Savannah Widow's Society, formed in 1822, provided care for women whether they had children or not; the lots for its housing were donated by the city. Several orphanages were established between 1810 and 1844, and the Union Society, one of the city's oldest charitable organizations, established the Bethesda Orphanage in 1854, during the height of the worst yellow fever epidemic in Savannah's history. By 1860 there were 45 charitable societies or institutions in operation.[5]

With the invention of the cotton gin, the agrarian utopia of Oglethorpe passed into the hands of New England merchants and immigrants from Ireland, Germany and other European countries and evolved into a cosmopolitan commercial center. The 1848 census reveals that among Savannah's population of 2,201 were 552 native Georgians, 682 from other parts of the United States and 807 who had been born abroad.[6] In 1860 only 2% of Georgia's population was foreign-born, compared to 27% of Savannah's 22,292 residents, largely due to the influx of Irish in the 1840s. Yet she was distinctly Southern in her way of life.[7]

Among the Northerners who came to Savannah was John Henry Salah Branch of Providence, Rhode Island, sometime prior to 1835. The oldest son of Sandford and Matilda Cady Branch, he began his career in Savannah as a dry goods merchant. His business prospered, and on March 15, 1837, he married a local girl, Charlotte Sarah Sawyer.

Charlotte and her mother were of modest means and had experienced much sadness. Sarah McDevit Sawyer, from County Tyrone, Ireland, married Walker Colburn Sawyer, a New Hampshire sailor, and on September 20, 1814, she gave birth to their only child, Charlotte. Walker Sawyer died aboard ship four years later and was buried at sea. Charlotte grew up in Savannah, where her mother owned a millinery shop. She learned the trade of dressmaking, and their family business made a good living.[8]

Charlotte and Henry enjoyed Savannah's Golden Age, the period from 1830–1860, the zenith of the plantation system, when land values increased, commodity markets rose constantly and fortunes were made.

Their first son, John Lufburrow, was born on the Sabbath, March 4, 1838. Sanford Walker, known affectionately as Santy, was born on March 17, 1840, and Hamilton McDevit, called Hammie, was born precisely three years later, on March 17, 1843.

Branch's business grew, although occasionally he was forced to barter to settle the debts of his customers. Though not previously a slaveholder, in 1839 he accepted in payment a young slave girl named Sally. She would remain as a member of the family far into the future.

Tragedy struck the family in 1847, suddenly and without warning. John Henry Branch, in his prime at age 43, died of "convulsions." Charlotte, age 33, was a widow with three small children. Her husband seems to have left her well provided for, and she apparently sold his business. In 1850, she, her boys and her mother were living together at 180 (now 212) Broughton Street, where they ran a millinery and dressmaker's shop in the three-story dwelling. The two upper floors were home to the extended family and two apprentices—Georgia Elkins was then about ten years old, and Sarah Allen was about twelve.

It was a comfortable middle-class existence in the heart of the city, where life centered around church, community and jobs. The Branches attended Independent Presbyterian Church at the corner of South Broad and Bull. The wide dirt street in front of their house was a constant scene of activity with the horse-drawn conveyances of the rich, wagons loading and unloading merchandise and street vendors plying their wares. In wet weather the city plowed the streets to aid the runoff, and the road crews were followed by little boys wading in the furrows, up to their knees in water. Gangs of stevedores on the river docks handled cotton headed to European markets, while at the wharf of the Central Railroad others loaded freight bound inland.

This was the world in which John, Sanford and Hamilton spent their boyhood. Like the sons of the other merchants, they played in the squares and on the fortifications that had been built around the city for the War of 1812. They attended public schools, probably Chatham Academy, founded in 1813, and went to Sunday school. Even as children they exhibited a patriotic character, as evidenced by the certificates they received in 1850 for contributing one dollar each to the Washington National Monument Society toward completion of the obelisk to Gen. George Washington on the Mall in the District of Columbia. Their great-grandfather, Stephen Branch, had been one of the rebels of Capt. Willett's company on the green in Lexington, Massachusetts, that April 19th morning in 1775. Their mother considered them her most cherished possessions, and amid an atmosphere of love and nurturing, they passed a happy, though fatherless childhood.

John, as the eldest, was given preference for an education. Upon him rested the family's hopes; a good career was of the utmost importance. He went away to school in Wilmington, Delaware, in January 1850. On January 8, Charlotte wrote to her son, "It is very painful to be seperated from you . . . but I submit to it fully believeing it is for your benefit, for you will there have advantages of study that you cannot have here. . . . When I look at you and think what a responsable situation you are placed in (that of an older brother) I allmost tremble for you, I know it is an arduous one, but then think what an honour to be guide to your two dear little brothers. What a comefort when you are a man (if God should spare your life) to think you have never set them a bad example."[9] On his sixteenth birthday, in a letter written from New York, Charlotte exhorted him to "govern his passions" and "remember the eye of God is on you in every place." In the same letter she wrote, "I have just thought of something which a lady told me this evening which I must tell you as it will show you how much Sanford loves you. She sayed that one day she sayed to Sanford, you are a smart boy. He looked at her for a second. Who me do you mean? Why if you were to see my brother John you would see a smart boy and then he went on to tell her how smart and good and beautiful you were. Oh think of that and never let your lips pronounce the harsh words they once did to him."[10]

John attended Georgia Military Institute 1853–1855. He was a good student and studied math and engineering, careers that would ensure a successful life. While there he met Tallulah Hansell, the daughter of a prominent Marietta attorney and judge. Lula was quite attractive, and the family were known for their open hospitality to cadets at the institute. She had many friends among the boys, but none as close as John Branch. The two spent hours together, and he confided in Lula his dreams and aspirations, but after two years, at age seventeen, he returned to Savannah to take his place as breadwinner of the family.

During the 1850s the South felt more and more ignored by a federal congress that largely represented industrial interests and had little empathy with an agrarian society. Secession was a word heard more and more frequently among politicians, and Savannahians, with their long military tradition, were not to be caught off guard.

John Branch was attracted to the Oglethorpe Light Infantry, which was established in 1855 by Georgia Military Institute graduates, now embarked on careers as doctors and lawyers and merchants, to keep up their military skills. The idea seemed destined to failure, as Savannah already had her share of prestigious militia units, but they felt that if they were to make theirs the best—a crack company well drilled and disciplined—they would attract a full company of members. Every younger brother over the age of sixteen was enticed to join. Sanford was recruited, but Hamilton, age fourteen, was too young. Soon they had a roster of fifty members.

"From the very first day's recruiting we felt sure of success," wrote Charleton Way, the junior second lieutenant. "We proceeded to organize, select a name, elect our officers formally and begin our drills. We used to meet in an informal manner at Capt. Grant's office, or at the store of Monsieur Pierre Berane, corner of Bay and Drayton, and we drilled in the old St. John's Church building on South Broad street, next door to the Waldburg house. Then the city fathers, recognizing that we had come to stay, gave us a habitation and a home in the third story of the Exchange building. We were the first company to adopt and drill by Hardee's Tactics, and so people were anxious to see the new uniforms and the new style of drilling." [11]

The Oglethorpes were a family company, comprising many friends and fellow worshippers from the Independent Presbyterian Church. The first captain, John N. Lewis, was deemed incompetent by the men under him, and he was replaced early in 1856 by a 39-year-old Savannah attorney, Francis Stebbins Bartow. [12] Bartow quickly pulled the company together, and, with his enthusiasm and resolve, the young men attained much praise and attention for their improved military bearing. Their first parade was held on January 8, 1856, with John Branch as second sergeant and Sanford as a private. As their reputation grew, the best of Savannah flocked to their colors.

By their first anniversary in 1857 John Branch had been promoted to fourth lieutenant, and his dedication impressed Bartow. The Oglethorpes held an anniversary ball supported by the elite, and John entered the society class of Savannah. At that time he was a bookkeeper for Padelford, Fay & Co., commission and forwarding merchants, at 104 Bay Street. By 1860 he was employed by S.B. Levy, another commission merchant at 96 Bay Street, an ambitious young man whose future seemed bright and successful. [13] The company was incorporated by an act of the state legislature on December 11, 1858, and on October 6, 1859, John Branch was commissioned fourth lieutenant of the Oglethorpe Light Infantry.

Sanford drilled under his brother in the Oglethorpes and clerked in a hardware store, then later clerked for druggist James H. Carter, whose apothecary was just a few doors from Charlotte's shop. [14] Hammie, who was too young for the militia, clerked in a shoe and boot store. Neither he nor Sanford had the benefit of education that John had received, but they were intelligent boys who were willing to work.

The upcoming presidential election of 1860 was a hot topic on the streets of Savannah that summer and fall. When Abraham Lincoln won the election, her citizens were deeply affected. The city council stockpiled ammunition for the militia companies and selected a site for a city magazine. A public meeting held at the Masonic Hall at the corner of Bull and Broughton, drew a large crowd, with more congregated outside than inside. Capt. Bartow spoke for all Savannahians when he said, "If any man is to peril life, fortune and honor in defense of our rights, I claim to be one of these men. . . . I do not wish to destroy the government. I am a Union man in every fiber of my heart. . . but I will peril all—ALL—before I will abandon our rights in the Union or submit to be governed by an unprincipled majority."[15]

The band played "Dixie" and "La Marseillaise" while citizens held torches and cheered. It was resolved that there should be a state convention to decide how to resist Lincoln's election. Bartow, by then a state politician, convinced Savannah to take the lead in what would become a secessionist movement.[16]

When news of South Carolina's secession reached Savannah on December 20, the city went wild. In Johnson Square the whole city acted on its anger at Northern pomposity. The colonial flag of Georgia, a white state seal on a blue background, was hoisted at the Nathaniel Greene monument. Beneath it a platform for speakers was graced by a large framed picture of a rattlesnake with the words "Don't Tread On Me," a reminder of earlier rebels. Badges and palmetto cockades with the same inscription were prevalent, and the word secession was heard in many conversations. Many patriotic speeches were made by men of status as well as law students exercising their oratory abilities and youths anxious to join the military service of their state.[17] The meeting ended, but feelings brewed. Georgia moved inexorably into the fray.

On March 4, 1850, Charlotte had unwittingly foreshadowed events to come in a letter to her children written while she was away on a visit. "John's birthday—he is 12 today. God grant he may live to be a good man and useful in his day and generation. I hope I shall be at home on my dear Sanford and Hamilton's birthday. Santie will be 10 on the 17th and Hamilton 7. Will they all live to be useful good men? If I thought they would not, I should pray God to take them out of the world, before the evil days come."[18]

In 1861, when Charlotte's boys had barely attained manhood, the evil days dawned in a storm of conflict that tore asunder all in its path and changed forever the course of the lives of those who survived its wrath.

With all of her sons gone to war, Charlotte penned this passionate song.

TO MY SONS IN VIRGINIA
(to the tune of Bonnie Blue Flag)

My children I have sent thee forth
To battle for the right
God gave each youthful arm the power
He gives to men of might
Anxious will be my throbbing heart
At every passing tale
Thy Mother's soul shall falter not
Although her cheeks grow pale

My hand upon your bended heads
In blessing I have laid
And to the righteous Lord of Hosts
This was the prayer I made
Oh let my children gracious God
Be Thy peculiar care
Be with them in the battlefield
Be with them through the war

Keep from their young and manly forms
The scrouge Disease away
Keep stainless still their honour bright
Keep pure their hearts I pray
I did not ask He'd give the strength
All valiant deeds to dare
I felt full well my gallant boys
Knew no such word as fear

Boys you have won a high renown
Think of your freeborn Sire
Strike for the Mother that gave you birth
Your native home and fires
Think of their watchword who assail
Press hard the savage foe
Nor pause until its stars grow pale,
Their treacherous flag lies low.

C.S.B.

CHAPTER ONE

The Corps Made a Fine Appearance

It was the third of January, 1861, months before Fort Sumter would be fired upon. The newly completed Fort Pulaski on Cockspur Island in the Savannah River was there for the taking. In the first overt act of war against federal authorities, the prize was claimed by Capt. Francis S. Bartow and a detachment of the Oglethorpe Light Infantry, Savannah's esteemed militia unit.

John Lufburrow Branch, age 22, the third lieutenant, marched to the wharf at the end of West Broad Street with his friends on that cold, rainy day and boarded the sidewheeler *Ida* with baggage and arms. As they prepared to disembark at the north wharf on Cockspur Island, about twelve miles down the river, the sun burst from behind the clouds, as if it endorsed the venture.

The few men of the caretaker force at the fort were under the command of an ordnance sergeant who surrendered gratefully. Once inside the fort, the Oglethorpes found not a single serviceable gun. The moat was filled with mud and overgrown with marsh grass.

The Oglethorpes diligently remounted some old naval guns dating from 1840 and established daily boat contact with Savannah. Slaves were brought out from the rice plantations to clear the moat of grass. They stowed their ammunition in the magazines, sorted their camp baggage and drilled in the manual of arms under the able supervision of the Chatham Artillery. Over the weeks, they would rotate duty with the militia companies remaining in Savannah as citizen soldiers, the Republican Blues, Georgia Hussars, Savannah Volunteer Guards, Chatham and Savannah Artillery, Irish Jasper Greens, City Light Guard, Phoenix Riflemen and Irish Volunteers.[19]

The O.L.I. settled into their first wartime garrison, alert and ready for a challenge. For five years the unit had drilled for this—the defense of Georgia.

Capt. Bartow, a politician who favored secession, left the O.L.I. in charge of Fort Pulaski and hurried to Milledgeville, then the capital of Georgia, where the Georgia Secession Convention was to meet in the State House on January 16, 1861. Nearly every prominent public figure in the state was a member.

There, in Fort Pulaski, John Branch decided to pursue a military career. The serious, responsible young graduate of the Georgia Military Institute was becoming a soldier, and he requested an appointment in the regular Confederate service. Bartow acted in his favor.

Capt. Francis S. Bartow to Lt. John L. Branch

Milledgeville January 11, 1861
My Dear Branch

I received your letter this morning, and I make time for a short answer. I am glad to hear that you had no trouble at the fort. Keep the company in good order. There will be I think some sharp work, before this business is over. I have no belief in peaceable secession. I will be with you at the first moment when needed. I will keep a look out for you. Don't give up your business yet. There is plenty of time. I will let you know when there is any opening. So far there is nothing but volunteer service. We were occupied all day yesterday in organizing the commissions today in hearing two long speeches from Mr. [James Lawrence] Orr of SC and Mr. [John Gill] Shorter of Alabama. We have so far done nothing. Tomorrow I shall insist on going to work & having the ordinance of secession passed by Saturday. We have a decided majority & I hope we may have unanimity.

I am very tired of this place and would much rather be at Fort Pulaski. Give my love to all my children [the boys of the O.L.I.].

Affectionately yours
F.S. Bartow

Bartow and Georgia governor Joseph Brown agreed on the issue of secession, but they fell out entirely over the disposition of state militia units. Brown wanted supreme command over the Georgia militia, demanding that they be kept in state. Bartow insisted that the Oglethorpes would offer their services to the Confederacy as part of the provisional army. They exchanged heated correspondence, which the newspapers were quick to publish, resulting in strained relations between Savannahians and their governor. The bickering continued for weeks.[20]

Capt. Francis S. Bartow to Lt. John Branch

Savannah January 28, 1861

My Dear Branch

I think I have secured a place for you but say nothing about it. I will be down Wednesday. Don't make any change in your business arrangements—for [everything] in this world is uncertain especially politicians. One thing I promise, that if there is any fighting to be done, you shall have a chance with me—in some way. Don't let the OLI go down—I wish you could make a Battalion of them—I think I see how to use them. But I will talk this over with you when we meet. In the meantime keep up the Company.

Faithfully your Friend
F.S. Bartow

On February 7, 1861, John was appointed first lieutenant in the 2nd Georgia.

Capt. Francis S. Bartow to Lt. John Branch

Montgomery Feb. 12, 1861

My Dear Branch,

I received your letter yesterday, dated from Oglethorpe Barracks, & informing me of your appointment. I congratulate you on this gratification of your desire to enter the Military Service. I have acted in permitting your wishes, rather from my great desire to oblige you, than because my judgement was satisfied that you had made a wise selection of a profession. If the present unhappy state of the country shall terminate in war, why then I heartily approve as you know—But if we have no war, as is quite probable—Then the military service is the last place I would advise a friend to enter. However supposing you to be fixed in your determination I will do all I can, to assure you a position & promote your interests.

What the picking of this government will be cannot be determined until our new President is inaugurated—and the executive departments organized. I hope we shall have no difficulty in transferring our state officers, but I regret to see that Gov. Brown's appointments are objectionable, and may create trouble here, but let this remain with you.

I advise you by all means to remain in Col. [William J.] Hardee's regiment. I have many just reasons for this counsel, & I desire to impress it on you as very important to you. And now go to work like a man and study your profession. Don't stop at mere tactics—but put your mind on all that you ought to know. In this matter you will find Col. Hardee a safe counsellor and guide. Above all take care to preserve your moral habits from all taint & your good manners from the slightest deterioration. A soldier should be a model of honour & propriety & every accomplishment. You see I have time to give you a little lecture though greatly pressed by business. I hope though your relation with me as an officer has ceased, that instead ties of friendship will now remain. The past has been pleasant & I trust the future may be equally so. I shall always watch your career with the interest of true friendship. Write to me sometime. You have not half the work I have. Remember me to your Mother & brothers—& believe me always your friend

F.S. Bartow

Col. William J. Hardee, author of *Hardee's Tactics for Infantry*, had been a U.S. Army officer. He briefly commanded the 1st Georgia Infantry before becoming a lieutenant general in the Confederate States Army. John took a commission in the 1st Georgia on Feb. 16, 1861, under the command of his old classmate from the Georgia Military Institute, Col. Charles Hart Olmstead.

Capt. Francis S. Bartow to Lt. John Branch

Montgomery March 1, '61

My Dear Branch

I received your letter this morning. I have not been unmindful of you & [Thomas Spalding] McIntosh. Whatever influence I have shall be used for you and I think not in vain—But I most probably have to get you appointed in the army of this government. We hope organizations will not be received as organizations into the provisional army—and I think there is good reason for it—But I am sorry for the disappointments this means to many.

By our Constitution the President has the appointing power & therefore it is out of the power of Congress to transfer any body. You see the difficulty—but I will take care of as many as I can. Show this letter to McIntosh. Your Col. [Hardee] is here and I hope he will be put in a position to give him some power.

I am Truly Yours
F. S. Bartow

John was home for a visit in March. When he returned to Fort Pulaski, his mother wrote to him, concerned as always about his comfort, and enclosed word from his brothers, Hamilton (Hammie, age seventeen) and Sanford (Santy, age twenty).

Charlotte Branch to Lt. John Branch

Savannah March 30, 1861

My Dear Son

All of your communications have been rec. and contents noted. I suppose you have not had time to think of us much less to write. You will see by the basket that we have not forgotten that you are at (Fort Pulasky). Santy has asked me several times if I was not going to send you something good to eat, Hammie says no that you will never make a good soldier until you learn to live on soldiers fare.

My dear child my heart is full allmost to bursting when I think that you are now really gone from me—and that ere long home ties will be all most forgotten and worst of all that in the gay life of a soldier you will loose the religious infusions of your childhood. Oh let me entreat you not to forget God my child he is the only sure help at all times he will answer if you call upon him in earnest. It does not make a coward of a man to love and serve God. It makes a truely noble and brave man. Don't be vexed in reading this letter but remember who is the writer and what the love she bears you and how much of her happiness depends on her presious children and particularly on you.

This I hope will find you well and comfortably fixed if I could only come and fix you up a little. Santy and Hammie will attend Nicholl's Easter Ball on Monday night. I hear that it will be well attended. There has been so little amusement this winter that I suppose all are glad of an opportunaty to see and be seen. I do not now of anything new to write about. Walter Chisholm is better. No deaths, no marriages that I hear off: The boys got their new unaform today it is very neet. (When will Fort Sumpter be evacuated)—

. . . If you have time drop me a line or two and be sure to send this basket back, as I shall want it another time. All send love to you. I have many many enquiries of you dayly. As ever my dear child

Your affectionate Mother, C S Branch

[P.S.] When do you think you will be up. Hammie says all the boys but you were in town today, how was that. (Mr. McIver was in town on Wednesday did you see him.) I forgot to say that (I believe) Santy and Hammie will take Miss McI. and Julia Smith to the ball. CSB

An Easter soirée hosted by Mr. J.S. Nichols at St. Andrews Hall on April 1 was announced in the *Savannah Morning News* on March 30, 1861. "Among the most delightful episodes of Savannah life . . . conducted in a manner which never fails to afford to every one present the greatest possible amount of enjoyment."

Lt. John L. Branch to Charlotte Branch

Fort Pulaski April 3rd 1861
Dear Mother

I have received the basket and your several letters particularly the long and interesting one of the 1st inst. . . . The basket was a complete success also particularly the Pies. "Our Mess" the Secession Mess (because we seceded from the old fogies) is composed of most of the young Lieutenants who voted thanks to you through me which you will please accept in this name. We are getting along very well here except that we have (but you must tell no one) a few cases of measles among the men. Give my love to Cousin Laura [Lufburrow] and my tender regards to Miss Jinnie [McLaughlin]. Tell her when next she writes to Miss Kentucky to assure her of my increased attachment. Love to Grandmother [Sarah Sawyer] and all at home.

As ever Your aff. son, John
1st Lieut. 1st Reg. G A

Please send me some stamps both red and blue. JLB

Capt. Francis S. Bartow to Lt. John L. Branch

Savannah, April 7, 1861

My Dear John

I received your letter a day or two since. When you were last in town, I was not at home, and I regretted very much that I did not see you. I have the assurance of the Secretary of War [Leroy P. Walker] that you shall have your appointment, & therefore I am without anxiety on that account. I do not know why it was not make the last time, but it will come in due time. I have not the least doubt as I have his letter to this effect. I am glad you like your profession. I hope you will continue to like it. The heart is the greatest motive power and difficulties are easily surpassed where the way is pleasant. I think you have the qualities for success in military life. But you must not rely on natural gifts however great. Acquire an accurate knowledge of every detail, & pursue an exact system in every particular. Be careful to choose in your own conduct attention to every duty, & exact from those under you the same fidelity. Understand yourself thoroughly everything you have to order others to do—from the smallest detail up to the most complicated work. Be rigid & uncompromising in all matters necessary to duty and discipline, & yet kind and careful of your men. Their health—their comforts, their happiness depends on strict adherence to military rules. At the same time all officers should remember that men cannot & ought not to be turned into machines. Their moral and intellectual wants must be satisfied as far as possible. Study to do good in every way you can, without making the mistake of improper laxity in the inforcement of all the rules of war. Resist familiarity in your intercourse with both superiors & inferiors. You may be courteous & kind without giving any one the advantage of you. Think more than speak. Give no random opinions. Never use oaths or violent expressions of any kind. Gentleness combined with firmness is the texture of the finest nature.

I hope you will forgive this didactic letter. I feel so kindly to you, so much like a brother, that you must attribute my counsel to nothing but affection. I shall always feel a personal interest in whatever you do.

We have rumors of war, but I do not look for it yet. I trust Heaven may save us from civil strife. I cannot bear to think of it. But we can make no safe calculations on such men as are in power at Washington. If war begins it will be at [Fort] Pickens [in Pensacola, Florida]. I do not expect any attempt on Georgia. Should we have war—I will be in the fight, it matters not in what position. But let us hope we may not have to fight our countrymen. I shall hope to see you before I return to Montgomery.

I am truly Your friend
Francis S. Bartow

Charlotte Branch to Lt. John L. Branch

April 10th, 61
My Dear Son,

I cannot help writing to you, it may annoy you, I am so anxious that I can't help writing, there has been a report in town that the soldiers at the fort were to be sent to Florida or Texas and the volunteers were to be sent to the Fort, there are so many stories afloat that I don't know what to believe. Do write occasionally if only to say you are well. I have not seen any one from the Fort since I saw you, Neither of the young men send me word you were well (that is [John MacPherson] Berrien and [Thomas] McIntosh) and neither of them came to see me.

Don't think me foolish my son in writing to you when I really have nothing to write about. I am satisfied now that there will be war and if there is I would not have the slightest obstacle in the way to prevent my Sons from going where duty called them, no not if my heart should brake, May the God of Battles aid us, he is the God of all the earth let us entreat his favour, and try an to live that we may be ready to glorify him either in life or death. Then will all be well with us, with earnest Prayer for you all I am as ever

your affectionate Mother
C S Branch

Lt. John L. Branch to Charlotte Branch

Fort Pulaski April 12th 1861
Dear Mother

I received your letter this morning as it was delayed, why I know not. You need never fear that your letters at any time will prove tiresome to me for I can never be so lost to all true manliness as to forget that you are my mother so please never write that any more. I would have written before but I am so busy that I have hardly time to eat and not time to sleep *as much as I want to*. We are working almost night and day preparing for the fight which we hourly expect. I have command of one face of the fort comprising 7 guns manned by one company and if we have all engagement will prove to the Northern Branches that if I am as they think a traitor that I am at least *a man* but I am called away to pick out a boat's crew to carry Capt [Daniel] Gill [Chandler] up to town so I must go. Kiss all hands for me. Good bye. You know I never say all that I feel, so simply Good bye

Your aff. son
JL Branch

The Northern and Southern parts of the family had at some point become estranged. The whole story of why John thought the Northern Branches considered him a traitor is not known.

John received his commission as a second lieutenant in the 1st Confederate States Infantry on April 10, 1861.

Capt. Francis S. Bartow to 2Lt. John L. Branch

Montgomery May 1, 1861
My Dear Branch

I have seen the Secretary of War. He promises to promote you speedily & I rely on his promise. He appears to have labored under some mistake in your appointment. I advise you therefore to accept without delay the appointment ordered you & to report for duty—Do not hesitate about it. Say to McIntosh that I am again promised his appointment. I have taken great trouble about this matter & I hope you will follow my counsel.

Yours Truly
F S Bartow

Bartow wasted no time in his endeavor to get the Oglethorpes in the provisional army. He pushed a bill through the Confederate Congress in Montgomery, Alabama, authorizing President Jefferson Davis to accept individual military commands into Confederate service if they expressed a desire to enlist for the duration of the war. Prior to this, militia units had signed on for six months or one year.

The bill passed. Bartow telegraphed Savannah with the news, and Lt. James Hamilton Couper, in command of the O.L.I., assembled the corps at their barracks on Liberty Street (now Oglethorpe Avenue). At 4:00 P.M. on the afternoon of May 10, 1861, the dispatch was read. Lt. Couper offered a resolution that the

Corps enlist "for the duration of the war." [21]

War fever had become rife in Savannah with the firing on Fort Sumter and the occupation of Fort Pulaski by the city's own troops. The contagion infected Sanford and Hamilton Branch as well. Sanford, already a member of the corps, had been at the fort part of the previous months. Hammie, now eighteen, was underage, and Capt. Bartow was reluctant to take him into the company because his two brothers were already going. But at the insistence of all three boys, Bartow approached Charlotte Branch and requested her permission for the boy to enlist. She gave her consent, stating that she would never stand in the way of her sons' duty to their country.[22]

Both joined their brother's company, mustering in with Sanford as second corporal and Hammie as a private on May 21. The Branch boys were off to war.

CHAPTER TWO

All I Hope Is That We May Meet Them Soon

The Oglethorpe Light Infantry barracks on Liberty Street were a scene of bustle and excitement on the morning of May 21, 1861. The youthful members packed equipment and polished accoutrements in preparation for their departure from Savannah. Once ready, the boys were mustered by Maj. William Montgomery Gardner and assembled at their parade ground on the corner of South Broad and Whitaker. Cumbersome knapsacks and glinting steel highlighted the image of each soldier in their smart blue-black dress uniforms.

The O.L.I. was sworn into Confederate service as two separate companies. Co. A was destined for the war front; Co. B would remain in Savannah. On the departure day, Co. B escorted Co. A off with plenty of pomp and circumstance.[23]

At noon, members of the ten militia units of Savannah formed a corridor on South Broad Street. Both companies of the Oglethorpe Light Infantry entered the head of the street and marched down the line of colorfully uniformed ranks to the tune of "Bold Soldier Boy" under the command of Capt. Bartow. They continued down South Broad to Bull Street, turned onto Gaston to the northwest corner of Whitaker. All along the route, as Savannah cheered its young warriors, each chest grew a little fuller and postures became more erect with pride. The companies drew up on line and halted at the residence of Hon. Thomas Holcombe, mayor of Savannah, where huge crowds watched the presentation of a beautiful silk flag made by the young ladies of the city.[24]

Capt. Bartow accepted the symbol of a new nation, the Stars and Bars, and placed it in the hands of Color Sgt. Charles H. Daniell. He then spoke of the trials and hardships they would encounter and announced that if any man there was not prepared to face the test he could leave the ranks. None did.

The flag unfurled amid cheers, waving handkerchiefs and prayers for victory as the Oglethorpes marched to the Central Railroad depot, escorted by the entire militia of Savannah. With laurel wreaths draped from their bayonets, they boarded the cars for Virginia, where tradition would meet the merciless forces of war.

Georgia governor Joe Brown had threatened to have the Oglethorpes stopped at the state line if they attempted to take arms out of the state. To avoid interception in Augusta, Capt. Bartow chose a route through South Carolina, stopping in Charleston for a grand reception and banquet in the company's honor.[25] It was at the Charleston banquet that Bartow uttered his famous remark, "I go to illustrate Georgia." At every stop they were cheered by ladies who pinned cockades on their lapels.

Three days later they detrained in Richmond, where inexperienced hometown companies from all over the South were organized into regiments and brigades and drilled into some semblance of military bearing by Virginia Military Institute cadets who served as drill instructors. Companies with the Oglethorpes' military bearing and experience were few, and the tall lowcountrymen made quite an impression.

Pvt. Hamilton Branch to Charlotte Branch

Camp near Richmond May 25/61
Dear Mother

We arrived here on Thursday night at 12 M[idnight]. All safe and sound. We were received in Petersburg, Va. splendidly, the men were all over at the cemetery burying a Captain who killed himself at Norfolk and therefore the ladies turn out to receive us and it was a reception. They literally covered us with flowers and followed us down to the depot and there made themselves quite sociable and pleasant.

On our arrival here we marched up to the Exchange Ballard House where we eat supper. We then marched out three miles to our present camp ground. It is situated in the middle of a large open space with not a tree in it during the day it is very warm in deed and during the night it is exceedingly cold the Captain was very mad the first day they wanted to put us in some houses that were built for some Louisiana troops. They were full of fleas and smell very badly the captain refused to go into them and so we had to pitch our tents at 12 o'clock. The Atlanta Greys, a very fine company, are here. They will be in our regiment which will be the crack regiment. All along the route we were complimented very highly on our soldierly appearance and the splendid manner in which we were equipped so that I have got very proud and don't talk to common folks. The Atlanta Greys say that one of there reasons for coming was that they understand that Capt. Bartow was to be their Col. We received a letter this morning saying that we could move to Reserves encampment which is a splendid place if we still desired but that as we were a well drilled and disciplined Corps we were liable to be ordered off at a moments warning therefore he would leave it with the captain. Love to all.

Your devoted son
H.M. Branch

Give my love to Grandmother [Sarah Sawyer], Cousin L[aura Lufburrow]. Cousin O[rlando Lufburrow]. Aunt L[izzie Schaaf]. Mr. [Worthington C.] B[utler] and all friends. Hammie

The Union army promised mischief at the audacity of Virginia's secession, and under the command of Gen. Winfield Scott, the regular army and Lincoln's newly uniformed volunteers took the dare. On May 24 the Union troops occupied Alexandria, Virginia.

Events moved swiftly. Gen. Pierre G.T. Beauregard was appointed to command Confederate forces on the "Alexandria Line" on May 31. The popular belief was that this was to be a war fought and won in a single engagement, and it appeared that northern Virginia would be the decisive ground. The Georgians in camp around Richmond waited impatiently to get their quota of troops to form a brigade and move to the front.

Cpl. Sanford Branch to Charlotte Branch

[Undated, probably June 1, 1861]
Dear Mother

I expect you wonder at not hearing from me before but as Hamilton wrote last week I thought I would wait until this. John arrived here on

Saturday night, everybody was glad to see him.

We have 9 companys now in our regiment as soon as we get one more we will leave Richmond where for I do not know. We are the favorites with everybody particularly the Ladies. About 500 Ladies visit our camp every day. Some of the men have dinner in town. Our men are all well with one exception. He is at the Sisters of Charity where he receives every attension and is getting well. I have been offered & refused the position of Hospital Stewart with rank & pay of 1st Sargeant. I came here to fight & not to put up prescriptions.

I have a first rate mess, only too meny—7 in one of our tents crowds us so that when we all lay down we are so tightly packed that in the morning we have to call in the corporal of the Guard to pull the first one out. This is my mess Sargeant [Frederick]Bliss, Corporal Branch [himself], Privates [Alfred or Edward] Davis, [Addison R.] Tinsley, [John W.] Fleming, [Thomas] Purse & [Julius A.] Ferrill. In my next I will send you a bill of fare. Give my love to all and except the largest for yourself.

Your aff. son, S.W. Branch

While the young men waited to be called into the fray, the traditionally charitable citizens of Savannah prepared to meet the necessary demands of war. On the homefront, the work fell largely to the women. Many patriotic societies were formed to sew uniforms, socks, underclothing and other items, and when camps and hospitals sprang up around the city, the ladies added bandages and cartridges to their growing list of "war work." A Ladies Military Fair held at the Masonic Hall in the spring of 1861was a notable success, raising $6,000 from the sale of food and various articles.

The largest patriotic group was the Savannah Relief Committee, which established a base of supply in Richmond for the boys from Savannah. Like many others, Charlotte Branch threw herself completely into the activities of the relief associations, giving freely of her time, talent, and material to be certain that her boys were provided for while away at the front.

Capt. Daniel G. Chandler to Charlotte Branch

Brunswick Ga. June 3rd, 1861
Mrs. Charlotte S. Branch & others
Dear friends

Your highly esteemed favors of a box of clothing reached us yesterday for which you will please accept our sincere thanks. The preasent was the more acceptable on account of the scarcity of such articles here. Many will not procure such conveniences here from the fact that they are not in this market, My command are well (with the exception of measles) I have 8 cases in my company and greatly fear that there will be twenty more in a few days as most of my men have never had measles and worst of all we have here no hospittle accomodations and have to manage them mostlly in the open air. My self and company miss greatly the re'd and sympathy of our Savannah friends and fear that we will not be able to repay the debt of gratitude which we owe to the noble and patriotic Ladies of Savannah. All that we can say is God bless them may there lives be as prosperous and Happy as they have been patriotic and honorable.

> With great respect I remain
> your most obt. & very
> Humble Sevt.
> D. G. Chandler, Capt.
> Commanding Banks Co. Guards

Orders finally came through for the Oglethorpes to head north.

Pvt. Hamilton Branch to Charlotte Branch

Camp Georgia 8 AM June 4/61
Dear Dear Mother

We leave for Harpers Ferry this afternoon. We have just received the orders to leave as soon as possible; will leave on the first train. We will have to pass Manassas Gap and Fairfax Station so that we stand a pretty good chance of getting in a fight. In truth we can hardly get on without it. We the OLI will be the advance guard to draw the enemys fire. We will have to march through a nice tract of Country for about 20 miles, that will show what kind of stuff we are made of. We will have to march this distance or go on the cars by the way of Washington which our boys would like very much to do but can not. In the last fight at Fairfax [June 1] we had one Captain killed and we killed over 20 of their men and caught 15 of their horses so you see we got the best of them as we always will.

The President says we are a fine body of men and he will rely on our courage strength and rediness to go, as a safeguard against defeat. He says we shall have a place in the picture and a good place too. We have just been ordered to obey Lieut. J.L. Branch as Adjutant of this Post. Two Tennessee Regiments left here last evening for the seat of war. The Georgians are coming in by hundreds, we now have about 2 thousand here. some of them are encamped on our old Camp ground. the following companies are in our Regiment as lead out this morning. 1) Oglethorpe Light Infantry, 2) Echols Guard, 3) Atlanta Guards, 4) Floyd Infantry, 5) Pulaski Volunteers, 6) Rome Light Guards 7) Miller Rifles, 8) Oglethorpe Rifles 9) Macon Guards. The other company has not arrived yet.

We are all well. Sant. has had a sore eye but he is well. the Doct. says he caught cold in it. Fred Bliss and Tom Purse had the same but are well now. You can tell all the Folks that the boys are all well. We had a splendid rain last night it was very much needed. I will put on the machine you sent as soon as I get to Harpers Ferry. Give my Love to Grandmother, Cousin Laura, Aunt Lizzie [Schaaf], Aunt Am all the folks home and all the girls. Tell them we have lots of sweethearts here and in Petersburg, and also to all inquiring friends. Don't show this letter about town the boys don't like that idea at all they say they will have to stop writing if they keep on showing their letters.

Your loving son
Hammie

The O.L.I., who were nicknamed "Bartow's Beardless Boys" and "Captain Bartow's Independent Company," became Co. B of the 8th Georgia, one of three Georgia regiments under the command of their old captain. Bartow promoted John Branch to adjutant of the 8th Georgia, which became part of the Army of the Shenandoah. The 8th was held in reserve at Camp Hollingsworth, near Winchester, Virginia, a strategic point from which they could be at the ready against any action from Union forces through Maryland or quickly rushed by train to the battleline drawn between Alexandria and Manassas Junction.

The camp, named for local resident Isaac Hollingsworth, was within sight of his home, called Abram's Delight. Bartow made his headquarters there, in a room used by Col. George Washington in 1760.[26]

Charlotte Branch to Lt. John L. Branch

Sav June 5th 61
My Dear John
    Your telegraph afforded me much satisfaction as it assured us of your

safe arrival and of the good health of all the rest.

Tell the boys Miss Ellen Philbrick told me yesterday that she saw both of them out at their camp, they had a hard time to get home from *Boating*. Mrs. P. would not even look out of the window to see [Col. Elmer] Elsworths Funeral which passed right by the house. They were detained in Washington 36 hours trying to get a passport, they say all is confusion there that no one appears to know who is the proper person to go to about *anything*.

I am pressed for time write when you can as we are very anxious.

May the good God take care of my dear dear children and may they be blest here and hereafter, all the family and many many friends send love to you.

> As ever your affectionate Mother
> C S Branch

[P.S.] Tell Hammie I rec his dispatch and am much obliged to him, My dear Santy has not sent me a line or any message ever since he left. I am very anxious to hear from him. CSB

Col. Ellsworth of the 11th New York Volunteer Infantry climbed onto the roof of the Marshall House in Alexandria, Virginia, to remove a Confederate flag placed there. When he refused to leave, he was fatally shot by the proprietor.[27]

Charlotte Branch to Adj. John L. Branch

Sav June 7, 61

My Own Dear Son,

I have just rec a letter from Hammie yours I rec yesterday it is useless for me to say how much pleasure it gave me.

My Own Dear children you are in all my thoughts what a time of trial to you and to me, My all in this life is in this struggle, for what is my life—nothing to your lives. May God keep you and save you and bring you home safe to live for his glory; and Oh may your hearts be turned to him who is the giver of every good and perfect good and then whether living or dying all will be right with you. I do not wish to make you feel gloomy far from it. The [good] Christian is the man to be truely happy.

I do not know of any news; there have been many reports about the OLI away. Then some good, others not. One was that 2 of them had been caught sleeping on duty and were to be shot for it, I do not believe that. Do write when you have time and do my child find time to read your bible and to pray.

Your Grandmother is going over to Carolina to see Lotty Hardee. She will be gone but a few days. I wish she could go somewhere where she would be very quiet she gets so much excited and worries so much about you boys. We are very anxious to learn of your arrivall at your destination—

We are all well but very lonesome and shall be so glad when you all return home. Each of the girls send love to you and to your brothers. Every one appears to be interested in the OLI, that is of our people. Mr. Tom Farman [Thomas M. Forman] has just returned from R[ichmond], and speaks very highly of your Corps and says you are behaved so well, but that he thinks you will be spoiled as the people make so much of you there. *Embrace your brothers for me* (Arlanda says consider *yourself kissed*). My best affections are with you boys.

With a mothers love as ever yours

C S Branch

The young Confederates, many away from home for the first time, were itching to get a crack at "the Yankees." But, like Hammie Branch, the first enemy most encountered was sickness brought on by poor sanitation and contagious disease.

Pvt. Hamilton Branch to Charlotte Branch

Winchester Va. June 10th/61
My Dear Dear Mother,
    I wrote you last from Richmond, we did not leave there until the next morning after I wrote. We arrived at Manassas Junction the next morning at 1 AM but could not get on as our Locomotive . . . [needed] Wood and we could not get him to start again and we had to send for another Engine which arrived about 2 PM and we started for Strausburg [Strasburg, Virginia], on the way [to] which place I was taken sick caused by indigestion. On our arrival at Strausburg I felt so badly that I complained to Lieut. [Joseph] West and he told me to go to bed in my tent as soon as it was pitched, which I did and slept until next morning. the next morning we started for this place which is about 18 miles from Strausburg. The most of the troops came in waggons and stages but most of our boys walked. I tried to get Lieut. West to let me walk but he and John both sayed the Col.

had given orders for me to ride and so I had to be a baby and ride to this place. when I got here I went out to Camp and got permission to come in town which I did and walked through town and back to meet the boys, about 2 miles. I was a great deal better then when I met the boys. I marched along back with them to the Fair Grounds where we were to camp. when we got there I had to go to the Atlanta Grays House and lie down. Doct. West was taken sick and could not give me any more medicine so that the Doct. in the house with me gave me 3 Carthartic pills.

The next day a kind gentelman, Mr. Ray, came out and offered to carry any sick from our Company in town with him to Private families. Capt. B[artow] then sayed as he had to camp the next morning (yes today) at 10 o'clock that all that were sick must go in town he sent four of us William [H. or M.] Pat[t]erson and me were left at this house the owner is the Rev. Mr. Graham a Presbyterian Minister in this place of whom I cannot speak too highly nor of his wife nor his mother Mrs. [Ann Tucker] Magill who is some relation of the Formans and Bryans. Dr. Alf Tucker now in Savannah is a brother of hers. When I get to the Ferry which will be in a day or two I will write you more about these kind folks. I have got to stay here after I am well until Bill [William Pender, a negro manservant] gets well. He has had Chills & fever. I did not have an opperation for almost a week. I took a powder day before yesterday which worked me but I have not had one since. I have just taken another powder which I think will fix me. if so I will be well in the morning. I wish I could tell you how kind these folks are to me. Mrs. Magill says she wishes you would come on. She knows she could take good care of you. Don't come mother. the only thing that has been the matter with me was headache and dizziness nothing serious. Give my love to all. I must close. it is only 30 miles to the Ferry. As ever,

Your loving son
Hammie

Adj. John L. Branch to Charlotte Branch

Camp Defiance near
Harpers Ferry June 10th 1861
My Dear Mother

I have never received a line from you since I left home although I have telegraphed you twice and written once. We arrived here yesterday after a journey of 3 days from Richmond of which we marched 20 miles. I do not mean *we* exactly for I rode. Hammie had been a little sick and we sent him in a stage. When I arrived at Winchester I found him still sick and we left him with the Presbyterian Minister Rev. Mr. Grahame who with his wife & mother in law was very kind and when we left he was so far recovered as to be up and he was left only to look after two sick men who we left and to pick up a little. The Regiment is encamped on a young mountain almost grown in a wheat field in the most beautiful scenery you can imagine, just overlooking the Potomac. There are several Regiments around us but we have the best reputation of any Regiment that has entered Virginia yet as being well behaved orderly and sober. You never see a man of the *8th Ga.* drunk or noisy in the streets. I am as busy as a man can be and as it is time to have dress Parade I will say Goodbye. I will try & write soon. Tell [John T.] McFarland that I have his appointment [as assistant surgeon] here to come on immediately.

Your aff son, J L Branch

Charlotte Branch to John, Sanford, and Hamilton Branch

Sav June 13, 61

My Darling Precious Children

This as you see is fast day. May it be really kept as a fast unto the Lord Our God and may we all bow down and humiliate ourselves before him who is our onlly help, blessed are they who do so.—

We had a prayer meeting this morning at half past 6 o'clock which was well attended. Mr. Thomas, Mr. Carr . . . —and Rev. Mr. [Charles B.] King offered fervant prayer to God for our country. I wish you could have heard them, especially Mr. Carr. Oh how earnestly he prayed for all but particularly for your company and for your leader your helmed commander as he stiled (Capt. Bartow) May the prayers be answered. We shall have service in all the churches in the citty to day—

Bishop [Stephen] Elliott [the rector of Christ Church, Savannah] delivered a most eloquent sermon to the Pulaski Guard last Sunday; they are to go to Virginia soon. I heard yesterday that the Troup Artillery were ordered to Virginia.

This much I had written before church time. We had as usuall a most excellent sermon, a number of soldiers were in church I wondered as I looked at them if my own dear soldier boys were listening to a sermon or attending any religious service. I trust so, you were remembered before a throne of grace—

I enclose . . . a ps. . . . I thought you would like to see: it is pretty severe on the Gov[ernor] but I am really down upon him myself now. I saw Mr. [Thomas F.] Stevens this morning he had just seen Mr. [Benjamin L.] Cole who had a letter from his son [Hollie], Mr. [James] Hine brought James's letter and read a part of it to me yesterday. I was very glad to hear that you were all well and had arrived so far on your journey. Was some what disappointed (*yes more than somewhat*) that I did not get a letter. I do not want to tax you my dear boys but would like to rec as many letters as you can make time to write me. You will excuse the anxiety when you think how anxious your Mother is. We have just taken our fast diner which was a very simple one, tea and bread and scrambled eggs. We had but three at the table. M[other] is over in Carolina at Mrs. Hardees. Georgia [Elkins, an apprentice in Charlotte's millinery shop] afraid we would not have enough to eat perhaps so she went out to dine.

As ever most devotedly your Mother

CS Branch

Charlotte Branch to Adj. John L. Branch

Sav June 13 61

My Dear John

I wrote to [William] Jones and [George] Snider this morning to see [George] Whit[field] Stevens to see about buying a horse for you if you had not allready got one. I have felt very bad about not telagraphing you in reply to your's that I would send the money. I do not know now if I have done right. Jimmy is in Richmond and I wrote to him to pay for the horse and I would pay it when he came home or to draw on me for the amount.

I rec a letter from Capt. C[h]andler of the Banks Co. Guards in acknowledgement of a box of clothes I sent to Brunswick, he is very grateful. Says he misses the kind ladies of Savannah very much, there were a number of contributors to the box I sent, among them Miss A[da] Scriven. The Capt. says he had 8 men sick with measles and has no hospital for them. He says very few of his men have had measles. I suppose they will all have it. I have not the money now but Mr. Davis will lend it to me. Most devotedly

your affectionate Mother

C S Branch

[P.S.] I did not send the letter hopeing to rec a letter from you, that is some of you. Mr. Hine, Mr. Cole, Mr. [Franklin] Krenson and Mr. [John C.] Ferrill and others have rec letters. Mr. Gilbert Butler told me this morning he did not care if the boys did not choose to write why they might let it alone. I can't say that, I am most anxious to get news of you. Oh John do not let an opportunaty pass to drop me a line. Think of me, love me as I love you. I ask no more than that. I do beg you to take care of yourselves.

Your devoted Mother, C S Branch

Adj. John L. Branch to Charlotte Branch

Harper's Ferry
June 14th, 1861
Dear Mother

I received your welcome letter this morning. I asked you for the money because I really needed it to buy my horse & equipments. I thought that I had about two Hundred Dollars in the Savings Bank and that if you could borrow the rest I could repay it in a month or two If you can possibly send it to me. Please do so as I am mortified every day by the enquiry why do you not get a horse? I will be the onlly officer not mounted in a day or two. We evacuate this place today & march to Winchester. This morning our troops blew up two Bridges & burnt the Rifle works. We leave in a few minutes. This place is of no importance and I am surprised that it was held so long. Give my love to all.

Your aff. & not extravagant son
J L Branch

P S Sanford says that if he has any money in the Bank you can draw it & lend it to me. I hope you can get it without troubling Mr. Davis but it is very important to me and if I do not get it I shall resign as Adjutant but get attached to one of the companies. I know that you are doing all you can for me and if you do not succeed do not let it worry you for I shall get along very well any how even if I do resign. Hammie awaits us at Winchester. [Sanford] Branch well, he will write to you when we get to W.

Your Aff son,
J L Branch

[P.P.S.] Alexander & George Butler are well so is [John] M[acPherson] Berrien, Bob Grant, and all the camp. Sid Goodwin got yesterday accidentally scratched with a bayonet. it is a mere scratch I write this so as to correct any false report. JLB

Francis Bartow was appointed a colonel, then brigadier general. His brigade was organized at Camp Defiance in Frederick County, Virginia, on June 17, 1861.

Charlotte Branch to Pvt. Hamilton Branch

Sav June 17, 1861
My Dear Child
    Yours of the 10th came to hand on Friday 15, it grieved me to learn that you were sick. I have tried to comfort myself with your assurance that it was not a serious illness. . . . [M]y heart is with you but alas my willing hands are far away, and others strangers must minister to your comfort in the hour of sickness. . . . I am most gratefull to them for all the kindness they showed you. I must try and do all I can for the soldiers among us, trusting that in my childrens hour of need they will receive from others. We met at Mrs. Bartows on Saturday in answer to a call from her in the newspapers. the business before us was to see who would make clothes [&] unaforms for the OLI. There was a very large meeting all appeared to be anxious to do what they could. I shall make four suits, one a piece for each of you, one for a young man by the name of Carolin [James E. Carrolan] whom I am interested in and the other is for a man I don't know, a stranger Francis Lunts or Lents [Lentz, a Swiss grocery clerk who was boarding in Savannah]. you know these 2 men have no friends and so some body must make for them— . . . I have been so busy all the morning attending to the uniform that I can't write more now. My Dear Dear boys you do not know how anxious I am to see you all I will write to John as soon as I see [John T.] McFarland. I trust I shall get a letter tomorrow from Santy. Please remember to write me about each other when you write. I got your letter and John's at the same time neither of you mentioned Santy please do so hereafter. God bless you and my other two dear boys.

As ever your affectionate
Mother C S Branch

Pvt. Hamilton Branch to Charlotte Branch

Winchester Va. June 20/61

My Dear Dear Mother

I received your letter last week, but have not been well enough before to answer it. I was taken worse after I wrote you last and continued so three or four days but have been up now two days. I expect to go out to camp tomorrow the boys are now encamped about 4 miles from town but they will move in tomorrow. John will send his horse in for me he and Doc are perfectly well. Mother, Rev. Mr. & Mrs. Graham & Mrs. Magill have been so kind to me there was nothing I wanted but they got it for me and were sending and coming up all the time to see if there was nothing they could do for me. They were so kind Mrs. Magill would come up and sit and read the Bible and pray for us and then talk to us about Jesus. She sayed she could not help doing so because she knew that if you were here you would do the same thing they are all Presbyterians.

The Ladies and Children, that is most of them, are very much frightened because they think the Federal Army is marching on this place. A great many have left and others are getting ready to leave, but some of the ladies say they will not leave. They believe that our little army can whip 5 times its number and they intend to stay—Hurrah for them.

I am having a nice time now that I am walking about. I am with the young ladies all the time. They take me out to walk every morning and evening. I never walk far as I am pretty weak. I am going this morning with Miss Jennie and Miss Ella to Shawnee Springs [in Winchester] to drink some of the water. They say that if you drink this water you are obliged to come back here. The young ladies in this town are very nice. One of them gave me a very nice pen holder (silver) and pen. It is a very nice one. They say that as soon as I get out to camp they intend coming out to see, and bring plenty of good things so much for them.

We do not know how long we will be here we expect to leave every day. Uncle Tom [the Union army] is sayd to be in Maryland. They crossed over the river the other morning, our boys were then about 8 miles from them as soon as they heard it they crossed back and have not been seen since they were pursued by 500 of our Cavalry but they ran too fast. All well.

Give my love to all the folks, Cousins O[rlando] & L[aura], Aunt Lama Mr. B. Aunt A. Mr. L, Mrs. [Alicia C.] Dillon, Mrs. [Leocadia] Blois [a music teacher]. tell them I am getting on finely. Mrs. Thomason and every body I know. I am sorry to hear that the Savannah people are all down on the OLI [for leaving state service for Confederate service]. Col B[artow] is now acting General. He has command of five Regiments. but I must close Mother, do write soon. I can not write often as funds are pretty low and they say the paymaster is not coming around.

Your loving son
Hammie B.

Charlotte Branch to Sanford and Hamilton Branch

Sav June 20th 61
My Dear Santy & Hammie

As I was not able to get John's letter off yesterday I added a few lines to you. We have most deploreable stories of the destination of your company. Do write and let us know what the actual state of affairs is; How are you both off for clothes, I do hope you will get this letter soon, it is very bad that you do not get my letters. I have rec all but the first letters that John wrote. Mrs. Hine has had 4 letters from James this week. if you only knew how much gratification it was to me to get letters you would try to write oftener.

My dear Santy do try and write to me. John says you make a fine soldier (enduring all the privations I suppose well, as he says you are growing fat). My dear Hammie how sick you must have been to be away from home. Oh how my heart yearns to your kind friends I suppose they would hardly believe it as I have never yet written to them; God will bless them for all they have done for you, a stranger. The uniforms have been sent. I hope they will do service. I do not think them very pretty. Santy I commenced to put the chevrons on your sleeves and then changed my mind as I did not know how many to put on so put braid and thread in your inside pocket, so that you could have it put on your self. James Hine writes that there will be an election in the company for Capt. I suppose. I do hope there will not be any devision in feeling in regard to the election. He says there are two tickets secession and submission. I hope this is not so. I think you ought to be unanimous in your choice of a commander let division be among our enemies not among us. —Morty [Davis] told me yesterday that he had a letter from Fred [Bliss] and that all were well. It is late so I must close.

With sincere love
Your Mother C S Branch

Adj. John L. Branch to Charlotte Branch

Camp near Winchester

Dear Mother

I received your letter by [Private] Henry Graybill yesterday. I drew yesterday a check on the Bank for One Hundred and Fifty Dollars which as soon as I can I will return. I am as busy as you can imagine. M. Beman is sick in town and I have his work as well as my own to attend to. It is pretty hard but "we have to grin & bear it in the service." Sanford is very well and Hammie improving very fast. He will soon be all right again. I will write again tomorrow, if I can find time.

As ever your aff son

J L Branch

Charlotte Branch to Cpl. Sanford Branch

Sav June 21st 61

My Own Dear Santy

Why don't you write to me. I have only had one letter from you since you left Savannah. Which will be one month tomorrow. It is useless to say to you how anxious I am your own heart will tell you that. We hear many rumours . . . which are not confirmed afterward, they help to keep us in an unhealthy state of excitement, still I try not to be made unhappy by them.

There is not a particle of news in town to write so that I suppose you boys will think these letters had better be stereotiped. I think I see Hammie laughing at the letter being allways about the same, yet what else can I write about. You boys are all this world contains worth careing for, for me you are my all. Oh be watchfull of each other both *morrally* and phisecally, remember that what ever you do that is wrong will not injure you but only reflect on your Mother. John writes me that *the regimen[t]* is really the best and most exemplary from Georgia. may it continue to be so.

I do wish . . . you boys would make an effort to write oftener. I know that there is much uneasiness about you all.—Mrs. [Emma] Bliss felt very bad at not receiving letters oftener and Mrs. [Jane] Bogart too is very uneasy there have been reports that he[r son,] J[ohn H.] Bogart was ill, very ill.

Trusting that all will work well with you and that we shall all meet in health and happiness I am my own dear son

Your affectionate Mother, C.S. Branch

Adj. John L. Branch to Charlotte Branch

Camp near Winchester
June 24th 1861
Dear Mother

. . . I wrote you last the day we left Harper's Ferry. On the first day we marched but 9 miles, on the next 16. We heard that the enemy had crossed the River and were advancing upon Winchester when we immediately changed our course and marched towards them to Bunker's Hill within 16 miles of them when they [Patterson] although having over 20,000 men against not quite 10,000 recrossed the river and left us to march back to Winchester, where we now are awaiting further developments, all very much chagrined at the result.

There are some rumors in town today of Peace Prospects. The men generally, and this Regiment particularly, would be dissatisfied with it as we want one good fight to show Joe Brown what we are. I found upon arriving here that Hammie had been quite sick but was slowly recovering. He is still quite weak. I have borrowed some money here and bought a nice little gray mare. . . . Sanford is very well and makes a very good soldier. He has grown quite fat. Hammie is treated by his friends the Grahames and Magills as though he was one of the family. They have become very much attached to him. He will be able to rejoin his Regiment in a few days.

I suppose it is very hot with you now. We are having it as hot here in the middle of the day as it is in Savannah but the nights are very cool & pleasant. We, that is the Soldiers, drill 4 hours a day pretty good work for us. Col. Bartow is in command of the 2nd Brigade but he has not given up his Regiment. The Brigade consists of our & Gartrell's Ga. Regt, The 4th Alabama and Col. Duncan & Capt. Pope's (2 Battallions) Kentuckians with a Virginia Battery of Artillery. Quite a nice set for [Union generals Robert] Patterson, [George] Cadwalader or [George B.] McClelland either to meet. I forgot to tell you that we form a portion of the Army of the Shenandoah, A romantic name.

Give my love to Grandmother, Sarah, Georgia and Miss Bridget, Miss [Gertrude] Dillon & family and in fact to all that I care about. Tell Gertrude that I would like some of those "what nots" that she sent me at the Fort but I will wait untill I come home for them & now Goodbye.

As ever Your aff. son J L Branch

Cpl. Sanford Branch to Charlotte Branch

Camp Starvation
Jun 27 1861
Dear Mother

Your letter was received yesterday. It has been about 10 days since we recd a mail before. We moved camp yesterday and am now situated in a beautiful grove about 1 1/2 miles from Winchester how long we will stay here I do not know. Hamilton is quite well again, although he is still on *the* leave of absence he came out to Dress Parade 3 or 4 days ago with 5 young ladies, some quite handsome. He speaks very highly of the family where he is staying & I think he was very fortunate in getting sick for while we were marching from 12 to 18 miles a day he was in the city riding around with the Ladies and living on the Fat of the Land. Big [brother] is also having a nice time he is chief cook & everything else, Adjutant on the staff now that Bartow is acting Brigadier General. He went to a Ball Last night and I expect had a pleasant time.

We had a Brigade Review on the 24th, the Line extended a 1/2 mile. Our Brigade consists of the 7th and 8th Georgia, 4th Alabama & 6 companies of Kentuckians with 3 companys of Virginia Artillery. We were all very much disappointed in not having a fight at Bunkers Hill. We were within 3 miles of the enemy reported to be 25 thousand strong while were but 8 thousand. While on the second day march from Harpers Ferry General [Joseph E.] Johns[t]on heard that They had crossed the Potomac and were advancing on Winchester when he made his flank movement which military men say was one of the boldest moves ever made. That morning so certain was Johns[t]on of a battle that he requested the Colonels of Regiments to announce the fact to their commands which Bartow did saying that he did not doubt the courage of his men but on the contrary was afraid that they would rush heedlessly into danger. Johns[t]on then commenced forming his line of Battle where it was discovered much to our chagrin that the enemy were retreating.

All I hope is that we may meet them soon, and now as [Edward W.] Ned Davis & Fred [Bliss] are waiting for me to go in swimming I must stop. Hoping you will excuse this long & well written letter. I am your affectionate son

SWB

N.B. Give my love to Grandmother and all the rest. The money sent came just in. please except my thanks for it. Your son SWB

N B B Present my regards to Miss [Sarah E.] Sallie Davis . . .

Pvt. Hamilton Branch to Charlotte Branch

Winchester Va.
June 27/61
My Dear Dear Mother

I received your letters of the 13th & 19th yesterday also the poetry which is splendid [see page xx]. I did not get either of the pieces you sent. If you can get me all or any of the pieces that have been written about this affair please send them to me, also a copy of [Governor] Brown's letter against us. I have never seen that. If you can get any of them please do so for me.

I am now perfectlly well although they will not let me go out to camp, they say I am too weak yet. Just think I have been staying with these kind folks almost three weeks we have with us here now three more soldiers; a Mr. Witherspoon a Presbyterian Minister from Mississippi who is here with his brother who is sick and a Mr. Frierson who is also sick he is from Miss. also. There are about 300 from Miss. sick. 12 or 13 have died. The 7th Georgia Regiment lost one man yesterday [Andrew J. Camp]. He was packing up to move camp when his pistol fell shot him in the breast killing him instantly. We have one in our Regiment (Stephens Light Guard) pretty sick. The OLI are well.

We moved our encampment yesterday we were encamped 1 mile south of the City that is the 7th & 8th Geo. and a battalion of Ken. under Col. Duncan and an Artillery Co. We are now encamped 1 mile east of the town. I went out on Sunday to report myself for duty. They expected to leave for Martinsburg they were all packed the enemy crossed the river but recrossed therefore we did not go when I reported they refused to let me go and ordered me to go back to town. When Carolin heard it he came to me and asked me if he was missing after the fight if I would not write to his brother and let him know, but they did not go to fight. Lentz is the man that stayed in Aunt Lizzie [Schaaf]'s old house (that used to swing his hands and body so when he walked).

They say that we are to stay here until after the 4th of July. Gen. Johns[t]on reviewed our brigade the day before yesterday. They did look splendid. The 8th is the best Regiment that has ever been in these parts so every body says, the 9th Ga. is expected here today. They will be in our brigade which will give us three Geo. Regiments. Sant. and John are well I saw them yesterday as they marched through town. Mrs. Magill sends love to you, she says that she can sympathize with you. . . .

I made a bet the day before yesterday with a young lady she bet me anything she could give me in the world that we would have peace after Congress met. I made another yesterday with another young lady she bet herself against myself that we would have peace after Congress met so that you stand a pretty good chance of having a Virginia daughter. . . . tell all my friends to write to me but not to expect answers as we seldom get a chance to write and seldom can get silver and they will not take anything else in the P.O.

As ever your loving son
Hammie

P.S. Make my uniform to fit. Have you my measure. What color is it. Hammie

Charlotte Branch to Adj. John L. Branch

Sav June 29th 61
My Dear Son

Yours of the 24th came to hand today. I assure you your letters are welcome by all. I do wish you boys could see all the family, with what eagerness they look when Edward [a servant or freedman] comes in from the Post Office and if he has only a paper all look so disappointed. (All the family white and black).

My dear Hammie must have been very sick. Oh how I wish I could have been with him, I am very grateful to the kind people who have done so much for him, he has written much of them, and I am ashamed to think I have not written a line to thank them for all they have done for my poor child. My little Hammie. God bless them all How I wish I could see them. If you see them again you must tell them how thankfull I am to them.

You say there is some talk of peace and there is here but I really do not think there will be peace. The NY papers say the Crittendon resolutions or rather the proposition [U.S. senator John Crittendon] made with his offer to us [of a compromise that protected slavery in the south]. we can never except anything but an acknowledgement of our Independence. This I don't think they will acknowledge until they are whiped into it. And now I also don't think me unmindful of my own dear children when I·tell you that I want them whipped. They will never respect a peace on any other grounds. I have my all at stake still I do feel that I wish we may conquer a peace from the cowards.

You do not say much about yourself, how you get along with your duties, I trust you find yourself equal to them and I allso hope you do not forget the source that you must apply to for aid—God can help you to all that you knead both spiritual and physical. You sayed in your letter from Harper's Ferry that Santy would write when he got to W. which I supposed meant Winchester but now I think you must have meant Washington, but seriously why don't he write. Every one of his friends are complaining about him. Mr. Habersham sayed to day to tell Santy that he must write to me at once that I think he ought to have written to me if he did not to any one else. Do John beg him to write to his poor Mother. Ma is not very well, in fact I think she has failed very much lately. John, she loves you boys very much— Ma, Sarah, Georgia, and anybody/ not Bridget/ send their love to you they all say tell the boys to make haste and whip the Yankees and come home. . . .

What did you pay for your horse and who did you borrow from. Do let me know. Tell your brothers to write me what they stand in kneed of. With abiding love, as is above all earthly love for you and Sand. H[ammie], &

I am ever your Mother, CS Branch

CHAPTER THREE

John Our Beloved Has Been Killed

The opening days of July 1861 found the Confederate forces in a tense situation. The Army of the Shenandoah under Gen. Joseph E. Johnston, about 11,000 men strong, was keeping Maj. Gen. Robert Patterson's Union army at bay north of Winchester. The Confederate Army of the Potomac, commanded by Gen. P.G.T. Beauregard, had been building fortifications and massing troops at Manassas Junction, which had grown to a military depot of about 22,000 troops. Beauregard's army was organized into six brigades, the main body of which occupied entrenchments along Bull Run, a sluggish stream, from Union Mills on the far left to the Stone Bridge. A Union advance was expected hourly; anticipation mounted.

For the 8th Georgia the monotonous camp life, parades, and drill had been supplemented by the confidence-building sparring against Patterson. They were eager for action. For the Branch brothers it was the adventure of their lives. A commissioned officer, a corporal and a private, their letters reflect all three points of view. John chafed at the cautiousness of his older commanders while Sanford and Hammie typified the youthful ranks threatening to kick over the traces in their eagerness to experience the exhilaration of battle.

Charlotte Branch to Pvt. Hamilton Branch

Sav July 2nd 61

My Dear Hammie

I am really ashamed that I have not written to Mr. [Rev. James A.] Graham and his family before this but I had no idea you were so sick from the way you wrote. I supposed you were only a little sick you ought not to have decieved me allthough I do not see how I could have come on. yet I should have tryed. Hammie do find out what the expenses of your sickness was. I have written to Mr. Graham to request him to let me know. I had your wire grass hat fixed with a palmetto band instead of the ribbon. It looks very nicely. I had it fixed to send to Mr. Graham then I thought I would write to you first to see if it will be suitable. I allso have a palmetto work box to send to Mrs. Magill if you think it best, tell me who the family are comprised of, are there any children or young folks and how many and all about them. I am so sorry that you have not rec my letters, I think it is so unpleasant not to have news from home. The Troup Artillery left today for Richmond. The Chatham Artillery escorted them to the depot, I was so glad that they did.

Old Joe Brown gave them permission to take rifles or their cannon or I suppose anything else, all the arms in the state perhaps. Well never mind, the OLI will show him what they are made off. God bless you my child and bring you and my other dear sons safely back to me. This is the constant prayer of your Mother

C S Branch

Pvt. Hamilton Branch to Charlotte Branch

Winchester July 2/61

My Dear Dear Mother

I wrote you last from Darkesville or Bucklestown [now West Virginia] a place about 6 or 7 miles from Martinsburg. we stayed there (until Sunday) 4 days expecting every day to have a fight but nobody came to attack us. on Saturday evening it was reported that the advance column of the enemy was advancing on us and that we would be attacked before night. we were drawn up in line of battle but no enemy came and we had to go to bed without a fight—on Sunday morning Genl Johns[t]on issued a proclamation saying that for 4 days he had offered battle to the enemy (who had superior numbers) and they had declined and he would now retire to his old position, which we accordingly did and are now having embankments thrown up by the militia and prisoners. we intend to stand here until the last—the enemy have been reinforced and have now about 25 or 30,000. We have 11,000. we expect some reinforcements to day. I here that 2 Geo. Reg. will arrive this afternoon also that the Washington Artillery Battalion [of New Orleans] will arrive today. I here that we are to have 10,000 more men. we need them certain. we all think Genl Johns[t]on ought to have attacked them at first before they were reinforced and not have stayed idle 4 days, the prisoners all seem satisfied. they say they were half starved and that they intended to be taken prisoners, that is the army, all of them, whenever they get a chance.

We are all well. I got my uniform yesterday. the white shirts came just in time. I am staying in town again gaining strength. I will go out to camp tomorrow or next day. It is raining very hard now. I suppose the boys at camp are drenched. Ma when you write I want you to tell me if in 1854 there were not people who stayed in Savh during the summer and did not have the yellow Fever and wether Sarah Cornwell and others did not have Black Vomit and yet got well. Write soon and answer me. and whether we have the yellow Fever in Savh—every summer or not. Love to all. we do not expect the enemy for a fortnight yet

Your loving son
Hammie

[P.S.] John and Santy are well as are all the boys but John Richardson. Hammie

[P.P.S.] Give my love to all. One of our men [Bayard] Strickland died Saturday and was burried on Sunday he died at [former U.S.] Senator [James M.] Mason's. He was the red whiskered man who stayed at Gilleland's and Feldons. Mac Berrien is sick at Senator Mason's. Hammie

It was acknowledged even in the Union army high command that many early enlistees allowed themselves to be captured. The policy was that prisoners of war were paroled and exchanged for those held by the enemy. U.S. Secretary of War Edwin M. Stanton admitted, "There is reason to fear that many voluntarily surrender for the sake of getting home."[28]

Charlotte Branch to Pvt. Hamilton Branch

[Undated, in answer to his previous letter]

I will answer your questions honestly and truely and what I write can be relyed upon. I was a very little child when the Yellow Fever raged in Sav. in 1820. (it was caused by the dreadful rains after the great fire when so large a portion of the citty was laid in ruins.] Many of the building had deep cellars in which were large quantitites of vegatable matter which had been partially burned the rains filled these cellars and rotted the contents of them which [generated] feaver, that I have heard from the Old Folks who new all about it. I was born in this citty and never saw a case of Yellow Fever until the summer of 1854, when we had it in Savannah as an Epidemic for the first time in my recolections (when I was about 11 years of age I remember that it raged there were 8 cases in full near where I went to school but I did not think any one was alarmed about it as we all attended school as usual) I know severall families who did not have a single case of Yellow fever during the persistence of that disease in 1854. Sarah Cornwall's and severall others had black vomit who recovered and are still liveing—.

I do most positively and solemnly say that we do not have Yellow Fever yearly in Savannah and further that when we do have it it is a special visitation of Divine Providence just as any other citty is visited by any Epidemic—There is no logical cause today we should have it, I know many families who have never been 20 miles out of Savannah and who have never had a case of it in their families. I have answered all your questions and I say further that I believe Savannah to be as healthy as any place in the Southern Confederacy or in the United States.

Very sincerely and
affectionately your Mother
C.S. Branch

Pvt. Hamilton Branch to Charlotte Branch

Near Darkesville, Va.
July 5/61
My Dear Dear Mother

I received your letter to John, Santy and myself a day or two ago. the boys were in camp and did not send it in and therefore I did not get it until

I went out, which was the day we left Winchester. We are all well and in fine spirits. we have not had a fight yet although our pickets are bringing in prisoners all the time. they have brought in 7 already today.

Mother you must not believe any reports you hear about our having fights until you hear from some of us. I will always write you after every battle, if I can possible do so. don't let these reports worry you.

In the last fight we had up here [Falling Waters, West Virginia, July 2] there was only a part of one Virginia Regt. engaged in the fight, about 350 men. They say we had about 8000 men. We took 54 prisoners that I saw, on our way to Winchester. how many more I do not know. we cut them down like anything. they say that they had 2 killed and three wounded. we know they had more.

Our dead we had to leave on the field, viz 2. one of these dead men came into camp yesterday he says that he was only stunned. amongst the prisoners there are 1 surgeon who they all say is some relation to John Brown, 1 Lieut, 1 Sgt, 1 Spy, 2 Deserters, and 48 privates. they are all in Winchester.

Mother how I wish I could see you once more. dont think of coming on here.

from your loving son,
Hammie

Cpl. Sanford Branch to Charlotte Branch

Camp
July 8, 1861
Dear Mother,

As to day is a general holiday [declared by Joseph E. Johnston] I embrace the opportunity to write you a few lines we have just returned from Dark[e]sville, which is about 5 miles from Martinsburg where the enemy are in force, about 15,000 and strongly entrenched. We remained there about 4 days offering them battle but they declined to fight and we were too weak (about 10 thousand) to attack there in their position.

So we have fallen back to our former position about Four miles from Winchester and 19 from Dark[e]sville. We left there at Eleven & arrived here at Six O Clock pretty good Marching, considering the heat & Rock Roads. Hamilton went with us. The afternoon before we left Dark[e]sville it was reported that the Enemy were advancing the Line of Battle was formed but we were disappointed. it was only a skirmish with the pickets.

I had borrowed Johns horse and rode over to Bunker Hill about 4 miles, where I had a very pleasant time. In entering the village I looked for the finest house and having found it rode up and alighted, Knocked at the door, and asked for the Lady of the house. A beautiful creature made her appearance. I introduced myself as Adjutant of the 8th Georgia And inquired for a Tavern or Hotel (I knew there were none in the place) she said there was no public Houses in the village but would be glad to have me dine with them. Of course I hesitated but accepted. The result was I had Turkey & green corn for Dinner, while my less fortunate messmates fasted on Boiled Beaf & half baked Bread.

I am entirely out of Socks as well as money. The regiment are in fine health & spirits, only spoiling for a fight. John is getting very popular. I would not be surprised if he should be a General or Colonel yet.

Love to all
Your affectionate Son
S W Branch

Adj. John L. Branch to Charlotte Branch

Winchester
July 14, 1861
Dear Mother:

I wrote you on yesterday that I would write today if I had time, and while the rest are at Church, I will have a little leisure to fulfill my promise.

Since my last, we have had our usual amount of marching and counter-marching, advancing and retreating. We, the soldiers and Subaltern officers, call it retreating, but the Generals call it "Resuming our former position."

About 10 days ago, we received notice that Patterson had crossed the Potomac at Williamsport, and had occupied Martinsburg on our side. Our army was immediately put in motion, and we marched to within 7 miles of them and halted.

Our brigade was stationed in a wheat field, where we lay during that time with very little shade in the day time and no protection from the dew and rain at night. As long as there was a prospect of a fight, we did not mind it, and even preferred it to returning to our tents here.

Our scouts would take from two to five prisoners every day. Generally they were very poor apologies for soldiers, mostly small, dried-up Pennsylvania Dutchmen, and all telling the same story they were hunting for something *to eat*—when they were taken. About 40 of them have been working on our entrenchments here since they arrived, asking us to keep them until after the 22nd of June, as their term of enlistment expires then. In fact, we generallly suppose that the reason that Patterson has not advanced upon us is that most of his volunteers are for three months, and are unwilling to fight when their term is so near over.

After a march of about 20 miles in bad weather, a Bivouac of four days, to have to march back was a great disappointment, and was for a little time very demoralizing in its effect, but our army has fully recovered its spirits. As ever yours,

Affectionately your son,

J.L. Branch

Pvt. Hamilton Branch to Charlotte Branch

Winchester July 15/61

My Dear Mother,

I have written you 4 or 5 letters in the last 2 weeks and have not received one from you. Jon has received 2 or 3. Santy gave me some silver the other day. John gave me 5 dollars also the other day. I am going out to camp today to stay. I should not be surprised if some of our boys were sent home they are so sickly. I hope Grandma is well ere this. We have not had a fight yet. we have thrown up embankments about a mile from town on the Martinsburg road. Genl Patterson is still at Martinsburg. he has a great deal larger army than we and yet he is afraid to advance on us. I would not be surprised if we were in Baltimore in about two weeks from now. This is onlly my belief, it is reported here that Jeff Davis has told Genl Johns[t]on not to have a fight if he could help it until he came here. They expect him this week. we are receiving reinforcements every day 2200 came last night. we will soon have enough to go to Baltimore with. Genl Patterson is receiving reinforcements also there was a small fight the other night [at Falling Waters] between some of our cavalry and some of theirs. we killed 3 and took 2 with splendid horses prisoners. we did not have a man hurt in the late fight at Martinsburg. They had over 100 killed and 54 taken prisoners we had 2 killed and 13 wounded. one of the killed walked into camp the day after the fight and sayed he was ready for them to take another shot at him.

. . . I am sorry to hear that there have been any deaths at the Fort. Give my love to all home and to all my friends. Kiss Cousin Laura [Lufburrow] for me. how is Aunt [Mary] and Uncle [Matthew] Luff[burrow]. Give my love to them.

Your loving son
Hammie

[P.S.] John and Santy are well. Write to Cousin Eleanor [Hull] and ask her to get me a large size State of Florida button with the Coat of arms on it and Ma please send it to me. I want to put it on my coat. I have a Maryland, Mississippi, Alabama, & Virginia button on my coat. I am going to try and get one from each of the C.S. Hammie

Charlotte Branch to Cpl. Sanford Branch

Sav July 15th 61

My Own Dear Son

Your letter was most welcome. You write so seldom that it makes me feel very anxious about you. I am afraid you are forgetting your Mother. No I don't think that but I do wish you would write oftener for it is so gratifying to me to get letters from you all. It is almost 2 months since you left home and you have written me but 3 letters. You ought not to hate to write to me. I am sure your letters are very good ones. You did not say anything of Fred's being sick. Mrs. Bliss has heard that he was very sick is it so. Poor Bayard Strickland I was very sorry to hear that he was sick. I hardly believed that he was, as you did not either of you say a word about him. I heard the day before I got Hammies letter that he Strickland was dead. I hope he had every attention from you boys that you could pay him under the circumstances.

I have been having some blue check shirts made to send on to the OLI. I say *I* have, as I bought the most of the material but a number of ladies have made them. among those who have is Miss Sallie Davis & of those she made she marked for you with a little pc. of white tape and your name written on it so you must look out for it. . . . [This part of letter is torn away] I send you and Hammie in a valice 2 apiece. if you have more of the check shirts than you want, give John one of those I send if he wants it. tell him if he wants anything to write me word. I have asked you all to do so; You say you are out of socks and money. I sent 4 pr. of socks with your unaform did you not get them. I hope you have rec the 10$ I sent by letter to each of you—

Mr & Mrs Hine will leve on Wednesday for Virginia—I envy them. I believe I am the only [mother] who can't do as I would like. I wish I could be with you my own dear boys. I would be so much use. I could keep your clothes in order and make your meals so much better.

You do not say what you think of the clothes. I do not like them but suppose they will be useful. I had no hand in choosing the material. I hope you are able to keep clean as I have just had a terrible account of the want of cleanliness in some of the regiments. It is worrying me for fear that you are suffering for want of change of apparel. I have been [interrupted] by a visit from a young lady sent, so I fear this will not go by today's mail. Lotts of folks send love to you. all our own folks say tell the boys that we are all anxious to welcome them home.

Miss Kenady says did you get the brest of the turkey. says she hopes so—Was that dinner you had at Bunker Hill the first green corn you had had.

Bless you my own dear child. I intend to write to John but have not time. I hope I shall get a letter from him in a day or two—My son from your affectionate Mother

C S Branch

Charlotte Branch to Cpl. Sanford Branch

Sav July 17, 61

My Dear Dear Santy,

In utmost haste I just write to say a few words to you. I saw Morty [Davis] last night he had just rec a letter from you but it was written on the 5th, he says he prizes it very much as it is the first he has ever rec from you. Sallie [Davis] sends her love to you, and the two other Branches. If John wants any of those check shirts you had better let him have one of yours and Hammie let him have one of his and you take the one Sallie made for you and H. can take one of the other kind, and I can send others afterward.

All are well but me I am suffering with my face.

Most affectionately your mother
C S Branch

Charlotte Branch to Adj. John L. Branch

Sav July 17, 1861

My Dear Dear Son

I thought I would just write a few lines to you. The town is all excited to day One thousand soldiers are expected every hour, and all most all Savannah is in the street. I have been very busy getting off the box of shirts, if you want any of the check shirts take them, as I furnished half the material although they were made for the OLI. I am not at all well today. Have been suffering with face ake all night. But John my heart akes dreadfully. I am so sad to think of the fate of the first Georgia Reg. May God protect you my dear dear boys is the earnest prayer of your poor Mother

C S Branch

After Union gunboats landed at Hilton Head, S.C., the defense of Savannah was a prime concern and caution was exercised along the coast. Governor Brown requested Secretary of War Walker to order 5,000 troops to Fort Pulaski for the defense of the approaches to Savannah. A front line of earthworks and batteries were constructed from Red Bluff, South Carolina, to Tybee, and across Wilmington Island to Wassaw Island. A battery on Green Island and Fort McAllister on the Ogeechee completed the outer lines of defenses.[29]

The 1st Georgia under Col. James N. Ramsey was involved in an engagement at Beverly, Virginia (W.Va.). On July 13, the regiment lost its brigade commander, Gen. Robert Garnett, while fighting a rearguard action at Carrick's Ford. Nearly thirty men were killed or wounded. The *Savannah Morning News* carried an erroneous article declaring the clash a disaster with 100 killed and wounded.[30]

Charlotte Branch to Boys

Sav July 17, 61

My Dear Boys

I have not time to write a word hardly to you. The sad news in regard to the 1st Georgia Regiment has made us all very sad. God bless you my own dear ones. I send a box of segars apiece to John & Santy, and enclose 5$ for you. I did not like to send without sending you anything so send you the five so that you can buy what you want with the same amount that I

spent for them. I trust I shall see you all soon. With the earnest love of your
mother

C S Branch

[P.S.] Molena sends love to the boys. Mrs. A[nthony] Porter and I went
down to day and bought these segars. . . . Edward is nailing up the box, he
says tell the boys I wish they was home again. Hammie the black valise is
yours in it is a box for Capt. [Joseph J.] West and 7 shirts which a lady sent
for the use of the sick.

On July 16 Beauregard received word that he would be attacked by Gen. Irvin
McDowell with a force of about 18,000, an army far superior to the Confederates
in number. He sent word to Johnston in Winchester to elude Patterson and come
at once to Manassas with the Army of the Shenandoah.

Johnston received the dispatch at 1 A.M. on July 18. A forced march got his
army to Piedmont Station, where he ordered his commanders to entrain for
Manassas Junction. Col. Bartow began loading his brigade on the evening of July
19, but only two regiments could make the first carload—the 7th and 8th Georgia.
Feeling themselves to be lucky, they arrived at the battlefield at 1 A.M. on July 20.
The rest of Bartow's brigade would arrive too late to fight.

Pvt. Hamilton Branch to Charlotte Branch

Manassas Junction July 20
Dear Dear Mother

I wrote you last from Winchester. the day after I wrote we moved our
camp from its old place to the fortifications which are on the road to
Martinsburg. it was reported that Genl Patterson was advancing with his
whole command on Winchester. we stayed there a day but he did not come.
it was then reported that 6000 were coming down from Charlestown so
that we were sent down there on the Berryville road about 2 miles to look
after these fellows. We pulled down about 2 miles of fences so as to have
a good battle ground but no enemy appeared, as they had gone around as
if they were going to Alexandria.

Beauregard had been attacked by the Yanks [July 18 at Blackburn's
Ford] and had telegraphed up for us so that we started immediately for this
place. we marched all night and day, crossed a mountain [at Ashby's Gap]
and forded [the Shenandoah] river, and arrived at Piedmont [now

Delaplane] the next morning. on our way we passed through Paris. we stayed at Piedmont until last night 7 O Clock when we took the cars for this place. We arrived here about 1 O Clock this morning and expect to leave this evening for the battle field where Beauregard and his army now are, about 3 miles from here.

Beauregard had a little fight day before yesterday. he killed about 1000 took 500 Minnie muskets, $700 in gold & Gold Watches, 100 Knapsacks, 150 hats & caps. the Mississippi and Alabama Boys made a sad mistake. they fired into one another and killed 5 Alabamians.

I expect we will have a fight before long. Our boys are dieing for a fight. I have just gotten through washing my undercloths. the clothes I have on my back are the only ones I have with me. I left all the rest in Winchester. we were only allowed to bring our blankets with us. I left some of my clothes with Mr. Graham and some next door with Mrs. Meredith. The people did not like it if you did not let them keep something for you.

John and Santy are well. We left some boys in Winchester pretty sick. John Wright and John Chisholm are there sick.

Give my love to everybody. tell them that if I never see them again to try and forgive me if I ever have done them any harm. God bless you and keep you and all our folks is the constant prayer of

Your affectionate son
Hammie

N B I do not know as we will have a fight soon, but as they have attacked us once I suppose we shall have to return the compliment. We are sleeping in the open air our tents are in Winchester. I have not heard any of the boys complain. The eating is pretty hard and sometimes we have to go without it for a day or two, but we do not complain. They did complain of Johns[t]on's retreating so much, but that was all.

Union general Patterson was ordered to keep Johnston occupied in Winchester while McDowell attacked Beauregard. When Johnston received word that Patterson was advancing, he feared the federal forces would interpose themselves between himself and Beauregard to the east, so he sent troops to Berryville to meet the advance and stop them; yet Patterson did not move. Johnston was able to slip away and join Beauregard, uniting the two Confederate armies.[31]

The night of July 20 Bartow addressed his boys as a father might his children.

Beauregard had promised they would be in on the opening phase of the fighting. "But remember boys," he cautioned, "that battle and fighting mean death, and probably before sunrise some of us will be dead."[32]

When morning arrived, Bartow was distressed at the inaction on his front. Finding the battle had commenced on the extreme left two hours earlier, he hastily roused his troops and set off at the double-quick. Finally he reached the battleline and took position at the summit of Matthews Hill, on Gen. Bernard Bee's right. The 8th Georgia rested on the crest of the hill. They gamely prepared to attack, with a battery under command of Ephraim Alburtis opening fire on two Union batteries in their front. A charge was ordered against the Union batteries, and the Oglethorpes came under heavy fire. Gen. Bartow fell mortally wounded.

Sanford saw his brother fall and was instantly oblivious to the killing field around him. The other Oglethorpes beside him, the gun in his hands, the advancing enemy, his own safety—all were forgotten in that dreadful moment. He ran to where John lay and, with the help of friends, carried him to the rear. But John was mortally wounded and bleeding severely. As the regiment was pushed back, Sanford urged his comrades to retreat before they were captured, but he would not leave his brother so long as John was alive. Soon Union troops flooded past him, and he was taken prisoner. He asked that he be allowed to remain with his dying brother until the end came, pledging his honor not to escape. But when the tide of war turned in favor of the Confederates and the Union forces had to retreat, Sanford was dragged from John's side. The lifeless body was left to be attended to by young Hamilton Branch.[33]

Pvt. Hamilton Branch to Charlotte Branch

Camp near Manassas Junction July 23/61
My Dear Dear Mother

I wrote you last from Manassas we were then 1 mile from the Junction since then the cold hand of death has been in our family. John our beloved has been killed, poor fellow.

On Sunday morning we were ordered to march to the field of battle. We marched about 15 miles in all directions and at last got within sight of the enemy. we were then on the top of a hill with the Washington Artillery a little below us on the same hill. Sherman's battery [actually Reynold's Rhode Island battery in Burnside's Brigade] was opposite to us, and oppened on us with there rifle cannon. Col. Gardner told us to lie down, which we did and stayed there almost an hour with the shot and shell flying all around and above us. they fell within 30 and 40 feet of us all the time. 1 fell about 10 feet in front of us and covered us with dirt. Genl Bee who was engageing the enemy and getting the worst of it sent up to Genl Bartow to send him a regiment to sustain him on the right. The Genl told Col. Gardner to take the 8th and go to his aid. To do this we had to pass between the fire of the two batteries, which we did at the double quick, Genl Beauregard looking at us. when we arrived at Genl Bee's position he told us to charge down a hill, and up another one to a thicket which was on the left and front of the enemy. We did this through a perfect hailstorm of bullets. We gained the thicket and commenced fireing, the enemy returning the fire with all there arms (they had about 6000, we about 600)

Here Col. Gardner fell with his leg broken, and John with a wound in his breast. I did not see him fall, but some of the boys did and carryed him down to the branch and gave him some water, where they all left him but Santy who stayed with him untill the enemy came and took him prisoner. I have not heard from Santy yet but no doubt he is all right, as they treat our prisoners well. I did not know John was wounded until after we had retreated from our position which was just after he fell.

We buried them the next day on the battlefield in one grave in the following order: John on the right, next George Butler, next Willie Crane, next Bryan Morrell, next Tom Purse, next Julius Ferrill. Capt. West read the burial service. The men all feel John's loss so much. he was loved by everybody who knew him. I have his sword, sash, horse and pocketbook. I think Santy must of taken anything else that he had. His pocket book was in his pocket underneath him. John has been very kind to me ever since he came here. he would let me ride on his horse on marches. I will send a list of the wounded by next mail with some more of John's hair. What shall I do with John's things. shall I bring them home when I come after the war?

I was struck twice but God protected me. Once I was hit in the breast but it did not go in. The other hit me on the leg but did not go in.

Your loving son,
Hammie

[P.S.] We whipped them. they had about 7000 killed, we 2000.

Pvt. Hamilton Branch to Charlotte Branch
. . . a Continuation of His Battle Account

Manassas July 25

My Dear Dear Mother

We stayed in the woods about three quarters of an hour, when we were told to retreat, which we did in as good order as we could on acc of the woods. when we got out we were met by Genl Bee who sayed he had orders from Genl Beauregard for us to lie under cover, and rally and act as a reserve. we were then in a field with bombs flying all around us.

We marched up a hill rite in the face of the enemy with there musket balls hailing down all around us. It was here that poor Tom Purse was killed. He was walking in front of me about 10 feet, when he fell on his knees and stuck his head in the ground. I had seen men do the same dodging bomb shells and I though he was doing the same thing. As I passed him, I thought I would look and see who it was and tell him to come on as the balls were raining all around us. I looked and saw he was dead and that it was Tom.

We marched up to the top of the hill with about 80 men and layed down behind the Hampton Legion and 7th Geo. as a reserve. It was here that the ball hit me in the breast. Col. Bartow was in command of the forces in front of us and, seeing the Confederate Flag waving from a point that we were firing on, ordered our flag to the front. we carried it there and had no sooner planted it than the Stars and Bars on the other side was pulled down and the Stars and Stripes displayed, and a volley poured into us which killed 4 or 5 of the Hampton L. They then retired but were brought back and fired like tigers. When we left this place we were ordered by Genl Beauregard to the rear. We would have been taken out of the thicket sooner but Genl Bee could not get his Aid to come in to get us. when we did retire we were fired into by the 4th Alabama.

The man that took Santy prisoner is himself a prisoner, although Santy was carried on. Sid Goodwin was talking with this man yesterday and he asked him where he was from. Sid told him and he sayed he took a man from there prisoner, and Sid asked him what his name was. he sayed Brant or something like it. Sid sayd Branch and he sayed that was it. he sayed he was sitting by a ditch by a dead or dying comrade when he took him. He then went on to describe him.

The wounded include Frank Bevill, John [A.] Belvin, [Samuel J.] McDonald, John Martin, Holly Cole, [William F.] Billy Shel[l]man, John

Krenson, Jon Fleming, Bartly Donovan, Addie Tinsley, Hollie Estill, Lentz, Carrolan, Raysor, Joe Godfrey, Lippman, Jim Hunter, Franklin M., Ned Davis, [Charles C.] Hardwick, C.C. Girardeau, Joe King, R. Q. Baker, [J.S.] Montmullin, and 4 others who I can not remember now. they have all been taken care of. There was also 3 taken prisoners.

27 wounded
5 killed
3 prisoners
35 total

There were also others who were slightly wounded. To go over the ground we went that day, and know where the enemy were and in what numbers, it seems as if it was a miracle that saved us. the thicket we were in is torn to pieces.

Genl Beauregard says it was a splendid charge. Genl Johns[t]on says he never saw such a gallant charge. it seems as if we [were] sent forward as a Forlorn Hope to draw the enemys fire.

The victory was complete but was dearly won. The battlefield was covered with there dead. The 8th destroyed two regiments—the 6th Massachusetts and a Rhode Island Regiment.

We are all well as ever.

Your loving son
Hammie

[P.S.] Love to all.

Actual casualties were 460 Union killed, 387 Confederate killed. Total loss in Bartow's brigade was 60 killed. Casualties in the 8th Georgia were 207 killed and wounded out of 500, the highest loss of any regiment engaged.[34]

Sarah L. Hine to Charlotte Branch

Richmond July 24th 1861
Charlotte,
    my poor Charlotte what shall I say to you. "The Lord reigns," shall I try again *"The Lord reigns."* His love is as boundless as his power is Infinate, my dear friend you must trust him, cling to him, hold fast to the hours of his altar. He is able to hold you up, to sustain you, yea even to *comfort you*. I hope and believe you will find him so. If my poor prayers can avail I *know*

you will. In a letter to [our daughter] Josie day before yesterday James sent the passport of that day's despatches which said the Oglethorpes all well. We were wilfully deceived. The truth is they did not know themselves. We did not hear the sad tidings until yesterday evening, then Charlie Graybill told [my husband] James that John Branch was dead. My heart almost forgot to beat when he told me, it seemed as if it was freezing with horror, he said Montmullin told him who had come down wounded. James & I immediately started out together to try & learn something about it, he had gone out we could not see him. His mother said her son thought so but from what he had told her she did not. She thought it would be best to telegraph the news to Savannah but not let you know it. We thought differently, hoping it was not true. When the evening train came in late, young [Hollie] Cole & [James] Hunter [Jr.] came slightly wounded. James & I stood at the depot for two hours waiting for it. We came up at dusk, but as soon as it arrived, he went out & found the boys. They but confirmed the awful news, said poor John fell one of the first, even before Gen. Bartow. Hamilton they said was well, they believed Sandford was. the well ones were pursuing the enemy, not in danger in that pursuit, for the enemy had thrown away their arms & were running, the first time an American army was ever known to *run*.

I have not heard a word from [our son] James B. since we left home, only that he was left sick at Winchester. His father has tried in vain to get a passport to go there but the Sec. of War is inflexible, he has a certificate from the Mayor of Sav. as to who he is, has warm friends here from Florida, some holding high offices in the government. The Rev. Dr. Taylor a resident of this city is ready to vouch for him & some Savannahians here, but the Sec. has not granted a passport to any this week except to go after their dead, or mortally wounded, and then it must be their *own* dead. We could go to Winchester, only that the route lies through Manassas. Today he will apply for one for Manassas & go there on your behalf & look after your boy & send his remains on to you by Express as soon as they can be prepared for transportation. If you have any choice about a coffin or any thing else telegraph to us. If he gets a passport to day he cannot leave until tomorrow, & he may not be able to get it for some days yet. Should he get to the scene & ready to act before this could reach you he will telegraph to you for instructions. Address him care Rev. D. Taylor Richmond.

It is now six in the morning & he is out trying to find other boys who were expected last night, hoping to get something more reliable about

Sandford. As soon as he does he will despatch to the Mayor hoping John's death will be broken to you as gently as may be, but Oh how awful the shock will be. My very heart bleeds for you. I have passed a restless unhappy night & could not sleep for thinking of you. May the living God sustain you, He only can, and your poor heartbroken Mother. How will she bear it. She must rest in the arms of Divine love. The sympathizing Saviour is your friend & hers. I trust you will realize him to be such. I wish I could see you.

> "When hearts we love are revelling in gladness
> Though far away we are content & blest;
> But when they tremble at the breath of sadness
> We long to press the sufferers to our breast."

Evening.

Mr. Hunter says John's body is on the way here. I was glad to hear it, as James applied again to the Sec. of War for a passport & he said he must refuse, that Beauregard's orders were explicit, he had not granted a passport this week. Though we had heard people could go for their dead it seems it was not so. He said he did not suffer any one to go, even for Gen. Bartow, but telegraphed. He said the dead and the living were all properly cared for and if friends wanted the remains of any they should be promptly forwarded. Two or three are here from Sav. who left there Monday morning who heard the news that morning, some thirty six hours before we heard it here. This only confirms me in what I have heard before that the comfort of the soldiers & the parents are consulted as much as possible. We can hear nothing of Sandford one way or the other. I hope ere this reaches you, you will have heard that he is well. Hammy was struck by a ball right on the heart but it was a spent ball & did not hurt him in the least. It was slightly black & blue.

My letter is perfectly unsatisfactory to me but I don't know what to say. If I could frame words of comfort Oh how gladly I would do it. Yet I know none but God can relieve such sorrow. With most affectionate love & sympathy from James and myself your friend,

Sarah L. Hine

[P.S.] [Our daughter] Cornelia sends her love & says tell you she hopes it is not true. Alas!

Virginia Magill to Pvt. Hamilton Branch

Winchester July 25th 1861
Dear Mr. Branch

Mr. Paterson brought us over a list of the killed and wounded from your company this evening, and I was shocked to find among other friends the name of your brother. You do not know how distressed we all were to hear this, and how sincerely we do sympathise with your Mother and yourself but above all with your dear Mother in this sad bereavement. All of my acquaintances in your company with the exception of Lieutenant Beman your brother and yourself were either killed or mortally wounded. I knew your brother and yourself better than any of the others and of course felt more anxious for your safety. Oh! War is an awful thing and when I think of the crushed and broken hearts with which this country is filled this night it makes me sick at heart. It is hard to realize that one so bright and joyous as your brother was when I last saw him should have been so suddenly called from time to eternity, and oh Mr. Branch do let this sad affliction, for well I know what a blow it must have been to you, make you at once "prepare to meet your God." Do not put it off any longer make your peace with your heavenly Father and then whatever happens will be for your good. Think what a comfort it would be to your Mother if both your brother and yourself should now be brought into the fold of Christ. Excuse my writing so plainly to you, I am so anxious that you should now make a friend of that blessed Saviour who is willing and waiting to receive you, and who has promised that if you do come to him he will not cast you out.

You have been so much with us since you have been in Virginia that I feel as if you were no longer a stranger but a very dear friend to us all. Will you please write to me as soon as you have time and tell me the particulars of your brother's death, whether he was killed at once, and if he was at all conscious. I hope Mr. [John A.] Belvin and Mr. [Samuel J.] McDonald may prove not to have been so badly wounded as was at first thought. I feel distressed about Mr. Ferrill, I had become so well acquainted with him. I had two cousins and many friends shot in the battle and my heart has felt so sore that I have hardly been able to rejoice in our glorious victory. God grant that we may be permitted to have peace without further bloodshed. Colonel Bartow must have been a great loss to your regiment. I suppose you must have been in the thickest of the fight as you lost so heavily. I feel as if one victory was dearly bought at the expense of our gallant young men who have fallen.

Do take care of yourselves and do not rashly or unnecessarily expose yourselves. I shall look anxiously for a letter from you, and hope you will write soon and tell us about all of our friends in your company. God bless you all and keep you in safety is the prayer of your sincere friend.

Virginia Magill

P.S. Direct care of Rev. James A. Graham, all the family send much love and their sincere sympathies to you both.

Carrie McIver to Sarah Allen [Charlotte's apprentice]

Dorchester [SC] July 26th/61
My dear Sarah,

What can I say what shall I say—is my noble cousin among the slain? Can it be so! The papers confirm this news but I hope even against hope. "Man proposes but God disposes." *His* will is not ours—and may He help his poor bereaved Mother and grandmother to bear this paralyzing stroke of affliction. And what of Sanford have you news of him? Hammy I see is safe (for the present). Have you heard from Aunt C[harlotte]. Do write me by return of mail and tell me all you know of my cousins—I do not sleep for very suspense as well as anguish of heart. My heart bleeds for Aunt C. in this her hour of trial. And Oh I do pity Mrs. Sawyer how does she endure this? Will it not kill her? Should I be able to be of any service to her write and we will come to you. I should have started to her immediately were it not for the children. I thought unless I could be of service to her—the children would be more trouble there, than my presence would do good. Should she need me or should Aunt C. return with John's remains and *wish it* I will come down for a day or two. Tell aunt C. so if she does return, but do write instantly about Sanford. I shall await the next mail for a letter from you anxiously—All well—Mr. Mc. joins me in the deepest sympathy for your bereaved family. In haste and affection

Carrie S. McIver

Direct to —— and mark the letter *in haste*

Cpl. Sanford Branch to Charlotte Branch

Washington, DC
Old Capital Prison
July 26, 61
My Dear Dear Mother:

I scarcely know how to begin this sad, sad letter. You must have heard of the terrible loss which has befallen us before now. I will give you the particulars as nearly as I remember them.

We left Manassas Junction on Sunday morning about four o'clock and marched about ten miles, where we could see the enemys battery. After we had been there about fifteen minutes, we were ordered to the front to support General Bee. We gained a small piece of woods when I left the left of the company and advanced in front.

Discharged my gun and loaded when I thought I would look behind me to see if any of my Company had fallen. But, Mother, just think of my horror to see John, Dear John, reel and fall. I dropped my gun and ran to him. I got there just after Dr. West, who Dear John asked whether there was any chance or not. When told he must die, he replied, "Very well—he would die like a soldier and a man."

With the assistance of friends, I carried him to the rear of the regiment when, at my earnest request, all my friends left me, but Mr. Lewis Eastmead, who refused to go. My poor brother lived about 3/4 hour. He was perfectly sensible about half the time. He died in my arms. His last words were about you and Hamilton.

I cannot write any more now, as I was taken prisoner, standing by his body, and am now in Washington City. Please have my watch sold and send me 50 dollars. I hope to be exchanged in a short time.

And now Dear Mother, do for my sake, try and bear our terrible loss as well as you can. Remember he is in a better world.

Your affectionate Son,
Sanford W. Branch

According to Rev. John Jones, chaplain of the 8th Georgia, John "was shot in the right side, the ball wounding his right arm and then passing through his sash into the right side. He bled freely and suffered severely. When hearing the cries of the wounded around him for water, he took his canteen and said to his brother, 'Give them every drop of water in my canteen.'" [35]

CHAPTER FOUR

Death Loves a Shining Mark

On July 22, 1861, news of the Confederate victory at Manassas Junction was telegraphed to Savannah, yet the cost of its triumph left a stunned and mourning populace. Among the dead were six young men of the Oglethorpe Light Infantry, all friends, all members of the same Sunday school class at Independent Presbyterian Church. The closely knit community of families clung to one another for solace.

Charlotte Branch was plunged into a nightmare. Despite her anguish, she immediately prepared to make the long journey to Virginia. Her first concern was to get to the battlefield and recover her son's body. She appealed to Mayor Holcombe for a pass and, accompanied by Sarah Allen, departed on the evening of July 22. Along the way she shared her sorrow with travelling companions, and the compassion of friends gave her safe harbor in Richmond. Other Savannahians, including her friends Sarah Hine and Heman Crane, were already in the capital city organizing the Savannah Relief Committee to provide a place for soldiers on leave to receive packages, obtain clothing and food, and maintain contact with their families.

Once in Richmond she learned of Beauregard's orders barring anyone from the vicinity of Manassas. The army was still reeling, trying to deal with the aftermath of a battle much bigger than any had anticipated. Heartsick at the thought of her boy lying in an unmarked grave, she nevertheless turned her attention to the living. Sanford's fate was uncertain, but Hammie was safe. She attempted to visit the army camp and console her youngest son.

While Charlotte was absent, friends who heard the devastating news poured their hearts out in condolence letters and visited the home to express their sympathy to Charlotte's mother, Sarah Sawyer. Rev. Isaac Axson of the Independent Presbyterian Church had told her of her grandson's death.

Savannah was a city in mourning. The O.L.I. barracks on Liberty Street were draped in black crepe, and the members of Co. B resolved to wear a black arm band for thirty days. The newspapers gave detailed accounts of the battle, and wrote "in memoriums" of the young martyrs.

Gen. Bartow's body left Richmond on July 23 accompanied by his brother-in-law, Lt. J.M. Berrien. At a stop in Charleston the public buildings were draped in mourning, and the whole community turned out to pay its respects as he lay in state there. Company B of the O.L.I. served as honor guard and the Chatham Artillery fired minute-guns as the cortege moved through the streets of Savannah on July 27. The funeral took place the next day, with all of the city companies and detachments serving in the area in attendance. Services were conducted by Right Reverend Stephen Elliott, Bishop of Georgia, at Christ Church, and interment was at Laurel Grove Cemetery in the city.[36]

John's death left a tremendous void in the lives of those who had known him. From all who knew him we are given a portrait of a sensitive, thoughtful and promising young man, so representative of the best Georgia had to offer in the early days of the conflict. His fate was but one story of hundreds and thousands that would be played out tearfully in households all across the South for the next four years.

Laura Lufburrow to Charlotte Branch

Savh July 29th 1861

We have just received Sally's [Sarah Allen's] letter my darling friend which brings its welcome with it. It is a great comfort to us to know that you are as well off as you are. You do not know how very anxious we were to hear from you. Despatches are so little to be depended on. I hope that ere this reaches you, you will have seen dear Hammie, dear boy I know it would be such a comfort to you to have him with you, & sincerely hope he will be allowed to come home. We received a letter from him on Saturday written to you. of course we opened it, it contained a piece of dear John's hair. Oh Miss Charlotte it almost breaks my heart to think that I never, never, shall see that blessed face again in life. I cannot realize it. Never hear him say again *"Cousin Laura you are an angel"* that always expressed his thanks for anything I ever did for him. . . . Dear Sandy can nothing be done for his release? Our grief for John was interrupted by hearing of him as a prisoner. We did not know how to feel about it, but can only hope for the best.

Your Mother is a great deal better than we had any idea she would be. She says I must tell you that she feels satisfied that John's body can be put into a coffin & buried there & his grave marked. it would be best to let him lie till fall. There are so many around talking that it is almost impossible for me to write. I only wish I could be with you. I cannot say half I feel, but you know that my strongest sympathies are with you. . . . All send a great deal of love to you & Sally too. If there is anything that Lan [Orlando] or I can do for you do let us know at once. May God bless & keep you my dearest friend is the earnest prayer of your ever loving friend

Laura L. Lufburrow

P.S. Gen. Bartow's remains were put in their last resting place yesterday afternoon.

One of the most affected by John's death was a former sweetheart, Tallulah Hansell of Marietta. The daughter of the prominent Georgian judge William Young Hansell, Lula was born in 1838 and attended a girls school in Huntsville, Alabama, before going to Kennesaw Female Seminary. Her brother, Andrew Jackson Hansell, served as adjutant general of Georgia during the war.

She had known John in his cadet days at Georgia Military Institute. Many a happy hour had passed between the youths, and they shared a close and loving friendship. They grew apart when John returned to Savannah in 1855, yet they resumed their correspondence in 1859.

Tallulah Hansell to Charlotte Branch

Oglethorpe, Ga.
August 1st/61
Dear Madame,
    Though personally unknown to you, the writer fain would hope that she

is not altogether a *stranger*, for she would not wish to intrude on grief as sacred as is yours. —When news of the glorious victory at Manassas thrilled every patriot heart, before the words of exultation and rejoicing had been uttered, the news of the *martyrs* who had bought the victory with their blood trembled along the wire and the glad words quivering on her lips died unspoken. When the tidings came to my quiet country home, "Bartow had fallen," a shadow fell on our household, for he had often been a loved and honored guest. But to *me* the next words were far more chilling, for *your boy*—Oh! *weeping Mother*—*was my friend*! I *felt* that he was dead before I knew that he was in the battle, felt it so that the night before I learned his fate, I could not sleep at all. and when the mail was brought in at noon, I did not *dare* to unfold the paper, for some minutes. *Then*, I felt that your heart must be crushed by this terrible blow.

I was *his friend*, and the weight on my own heart tells me how bowed & broken his *Mothers* must be. We knew and loved each other as dear friends while we were boy and girl almost, in Marietta. Frank, noble, and generous, a warm friend. What wonder that we all loved him! In our house he was a frequent and ever welcome guest, and many a pleasant hour we passed together. Once, in consequence of gossiping tongues there was a slight misunderstanding, but at the first word from me, he grasped my hands in his, and begged pardon for ever listening to the tales so untrue. We were but *firmer* friends from the brief estrangement.

When we parted five years ago, he gave me his likeness, bidding me "keep it for the sake of a friend who can never forget you." It lies open before me now! This picture with the semblance of life; the dark, bright fearless eyes, the firm, kind mouth, the white brow with its framework of rich brown hair. This picture mocks my sorrow. It looks so full of life and youth, and *he* whose shadow it is pale and dead. The bright eyes closed in dreamless slumber, the lips forever sealed! *I cannot realize it!*

Very often I have heard him say "*No boy on earth ever had such a Mother as mine*"—and I have seen his merry flashing eyes grow soft and misty when he spoke of you. He brought books to me that *you* had marked—and seemed so fond and proud of his Mother, often expressing a wish for me to know you, for he always added "*you could not help loving her*"—The year before the last (59) we corresponded for several months—and though he seemed less *merry*, the *man*, had still the warm kind heart that I loved in my "boy-friend." If among his papers you find these letters, please destroy or return them to me. I would not ask it but they relate to a *third person*, a mutual friend. But for months the correspondence has ceased. I know not why. We never have doubted each others friendly interest.

To you, the Mother he so much loved, I now offer my *most sincere sympathy*. Many weep over your boys death, but honor the brave spirit that faltered not on the battle field. Our tears flow, but we know that *he* would have sought no *nobler* fate than to die for his land & home! Rest, brother and friend, in an honored grave, and know that friends honor thy noble daring, while their tears gush forth, and water thy resting place. Mother of the gallant hero, To an all merciful God I commend you. *He* can bind up thy bleeding heart, and He alone can do it! May His Comforter be with thee in these dark hours!

My family all tender their sympathy to yourself and family. *If you can in time*, feel able to write me, please tell me of his life latelly, and the particulars of his death. If I have intruded, forgive me, and believe that my motive is pure. I cast this simple tribute on his grave, feeling how poorly I have expressed the sorrow I feel, and the sympathy I would offer.

Praying that our kind Heavenly Father will comfort your aching heart— and that in the shining realms of glory with him we have loved and lost, we may sing praises to our Redeemer—I beg to be allowed to call myself your unseen but *sympathizing friend*

Tallulah Hansell

Charlotte Branch to Pvt. Hamilton Branch

Richmond Aug 30 61

My Darling Boys

I have been very lonely without you, do write and let me know how you are geting along. Hammie would not you like to go home with me? I do wish I could take you home. don't you think I had better make an aplication for your discharge? write just as you feel about it. Whit Stevens says that the tent John ocupied was his own, that is he says that he is very sure John bought it. he allso says that the Old man (negro man) that is wating on Coll Gardner has the keys of Johns trunk and that Johns trunk is at the Old Mans house in Winchester. now had you not better have it sent down to me? Whitfield [Stevens] Allso says that Johns valise is with the baggage at the camp. he thinks you must do as you think best about the horse. Mr. S[tevens] and his son both think it will be best to sell it, perhaps it would be as well to keep the saddle and bridle which I could take home.

Oh my Dear child I am so sad and lonely. I had some thought of going up to Winchester to morrow with Mr. H[enry] Fre[e]man who is here and is going there to attend to George Padelford's effects and to mark his grave. I believe I should go but that I should have to travell on Sunday. it would be so excellent an opportunity for me to go and attend to these things myself.

My dear precious boy do take care of yourself and dont be careless of yourself, and above all remember your testatment and do please remember your Creator now in the day of your youth. God bless you my own dear precious child. I have not heard from Santy yet. . . .

As ever your devoted Mother
C.S. Branch

Charlotte Branch to Pvt. Hamilton Branch

Richmond, Aug 4th 61
My Dear Darling Hammie,

God be praised for the blessed inteligence I have just recieved by telegraph from you that Santy is safe.

I trust my child that you do give thanks to God for the safety of your *only brother*. My dear Hammie let us endeavour to live lives of close obediance to God who is our only help. I shall go mourning all my days for my dear John, yet I trust he is a glorified spirit, and if so then death is gain to him— Oh how much I thank you for telegraphing as I shall spend a much more quiet night.

Mr. W. Stevens says the acting Adj. of your regiment is using Johns horse and that the horse is not taken care of. Do attend to it and consult with Mr. Stevens and Mr. Hine as to what is best to do with it. Mr. Charles Green has a plantation about a mile from you where the horse might be kept. perhaps, if you think it best to, wate until Santy can say what he would rather have done with it.

Oh I am so happy to know that Santy is safe. I trust you will love each other better than ever.

God bless you my own dear precious child. As ever your affectionate Mother

C.S. Branch

Sanford remained a prisoner at Old Capitol Prison in Washington, D.C.

Eleanor Hull to Sarah Allen

New Boston Aug 5th/61
My dear Sarah,

I have written Aunt C. twice within the last two months but having heard nothing from her concluded she could not be in Savh. I heard last week that she had gone to Virginia.

Sad indeed were the tidings brought to me that our dear noble John had fallen on the battlefield. I cannot realize it is so, and yet it is the one thought of my mind. I see it written everywhere both night and day. Poor boy! he did not live to know he had won a single battle. It was too dearly a bought victory for me to rejoice in it. I am glad Aunt C. went on to Va. It was best for her. Poor Aunt! I feel her heart is well nigh broken; but the God in whom she trusts will give her strength to rise above this heavy stroke and grant the consolation so needed in this her hour of affliction. And Mrs. Sawyer too will feel it sadly, how did she bear it? I fear it will almost kill her. We see by the papers that Sanford is a prisoner and Hammie is unhurt. Oh! I am very thankful to hear no worse. I hope Santy will soon be released. Poor Hammie must have felt so alone after the battle was over. I trust they will be permitted to return soon.

I wrote Sister [Carrie McIver] last week in regard to having bonnets & I would like either blk [black] straw or colored straw with blk. trimmings or anything you may have suitable. I suppose it will be difficult to procure just what we would wish at this time. I have a mourning gingham which is the only piece of black to be obtained here. I hardly know what to say about other dresses. It will depend upon the bonnets. I have written Sister respecting this. We all expect to start for Dorchester [S.C.] in the course of ten days or two weeks and Mr. H. and myself will certainly come down to S[avannah] to see Aunt C.—If I can get a bonnet and one dress before we go. you must not trouble yourself farther as we have silk mantillas that will answer. Mother will not get anything until I go to S.— I need not tell you that we wish to wear this for our dear cousin, our almost brother. We may be in Liberty [County, Ga.] by the 14th or 15th and I would like to find our bonnets at Mr. B. as it will save Mr. McIver the trouble of sending again for them. Direct to Mr. A.M. McIver—I feel very anxious to hear from Aunt C. and to learn the particulars—

Mr. H[ull] has been compelled to disband his company on account of health. Most of his men have joined a company just organized in Lake City

[Florida]and have been ordered to Fernandina [Florida]. He leaves today for Fernandina with fourteen new recruits. Give our best love and sympathy to dear Aunt C. and Mrs. Sawyer.

> In haste truly your friend
> Eleanor C.H.

Mourning attire for close relatives was complete black for a minimum of three to six months, depending on the relationship of the deceased. The Hulls and McIvers were not blood relatives, but showed their respect by wearing appropriate clothing due to the devotion of the families.

Charlotte Branch to Pvt. Hamilton Branch

Richmond 6, Aug
My Dear Hammie

Sarah [Allen] will leave for home in the morning with Mr. Stevens, I shall then be very lonely so have made up my mind to come up to Brisco or Bristo whichever it is. then I shall be quite near to you. if it is posable for you to go there you could procure board for me. I shall come on Thursday or Friday but will write you to morrow night again, I rec a letter from Mr. Axson yesterday and one from Gertrude [Dillon] today she says that Mrs. [Leocadia] Blois has written to me and Maria [Blois] to you. I have not rec them yet. Have you seen the list of the Confederate prisoners— I will send you the list if I can find it. I send a [Savannah] Republican [newspaper].

Oh my child how desolate I feel. My children have been my all and how can I live without them. Love God my child and try and live very near to him and may God bless you is the prayer of your mother

> Charlotte S. Sawyer

[P.S.] I expect to get a letter very soon from Washington.

The Confederate army camped at Bristoe Station, Virginia, near Manassas, for the fall and winter of 1861–62. Charlotte corresponded with various people in Washington in her attempts to contact Sanford.

Adela McLaughlin to Charlotte Branch

Augusta August 6th
My Dear dear Mrs. Branch,

Will you allow a comparative stranger to say a few very few words to you. Our hearts are so full for you that we feel we can have no relief until we express our *great great* sincere heartfelt sympathy with you. Your son I had never seen but once but in a single moment years of feeling and admiration for him sprung up. I have known him through others, through our dear Hammie & you will certainly excuse me when I tell you we are bereaved, when I tell you we feel for you, when I tell you our hearts have gone out to our Blessed Savior in his mercy upon you. Remember dear one that when on earth he was ever ready & willing to sympathize with us & if when he was poor weak flesh with us he could feel for us, that he can now more thousand fold more feel & pity us that he is our spiritual Savour.

Oh! my dear Mrs. Branch excuse me, when I tell you my heart has bled for you since your affliction & that I have prayed God! to have mercy upon you & comfort you & your dear boys since this great affliction. Remember this is a short life. he has only gone a little while before you & that God in his infinate goodness & mercy saves a soul in its dying hour, Let this then be your consolation. Feel that your fervant prayers for his soul have been answered & believe that no one feels more sincerelly for you than myself & our Jimmie. Excuse me if I have presumed too much. I felt & must give bent to my feelings, When I know & feel they are sincere. Yours in much love & sympathy,

Adela McLaughlin

Charlotte Branch to Pvt. Hamilton Branch

[James H. Binford's house, Richmond]
Richmond Aug 7, 61
My Own Dear Son,

I really have very little to write, still do not like to loose an opportunity of saying a word to you. . . .

I am wating to see Mr. Henry Freman then I shall come up to Bristoe. Ca— [unclear] came yesterday. he called to see me and offered to go up with me. he says he has come on to be one of Gen. [Robert] Toombs aids. George Snider arrived this evening he sent me word he would be to see me in the morning. Holly [Cole] tells me that a young man by the name of Wm. Mell came on to join the OLI. he allso says that Comp B. is impatiently wating to here from Capt. West that they are affraid they will be sent on the coast then they wont be able to come.

I am very sad and lonely. God bless you my own dear child and keep and take care of you. I have not heard anything further from Santy except that the enemies sayd today, that is a correspondant from Washington, that the secession Ladies [Southern sympathizers] had sent boquets to the Confederate prisoners at the Old Capital. I hope they send them something better than that. My child I am crazy to see Santy. I trust it will not be long before I do see him. Do write when you can. As ever your affectionate Mother

C.S. Branch

Charlotte Branch to Pvt. Hamilton Branch

Richmond Aug 9th 61

My Dear Son,

I do not know when I shall leve for Brisco [Bristoe Station, Va.] as I have not seen Mr. Freman yet or have I heard further from Santy. I rec several letters today from Savannah, one from Georgia [Elkins] one from Gertrude D[illon]. The others were from Mrs. [Virginia] Magill, your cousin Carry Mc I[ver] and one from Miss Talula Hansell, Johns friend. I would send it to you but am affraid you might loose it, I shall write to Mrs. Magill very soon. I enclose your cousin Carries. Gertrude wrote that Ma had made a cake for you but that George Snider could not bring it. I send you some candy and 2 cans of peaches, I hope they will be good. I want to be neer you my child, I do wish the war was over. I am very lonely, very. Pray for me my child that God will comefort me—

My son you say you want to be revenged dont feel that way. Remember God has sayed vengence is mine I will repay. Leve it all to him. just do your duty and all will be right. We must learn to say though he slay me yet will I trust him. This is what I am trying to do. I hope the holy spirit will help me. May your heavenly Father bless you my darling child. With earnest love as ever

your devoted Mother,
C.S. Branch

[P.S.] Remember me to all who care for me. Mr. [Ralph B.] Sand[i]ford and others. I am sorry for Dr. West. CSB

Sarah Allen to Charlotte Branch

Savannah, August 9th/61
My Dear Friend,

We had a fine trip arrived home yesterday. We made every connection. They received the despatch that I had left and thought I would be there today, and they were all astonished when I walked in. Found Mrs. S[awyer] well. They all say she has been remarkably well since you left. The house has been full of company all the time. I think it was well you were not here for from what they say it was enough to leve anyone crazy.

Georgia & I went to meeting last night. You may believe I thought of you and of the great change since we last sat there together. God grant you every comfort before you return to that seat. . . .

There was quite a little party here yesterday afternoon. Mrs. Bennet, Butler, 2 Smiths, 2 Dillons, 2 Bliss. They have heard from Mr. Smith He says he dont know when he can come home. He says he cant do anything with his stock. Mrs. S. says she would rather shoot them all than that Lincoln should have them. Mrs. Butler and Mrs. Laura Luff. have both written to you. Mr. O[rlando] H. L[uffburrow] came last evening to say he saw Mr. [Samuel] Dasher who brought the letter from Manassas and that they had heard from Santy. He was astonished when I stepped forward and told him I was ahead of him. He says I had better go up with them Saturday. I told I must stay and hear Mr. Axson. he said he would let me hear as long a sermon as I would wish. I said quality was better than quantity.

The girls are quite in love with Mrs. [Mary] O'Brien. They say she is so lovely. She had gone home when I came. But she came after Tea. She sympathises with you deeply. Georgia Olmstead Banks has been here twice Mrs. Tucker told Miss Josie [Hine] she would like to come but did not know what to do. I just received a letter from Eleanor [Hull]. she has heard of John's death and the safety of the others. She feels very bad. they are coming to Dorchester and said she would come in to see you. They have had 2 letters from Carrie saying if she was needed she would come right in. They have sent for mourning. Eleanor says feels as if John was her brother. Every one sure enough feels for you. But as you say that does not avail much. God alone who gave you your dear child can comfort now that he has taken him, as I trust, to Himself. Do let us know if you hear anything of Santy. Remember me to Hammy. Everybody sends love to you and Hammy. I must close now as it is time to send the letter. Write soon and often.

Your aff. Friend
Sarah J. Allen

Philip Fendall to Charlotte Branch

Washington 13 August 1861.

Madam,

Your affecting letter of the 2nd instant reached me this morning.

I immediately endeavoured to see your son, if he should be here, with the desire of offering to him any aid which might be acceptable. The effort was unsuccessful. But I have just left Judge Wayne, who informs me that he saw your son and other military prisoners from the same neighborhood, shortlly after their arrival here; and that your son was quite well. The Judge has repeatedly endeavoured to see them again, and to render them any desireable assistance; but has hitherto been foiled by the stringent regulations which, in the progress of public events, it has been deemed expedient to adopt. I am to join him in another and early effort for an interview with your son, which, we cannot but hope, will be permitted.

But as it may mitigate your distress to know, if nothing else, that your son is safe and in good health, I give you this information at once, instead of waiting till I can say more. Meanwhile I assure you of my continued efforts in his behalf.

Permit me to suggest, as well on account of your son as of others similarly situated, that it will be prudent to withhold from the newspapers the names of persons taking an active interest in his case.

Deeply sympathizing in your affliction, and solicitous for its alleviation,

I am, Madam,
Very respectfully,
Your Obt. Servt.
Philip R. Fendall

Charlotte Branch to Pvt. Hamilton Branch

Richmond Aug 13, 61
My Dear Son,

I wrote you several days since and when I wrote sent several letters I had rec from home, I have been sorry I did not send them by mail. I rec a letter from Sarah today which I send. I was told that there was a ps. in one of the papers today stating that the Confederate prisoners were on parole in Washington but not to leve the city. That is done that they may support themselves. what will Santy do poor fellow. My heart akes for him for all of them. I have not heard from either of the letters I sent to Washington. I wrote to Mr. Breckinridge Mr. Fend[a]ll and to Santy and telegraphed too. Oh my child my child would that he was released.

I really have not any thing to write about so will stop. I must come to Bristo. I am not certain when I can come as I have been quite sick, I send the oil it is the best I can get. Thank you my child for your prayer for your Mother. Please try and be consistant in your religious duties. dont be ashamed to pray to that God who has so mercifully protected you. ever trust him. He will take care of you. I should be so very glad to see Fred [Bliss] and Mr. [Ralph] Sandaford. Remember me to all friends God bless you my own dear darling child is the prayer of

your Mother,
C.S. Branch

Carrie McIver to Charlotte Branch

Dorchester Aug 14th/61
My *dear dear* Aunt,

I have been trying to find out your address for some time and have just succeeded. What *shall* I say to express my deepest sympathy for you, in this your hour of darkness and distress! I feel that words avail me nothing. Surely there can be no sorrow like *your* sorrow! I almost forget my own grief for the death of my heroic cousin, and the captivity of another equally as dear, to condole with you on your irreparable loss. Ah! this is surely an unholy war, and I feel that a just retribution will sooner or later overtake those who have been the cause of it. You gave to your country your *all*. It was no common share of patriotism that induced this great sacrifice—it was an act worthy of a Spartan mother. *I* knew how you loved your boys, and could estimate the value of your gift upon your country's altar. A portion of that sacrifice has already been received—but God grant the rest may be left—

I can not realize that our dear John is no more—that he now lies on the Plains of Manassas pierced by the balls from those guns which (one would think) should have protected him. He died amid "the din and tramp of war" a fitting place for a spirit as brave & gallant as his—he died in a glorious cause and I feel assured that he (as well as others) died not in vain. The blood shed on Manassas Plains will yet bring *our* new government out of all its trials and tribulations, purified from its dross—and we shall yet be numbered among the great nations of the earth. . . .

Have you heard anything *from* Sanford, and is there any immediate prospect of an exchange of prisoners? Poor Santy, what *must* have been *his* feelings, and Hammy must have felt desolate and alone after the battle was over. Have you seen him, is he with you? Oh I do long to hear from you! I had sent you a letter on the *Monday* before I received news of the battle, inquiring about you and *yours*; presume it did not reach you ere you left. On hearing of your departure, I sat down and wrote Sarah [Allen]—she too had left. Laura very kindly answered the letter. I then wrote Laura asking for your address. She was *then* out of town but finally received my letter, and I have just received her reply. Sis [Eleanor Hull] does not yet know your address, but as I am expecting herself & husband, & baby with mother, *this week*, will not write her again. I should have gone down to Sav. to be with your mother had my children been old enough to leave; but I could not leave baby and as she was quite sick from teething, could not carry her from home, well. The children are doing well now and Mr. Mc. and myself are moving about but not very well. We daily talk of you and the boys, and hourly nay constantly think of you. I received a letter from Mrs. Dr. Walthour a few days since, and she says there is no one she thinks of more or sympathizes with, in all these troubles than you. Hoping this will reach its place of destination and meet with a speedy reply, I close. I wish to know all you know of John's death and Santy's capture and Hammy's whereabouts.

Yours in sympathy
Carrie

The following letter was never delivered. It was given to Joseph F. Waring, who carried it in his pocket for the rest of the war.

Sarah Sawyer to Cpl. Sanford Branch

undated, c. August 1861

My Dear Sandford,

I cannot express to you how happy I have been made by hearing from you and having it in my power to write. You will rec. an undershirt, 2 pr. socks and twenty dollars in Gold. Your mother is at Bristoe Manassas and seen Hammie several times and has visited John's grave. She left here the night after the Battle. Make your wants known to any friend who offers, as all will be made right then. If you can write to your Mother or me do so. Your brother was burried with the Oglethorpes Ferrill, Purse, Morrell, Crane & Butler.

Tell [Lewis] Eastmead I shall write his mother. Old Mr. [Matthew] Lufburrow has been very ill but is better. Young [William] Ivey's body was brought home on Tuesday, died from wounds received [at 1st Manassas].

Good Bye my dear grandson. Believe you are never forgotten for a moment by dear

Grandmother S.S.

May God bless you dear Boy.

Philip Fendall to Charlotte Branch

Washington 15 August 1861

Madam,

In my letter of Tuesday I intimated that I would again endeavour to obtain an interview with your son. I have just succeeded, in company with Judge Wayne, in doing so. I found your son quite well, and as contented as one in his circumstances can be expected to be. I was desirous to relieve any wants he might have, or in any way to promote his comfort, but he assured me that he wanted nothing and promised if he should, at any time, want anything he would so inform me; in which case I shall very cheerfully supply him. I shall soon repeat the visit. Your son will himself write to you.

Yours very respectfully,

P. R. Fendall

Charlotte Branch to Pvt. Hamilton Branch

Bristo Aug 18 61

. My Dear Hammie

I have looked daily and hourly for you ever since I have been here, I do wish you could come. you sayed in your last that there was very fiew clothes of Johns. where are his cloak and his shawll. He had 2 dozen shirts when he left home and plenty of drawers and 4 flannell shirts, several pr. of white pants a new pr. of blue cloth unaform pants and pr. of light ones. I do wish if you cant come you would write to me for I am most desolate and lonely.

Most affectionately

your Mother

C.S. Branch

Mary H. O'Brien lived in Savannah with her daughter, Mary Catherine, and her son-in-law, Henry Brigham, a commission merchant from New York. They are not related to the Branches. To call a friend "cousin" or "aunt" was common practice in this period.

Mary H. O'Brien to Charlotte Branch

Savannah Aug 19th 1861

My Dear Cousin,

I feel that I ought to have written to you before this, and would have done so, if for a moment I could have given you any consolation, but I felt quite unable for such a task. I know my dear cousin, that your faith and trust in *one* who alone can help you, in your deep distress, and he is ever ready to help all, who trust in him. and all I can do is to pray to the same Almighty spirit for you that he may strenghten and support you in every trial and that it may please him to spare to you those dear one's whom he so graciously pleased to save in the battle, and that he will permit them to return to their home and smooth the remainder of your life, for I think none other earthly beings ever can tender you any pleasure. with deep heartfelt sympathy I think of what you have to endure. Oh! I hope you will not sink under it. May God in his infinite mercy help you.

How often I thought when I saw you with your three dear boys that you were as truly happy as any one could be. alas! how short lived is anything like happiness here. Yet in all this sadness, one blessed pleasure still is ours.

it is that we can speak any where and at any time and mourn for our dear departed when every heart will feel and say, well may she weep for such a good son. There is something Heavenly in it. I pray that we may be prepared to follow.

My dear C. I have been obliged to leave your dear Mother, for the present. Mr. Brigham has gone to Kentucky on business and will be absent for two or three weeks, the baby is not well and I feel that I must be here to assist Kate but I shall see your dear Mother very often she keeps up well considering how feeble she is—I hope you will soon see poor Sandford. I am glad to hear the prisoners are well treated. I hope you will be able to see Hammie often, give my love to him when you see him, tell him we all think and speak often of him and wish for his safe return—with much love to you my dear Cousin, I remain ever yours—

Mary H. OBrien

Rev. Isaac S.K. Axson to Charlotte Branch

Savannah Ga. Aug 21,1861

My dear Mrs. Branch

I have just returned from your Mother's, who really seems to be sustained under the pressure of your affliction beyond which in her feebleness could have been anticipated; but "God does not suffer the bruised reed to break"; —and I trust you will continue to realize a similar fulfilment of his precious promise, although doubtless every week will make you more to realize the heaviness of your visitation, & will exercise & test to the very utmost your patience. But he hath said I will never leave you nor forsake you; cast your burdens then upon the Lord, who perfectly understands your case, and whose purposes touching his people though they may seem to be involved in mystery are based on Mercy & cannot be thwarted nor delayed in their execution if any of the wrath or unrighteousness of evil does. Grace will be measured out to you, I doubt not, proportioned to your tribulations; & I hope as the ultimate issue when you let testify to the goodness & fidelity of Him who keepeth covenants.

Your mother read me a copy of a letter from Sanford, the original of which was remailed to him—it is doubtless a severe trial to him to be held in confinement:—and the very childishness of folly are the fools of the Washington Administration to decline an exchange of prisoners on the grounds alledged. Our men, under these circumstances must have patience, & show an equal heroism in bearing the discomforts of captivity as they did in facing the danger of the battlefield—the same God lives who was with the young man *Joseph* in the Egyptian Prison House, & when his purposes have been subserved, he will "loose the prisoners"—Have faith then in God, & you will let yet praise Him for the help of his Countenance—

Very truly yours
I.S.K. Axson

Ann C. Magill to Charlotte Branch

The Meadows Aug 23
My afflicted Friend,

    Your letter was brought me last night & I hasten to answer it in the hope I may be made use of to speak some words of comfort to your stricken heart. You have indeed the sincere sympathy of our entire family, Mr. & Mrs. Graham & all my daughters & even the little children & servants, who were all so attached to Hammie that they feel for all whom he loved— *they* knew John too tho' not so well, but *we* all knew & admired him, & feel that we have lost a very dear friend—he told us he *expected* to be wounded, to carry an honourable scar from the battle & he should certainly return to us to be *nursed* as he could not bear the idea of going to a Hospital & would feel so at home with us, the girls told him to be sure & do so, we would take care of him & he rode off saying, now mind I'm in earnest, its no joke, I shall order myself to be brought here. that was the last we saw or heard of him till I returned from Martinsburg where I followed three bodies of my very dear Cousins who fell on the same day.

    [They] were brought immediately back & carried to their homes in Martinsburg. Hammie I expect has seen them at our house. Holmes & Tucker Conrad, brothers fell at the same instant almost in each others arms, the only sons of their parents, who in their old age can never cease to mourn their loss. Peyton Harrison the third of these noble young men left a lovely young wife & three little children to "plod their weary way" through this dark world without a Protector. He had left his will & little treasures with me for his wife in the event of his falling & I took them to her—poor child she was wild with grief—we both know what that *widowed* has to feel.

    We returned from Martinsburg expecting to find our house full of the wounded & perhaps your sons among them, but instead of that, the sad news of poor John's death & Sanford's imprisonment awaited us & also the death of many many other Friends. . . .

O what a fearful battle that was. I cannot tell you what a gloom has been cast over our Society. The Army had been in our midst so long, that all had made friends from among the strangers, as well as those who fell of our townsmen and kinsfolk. God forbid that any more blood shall be shed & grant us Peace speedily.

Your dear John was indeed a noble fellow, no wonder you were proud of him, few Mother's had such a son to lose, the widowed Mother's stay & prop too. . . .

Lay hold upon this hope. you have a *right* to believe & trust His promises & say to the evil one "Get behind me Satan" when he tempts you to doubt Him whose name is *Love*. . . . You must be so lonely in your sorrow, but you are not *alone* for I am persuaded our Saviour is with you & will give you the victory. Think of your other two noble boys who will try to make up to you the loss of their brother. "Jesus can more than make amends for all he takes away." Santy will soon be released & will go home with you & I wish you could take dear Hammie too. Mr. Graham & Ginnie [Magill] got his letters & thank him for them.

We have all come to the country about five miles from Winchester at my brothers for the benefit of the pure country air. We have all been sick from having so much sickness in town. The air has become impure. My family all join me in much love to you & Hammie. God grant that he & Santy may soon become Christians. May our Father give you all such consolation as you need, is the prayer of your Friend

Ann C. Magill.

[P.S.] We shall go home in a few days. Hamilton's clothes were sent to him by his direction, several weeks ago, but we have not heard whether they were recd.

Charlotte Branch to Pvt. Hamilton Branch

Bristoe Aug 26th 61

My Dear Dear Son

You cant immagine how disappointed I was that you did not come. if I had thought there would be any doubt about your coming I would have stayed all night at your camp. As it was we waited until 1/2 after 9 o'clock and then had to go as the camp was broken up and more than half of them had gone before we left. Oh Hammie I spent a dreadfull night. it is so terable to see so many sick. Mrs. Bayard's nephew was very low and is near, she brought him with her to take care of him, they burried 2 the morning we left. they died during the night, disease in camp is dreadful, dreadful everywhere but worse there, with not a comfort around them, so little attention. I rec 6 letters when I got back, I hope you will arrange soon to come to me. All at home want you to get a furlow if not a discharge. God bless you and keep you in health. I am not well today, having had a most terable fall yesterday. am most bruised and it hurts me much to draw a long breath. Still I have much to be thankful for it. is a miracle that I did not breake my neck.

Do arrange to come soon. Remember me to all my friends.

As ever your affectionate Mother
C.S. Branch

The 8th Georgia was at Camp Victory, near Manassas, from July 27, 1861, until they moved to Camp Bartow two and a half miles northeast of town, near the railroad. They remained here until relocating at Camp Mason's Hill in Fairfax County.[37]

Correline West to Charlotte Branch

Savannah Aug. 29th 1861
My dear Mrs. Branch,

I have earnestly wished to write to you long before this, but I could not find time, or strength, or courage to do so. . . .

I do pray God, to bless and keep you, to strengthen and sustain you, and in "this great and lone trouble" that he has shown you to turn again "and refresh you" as he has so often done, those that he loveth and chasteneth and scourgeth" ever since and before, the sweet Psalmist of Israel wrung out from his bruised and crowded spirit, these sacred and true words of comfort—

. . . How it would have done every Mother's heart good to have heard him—My boys have that sermon—do get it & read it—send them word dear Mrs. Branch where you are and they will come to see you.— intended telling them you came then I forgot it—I wish also I had an article I wrote called Oglethorpe to send you—I know you would like it—Bob & Jimmy have it—if you see them ask them to lend it to you.—

I have been reading every morning a precious book—"the words of Jesus," & the Faithful Promises—I wish you had it—it would do your soul good—"If need be" "only believe" and many other passages are so beautiful, heartcomforting & encouraging—

Oh! dear Mrs. Branch. We must . . . believe—it was your Father in Heaven, your blessed Saviour who saw "the need of the rendering of your very vitals, in the sacrifice on the altar of his country, of your glorious firstborn noble son— Oh! bitter, bitter, sad & sore trial to you to yield up that gallant boy! Oh ever think often of his splendid eyes—so clear, so bright, so beautiful—if ever Savannah owned a young man of whom she might be justly proud— it was John Branch—for purity, industry, valour, truth and chivalry —surely of him most truly it might be said—

None saw him, but to praise

None knew him but to love—

Death loves a shining mark—and when in the thick conflict—amid the din and cannon's roar he winged his fiery dart at your Son's noble heart— he knew he struck one observed of all—Oh! dear Mrs. Branch take comfort from these things—remember by whose will these trials are permitted— bear in mind that "He doeth all things well"

. . . Oh what times these are for all of us! They try men's souls and women's too—we have had cool delightful weather—and great health prevails—believe me dear Mrs. Branch yrs with love and sympathy

Correline West

Eleanor Hull to Charlotte Branch

Dorchester [S.C.] Aug 30th 1861

You must not think from my long silence my dearest Aunt that I have not thought of you in your great sorrow. Most sincerely do I sympathise with you and not a day, scarcely an hour has passed since the sad tiding from Manassas reached us, that I have not thought of and sympathized with you. I hoped the first despatches that came might not *all* be true, but the second confirmed it and I was forced to believe that our brave noble John had fallen since the first battle had been won in which he was engaged.

. . . I have secured letters from Lilla Hazlehurst and Sallie Scarlett in which they expressed much sympathy for you and spoke in the highest terms of our noble boy. Sallie told me to write you how much they *all* sympathize with you. She says Mr. [Francis] D. Scarlett shed tears when he heard that Gen. Bartow and John had fallen. . . . We all think of you and talk of you. Am very sorry I shall not see you. I expect to spend a day or two with your Mother if she is in Savh. I wrote Sarah [Allen] yesterday—We have been here a few days.

. . . Please dear Aunt excuse this short letter. I should have written longer and better had not the babies all been around me. We have such baby times. The Troup [Artillery] are encamped four miles from here so we see very little of Brother Mc[Iver]. Mother, sis & Mr. M. join me in much love and sympathy for you. In joy & sorrow ever your affectionate

Nora

[P.S.] Sister [Carrie] & her little ones are well. Write me to this place of yourself & Hammie. Have you heard more of Sanford?

CHAPTER FIVE

I Wish This Old War Was Over

Charlotte remained in the vicinity of Bristoe Station, Virginia, through the fall of 1861, nursing the boys of Co. B, Hamilton among them. She won the sobriquet "the Mother of the Oglethorpe Light Infantry" for her devotion. She never ceased in her efforts to contact Sanford, but was unsuccessful in obtaining permission to visit him. Her letters did not reach him, the federal authorities being ever vigilant in their ruling that Confederate captives were not as worthy of the same treatment as "legitimate" prisoners of war.

The early policy of the war toward prisoners was still being defined, and semantics complicated the issue. The Confederate Congress, having adopted conventional rules of war, was willing to exchange prisoners, yet the Lincoln administration hesitated. Secretary of War Stanton interpreted such an exchange to be a recognition of the South as a legitimate power; while the Union was trying to convince the Europeans that the Confederacy was "in rebellion," they could not recognize her soldiers as "prisoners of war." Stanton sought to try the Confederate soldiers as traitors and rebels, the exact position the British had taken in regard to American soldiers during the revolution in 1776. And he knew that many of the three-month U.S. volunteers who had been captured would be under no obligation to reenlist, as their enlistments would be up by the time they were exchanged; they would be of no use to the Union army.

Sanford remained at Old Capitol Prison in Washington, D.C., throughout the fall of 1861. The building had been erected in 1814 to house the U.S. Congress when the British burned the capitol. Later it served as a boardinghouse, then fell into disrepair. When the war began, many citizens of the District of Columbia were arrested as "disloyal" for supporting the right of the Southern states to secede, or as spies, and the building was used to confine these political prisoners.

Southern-sympathizing women in Washington, Baltimore and the part of Virginia under Union occupation (Arlington and Alexandria) aided Confederate prisoners, providing financial aid, food, and even clothing where Union authorities would allow. They smuggled letters out, relayed verbal messages between the prisoners and their families, and reported mistreatment. These determined ladies were liable to charges of "disloyalty" and could be and were imprisoned or banished. One of the most infamous sympathizers was Rose O'Neal Greenhow, the spy, who was confined at Old Capitol Prison while Sanford was there.[38]

Unknown Sympathizer to Charlotte Branch

Washington Oct. 21st/61
Madam

I heard through a lady who heard a letter read from a Lady in Baltimore who saw you at Manassas that you were now at Fairfax Courthouse endeavoring to send funds to your son who is a prisoner here, and that you were anxious to come here hoping that you might procure his release & that your younger son was well. I have just written him to that effect, presuming it would be a relief to him to hear from you, I deeply feel for you. I am the Lady whom you met on the cars on your way from Richmond to Manassas, I succeeded in delivering your message and card sent to your son here. I would not advise you to come here, but if you conclude to do so I should be very happy to meet with you. I will be on the look out. Present me very respectfully to Mr. [John] Richardson, [a commission merchant from Savannah,] who was accompanying you when I met you, for reasons which you will understand I will not sign my name to this. I hope to send it by one of the released prisoners, and write you desiring to relieve your anxiety, and to let you know that your son is well & has heard from you—
                                        I am sincerely, Your friend
                                        Mrs. xxxxx

The news of Savannah's loss at the battle of first Manassas spread slowly but inexorably across the country, eventually reaching even the furthest territories. James Carter was a druggist whose apothecary was two doors down from Charlotte's millinery shop. Sanford clerked for him prior to the war.[39]

James H. Carter to Charlotte Branch

Waco, Texas Nov 26 1861
My dear Mrs. Branch,

As we are so entirely cut off from the means of communication & getting any very direct & decided news from the states it has been only very recently that I have heard anything decided as regards the fate of many of my friends & relatives who are now battling for our right. I have just rec papers giving me a list of our Georgia troops who suffered at the Battle of Manassas. Oh! the sad deplorable fate of poor John. Ah! my dear friend, what shall I say to alleviate your sorrow; I feel it is not in human power to assuage your grief, but knowing your true Christian spirit & putting your trust & faith in the great ruler of the universe that you have received strength from the throne of God to bear your heavy affliction. Oh; how hard it is to part with those we love for only a short period but when a dear devoted son is taken from us forever the grief is heart rending, a mothers love, oh how deep, how lasting, you have been sorely & deeply afflicted a double share of misfortune; poor Sanford! a prisoner. I hope he is kindly treated but still I fear that our prisoners do not receive much kindness from such a set of vandals and heathens.

. . . My own illness has entirely incapacitated me from taking any part in the great struggle of our country; except contributing our mite in assisting our troops; but I hope it is God's will that I may yet be abel to strike a blow & avenge the many afflictions & misfortunes that the evil black hearted band has caused us to suffer; Mrs. Carter writes with me in much love to your dear Mother, cou. Laura [Lufburrow] & family, I have some idea of coming in if possible in January when I hope to see you.

Your sincere friend
James H. Carter

Carter refers to the treatment of captured Confederates in Arkansas, Missouri and Texas in the early months of the war by "the black-hearted band." They were treated as guerillas, and many were hanged without benefit of trial.

Heman A. Crane to Charlotte Branch

Richmond Nov 27th 1861
My Dear Mrs. Branch

I arrived here last night safely and delivered your note to Mrs. Hine. . . .
I found Mrs. Hine well, thinks she may go up to Manassas on Monday next.
I found Horace improved and anxius to go back to camp, but his friends
object and think he should remain here longer. I think he will go on
Monday next if not before.

I got Mr. [Thomas A.] Bulkley to go with me to the War Department
(Passport Office) this morning to assertain if Sanford could be permitted
to visit you at Manassas on his arrival here and find that he can. We have
stated the case fully and are assured that he can under the circumstances
have permission to go. I have no letters from home and nothing now to
report. Please remember me kindly to all.

Yours truly
H.A. Crane

[P.S.] I have bought a camp stove an oven and some other necessary
articles for the comfort of Horace and his mess which I think will be found
very valuable to them and contribute very much to their comfort. they can
cook in their tent with this stove in bad weather—it is made of boiler iron
very portable, not liable to brake or get out of order, and when moving can
pack most of their cooking utensils in it and take it up by the handle.

I expect to leave for home tomorrow or the next day—and now Mrs.
Branch allow me to commend to your care and kindness my dear son, my
only son Horace—should he get sick again while you remain near the camp
take him and care for him as you would for one of your own dear sons and
the gratitude of a father and mother shall be poured out in humble prayer
to God for his chosen blessings upon you and your own dear children. That
visit of ours to the graves of our beloved and lost children will never be
forgotten while life lasts. I said lost children, I should not say this—they
are not lost they are gone to Heaven and we are left to wep and mourn
(poor human nature) while they rejoice singing the praises of the redeemed
around the throne of God. Oh! how happy shall we be when we reach that
happy place and are gain united with them—shall it ever be? Shall I ever
reach that happy thrice happy home? My dear Saviour shall it ever be? I
dare even hope but hope through fear and trembling that one so vile and

unworthy as I am should even be permitted to enter there but the attonement of Christ has no limit and in that alone may we all hope.

H.A.C.

The blockade and coastal operations in Georgia and South Carolina heavily favored the Union by late 1861. Charleston Harbor was under seige. Hilton Head Island was occupied by Union forces who set up a large base from which to send land troops into Georgia and South Carolina. This was too close to Savannah for the comfort of her citizens.

Mary Wilbur, wife of Aaron Wilbur, an insurance agent in Savannah, expressed her concerns to Charlotte.

Mary E. Wilbur to Charlotte Branch

Savannah, Ga. Dec 4th 1861
Dear Friend—

. . . I have often thought of your solemn earnestness of manner, the "Thursday before the battle of Manassas," which was the last time I saw you. How strangely you seemed to be impressed with a conviction of the *coming sorrow*, and your irrepressible desire to go to Virginia. Since then, I have watched eagerly for all tidings of you, and I have longed to tell you, my dear friend that among the many loving hearts that sorrowed with you in the dark hours of your affliction, your Mary mingled her heartfelt prayers with theirs that the *"Comforter"* might come to you, and that you might be strengthened to bear this heavy burden, which God in his providence had given you. . . .

I called to see your dear Mother yesterday morning, and found her much better though still feeling some inconvenience from the effects of her *late fall*. I met *Mr. Eastmead* there, who was a fellow prisoner with *Sanford* in *Washington*. He has been recently released, and brought gratifying tidings of the expected release of Sanford which together with "Mr. Crane's" assurance that by this time it has taken place, has filled your mother's heart with that eager expectancy which makes the hours so tedious in their course until that day comes when she can again see him face to face. . . .

Yet still the cry seems to be *"No Peace."* Upon our *own coast*, the note of alarm is sounded, and an anxius unsettled people await the next movements of the *Foe*—Whether they will succeed in driving us away from our homes and in destroying them is a question, which the deep earnest spirit of resistance of our community and the efforts making for defence must answer *when the day of trial comes.*

... The late action of our [Soldiers' Relief and Aid] Society has devolved a heavy responsibility upon me, especially in the absence of our esteemed 1st Directress, "Mrs. Hine." Though in consequence of other interests & the excitement of the times our meetings are not largely attended, I trust I amy be enabled faithfully to perform my duty, and that as a body corporate we may be forward in every good wrod & work. There is a wider field of usefulness open before us, *now*, perhaps, than ever *before* and the calls upon Christian charity & self denial more than *ever urgent.* I hope we may have grace given us to labor & be strong in the Lord, waiting in diligent patience while the clouds hang heavy over us for the bright dawning of that day, when *"Peace, liberty & Independence,"* shall be re-echoed from hill to hill— and resound through the Valley of our beloved *"Southern Confederacy."*

... It will be a happy moment to me when I can again see your dear familiar face—though for aught I know there may be fiery trials *for both of us* ere that time—God grant us his sustaining grace for every day, be its burdens as they may and for you dear friend that you may experience day by day how sweet it is to be passive in His hands & know no will but *his.* ...

from your sincere friend
Mary E. Wilbur

Rebecca Ball to Charlotte Branch

Near Upperville [Virginia]
Dec 11th 1861
Dear Mrs. Branch,

We were very glad to receive your letter and to hear you were so comfortably fixed near your son. Though I suppose you do not see him often it must still be a great comfort to feel yourself near.

I intended answering your letter immediately, fearing you might leave Mr. [Robert] Weir's, but have been prevented in many ways. Uncle William [Ball] returned Monday from Richmond where he has been attending Convention, his arm is still improving tho he cannot yet use it or wear his coat sleeve. He met with one of the released prisoners who knew your son [Sanford] very well, he told him he was well & getting on finely. . . . I do hope most truly you may soon be permitted to welcome him from his captivity. It seems a hard fate for our noble southerners to be held in confinement by such a set, still it must be sweet to suffer for one's country and in such a righteous cause, and with such manifestations of the Divine assistance as we have already received we must blieve the day of release & retribution is not far distant.

I hope your son [Hammie] continues well and will be able to endure our disagreeable winter (rendered doubly so by the hardships he must have to bear) without much suffering, he must feel the difference between a comfortable Savannah home & the bleak hills of Centreville. I should think if our army is to winter there some kind of log huts would be provided for the troops, for even our Virginia soldiers accustomed as they are to our climate will find a great difference this winter; while those from the far south must suffer severely I should think.

I do not wonder at all that you cannot make up your mind to leave your son during the present anxious times, indeed I think it very natural you should remain. I hope you will not leave Virginia without paying us a visit, we hope to move into Upperville in a short time & then if you would come, you would be where you could get a daily mail & could at any time get to the cars should you wish to leave. . .

We are living in *war style* as regards furniture, but are really very comfortable and it would give us all pleasure to entertain you, we hope you will not disappoint us for we anticipate much pleasure in the enjoyment of your society. . . .

I have copied the pieces you wanted & sent them in this letter. . . . Did you ever notice the similarity of idea & connection in [the poems or essays] "The Exodus" & "The Battle of Manassas"? We noticed it & I was very glad "The Exodus" was published first, it came out some time before the other. I do not remember the date but I know it was first known after "The Battle," Miss Talley's piece from which 1 copy was published in September. I hope you will answer soon. with sincere wishes for the happiness of you & yours & hoping soon to see you believe me very truly yours

R. Ball

Rebecca notes that they are living *war style*. Most of the wealthier families in northern Virginia were raided and robbed of their fine furniture and items, so many loaded their best possessions on wagons and shipped them to areas of Virginia not jeopardized by Union troops.

Finally, late in 1861, after months of discussion, the authorities agreed on an exchange program. Sanford was paroled in early December and went home with his mother to await exchange. Hammie remained in Virginia with the 8th Georgia, where he passed a lonely Christmas with his comrades.

Pvt. Hamilton Branch to Charlotte Branch

Centreville Dec 25/61
Dear Dear Mother

Christmas, Oh Mother how I do miss you. it seems as if it has been a month since I last saw you. I did not know that I would miss you so much. Jim & myself were invited by Mrs. Hine to go down and eat Christmas dinner with her today. Jim could not go because he had already made other arrangements and I can not go because Eb [Ebenezer Starke] Law let a stick of wood fall of[f] the waggon on my foot and bruised it pretty badly. it will be well again in a day or two.

We have met with a sad accident. Lt. Col. [Thomas L.] Cooper while out looking at our winter quarters was thrown from his horse and his skull fractured and his whole body so badlly jarred that he died in a few hours. his body was escorted to the cars this morning by 5 men from each company. Although I did not like the col. as a military Commander I can not help feeling sad at his untimely end, he left camp in the afternoon well and happy, telling Capt. [Edward A.] Wilcox what he was a going to do, how he was agoing to have his wife come on as soon as we got into winter quarters and that he was going to have the plank hauled to us to floor our houses with, and that he did not like the place for our quarters and that he was going to try and get a better place for us, and at 8 oclock that night he was brought back insensible and at 2 AM he was dead. Although we did not like him we can have worse commanders than he was, though not perfect in military knowledge he was a perfect gentelman. Adjutant [Charles M.] Harper went home with the body.

What a different day I will spend this Christmas to what I did last Christmas. Last 25th I eat a big splendid diner and this 25th I will have no dinner at all but tomorrow I will make up for it. Sandy [Alexander N.] Shell received some pies and cakes from home and we bought a turkey a little while ago which we intend to have for dinner tomorrow and when the pies and cakes that Grandma sent me gets here and the cake Aunt Lizzie sent me arrives we will have another big dinner. Give my love to all and wish them a merry Christmas and Happy new year for me. Tell Aunt Lizzie that

I am very much oblidged to her for the cake and that when it arrives Ralph [Sandiford] and myself will have a good time eating it. There will be one thing different from last Christmas and that is last Christmas I was telegraphed for a half dozen times to come home beefore I came and this time I would come in a minute if I could. I wish this old war was over and I and the rest of us were back home again with our friends once more. Hoping this will find you arrived home safe and well I remain as ever your loving son

Hammie

N.B. Give my love to Doc tell him to write to me when he gets a chance. Mother you must excuse my not writing often as there is noting here to write about. Mrs. Hine has moved. she likes her new quarters very well.

Pvt. Hamilton Branch to Charlotte Branch

Centreville, Jan 2/61 [1862]
Dear Dear Mother

I wrote you day before Christmas and have not heard from you yet. I am expecting to get a letter from you every day there is nothing new here. I had a very nice dinner day after Christmas I have not received the cakes or pies yet. I do not know why I do not get them I hope I will get them before long as I have been looking for them and thinking what a nice time I would have when I got them but I am afraid that will be some time.

We are very busy building winter quarters and I can not write much as I do not have anytime to do anything. It is pretty hard work building winter quarters.

Horace [Crane] has got back to camp again he is looking very well indeed. Holly Cole, George [W.] Dell and [Lewis A.] Sessions went off sick yesterday. Capt. [Alexander F.] Butler's boy [bodyservant] arrived yesterday. I have not been down to see Mrs. Hine as I have not had any time. We are all pretty well I am as well as I ever was in my life. I miss you very much but still am glad for your sake that you went home as it is very cold out here, although they say it is the mildest winter there has been for some years. Give my love to all and please put the enclosed note in the P.O. God Bless you my Dear Mother

Your loving son
Hammie

Pvt. Hamilton Branch to Charlotte Branch

Centreville Jany 9/62

My Dear Mother

I received your letters of the 28th 1st & 3rd Inst. I was very glad to receive them as I had not heard from you since you left I did not receive the turkey nor the things in the [Georgia] Hussars Box nor Aunt Lizzies cake. I received the things in Dunwoodies Box. I suppose Hollie Cole has been around to see you before this, he has a thirty-day furough. We expect to move out to our huts tomorrow. we have the logs laid and have got to roof them and chink and daub them. We have just got back from picket. We have been out three days it rained two of the nights and snowed the other. the ground has been covered with snow three or four days. Bull and Cub Runs have been frozen over so that we can walk over on them.

Mother you must excuse my short letters as I have not time to write anything. I do hope that I will be allowed to go home with John's body. I wish you would write Capt. Butler and ask him to use his influence to get me leave to go. I do not think we will get any furloughs this winter. Give my love to all my friends. Lieut. [William F.] Shellman and James Hine both send love to you. Ralph sends his respects and says he is very sorry he did not get to see you oftener than he did. Write me when Cousin Lan will leave as he will get here before the letter will arrive. I do not think I will be able to see [Rev.] Mr. Ax[s]on as it is so muddy that I can not run around to find him. I should like very much to see him he is such a good man. Tell Dock to write to me he is a bad boy. Take good care of Bruce and Bunny. Tell Fanny to give Bruce plenty to eat and take care of him. God Bless you my dear Mother and preserve us so that we may all meet again. but if it is his will, that we may all meet in a better and happier world than this.

Your loving son

Hammie

The Georgia Hussars was a militia cavalry company from Chatham County. Orlando Lufburrow probably went to the camp as one of the Savannah Relief Committee representatives. Fanny was a young Negro girl who worked for the Branches. When she heard of John's death at the battle of Manassas, she fainted.[40]

Tallulah Hansell to Charlotte Branch

Oglethorpe Jan 16th, 1862
Mrs. Branch
My Dear Friend,

I know your heart will forgive the terms of friendship I use, if you could but read *mine*. I feel that you are indeed *my friend*, and will not doubt it sooner than I would have doubted the one so dear to both, over whose grave we mingle our tears. It is a sweet recollection to me that *he* never doubted me but *once,* and that when it seemed reasonable, even then when the tongues of meddling gossips, false as the tales they told, succeeded in effecting a brief estrangement, at the first word from me, he hastened to my side, and the shadow was truly but a "passing cloud"—Never again would he listen to the voice of detraction, and our friendship was true, and unwavering. I thank God for the love my dear friend bestowed upon me, & for the blessed bright hours now gone.

I cannot express to you my feelings when I received your letter written from Bristoe, Va. enclosing a copy of one from your son in Washington at the time. I felt more than words can ever convey to you, the loss I had sustained. I could hardly read it, when the words were like a dagger in my heart. . . .

The mail has been brought in, and your letter of the 14th inst. with its *precious* enclosure. How *can* I ever thank you for it? Let your *own heart* tell you how it is prized. I longed to ask for a lock of his hair, for any little thing that he had worn or loved, but I could not ask for it. And you have sent it to me, divining my wishes. I shall indeed treasure it, and wear it like a talisman. You could not have bestowed it [on] any one who would esteem it more highly. I have heard that he was engaged to be married. If this be true, there is another heart that throbs with pain, if I his *friend* feel his loss so keenly, her loss is indeed irreparable. May the kind All-pitying Father bind up her broken heart. I feel as if a dear Brother had left me—her grief I cannot imagine—nor would I intrude on its sacredness.

I owe you an apology for not sending a reply to your letter last year. It was for a long time a loiterer by the way, so that I knew not where to address you at the time. Just as I decided to enclose it to your son Hamilton, my sister Fannie was taken *extremely ill* with a sort of protracted nervous fever, and at the same time, my *Parents* were *very* sick. Every member of the household, including *all* our servants were sick with fever, at one time, excepting myself. To add to my cares, our phisician fell sick with fever, and the other doctors having gone to the Army, I was left with this heavy responsiblity of *prescribing* for as well as *nursing eight* sick persons. My sister was ill a long time, indeed is not yet well. I did not feel the reaction of the long sustained mental excitement, or bodily fatigue until the sick were out of danger. I sat up for thirteen nights consecutively, without taking rest in the day. Of course, as soon as the exciting cause was removed, I felt the loss of rest, and fatigue, and was taken sick on Christmas night. I have been *very sick*, but this week I am stronger and can *walk alone*, and hope soon to be quite well.

Several weeks ago, in Nov. I wrote a little "Tribute" to the memory of my friend, intending to send it to you in manuscript, but being unable to learn your address, I allowed a friend to have it published, hoping it would meet your eye. As it did not come out until Jan'y 4th in the "Southern Field and Fireside" of Augusta, I presume you have not seen; I enclose a copy of it, hoping you will there find a *partial* expression of my feelings. . . .

You *honor* me by your friendship—I will always try to *deserve* it. I feel a deep interest in yourself and your two brave, gallant boys, and trust that we may know each other better ere long—I say "better"—for I feel that I am not a stranger to them or you. . .

I *sincerely hope* you will pardon my *unwilling* silence, and write to me, as soon and as often as you can. Your letters are a mournful pleasure to me— mournful because our friendship was formed beside his tomb, as it were— and pleasant because you write of him, his virtues and many noble traits— to which I bear *willing testimony*. . . . Again, a *thousand* thanks that in your affliction and bereavement, you did not forget me, and for the beautiful and *precious* gift. It has been six years since "John" and I parted—then his hair and mine were *precisely* the same—I remember his stealing a little curl of mine, and placing it among his own brown locks defying me to detect my own—But I must stop—though memory brings back many a joyous hour—forever gone. . . .

I am dear Mrs. Branch, with earnest prayers for you, your very sincere friend and sympathizer.

Tallulah Hansell

There is no record that John was engaged. There is, however, an incomplete letter in the collection, unsigned, which reads: "an eye that I loved to look into I shall never fathom with affections gaze again. A voice that has whispered many a word of love in my ear is hushed to voiceless slumber and the red lip has passed from my caressing. Arms that have enfolded me in their pure embrace are now meekly folded on the unheaving breast and dust hath gone to dust." Perhaps it was from a fiancée.

Pvt. Hamilton Branch to Charlotte Branch

Mrs. Johnsons Jany 19/62
My Dear Mother

I received your two last letters but have not had time to answer them before. We have been so busy building our winter quarters. We have moved out to them now and our mess are in their house. We worked hard and steady at ours and had the good luck to draw the shingles to cover our house with. The regiment only split enough shingles to cover one shantee out of each company so that we had to draw to see which shantee should have them and we got them. Our shantee is now finished outside and all we have to do now is to finish the inside that is to level the ground and build our berths to sleep in. We have a nice large fire place in our house which keeps the whole shantee warm our house is about fifteen feet square an about 6 feet high at the eaves with a slanting roof our mess is composed of seven boys all present viz. H.A. Crane, W.B. Mell, J.E. Carrolan, G.H. Mock, A.N. Shell, R. B. Thompson and H.M. Branch.

There are to be eight shantees to each company and two for the officers of each company. I think we will have a nice home now we are right in the middle of a thick wood on Rocky Run near its Junction with Bull Run we are about a mile and a half from our old camp and about two miles from Centreville. We are near where the 2nd Ga. were encamped when you were here. Rocky Run is the little stream you crossed coming down the Turnpike between the Suspension Bridge and our camp. There is no bridge over it. I suppose you would like to know where I am. from the heading of this letter you will see that I am at the house Mr. Hine is at. [His son] James got permission from Capt. Butler to come down and stay two days. we came down yesterday and will go back tomorrow morning. Mr. & Mrs. Hine will leave in a day or two for Savannah. Mr. Hines looks pretty badly yet.

It has been raining for the last day or two and before that it was snowing almost every day. We had a terrible time coming down here and will have a bad time going back tomorrow. The mud is about 4 inches deep and in some places about 12 inches deep. I suppose you have seen Billy White.

He is off on 30 day furlough. A great many of our boys are off on furloughs now. You will please give the piece called Yankey Ran to Miss Josee Hine when you get through reading it. It belongs to James. I received the 2 dollars but did not get the stamps. the things in the Hussars Box are at there camp. I expect to get them in about a week there is also a box from you. I did not get Miss Fannie [Tarver]'s turkey. Give my love to all my friends tell Santy to write to me. And now my dear Mother write me often and I will write when I can. With much love

Your affect. son
Hammie

Sanford was still at home in Savannah. He could not return to his regiment until officially exchanged.

Rebecca Ball to Charlotte Branch

Hazel Plain Prince William Co. [Virginia]
Jan 27th 1862.
Dear Mrs. Branch,

As you will perceive by the heading of this page, I have moved a little nearer my old home since I last wrote you. I am now on a visit to my Grandmother Ball, and old lady of 82 years, who has been compelled in her declining days to leave her home & flee before the invaders of our soil, she (with her daughter her son & family) left home some months ago & since that time have been living in this County. They were obliged to leave home in great haste, consequentlly, barely saved their clothing & a few articles of bedding, their home has long been in the possession of the enemy & we have heard from reliable sources that everything has been destroyed & their servants taken off to Washington, the home of my childhood (near my Grandma's) has likewise been destroyed & even the flowers (which I regarded as something almost sacred having been reared & trained by my dear Mother's hands) could not escape the hands of the Vandals.

I was anxious to write you before I left Fauquier [County, Virginia] but could not very well do so. We were all truly glad when we read of your son [Sanford]'s release we often think & speak of you with affection & sympathy. I think I have a heart that can deeply feel for the woes of others, for since my early years I have known many & bitter sorrows. I once had as happy a home as any one could have, too happy for this world, I knew sorrow only by its name & looked forward to future years of bliss but I was disappointed, cloud after cloud arose until this world seemed nothing but misery. I ought not to write this to you I know for when I contrast my sufferings with yours they seem almost nothing. I know nothing can equal the anquish of a Mother's heart when she is bereaved of her children—

My Grandmother has a house very near the battlefield, almost on it. There are several encampments near there, two or three Georgia Regmts. among the number. I have enquired for the 8th Georgia & heard it was farther down toward Centreville. There is a Mrs. Harris from Georgia boarding here & there has been a Presbyterian minister, a Mr. Dunwiddie, (or some such name) here also. My Aunt Getta did not accompany me here tho I was very anxious she should, her spirits are very bad. I thought change of air would restore her to perfect health & a visit to friends here who are much attached to her might improve her spirits, she has never been the same since my dear Grandma's death. Aunt Getta told me to give her warmest love to you when I wrote & tell you to come on in Spring if not before.

Please direct your next letter to Groveton, Prince William as I expect to be here several weeks.

Yours R.F.B.

On February 2, 1862, the whole city of Savannah paid homage to the boys of Independence Presbyterian who had so violently lost their lives. A committee of citizens selected at a public meeting (Robert D. Walker, Dr. W.G. Bullock, Rev. I.E. Godfrey, Lyde Goodwin, and John E. Davis) had acted as representatives for the grief-stricken parents and brought back from the frozen field at Manassas the earthly remains of their most treasured possessions, their sons.

A gray day blanketed the crowd of mourners who stood at the depot to meet the funeral train. On the Exchange Hall building the Stars and Bars flew at half staff as an escort of each of Savannah's militia companies stood at attention while the coffins were unloaded. The remains lay in state in the Council Chamber of the Exchange Hall under a watchful honor guard until the following afternoon.

It was a moving and heartrending scene as the six coffins were escorted from the hall and placed in a single hearse drawn by six white horses, their bridles adorned with plumes. A procession of soldiers with arms reversed accompanied their comrades to the Independence Presbyterian Church where Rev. Axson performed the last rites. Then, to the dirge-like rhythm of a tolling bell and muffled drums, they proceeded to Laurel Grove Cemetery.[41]

The Savannah Morning News of February 3, 1861, reported the emotional and solemn occasion and explored its significance:

As we gazed upon all that solemn scene and ceremony, and asked ourselves, why is all this? an impulse for vengeance mingled with our feelings of sorrow. It was no idle display—no ordinary occasion—those to whom the honor was paid were no ordinary men. A stranger to the actors, the scene and its history, need not have been told there was more in its meaning than the hollow display of ordinary burial. . . . To us acquainted with the actors, with the dead, with the scene and its history, how sad, how sorrowful was it, to look upon all that was earthly of six brave, noble, chivalrous youths, friends at home, comrades in arms, slain side by side in one day, on one common battle-field, now borne in one common hearse to a common sepulchre!

Well do we remember the day when the little band to which they belonged took their departure from our city, to pitch their tents on the soil of Virginia. . . . It was in the sweet springtime, and they were in the sweet springtime of life. Many, as they looked on their slender forms and rosy cheeks, shuddered when they thought of the soldier's life—its toils, its fatigues, its exposure and its temptations; and they dreaded to see that band go forth. The flowers of spring were wreathed in richest boquets by the dear ones at home, and as they filed away, each one bore upon his bayonet a lovely wreath. We remember, too, the words that fell from the lips of their gallant commander, the lamented Bartow, when acknowledging the presentation of a beautiful flag from some of the young ladies of the city. . . . He told his comrades that they were going to lay themselves down to sleep on the bosom of Virginia. Who that heard his words did not feel them sink like lead in his bosom? Who has not called them to mind a thousand times since that brief day? Eight little months, big with history, but short, how short, have passed away, and many of that handful of heroes have "laid themselves down to sleep on the bosom of Virginia!"

Sanford, his mother and grandmother attended the reburial. Sanford had last seen his brother as he lay dying on the battlefield. Long denied proper mourning, he finally found release. For Charlotte, the nightmare was simply relived.

Hamilton had been unable to obtain a leave to accompany his brother's body home. He remained in winter quarters near Centreville, Virginia, during the early months of 1862, where the demands of camp life and the companionship of his brothers-in-arms were his solace against homesickness. His military career was furthered by a promotion to corporal while in quarters at Centreville; in January he was made a sergeant.

Sgt. Hamilton Branch to Charlotte Branch

On Picket Feb 8th/62
My Dear Mother

I have not heard from you for a very long time. The last letter I received from you was the one in the bundle Cousin Lan brought me. I am very much obliged to you for the candy and groundnuts. They were splendid. I would have written to you before but was waiting to hear from our furloughs. I thought every day, well I will write tomorrow anyhow whether I hear from them or not. I have not heard from them yet. They have not been returned yet and I don't believe they will be. I had some hopes of going home recruiting with Capt. Butler, who I expect will leave camp today for Savannah. [William D.] Coombs goes with him as he is the only married man in the company, but now that all my hopes are gone and I see there is no chance to get home I thought I would write. We are all well. We are on picket now. Billey Shellman is in command as Capt. Butler did not come out and Fred [Bliss] stayed with him to fix up some company matters. Major [Lucius M.] Lamar has been made Col. and Capt. [John R.] Towers Lt. Col. and Capt. [E.J.] Magruder Major. We would a great deal rather Magruder had been Lt. Col. Horace [Crane] was dissapointed, he was to have gone home with Capt. B. also. Mother I wish you would return my thanks to Mr. Butler for the shoes. They are splendid. A little too large but do first rate. Also return my thanks to Miss Fannie Tarver for the pulse warmers she sent me. Tell her that I hoped to return my thanks to her in person also return my thanks to Cousin Laura for the doughnuts she sent me by Cousin Lan. I do wish I could get some of them often. The cake Aunt Lizzie sent us was splendid.

I must close as Lieut. Shellman is going to camp to act as adjutant and will carry this for me. Give my love to all. . . . write often to your loving son
Hammie

Sgt. Hamilton Branch to Charlotte Branch

Winter Quarters Feb. 11/62
My Dear Mother

I received yours of the 2nd and 3rd today. I was very glad to receive it as I had not heard from you for so long a time. I did not know why you did not write but supposed it was because you expected me home. Oh how I do wish I could have come. At one time I thought I would be sure to get a furlough but no, I had to stay. A great many of the 12 months men are reinlisting and getting furloughs. now is the time for the enemy to advance while we are weak. They are now elated and on the strength of there victories may get courage enough into there men to attack us at Centreville. If they do they may whip us but not until they have killed many a brave boy. I do not apprehend any attack but I intend to write you all the news never mind what it is. I know Santy will think I am wrong, but Mother before I do this I want you to promise me that you will not let anything I write you worry you untill you hear it has happened. That is if I write as I will now, viz, that our regiment has been ordered to be ready to move and the commanders of companies have been ordered to see how many haversacks canteens spades pickaxes and axes they have in there companies. Rumor gives different reasons for this. One is that General Beauregard has telegraphed for a Brigade from this point and that our brigade will be sent. another is that we are a going to North Carolina. Now I do not want you when I write you such things as this [to] worry you but wait untill you hear that we have gone. That is that the thing I write you about has happened. I do not believe there is any truth about our going away, Another report is that the enemy are advancing and that there cavalry are now at Fairfax. I do not believe this either. The roads are getting in good order now though and if the weather keeps good the enemy can advance.

Sam[uel H.M.] Hall has been appointed Quartermaster Sargent and Jimmy Hines has been appointed Postmaster. Mother please send me some postage stamps, and if you ever send me anything send me some envelopes. I have plenty of paper and envelopes enough to last me a good while. There is nothing new. We returned from picket on Sunday. Yesterday I put up a blanket room in our house and took a good wash all over, and put on clean clothes. You do not know how much better it makes me feel. Jimmey Grant has not finished your picture yet. He has just gotten his paints up here and says that he will finish it as soon as he can. Jimmey Hunter has been appointed a Lieut. in the army. I will go and see Miss [Rebecca] Ball if I can find out where she is. I would like very much indeed to see her. I will try and find the house. if I can see Mr. Dunwoodie I can find out. I never leave camp now the weather has been so bad and there is no wheres to go.

Capt. [John R.] Towers has been appointed Lt. Col. and Capt. Magruder Major of our Regiment. Jimmey Hines sends his love to you. Give my love to all my friends who remember me. Tell Mr. Butler to ask Dinzey why he does not write to me. Why does not Mr. Butler answer my last letter. Why does not Doc write to me. I think he might tell Miss Gertrude D[illon] that I would like to hear from her. Give my thanks to the Miss Smiths for the socks. Give my love to all the homefolks and believe me your loving son

Hammie

[P.S.] The things in the Hussars Box have arrived. What bad news from North Carolina.

The bad news was Union general Ambrose E. Burnside's expedition against Hatteras, which threatened the North Carolina coast. He led an amphibious attack against Confederate forces at Roanoke Island on January 9, 1862. By February 12, federal forces had taken the island, moved into Albemarle Sound, and occupied New Berne and Elizabeth City.

Tallulah Hansell to Charlotte Branch

Oglethorpe, February 17th 1862
My Dear Mrs. Branch,

Your most welcome letter was cordially welcomed more than a week since, and I should have shown my high appreciation of your kindness at an earlier period, had it been in my power. I am Secretary of a "Soldier's Relief Society" of this county, and for the past two weeks I have been constantly engaged either in work for the Society, or in copying law papers for my dear Father, who is in very feeble health, and unable to write. My thoughts have been often with you, and particularly during the sad and trying scenes connected with removal and interment of the remains of my dear friend. . . .Were both your sons with you? I intended sending a copy of the "tribute" I sent you to your son at Manassas, but am unable to procure another printed one. I was *so* glad that you liked it—*it was written for you*-and published because not knowing your address, I hoped in that paper it might catch your eye. You were right in saying it came from *my heart*—It did come from the "innermost"—Not one word in it that is not written on memory's tablet. It seems to me so imperfect, so unworthy the *friend* I mourn, that I have at times almost regretted its publishment. You can therefore Judge how gratifying your approval of it is to me. . . .

I thank you, dear Lady, very much for the invitation to visit you. I sincerely trust that when the white winged dove of Peace returns to our land and coast, it may be in my power to accept it. . . . I have even among the troops in Savannah (three companies of our townspeople and country friends from the county are there) many friends and in Gen. [W.H.T.] Walker's Brigade, the Commissary Capt. [D.D.] Stockton is a brother-in-law. Of course we tremble and pray for their safety and success. Gove. Brown writes us that he considers Savannah *safe* & able to repel any attack made on her.

Are you acquainted with Rev. David H. Porter [a Presbyterian minister from Greene County, Alabama]? He is a special and very great friend and favorite of mine. I learned not long since that he was in miserable health, and am quite anxious to hear from him. I think his a most lovely character.

I enclose the copy of the "tribute" according to your request, and wish it was more worthy. If your sons are with you, please present my kindest regards to them. Do they resemble my friend? I have a favor to ask of you—Will you not plant a *white rose by his grave for me*—or a little tuft of *blue violets*? He always loved to see a white rose bud in my curls. Mother and Sister join me in love to you. Please give my regards to your Mother also. I know this is a very poor letter, but I have been reading over my dear friend's *letters*, and I feel very sad. May God comfort your heart! I am well acquainted with Capt. Butler—knew him in Marietta, and would be pleased to meet him again. Write to me whenever you can, and believe it will ever afford me pleasure to hear from you. With a fervent prayer that He who has afflicted, will bind up your bleeding heart, and comfort and sustain you and your loved ones in every scene in life—I am, dear Mrs. Branch—your warm and sympathizing friend—

Lula Hansell

CHAPTER SIX

Some Say That We Are Going to Richmond

Union forces settled into winter camp on the farmland of northern Virginia in 1861–62, displacing families and destroying property. Women and children were cut off from Confederate soldier fathers and sons and lived in constant fear of a visit from roving bands of federal cavalry and infantry. The Virginians began to understand what was in store for them—the war had come home.

Rebecca Ball to Charlotte Branch

Prince William County Feb 24th 1862
My dear Mrs. Branch,

Tho quite late tonight I must write a few lines in answer to your kind and most welcome letter which reached me yesterday in one from aunt Getta.

I did not answer your letter written from Richmond until I reached this place tho I intended & wished to do so very often. Soon after I reached here I wrote you and hope you have received my letter before this. I can not hope tonight, to write any thing of interest, my thoughts are too gloomy, the recent sad reverses with which we have been visited have cast me down very much yet I cannot feel (as some around me do) that *all is lost*, I am well convinced the South *can not* be conquered, while I fear we have but seen the beginning of horrors & will have to wade through years of bloodshed before peace will crown our efforts. I still endeavor to hope for the best & believe that God will overrule even ourdefeats for our eventural good.

Saturday evening it was reported here that Savannah had been taken, we did not place any confidence in the report 'tho we fear such a thing may occur. Where would you go in such an event? I do hope you will not be called upon to suffer the loss of Home and all its endearing surroundings, as we have done. You have had far greater trials to bear, and I feel that I should be very grateful to our Heavenly Father for having spared thus far those I love most tho they have been exposed to the dangers of the Battlefield, compared with these dear ones, what I have lost is nothing.

I do not wonder you found it hard to leave your son here. I believe his Regmt. is only a few miles from this place, my Uncle with whom I am staying, would have invited him here, could he have gotten to him but owing to the mud we are kept closely within doors, he has inquired for him from soldiers who have stopped here but none who knew him have yet called.

My Uncle & Aunt have heard me speak of you & feel a great interest in yourself & children. They have a son a prisoner in the Old Capital perhaps your son met with him. We would be delighted to hear any thing of him should your son have become acquainted with him, his name is Summerfield Ball, he has been there nearly six months. I know not why he has not been released. General [Gustavus W.] Smith has taken the matter in hand & written to General [Samuel] Cooper [the inspector general in Richmond] on the subject perhaps he may be able to procure his release.

My Aunt is kept in continual sorrow, not only on his account but she has two sons in the army who were members of my Brothers unfortunate co. & who refused to remain any longer inactive, we all feel they would meet with a sad & awful fate were they to be retaken. Persuade your son not to join until exchanged, I know if he does it will give you double sorrow on his account. My Uncle has so far recovered as to be able to rejoin his Co. the 1st of next month. Poor Aunt Getta dislikes so much to give him up yet we feel our country needs all who *can come* to her rescue.

My brother is now recruiting his Company & expects to have a larger one than formerly. I feel dreadfully about his joining, but he is determined, you know I have good reasons for uneasiness on his account owing to his unfortunate position. Since the death of my dear Parents, he has been doubly dear to me & has always been a most devoted Brother. I hope you will come on in the Spring & visit us wherever we may be. I shall remain here about two weeks longer. Please excuse my writing on two pieces of paper. I forgot to bring a supply with me & it is very hard to find here. I hope you & your sons are well, & my prayer is that they may be spared to you for many years. I am much obliged for the pieces, have not seen them yet, my Aunt wrote she had put them away for me, she sent her best love to you. I hope you will answer this very soon. Let me know where you will go if you leave Savannah. Hoping the blessings of Heaven may rest upon you & yours I am ever yours truly & affectionately,

Rebecca Ball

The Confederate army under the command of Gen. Joseph E. Johnston also passed the winter in camp. The cold weather and muddy roads kept the boys confined, the monotony broken only by an occasional snowball fight. During this period Hamilton wrote nearly every day, adding to his letter daily until he had an opportunity to mail it.

Sgt. Hamilton Branch to Charlotte Branch

Log Huts Feb 26/62
My Dear Mother,

I received yours of the 17th by the last mail. I was very glad indeed to get it as I had not heard from you for so long a time. 16 days, I did not know what to make of it. I thought that something must have happened to you but am very glad to hear that I was wrong. I am very much obliged to you for the bible but I would rather have had one out here that I would not value so much as I do that one as we do not know what moment we will leave here. almost everyday we here that we are going to fall back from here and now it looks as if there was some truth in it as it is reported that the Yankeys have taken Winchester and that our forces are falling back on Manassas. if this is so the report [is] that we are a going to fall back to the Rappahannock River, which is between here and Richmond. I do hope that this is not so.

I heard today that Santy was on his way here. [A false rumor.] Jesse Heidt arrived here a day or two ago. He is looking very well indeed. There is nothing new here except the reports of our going to fall back. while I am writing this I have heard that the sick are all to be sent back to the rear. I have been sick for about a week but am perfectly well now. If I was not afraid that we were going to have a fight here I would become suddenlly sick again. If we do have a fight you will here it before you receive this. It would be too bad to fall back from here and leave all our houses, blankets, and cloths for the Yankeys to have.

I have not seen any of Mr. Wares[Robert Weir] folks since you left. I do not know what has become of them. Mother please send me some stamps I have not had any for some time and have had to borrow from Jimmie Hines. Give my love to all my friends. . . . All the boys here are well and send there respects to you. Give my love to all the home folks and pray for your loving son

Hammie

Feb 27/62

There was no mail carried yesterday so mine of the 26th did not go. Therefore I thought I would open it and tell you that the report of us going to fall back is not true but that it is thought there is some move on hand. I have had the toothache twice the last week and so yesterday being on as Sergeant of the Guard I thought I would step up and see Lt. [Charles A.] Jones of Co. H and have my tooth pulled out. I did so and after 5 or 6 twists and pulls he finally got it out. He told me that I stood it like a man, that a great many would have moved about and given him trouble. Love to all

Your loving son
Hammie

By early March the worst of winter was past, and the army prepared to move. Johnston was ordered to reinforce Gen. John B. Magruder near Yorktown, Virginia, against Union major general George B. McClellan, the new commander of the Army of the Potomac.

Sgt. Hamilton Branch to Charlotte Branch

Camp Sam Jones March 7/62
My Dear Mother
I received yours of the 1st yesterday afternoon and was very glad to hear from you. I have been expecting to hear from you every day. There is nothing new here we are expecting to move every day we are kept ready

all the time so that we can move any moment. I can not find out where we are going to but think we will fall back of Manassas. . . . Hollie Cole has not arrived yet. We expect him every day. I think he will be here tomorrow. . . . We hear that nothing is allowd to come up from Richmond not even government stores. all the things that have been at the Junction are packed away in the cars ready to send away. We have sent off all our extra tents, guns, extra baggage and every thing that we cannot carry on our backs.

I had my likeness taken yesterday. It is a very [bad] likeness and a very poor picture. I will send it to Grandma by Sid Goodwin who will leave here for Savannah as soon as his and George [W.] Dickerson's Commissions come back from Richmond. Mother please return my thanks to my kind friends who have sent me the presents. I am very much obliged to them for thinking of me. Give my love to all my friends and all the homefolks. And may God bless and protect you is the sincere prayer of Your loving son

Hammie

Sgt. Hamilton Branch to Charlotte Branch

Camp Sam Jones Winter Quarters 8th Reg. Geo. Vols.
March 8th 1862 3 1/2 AM
My Dear Dear Mother

As I told you in my last I set down to write you that it is thought we will leave here in the morning, that is in about two or three hours from now. I am Corporal of the guard or I would not now be up. We have not been told that we are going but at the same time it has been hinted and as we have been required for the last week to be ready all the time of course it is not necessary to tell us that we are going as we are supposed to be ready to start at a moments warning. I am pretty sure that we will go this time as the Surgeon has packed all his medicines and other things up and the Quarter Master & Commissary have all there things ready to start. If we do go, I will not be able to mail this for a day or two that is untill we get to some post office. if not I will send it this morning. Sid Goodwin has not gone yet therefore I have not sent the likeness. Some of the boys think the likeness a good one. Hollie has not arrived yet. With much love to you my dear mother and all the rest I am as ever your loving son

Hammie

N.B If we go I will not be able to write with ink.

These were the first movements that would carry the 8th Georgia into the Peninsula Campaign.

On the Road 2 1/2 miles from Camp Sam Jones March 8th 10 1/2 PM

We left camp this morning at 7 oclock and marched to this place. It was pretty huge. We had to carry our knapsacks with everything we had in the world, mine had 4 blankets, a tick and a change of underclothes and an oilcloth. We arrived here about 10 AM and had to wait for the baggage train to get ahead of us. This consisted of the 1st & 2nd Divisions waggons the roads are bad and the horses so poor that this took until dark so that we have got to bivouac here. I have just returned from Centreville. I went there with Adjutant Shellman to see if we could not find some forage for his and Col. Lamar's horses. We do not know where we are a going to. Most people think to Warrenton as I have not gotten to a Post Office will write more tomorrow. Billey Shellman sends his kind regards as does also Ralph. As ever your loving son

Hammie

Bivouac near Bucktown March 9th 8 PM

This morning about 1 hour before day I got up being unable to sleep, it being so cold as the ground was wet and we being in an old field. About 8 oclock I was sent back to the Winter Quarters to look and see if I could find any guns and accoutrements that had been left there when I returned with them the regiment had gone. I put the guns into a waggon belonging to the 2nd Division and started with Jones Franklin one of the squad to try and catch up with the regiment but have not done so yet. We are now 5 [miles] from Gainesville having passed there about 2 hours ago. The regiment (I have been told by some men who were here) passed here about that time, therefore they must be pretty near Warrenton by this time. I do not know yet where we are going to but think to the Rappahannock River. Our party, Jones (One of the boys who we met on the road, he having to leave the Regiment being a little weak) and myself have made our beds and built a fire in a little pine wood and are a going to sleep and start in the morning for the Regiment.

Hammie

Warrenton Hotel
March 10th 9 PM

I got up this morning early and went over to a house near our bivouac and paid a half dollar and got a pretty good breakfast. Then started on the road again after the regiment. Arrived at this place at two oclock and found that the regiment had passed through here early this morning and that they were about 5 miles ahead. Met a good many of our boys here who had dropped out. Sid Goodwin, [J.F.] Stone, [Jesse] Heidt, [Benjamin S.] Purse and myself are a going to stay here tonight. I have tried to find Miss Fannie but have not. The Regiment have gone on towards Culpepper C.H. The enemy are at stone bridge, our pickets are this side of Gainesville. There is no mail here as the cars have stopped running here. All well,

Hammie.

At Dr. [John S.] Wellford's
9 PM March 11th/62

I left Warrenton at 10 oclock and marched about 3 miles when we had the good luck to meet up with a waggon which we six of us hired to carry our knapsacks to the springs. We paid him 3$ for carrying them when we got there he told me that he was not agoing our road any further, but that he could carry us within 10 miles of the Culpeper C.H. He did so and brought us to the Rappahanock River about a half mile from this place. We then walked up to the house. It was just dark. We knocked at the door and the gentelman himself came to the door. We asked him if we could get lodgings for the night. He sayed no (I do not blame him for we did look rough). One of the boys then told him that we had made a long march. He then asked us what regiment we belonged to. I told him the eighth Georgia. He then sayed come in gentelmen certainly. I can find a place for you when we got in he called for a light and told us to take our things off. He then sayed that he supposed we were hungry. He then carried us in and gave us a splendid dinner. We are now in a splendid room with good beds and two boys to waite on us. I will write more about this fine gentelman some other time. We will go from here to the C.H. All well.

Hammie

Gordonsville March 12 5 PM

I left the Dr. this morning and marched to Brandy [Station], there took the cars and went to Culpeper. There heard that our regiment had gone through there so I got on the cars for Gordonsville and came here. when I had gotten about 2 miles from the C.H. saw one of our boys sitting on a fence. He hallowed to me that our regiment was a going to stop there for the present, so as there is a train agoing back in a few moments, I am going back too. All well. I saw Mr. Witherspoon this morning. God bless you my dear Mother. Will write again in a day or two. Your loving son

Hammie

Sgt. Hamilton Branch to Charlotte Branch

Exchange Hotel Orange C.H.
10 PM March 13/62
My Dear Mother
    After mailing you a letter at Gordonsville, I left on the train for Culpeper C.H. I got off at Orange C.H. because I had heard that our division had left Culpeper for this place. Come up to this hotel and got some nice meals and stayed all night. Have heard that our division is still at Culpeper.

Hammie

Camp near Culpeper
8 1/2 PM March 14th
    Left Orange C.H. for this place, at 1/2 10 last night, as soon as I got in the cars I spread my blankets down and went to sleep when I awoke this morning I found that we had arrived at the C.C.H. Found that our division was camped about 1/2 mile from the town. Went out there and found all the boys well and having as nice a time as possible. They were all pretty tired and footsore, we have four small bell tents for the company, 48 men.

Hammie

Sibley tents were circular and mounted on a tripod, allowing for a fire in the center. They were designed to hold fifteen men.

Camp near Culpeper
8 PM March 15th/62
    Still at Culpeper. Have been on guard all day as sergeant of the guard. I went to town and bought some nice sponge cake and some nice pies. It has been raining hard all day and I am soaking wet.

Hammie

Bivouac Plenty

8 1/2 PM March 16

Left Culpeper C.H. this morning before breakfast and marched on very muddy roads to this bivouack which is about 10 miles from Culpeper. We have named this plenty because we arrived here very hungry, not having had anything to eat all day and have had a plenty to eat and have our haversacks full for the march tomorrow. Tomorrow is my birthday and allthough I cannot be with my dear relatives and friends they can no that I will think of them all day and that I am well and have a plenty to eat.

Hammie

Bivouack near Orange C.H.

7 PM March 17th/62

We left bivouack plenty yesterday morning at sunrise and after crossing over two or three creeks and one river arrived at this place about 1 1/2 miles from Oran[g]e C.H. I walked in to town as soon as we were dismissed and bought $2 worth of candy so that I had some thing nice for my [19th] birthday. Anyhow I expect we will stay here two or three days if not make a stand here.

Hammie

Bivouack near Orange

7 PM March 18th/62

Our bivouack last night was a mile and a half before we arrived at Orange C.H. This bivouack is 2 1/2 miles beyond Orange C.H. We left our bivouack of last night this morning at about 12 oclock and after marching through Orange C.H. arrived at this place. It is in a nice piece of woods so we will have plenty of wood anyhow. Col. Lamar says that we will stay here a week or two. I think a stand will be made at the Rapidan but do not know. All are well. We will get our four tents tomorrow. Hollie has not arrived yet. Give my love to all my friends. Bad news from Carolina and Florida. As ever your loving son

Hammie

The bad news referred to is Burnside's successful seizure of the coast of North Carolina and the fall of Fort Pickens in Pensacola, Florida.

Sgt. Hamilton Branch to Charlotte Branch

Bivouack Orange C.H.
March 20/62
My Dear Mother

I received your letter of the 8th yesterday and was very glad to hear from you. It was the first mail we had received since we left Centreville. I received your letter with the $10 before we left Winter Quarters and acknoledged the receipt of it before leaving there. I received the stamps in the letter yesterday. We are all well. It has been raining the last two days and we have been wet. Hollie and Willie White arrived this morning. I received the bundle by Hollie. It contained a shirt, two handkerchiefs and a pair of gloves but [not] the nutshell sent by Mrs. Dillon. The bundle had gotten torn open and the gloves fell out in Richmond, so Hollie told me, and I am afraid the nutshell has been lost. I am very sorry indeed. How was the nutshell put up, was it in the gloves or the pocket to the shirt or how. We are still here although we are not allowed to leave camp. Some say that we are going to Richmond, others that we are going to North Carolina but they are only camp rumors. Tell Grandma and Santy that I will write to them in a few days. Why does not cousin Lan write to me, and Mr. Butler also. There is no news here. Ralph, Billey S., Horace and all the boys send there respects to you. As ever your loving son

                                         Hammie

Sgt. Hamilton Branch to Charlotte Branch

Camp Orange C.H.
March 27/62
Dear Mother

I received your last letter in due time. We are all well. We have just been dismissed. we were drawn up in line with one blanket and four days rations. There were only two waggons to go every body thought that we would go to the relief of Stone Wall Jackson but the orders whatever they were have been countermanded and we have been dismissed but will have to be ready to march any time now. The Summer Campaign has commenced, and we will be on the go all the time. Hollie sends his regards. With Love to all I remain

                                   Your loving son, Hammie

On March 23, 1862, the battle of Kernstown opened the Valley Campaign for the Army of the Shenandoah under Gen. Thomas "Stonewall" Jackson.

Sgt. Hamilton Branch to Charlotte Branch

Camp near Orange C.H. Va.
April 1st/62
My Dear Mother

I wrote you two or three days ago by Lieut. S.P. Goodwin. I have written you two or three letters within the last ten days but am afraid that you will not receive them as they tell us that the mail does not go any farther than Richmond. But I thought that I would write you every three or four days and that perhaps one of them might accidentaly get to you when Sid. G. left here. We were drawn up in line with our knapsacks packed and our haversacks filled with hard bread. We expected then to have to march to Fredericksburg but after staying in line 5 or 6 hours we were dismissed and told to pitch our tents again but to keep ready to march at any moment. since then we have been expecting to be sent off every day but have not been yet.

It was reported that we would be sent to Richmond as soon as they could get the cars to carry us and that from Richmond we would be sent to North Carolina. Others said that we were going to Norfolk others that we would go to Staunton and others to Tennessee. But nobody knows where we will go to or whether we will leave here or not. Our division is the reserve division and of course will be sent wherever they are in need of help. Therefore we will be moving all about. Our late Brigadier General David R. Jones has been promoted to the command of our division, General G[ustavus] W. Smith having been sent somewhere else and Brigadier General Chas. Winder has been ordered to take command of our brigade. He is expected here every day. I like Col. Lamar and Major Magruder very much indeed. Col. Lamar never intends to surrender his regiment and therefore he just suits us. I do not like Lieut. Col. Towers and I do not think the boys like him much. Adjt. A.R. Harper has not returned yet and I do not think he will. Billie Shellman is still acting adjutant. He is liked very much by the whole regiment. The boys all wish Capt. Butler would come back. We have noone with us now but Fred. Charlie Hardwick is acting Adjutant General for Col. [George T.] Anderson who is in command of our brigade untill General Winder arrives.

Give my love to all my friends and if this comes through and you hear any one complaining of my not writting to them tell them I would write if I thought there was any chance of getting the letters through. The box sent by Mr. Crane has not arrived yet.

I visited Montpelier the residence of the late President Madison. It is a beautiful place. I met there an acquaintance of Mr. [Francis] Sorrells [of Savannah]. His name is Genl. Stewart [Stuart], the father of Genl. [J.E.B.] Stewart [Stuart] of our Cavalry. He showed me all over the house and told me which was the room he used as a study and which as a dinning room and which room he died in.

Give my love to Grandmother and ask her how she liked the picture I sent her. With love to all. I am your loving son

Hammie

[P.S.] Tell Mrs. Cole, White and Mrs. Bennett that Hollie, Billey and Billey are in the tent with me and talking to me and that they are quite well.

Sgt. Hamilton Branch to Charlotte Branch

Camp near Orange C.H.
April 5th/62
My Dear Mother

I have received yours of the 20th & 27th March. We are still here, and from present apperances will stay sometime allthough we do not know anything about it. We are all well. Jimmey Grant went off sick about a week ago. Lieut. Bliss has been unwell sometime and I think will go home as soon as Capt. Butler comes back. Charlie Go[u]lding will leave this morning on furlough to accompany the remains of his Uncle Col. [Edwin Ross] Go[u]ldin[g] of the 9th Reg. Ga. Vols. who died yesterday. Charlie will probably go to Savannah before he returns to camp. I asked Col. Lamar about Sanford. He says that he will do all in his power to get him back and that he would like very much to have him back. Lt. Col. Towers says he saw in the papers a bill which had been introduced in Congress to declare all the paroled prisoners free as the enemy had failed to keep up there bargain.

We have a brigade drill every fair day and have about a dozen ladies out to see the drill. We drill on the lawn in front of Montpelier the place I wrote you about in my last. I have not heard anything of the Wiers or Wilcoxens.

I want a pair of pants but here that Col. Lamar is agoing to get uniforms for the regiment from the Government and one pair will be as much as I care to carry this summer. My valise which was at Manassas was burnt up and all of my clothes that were in it, but I have two changes which is as much as I want to tote. I intend to send off two of my blankets off as soon as it gets a little warmer. The days are warm now but the nights very cold. As I am agoing to try and get Captain [Edward A.] Wilcox (who is agoing home) to put this in some office where you will get. I will mention the boys are all well, Shellman, Hardwick, Webb, Holmes, Burney, Cole, [Joseph H. Gnann], Bacon, A. & C. Boishirt, Carrolan, Crane, Chisholm, Dashers S. & W., Davises E. & J. & A., [Jones] Franklin, Goodwin, F. Krenson, Louis [probably Lewis, J.R.] Luddington, Law, [John J.] Griffin, Lacklison [Robert or K. Lachlison], Nickles, Mock, Mell, Price, Pattersons W. & W., Quantock, Remington, [J.F.] Stone, Sturtevant, F. & W., Shell, Sandiford, Tinsley, White, Wright, & Zettler, Parnell, Purse, Barnwell, Snider, Thompson, Hall. Lieut. Bliss is not sick, still he is unwell. The box from Mr. Crane has not arrived yet. I have written you 4 or five letters lately. Tell Cousin Lan to write to me. Give my love to all my friends and with much love

Your affectionate son
H.M. Branch

N.B. Take care of Bruce don't let anyone steal him. Hammie

Sgt. Hamilton Branch to Charlotte Branch

Camp near Orange
April 5th/62
My Dear Mother
    Please make me as soon as possible and send as quickly as you can two small Confederate flags either stars and bars or battle flags which ever you think will be the prettiest. I would rather have the stars and bars if you think it will be as pretty as the other. I want them 12 inches by 18 inches that is if stars and bars if not about 14 inches square please mother ask Miss Jinnie [McLaughlin] if she is in town to be so kind as to work 8th Ga. on the white Bar or on each side of the cross. I want both the flags alike. Please mother make them out of cloth that will be easiest to keep clean or can be washed. Also please sew three pieces of small ribbon on each flag so that

we can tie them on to our flag staffs.

Hollie Cole and myself have resigned our offices and have been appointed by the Col. at our request Markers for the regiment and that is what I want with the flags. Hollie has no own mother to write to for his and so I told him I would get you to make his too. Mother do not get too expensive cloth for these are hard times and I know you spend too much for me anyhow. If you send them by freight or express you had better direct care of Mr. Buckley [Thomas A. Bulkley] or Mr. [James M.] Selkirk [a railroad agent] and ask him to send them up by some of our company or regiment. We have the flag staffs. We are all well. The box sent by Mr. Crane has not arrived yet. Love to all.

As ever your loving son
Hammie

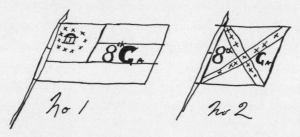

These are the styles. I prefer No. 1.

Mother if you make the stars and bars get Miss Jennie McL. or Miss Gertrude Dillon to work the coat of arms of Georgia on the field and I do not think there will be any need for the Ga. in the bar but just the 8 alone.

Mother please make this for me and send them as soon as possible.

Mother to get them done soon you might let one person be working the stars and 8 whilst another is working the coat of arms. I want them just alike mother if you please. Hammie

Sgt. Hamilton Branch to Charlotte Branch

Bivouac Short Nap
4 AM April 7th/62
My Dear Mother

Yesterday afternoon we received orders at 6 pm to get ready to march in fifteen minutes, with 1 blanket, and 4 days rations, to Fredericksburg which is about 40 miles in a northeasterly direction from Orange C.H. At 7 pm we started with the 1 blanket but without the 4 days rations being furnished to us. We marched very slowly until we got to Orange which as

I told you was about 2 1/2 miles from our camp. We had to let the waggons and artillery and some other brigades pass us and consequently it was 12 mid. when we arrived at Orange. We then started at a very fast rate and marched until 3 oclock this morning without stopping. We then were halted and the Col. [?] told us to build fires and go to sleep as he thought we would stay there 2 hours, we did so but had just lain down when the drum beat for us to fall in. We did so but as I heard that we were only agoing a 1/2 mile further and then agoing to halt for 2 hours, Horace and myself thought we would stay where we were until the 2 hours had past so we went to sleep and slept an hour and on awakeing seeing that day was breaking got up and started to find the regiment.

Bivouac Nary Grub
6 AM April 8/62

We marched about 8 miles yesterday without meeting the regiment but met the 1st Va who were just agoing to bivouac and they told us that our regiment was behind them some distance so we thought we would stop here and wait until they caught up with us, so we built a bivouac and went to sleep. It snowed and rained all night and our bivouac leaked and we had nothing to eat, so you can judge how we feal this morning—our blankets and ourselves all wet and nothing to eat.

Bivouac near Orange
April 9th/62

Seeing that Longstreet's Division was about turning back we started back to try and catch our regiment. We marched back about 5 miles when we met our regiment drawn up in line ready to march back to this place so we fell in. After marching 6 hours in the rain on the worst roads I ever saw and the cold freezing wind a blowing we arrived here almost dead. This has been one of the hardest marches we have made, one of our regiment died on the road and another one was found dead this morning. Our baggage has all been sent off and we are left here without any dry clothes to put on, but our boys have built fires and dried themselves and are alright again although pretty hungry. But I think we will get something to eat this evening. I do not know where we will go to from here but think to Richmond. But there is one thing I do know and that is that this thing they call strategy and strategic movements are about played out. We marched about 15 miles yesterday.

Bivouac near Orange
[April] 10/62

Our baggage which had been sent off came back yesterday evening so that we had a first rate night's sleep last night. The baggage has all been sent off again this morning but I have kept mine this time and intend to carry it untill it gets a little warmer, the baggage and artillery started for Richmond but wether they will go on or come back nobody but Genl. Johnston knows. I think we will go this time but do not know, we have been ordered to cook two days rations.

There was a trunk arrived in camp this morning marked W.D. Coombs. One of the boys thought it was his and oppened it but seeing my name on the pants and books thought that they were mine so turned the trunk over to me. A jar of syrup had broken and spilt all over the things and a jar of preserves also. The drawers and shirt and stockings came just in time and the pants are worth their weight in gold. I am now all right in the clothes line. I am very much obliged to you for the cake, candy, lemon syrup, pickles and groundnuts. I will finish them before we leave and try and finish the Grist and meal. The knife scissors and corkscrew and spoons are splendid and allso the emery paper as our guns were in an awful condition. The books the boys will help me carry if we move so that we will save them but the trunk will have to go up. I hear that my valise is at Gordonsville, but do not believe it. I do not know when I will be able to send this but will send it as soon as I can. I am glad you sent the map. It is just what I wanted.

Your son
Hammie

Bivouac No. 2 near Orange
[April] 11th/62

We left Bivouack No. 1 near Orange yesterday evening at 7 PM and marched down here to the cars to go to Richmond. We waited untill [Robert] Toombs Brigade and the 11th Ga. of our Brigade got on when we found out that there was no more trains left so we have got to stay here untill some of the trains get back. if the Yankeys come down they can get us because there are but four regiments left here. Lieut. Bliss has made so much fuss about our being appointed markers that we have concluded not to take it but take our old places. therefore I will not need the flags. We are now laying out in an open field waiting for the cars.

Hammie

Camp Winder, Richmond
April 12th/62

We left Orange C.H. (after laying or rather squatting in the cars about 4 hours) yesterday evening at 7 oclock and after riding all night arrived in Richmond this morning at 12. We marched through town with our band playing and the people huzzaing and arrived here at 1 PM. Hollie and myself ran the blockade and went to town. Jim Binford made us take dinner with him. Mrs. Binford is unwell. She says that you would not know me if you were to see me. We have had some hard times lately. I saw Mr. & Mrs. Hines and Lilla [Cornelia] this morning. They are quite well. I am agoing to try and go and see them. Capt. Butler also met us in Richmond. the recruits are with us also. We can not believe the news about Fort Pulaski, viz. that it has been taken without anyone being killed. I went and saw Mr. Bulkley this morning. He says that anything he can do for me he will do with pleasure.

I do not know where we will go to from here. We were to go to Yorktown but we hear that they have enough troops down there but I do not know whether it is so or not. I telegraphed you this morning not to make the flags. Fred Bliss made so much fuss about our resigning that we will not have the markership but have taken our old offices back, therefore you need not make the flags. Give my love to all my friends and write often to me as ever

your loving son, Hammie

On board the *A.W. Schultz*
April 14th/62
My Dear Mother

We left Camp Winder, Richmond at 4 PM yesterday and marched down Main St. from one end to the other with our band playing and the Citizens cheering. We got on board this boat at 9 PM and started for Yorktown. We have just passed Jamestown and are in sight of Williamsburg. I left two blankets and some clothes with Mrs. Hine. She was down to see us off. We expect to have a big fight as soon as we get to our destination which is near Yorktown. All the boys are well. I saw two of our old members, [John A.] Belvin & [A.J.] Franklin in Richmond. I gave Mrs. Hines a letter to mail to you

Your loving son
Hammie

Bivouac Lebanon Church
April 15th/62

We arrived at Kings Landing at 10 AM yesterday and marched to this camp which is 9 miles from the landing. We stacked arms and were told that we would have flour and bacon given us and that we must cook it up and be ready to march at dawn the next day. We did so and got up this morning early but did not move. I went about 3 miles to see [Capt. John P.W.] Reads Battery [at Fort Magruder]. There fort is called fort Savannah. Returned to bivouac and find that we will leave in a few moments.

                                                                    Hammie

The 8th had been sent to reinforce Maj. Gen. John B. Magruder on the Warwick River, south of Yorktown, Virginia. The Warwick was little more than a sluggish stream, twenty to thirty yards wide, running through a dense wooded swamp. Originally, two dams existed on the river, at Wynn's Mill and Lee's Mill. Confederate forces had built three more, flooding the stream to a hundred yards in width to discourage any frontal attacks by Union forces. The center of the line was located at Dam #1.

Magruder had only 11,000 troops to hold a line of defenses built to be fortified by 20,000. To offset this lack and the chance of Union troops getting through, he had constructed two additional lines of trenches and batteries. A redoubt was constructed to defend Dam #1, consisting of one 12-pound Napoleon of the Troup Artillery charged with double cannister. This battery had successfully held Union troops at bay and was referred to in reports as the "one gun battery."[42]

Behind this redoubt was a sand battery of two guns which were put out of commission early on. A third line of defense consisted of heavy works and trenches for the protection of infantry not engaged at the front. A picket post was established at the dam, within twenty steps of enemy lines. Relief pickets, who had to cross mud and water while exposed to enemy sharpshooters, were on duty for a twenty-four-hour shift. They were relieved under cover of darkness.

On either side of Dam #1 timber was felled for fifty to seventy-five yards, leaving a clear field of fire. Union forces under Gen. George B. McClellan established three sand batteries of four guns each, six hundred yards in front of the dam. Since April 5 Magruder's men had slept in the trenches, under arms for days, expecting an attack. Many nights they stood in the ditches or leaned on the parapet up to their knees in water.

McClellan had massed his Army of the Potomac around Yorktown for a push to Richmond. The Peninsula Campaign of 1862 had begun, but Magruder's forces were holding him up. It was around 3:30 P.M. on April 16 when McClellan ordered an attack to penetrate Confederate lines. He would hit them at Dam #1.

The Confederate forces sprang for cover as the woods filled with shells and noise. Sharpshooters pressed forward as six pieces of Union artillery opened on the Troup's Napoleon, behind which stood the 5th North Carolina in the third line of trenches. Maj. Gen. William F. Smith commanded the Second Division, Fourth Corps, which included the 3rd, 5th, and 6th Vermont Volunteer Infantry Regiments. As his Vermont brigade overran the battery and the North Carolina troops, a counterattack was hastily thrown forward by the 16th Georgia. This regiment began to falter, and the 8th Georgia came to their aid to save the day. With fixed bayonets and the steadiness of veterans the Oglethorpes advanced with the 7th, charging the rifle pits and routing the Vermonters.

Again Union troops massed for the attack and charged. The 8th coolly held the line, buying time for Confederate reinforcements to arrive. The Federals were forced back across the muddy, shallow stream and darkness put an end to the encounter.[43]

Sgt. Hamilton Branch to Charlotte Branch

Supporting a Battery
11 AM April 16/62

We marched about 1/2 a mile yesterday and bivouacked. We staid all night and this morning marched 1 mile and drew up in line in a pine woods. We staid there about 15 minutes and then left our baggage with one man from each company to guard it and marched to this place. We are in the rear of one of our batteries [including the Troup Artillery] which is now fighting a duel with the enemy. They have been fireing all the morning. The shell of the enemy, some of them that is, burst over the battery and the musket balls from them scatter all around us. Two of our regiment have been hit by them but not hurt. All well so far. God bless you and all of us and protect us in this our time of need is the prayer of your ever loving and affectionate son

H.M. Branch

Bivouack near breastworks
April 17/62

Left the rear of the battery about a 1000 yards and stacked arms to await a demonstration from the enemy. The enemy began shelling us and shelled us about 1 hour. They came very near us, one passing about 20 feet from Captain Butler and hitting about 5 feet from me but did not hurt any of us. The enemy then commenced a rappid fireing on our right and we were ordered to fall in and take arms. We then marched to the right and were ordered to sustain Col. [William T.] Wilson of the Seventh Ga. as we got in sight of the breastworks we saw some of the 7th a kind of giving back. We then charged towards them and gave several yells. This encouraged the 7th and they turned and charged the enemy. The enemy then ran and left our breastworks, which the 7th took possesion of. We were then drawn up in line about 50 yards in the rear of the breastworks in a very exposed position.

Col. Lamar then told us Boys if the 7th or any other Regiment left the breastworks that he intended to order us in them and that we must hold them. We told him we would and gave another cheer. The enemy all this time had recrossed to there side of the creek and were pouring a terrible fire upon us. We were then ordered to the left of the 7th and into the ditches. We went in and the enemy attempting to cross and charge our ditches we opened on them and they fled in confusion. There Artillery then attempted to shell us out, but to no effect. We staid in the ditches untill 11 PM expecting a charge but they did not attempt it. We then were relieved and retired to the rear about 200 yards behind a small breastwork and tried to sleep but could not, as we could not get any blankets and it was so cold. This morning we were relieved from the advance and are now about 500 yards in the rear laying by our stacks.

We ought to be, and I think we all are, very thankfull to the Lord that he has spared us. It was miraculous no one killed or wounded in our regiment. Every [body] says it was a miracle. The Kentucky had 12 wounded and the 7th Ga. 5 killed and some wounded, and I do not know how many the 5th North Carolina had killed but I think about 12 and 40 wounded. They were building breastworks and there guns were stacked of one side and the first they knew the enemy were right upon them and there Col. being killed the first one, confused them. Our boys behaved gallantly. We have killed about 50 of the enemy taken about 20 prisoners and wounded. I do not know how many. We expect the big fight every hour but do not know when it will come. With a thankfull heart to God for spareing our lives thus far and a prayerfull heart that he will continue to protect us, I remain your loving son

H.M. Branch

The Union returns listed 35 killed, 121 wounded, and 9 missing; 45 dead were returned to the Federals under a flag of truce.[44]

The 8th Georgia and Magruder's little Confederate army served without relief in the trenches through May 1. It rained steadily and mercilessly, filling the ditches with water and adding to the sick list. The raw cold was made worse by the order of no fires. The Oglethorpes were under constant shelling and sniping, without coffee, sugar or bread. A ration of flour and salt meat sustained the boys. Gen. Magruder paid their endurance this tribute in his report: "I have never seen, and I do not believe there ever has existed, an army which has shown itself for so long a time so superior to all hardships and dangers. The best drilled regulars the world has ever seen would have mutinied."[45]

Sgt. Hamilton Branch to Charlotte Branch

In trenches near Yorktown
April 19/62
My Dear Mother

I wrote you last on the 17th and sent it by [Paul] Kreuger one of our company and a member of our band who said he would give it to some sick person going to Richmond and ask them to put it in the office at Richmond. In it I gave you an account of the fight we had here and of our miraculous escape. Since writting that, we have learned from the prisoners some facts concerning their intentions. They intended an advance on us here so as to get in the rear of Yorktown. They paid 60 men $50 and a gold medal apiece to cross the creek and lead the advance. They promised to support them with a brigade. The 60 men belonged to Companys D, E, & K of the 3rd Vermont Regiment, about 40 of them are now laying in front of our trenches some 6 or 8 not 30 feet from me. We cannot burry them because the enemy are fireing at us [with] there sharpshooters all the time. We have been in the trenches now ever since yesterday 4 AM and do not know how long it will be before we will be relieved. We are all safe yet. We expect a big fight before long. Give my love to all my friends. And now hopeing that the Lord will bless and protect you my Dear Mother and all of us, I am as ever your loving and affectionate son

Hamilton Branch

Although the Oglethorpes were busy in Virginia, they were undoubtedly concerned about their home. Savannah was the next link in the chain of ports targeted by the Union fleet. Wilmington, North Carolina, was staving off gunboats with Fort Caswell. Charleston, South Carolina, was under a loose siege, and federal troops were building an ordnance and supply depot on Hilton Head Island, just fifteen miles from Savannah. It was from this place that Union general Quincy A. Gilmore planned an assault on Fort Pulaski, the lion guarding the gates to Savannah, using the latest weapon in the Union army—a rifled, long-range cannon. In March the Union batteries were constructed on Tybee Island, adjacent to the fort, just out of range of Confederate guns inside. Eight thousand troops were prepared to advance once the fort was shelled.

The Confederate forces inside Fort Pulaski were under the command of Col. Charles Olmstead, John Branch's old Georgia Military Institute classmate and fellow Oglethorpe.

Lt. Benjamin Theodore Cole [?] to Charlotte Branch

Fort Pulaski
March 28th 1862
Dear Mrs. Branch

You must not think hard of me for not writing before this. Several times have I made the attempt but being conscious that the receipt of any letter from me would cause you sorrow, I have not been able to finish. I am truly glad that you are again home. Sanfords being liberated must ease your mind very much. I earnestly hope my Dear Mrs. Branch that your mind is more quiet and that you have submitted to the will of Providence with that resignation and Christian spirit which has always characterized your life. I saw Sanford for a moment only, when I was in Savannah "over two months ago." I had not time to complete my business or I assure you I never would have gone away without seeing you. My situation here is not a very enviable one, but I do not complain. I am willing to share the fate of the garrison be it what it may.

The Yankees are upon all sides. Every now and then they honour us with a few rifle shells as yet none of our men have been hurt. Each battery which they have opened has sent shells over the Fort. I am still outside the Fort in a wooden building next my hospitals but the Col. has moved the sick into the Fort and I have orders to do the same tomorrow.

The health of this post is excellent. I have but little work & hope both for my sake and that of the men that this may continue.

Mat Hopkins rooms next to me. He has to go into the Fort also we do not like it as our quarters outside are so very pleasant. The mail will be closed in a few moments and as I have nothing new to write you I [trust] even you will excuse this short letter. I was very much afraid that the bundle which you entrusted to my care had been lost but am pleased to hear of its recovery. I lost my sword, some chap took a fancy to it on account of its ugliness I suppose.

Not knowing what may happen [to] me you will excuse my writing a few lines on business. I took up a due bill of $45.00 which I handed Hamilton. I purchased a trunk and almost ashamed am I to say that I had to pay $10.00 for it. This leaves me in debt to you still $45.00. I cannot give you an order for it, being without money on hand. Should I fall please show this to Father and he will attend to it. Remember me kindly to your Mother and Sanford. When you write Hamilton please do the same.

Should you have an opportunity to write I would be very glad to hear from you.

Ever yours truly
Theodore

On the morning of April 10, 1862, Gen. David Hunter demanded the fort's unconditional surrender. When Olmstead refused to surrender his force of 385 officers and men, the Federals began a bombardment that lasted thirty hours. The once impregnable masonry walls crumbled before technology—shells from the long-range rifled guns turned the southeastern wall into rubble. Olmstead realized his position was hopeless. Instead of forfeiting lives, he surrendered the fort on the afternoon of April 11, without a single death, along with forty-eight cannon and a large quantity of supplies. Many of those who surrendered were natives of the city and childhood friends of the Branch brothers.[46]

The Savannahians were shocked. Fort Pulaski, their source of pride, had proven vulnerable; the city was cut off from foreign trade, and the enemy was one step closer.

Sgt. Hamilton Branch to Charlotte Branch

Bivouac near Pitts
April 26/62
My Dear Mother
I have just received your letters of the 11th & 15th and received the one by Charlie Go[u]lding a day or two ago. I was very glad to hear from you.

It is the first mail we have received for a long time. I was very sorry to hear of the fall of Fort Pulaski. I never expected to hear of the fall of that Fort. I thought the men in that fort would hold out untill every man was killed or wounded and that the last man would blow the fort up. But no if it is as we hear they have proved themselves poor Georgians. Mother if the 8th Ga. had of been in that fort there would have been someone killed. Dont tell anyone that I say so for it may make those who have friends there feel badly. Mother it is too bad that 500 Georgians should surrender without a man being killed. It is two bad entirely. We have had a hard time since I last wrote you. We have been in the Pitts for the last ten days and it has almost used us up. But we are all well yet, although some of us are complaining. Give my love to all my friends. There is no mail from here and we have to send our letters by the sick. With much love. I am as ever your loving son

Hammie

Hollie, Horace, Billey S., Ralph and all the boys send there respects. Tell Miss Jennie that I will answer her letter the first chance I get. Excuse this short letter as the sick are agoing and I will have to stop. Love to all.

Hammie

Tallulah Hansell to Charlotte Branch

Oglethorpe.
April 29th/62
My Esteemed Friend—

It seems indeed a long time since I had the pleasure of reading your last letter which I assure you was most *acceptable*. . . . When your missive of friendship arrived, my Father was very sick, having had another threatening of Paralysis. He grew better, only to relapse, and two weeks since, as he was much better he left for the bracing atmosphere of Marietta my dear old home. I am glad to inform you that the change of climate, pure water, and mountain air, have already benefitted him greatly. He is with my Brother's family.

The very night that he left, we had a most terrific storm or succession of storms, that have injured our railroad, and broken off communication with the world around us. Occasionally some pedestrians would arrive with accounts of victories and defeats to our Confederate armies—ultimately raising our hopes or sinking our hearts. It was a deprivation very hard to bear, particularly when a straggler brought tidings of the attack on Fort Pulaski, in which was one of the best companies from our county. The "Wise Guards" was formed of men of good standing, belonging principally to the better class of farmers—and nearly *all* men of family. Communication has just been re–established to bring us the news of the *surrender! You* indeed can truly appreciate the sorrow this causes—and we have not even the poor satisfaction of *knowing where their prison is*. I sympathize deeply, not only with the distressed at home, but with the *captives*, whose *courage* has (by some newspaper scribblers) already been called into question. This is *brave*, truly—to assail men who offered *everything* on the shrine of liberty, and now as prisoners in the enemy's hands are deprived of the opportunity of *vindicating* themselves! Such attacks should disgrace their authors I think. I know Col. Olmstead well, and also the officers of the "Wise Guards" and believe them all to be true and brave men.

We have had within two months past three terrible freshets and the crops are greatly injured. Wheat and oats and rye are almost if not entirely ruined by *rust*. The rains have washed up corn and prevented farmwork, so *everything* seems unfavorable. Our first crop, usualy more than enough for home and neighbors—will be a failure. It is no longer a matter of *choice* as to what shall be prepared for table use—but a question of *"what can we get?"*. . .

Our victory at "Shiloh" under our greatest leader, has cheered us, but the taking of Huntsville [Alabama] was a heavy blow to me, as I was at school there, and have many and very dearly loved friends resident there. I have relatives there also, and some in the army near. A young cousin distinguished himself at "Shiloh" by his gallantry, Capt. R.H. Harris of Louisiana. He was at the "Institute" when your dear John was there.

Of the latter you judge correctly, I think, when you say that I *appreciated* him—I have had him often say "Miss Lula, you are the only person out of my own household, to whom I feel perfectly *candid*, because *I always know that you understand me.*" Very often he would talk to me as freely as to a sister, about his little troubles, plans for the future &c. I was always frank with him and sometimes he would laugh, and say "my Mother would like you, for being such a *little Presbyterian*, and talking to me so soberly. I think you two would make a good *preacher* of me." . . .

I wish I could see you and all your family, it would be a great pleasure, although a *mournful* one to me. I would be so glad to have you at my own home, but cannot ask you to come *now*, as it is the beginning of the sickly season with us. If we knew of a safe retreat in the up country we would be tempted to seek it—as we have never spent but one summer here, and suffered much from sickness. Do remember me most kindly to *all* your family with you, & to your "baby" when you write. I must beg you to write soon to me, and rest assured I will never defer a reply *voluntarily*. May the smiles of God rest on you & yours, and comfort your sad heart—ever prays your friend.

Lula H.

[P.S] Miss Lizzie Sneed of Savannah is here and spoke in glowing tones of "John's" popularity, and the gloom his death caused. I did not see the obituary notice of which you wrote and will thank you very sincerely for it. I have heard lately that Mr. Porter's health is much better. He preached a short time since at Beach Island. I knew Dr. Axson several years ago in Marietta. Mother and Fannie join me in love to your Mother yourself and family. Good-bye, May God avert the threatened danger from your home, and soon give an honourable & lasting peace.

Sgt. Hamilton Branch to Charlotte Branch

Camp Dam No. 1
April 29/62
My Dear Mother

I have not heard from you since I received your letter dated the 16th. I suppose the reason is because we have received but one mail since we have been on the penninsula. I have written to you four times since we have been down here and sent them all off by sick men to mail in Richmond I hope you will receive them. I have been in the hospital about a week but am all right again and will go back to duty tomorrow or next day. We have had a pretty tough time since we have been down here and will have untill this fight comes off. We will have a tough fight here as the fall of New Orleans will encourage them to fight. It is terrible to think that New Orleans should have been surrendered [to General Benjamin Butler] without a gun being fired.

We have been very lucky since we have been down here. God must have protected us for while all the other Regiments in our brigade have had 5 or 6 killed and some wounded, we have only had three wounded one had one finger of his left hand shot off, another two fingers and the other was shot through the thigh. Not a single Oglethorpe has been shot yet. I do not see how two such large armys can stay so close together without fighting. We have been here two weeks now and there has only been one little fight. I have seen Clacky Lovell and Capt. [B. Edward] Ed Stiles since I have been down here. They are both well. Billey Shellman is acting Adjutant of our regiment and Charlie Hardwick is acting assistant—adjutant—General . . . but I would not be surprised if they were both appointed to those offices. I have not heard from any of my young lady friends in Savannah for some time what is the matter have they all left the town. . . . As ever

> your loving son
> Hammie

On or about May 3, Hamilton's company was on picket duty in the trenches for three days with no relief. The rations ran out, and although they were nearly starved, the federal shelling was so heavy that it was impossible to get another picket line there to relieve them or to order them in. Sgt. Branch volunteered to go to the rear and bring back supplies. While returning with the rations he was wounded in the hand and furloughed home.

Sgt. Hamilton Branch to Charlotte Branch

Richmond
May 5/62
My Dear Mother

I was sent off (from Camp at Dam No. 1) to Richmond on sick list. I am not much sick only very weak and as the Regiment had to march I was sent off. I do not know what Genl. Johnston is agoing to do. All I know is that he is falling back from the peninsula.

I have been three days coming to Richmond. When I got to Kings Landing (the nearest landing to our camp, and the one from which our sick were being sent off from) it was so crowded with sick that I saw there was no chance to be sent off soon and as I met Mac Berrien who asked me to come aboard his ark and lie down (he had an ark loaded with ammunition for Richmond) I went and layed down and waited all day but no sick were sent off so I went to sleep on his berth and slept all night. In the morning I found that the sick had been sent off at midnight so I had to stay and come up with him.

We stopped at Jamestown a day and night. We had some splendid batteries on that Island. I went to the ruins of the first brick church built in Virginia and went through the graveyard. There are some queer old tombstones in this graveyard. Some written in Latin and some half Latin and English. One reads thus "Here lyeth William Sherwood, born at White Chappel, near London. A great sinner waiting a joyful resurrection."

I feel a great deal better than when I left camp. My bowels are wrong and my stomach very sore. I will be all right after a few days good eating. Horace is here also sick and several others of our boys. None much sick, only weak from exposure. Give my love to all my friends as ever

your loving son
Hammie

CHAPTER SEVEN

I Consider the Confederate Army . . . Invincible

Hamilton Branch returned home at the end of his first year of service. His mother's continuing grief over John's death convinced him that she needed one of her sons nearby. The Savannah Cadets were mustered into service in May 1861 for three years or the war, a war baby composed of underage boys for local defense. At age nineteen, Hammie was a veteran. His value was recognized, and he was offered a commission as second lieutenant in the Cadets. As the company most likely would serve near Savannah and the coast, he accepted the position.

Tallulah Hansell to Charlotte Branch

Oglethorpe, May 6th 1862
My Dear Kind Friend
    How can I find "words" with which to thank you for your letter and its very precious enclosure. could you only have seen me when I opened it. I think you would have felt my *high appreciation* of the likeness of one who had so much endeared himself to me, as your dear son had. How can you thus divine my wishes? I have a likeness of my beloved friend, that was *excellent* when taken, but I have longed to see him *as a man*. Still I could

not summon courage to ask it of you fearing that a rude touch might jar the bleeding chords of your heart, and you from your own heart have *felt* the wish I dared not express, and sent me this memento, that no one on earth but a *Mother*, could prize more highly. . . .

I do thank you, & thank you a thousand times for these dear mementos of him, and of your confidence and affection. It is a *very great* gratification to me to know that you have for his sake, given me a place in your heart. I prize your friendship, and that of your family. Do your sons resemble my friend? I am always glad to hear of them, and shall ever feel an interest in their welfare and happiness. I have a cousin at Yorktown, Maj. [William A.] Harris of the 14th Ga. Regt. and when he wrote he mentioned the 8th Ga. Although I have not seen your sons, I feel myself a *friend,* and hope they will ever regard me as such.

I cannot wonder that at this crisis in our national affairs, your son should feel anxious to be in service again, and sympathize with him. We have at length heard from my nephew Willie Hansell, of whom we had been without any news since the battle of "Shiloh." He was unhurt, but made a narrow escape from the Federal cavalry at Huntsville. He is Adjutant of an Ala. Regt. and with one of the captains was sent to H. to buy swords for the officers. As they entered H. a child said something about the "Yankees" being there. They turned their horses heads, but not until they had been seen. A cavalry company pursued them, but at a farm house they left their horses & saddles, and with two horses obtained there, they left & succeeded in making good their escape, as the Federalists stopped to search the farmhouse. I trust Savannah may escape the invaders, and feel great confidence in the gallantry of her defenders except in *Genl. Lawton,* of whom we have very bad accounts—

I have been nursing a sick sister for nearly two weeks. She has a young infant & four other children and as her husband is in the army I have my hands full. You must make due allowance therefore, for this letter. I feel quite indisposed today from being awake so many nights, and also from the anxiety of mind about our soldier friends. I have a very dear friend at Ft. Pillow, from whom I have not heard since the third day of the bombardment. He wrote then at his cannon. I was at school in Huntsville, and have many dear friends there so I am so constantly hoping for good tidings from them.

My Father returned yesterday and is somewhat stronger, I hope. Our little village is very unhealthy this spring, as we have typhoid fever here. I was a school girl when I saw Dr. [Isaac] Axson in Marietta, but was delighted with him. His son Edward who married Miss Hoyt I liked *very much*, as I did Miss H. Do you ever hear anything of the Kings of St. Simons? I knew & liked Mallery very much. He loved John dearly when they were in Marietta. He and I corresponded some time, but he dropped it & now I never hear anything of him. I hope dear Mrs. Branch that you will look upon me and my family as *old friends*, and that we may yet meet when this cruel, horrible war is over. . . . For the sake of the sleeping friend, I ask your love. Ever your true and constant & grateful friend—

Lula Hansell

Sgt. Hamilton Branch to Capt. Alexander F. Butler

Savannah May 19th/62
Capt. A.F. Butler
Dear Sir

I have been told by Col. [William S.] Rockwell that I will have to make an application to you for a discharge and enclose my commission and that you will attend to the rest for me as our Regimental muster roll will have to go to Richmond and our commissions be sent back to us. Before I can do that and as you will have time to answer this before that will be done, I will be very much obliged to you if you will answer this imediately and let me know if that will be the right way of doing. I dislike very much to leave my old company and in parting with you allow me to express my regret at leaving you, and allow me to express my admiration for the impartial manner in which you have always treated me and my company the O.L.I. Col. [Charleton H.] Way commands our regiment. Give my respects to Lieut. Shellman. By replying to this immediately you will much oblige your friend

2nd Lt. H.M. Branch
Co. A, 5[4]th Ga. Reg. C.S.A.

N.B. My company the Savannah Cadets have been mustered into the CSA for three years or the war. Please answer imediately and let me know if the way above stated is the way for me to go to work. Direct Box #500, Savannah.

Sarah Hine to Charlotte Branch
... on the Anniversary of John's Death

Warren[ton] July 21st 1862
My dear Charlotte

There are some ladies here spending the day with me but I have left them for others to entertain while I hold brief converse with you through the pen. Where could my thoughts be on this memorable day but with my suffering friend, and how is she spending it. I presume alone with God. May the Angel of his presence comfort her. I cannot say aught to you my dear friend in the way of consolation that has not been repeated to you over and again, and your own heart has so often applied to the rich fountain of His promises that it would be idle to direct your attention to them. There is one declaration of Holy writ which oftener than any other has comforted me when my soul has been overwhelmed with Life's sorrows and I have felt as if all the waves & billows of God's indignation were engulfing me, *"The Lord reigns"* I would fain repeat it to you Charlotte again & again, *the Lord reigns.* What could we ask for more, He is *our* Father, every interest of our lives is dear to Him. Not a hair of our heads can fall without his notice; and more ready to give good gifts to us than earthly parents are to give good gifts unto their children, can we doubt that he deals with us wisely & well.

. . . I wish I could write more but have not the time.

22nd. I would write a few lines yesterday, I thought of you all day, and must now close hurriedly. If Josie is in Sav. I want her to telegraph to me if she is sick; direct Richmond care Mrs. Ann L. Staples Sydney, head of Main St. I shall be in Richmond soon, James is there now. I want my letters directed there hereafter, but it is not necessary to direct letters to any ones care, as we are at the Office [of the Georgia Hospital & Relief Association] daily.

My husband is in Richmond now, he went down to meet James and let him come up to spend a few days with me before going into camp. I am so glad to see him once more, his general health is good but his throat is far from well. He wakes coughing every morning & the least dampness in the air keeps him hoarse. . . . I am very anxious about Josie & long to go to her, and would go at once if my husband and son were willing for me to change the climate just at the time of the August heats. I expect to go any way by the first of September if not before, dear Charlotte I trust in you to care for her as if she were your own, if she should go to Savannah and be prematurely sick. I have a comfortable hope that she has accepted the Saviour as her Redeemer, and is prepared for the rest of Heaven. . . .

I am with delightful people here who are all the time planning rides & pleasures for me. We make friends every where, Cornelia is a great favorite & every body loves my husband of course, I feel as if I had many friends in Va. and many ties here but I long for my own house once more.

With much love to you & Hammie & to your mother & Sanford when you see them & kind remembrances to all my friends.

Very affec. your friend
Sarah L. Hine

Lt. Hollie Cole to Lt. Hamilton Branch

Richmond Va. Aug 11/62
Dear Hammie

Your kind epistle came to hand this morning. I was glad to hear from you but how sorry to inform you that I cannot give you any information concerning your money for I am in the city and cannot get out to the Reg. You had better ask Capt. Butler. I am here suffering from my head.

Poor Bill Coombs died Sunday two weeks ago. He died at the 1st Ga. Hospital and I cronicle the death of another of our boys, poor Willie Borchert. He died at Petersburg two days ago. Charlie went to see him but got there too late to see him alive. He was burried in Petersburg. I must close. Good Bye. Write soon to your brother

Hollie

With Hamilton at home, Sanford grew even more impatient to return to the 8th Georgia. With exchange imminent, he went to Richmond to wait near the regiment so as to be ready to return to duty at once upon word from the commissioners.

Sgt. Sanford Branch to Charlotte Branch

Richmond Aug. 20, 62
Dear Mother

I arrived here all right—except a severe cold—on Monday haveing stoped at Augusta 2 days. There is no chance of my being exchanged in 10 days as the commissioners do not meet again in that time. I have been paying $4.50 per day but am now staying at a private House at $12.00 per week. I am disgusted with Richmond and often wish I was home again. The Regt. left on Wednesday last for Stonewall. I was very much disappointed in not seeing them. several of the boys are here on sick leave. I dont know when I shall be able to join the Regiment but it will be soon.

Your affect. son
Sanford

The 8th was encamped near Culpeper, Virginia, in preparation for the battle of Second Manassas.

Sgt. Sanford Branch to Charlotte Branch

Richmond Aug. 24, 62
Dear Mother

In Richmond yet. Saw Mr. [Julian A.] Hartridge last night, he and Mr. [Thomas F.] Stevens will go with me to the commissioner to day to see about my exchange so I expect to be able to join the Regiment soon. I am perfectly disgusted with Richmond. I do not think there will be a fight soon. It is reported here that [Union Gen. John] Pope is falling back towards Washington. If that is so it will prolong the war. If we could have wipted them I think the war would of ended in six months. I saw Ned Willis last night. He was a prisoner but escaped.

I may have to draw on you for a small amount as I was foolish enough to lend out $50 thinking I would not need it.

Your affect. son
Sanford

Sgt. Sanford Branch to Charlotte Branch

Richmond Aug. 28/62
Dear Mother

Still in Richmond. Was to have left today but the Yankee commissioner was sick and could not reach our commis. there will not be another meeting until next week. I am very anxious to leave this miserable place but am afraid that it will be some days before I can do so.

Quite a number of our boys were in town but almost all have left for the

Regiment—They all say I can get the position of 2nd Lieut. but I told [Charles F.] Borchert I would not run against him and I wont.

Mr. Branch has been very kind to me. I shall leave my trunk with him. Mr. Bulkley is absent at the Springs.

I have not called on Mrs. Binford yet but hope to do so before long.

Mr. Hartridge told me he wanted to see me this afternoon about something very important. What it is I cannot imagine for although I have seen him everyday he has not said a word about commission to me.

I may go up to Gordonsville and there wait for the exchange. The other prisoners are very anxious for me to do so. The expenses will be less and there we will be nearer the Regt. If I conclude to go I will let you know how to direct. Please give my love to all, Hammie and Grandma.

Your affectionate son
Sanford W. Branch

Sgt. Sanford Branch to Charlotte Branch

Orange C.H. Sept. 1st 62
Dear Mother

I arrived here yesterday and will wait here until we are exchanged which will be in a few days I hope.

The news from Manassas today is very good if the Reports we hear be true. It is Reported that the enemy in attempting to force our lines were repulced with heavy loss, 2000 prisoners & all their wagons. [Gen. Richard] Ewell is said to have lost a leg. I saw a negro the servant of Col. [J. Foster] Marshall [of the 1st South Carolina] who was killed. He says that [Maxcy] Gregg's Brigade was all cut to pieces. I will write at length in a few days.

Affectionately
S.W. Branch

Gregg's South Carolina brigade lost 116 killed, 606 wounded. Anderson's Brigade, of which the 8th Georgia was a part, lost 108 killed and 701 wounded, both high losses. After the battle of Second Manassas only ten to fifteen members of the Oglethorpe Light Infantry were left of the ninety-five who had gone to war a year earlier.

Tallulah Hansell to Charlotte Branch

Marietta, Ga. Sept 5th/62

My Highly Esteemed Friend

Since the reception of your last letter, which was warmly welcomed, I have longed many times for an opportunity of writing to you. . . . I have been in the midst of sickness ever since July—first acting as nurse, and for several weeks as a *patient*. Our family has been much afflicted with disease, principally bilious fever—dear sister Fannie is still confined to her bed. I am now able to sit up most of the time, but am weak and very much reduced. Our phisician advised our leaving Oglethorpe, and the first day we were all able to sit up, we came away, hoping to regain health and strength in this bracing mountain climate. Since our arrival here Father has been very sick, and indeed we are *all* invalids. . . .

I was truly glad to hear that your youngest boy, your "baby" was again with you. With the torturing recollections of the past, I know how your heart must ache to resign either one of your heart's remaining jewels. Has your son Sanford been yet exchanged? You must remember that I am interested in *all* your household band, for the sake of one we all loved. Oh! you can hardly tell what a trial it is for me to come back to Marietta where *we* had been so long together. Every street & walk has associations. I *would* not *forget*, yet can hardly dare to recall. I have not yet revisited the old homestead, now passed into the hands of entire strangers, nor the church to which we had so often gone in company. I dread these trials exceedingly. How many changes a few short years can bring to us!

In your letter you mentioned Mr. M.P. King—he was a warm friend of mine during his stay in M. John, Mallery and myself were constantly associated. After he went North to "West Point" he wrote to me regularly and frequently for some months. Suddenly and without any cause *that I ever knew*, the letters ceased and we have never met since. I am very *sensitive, too much so for a poor person*, and let the matter drop. I was sick when I heard of M.'s marriage, & when I got better & saw the notice I felt perfectly shocked to see that he *had married* on the first sad, sad anniversary of our sorrow and loss! I felt for a moment, so *bitterly*, that *John* could never have done that as Mallery had—but then I blushed for my want of *charity*, for unless I knew all the circumstances, I had no right whatever to censure. Our litle trio has thus been severed, and I am here a *stranger*, where my childhood & girlhood were passed. Can you wonder that I am sad?

Marietta is quite crowded with refugees from Kentucky, Tennessee & N. Orleans. I am not able yet to go into company much, but hope to form some pleasant acquaintances among them soon. I had the pleasure of meeting Mrs. Crane of Savh., a few days ago. She spoke of yourself & family in most kind and cordial terms. Hon. T[homas] Butler King also visits my Father occasionally. I like him very well. I am sorry, dear Mrs. Branch, to send you such an uninteresting letter, after waiting so long, but I am too much of a recluse to tell you anything of the outside world— & too unwell to be able to write at any length. I shall wait with anxiety [for] a letter from you hoping to hear that you have not thought unkindly of me. . . .

Many thanks for your thoughtful kindness in sending me a copy of the inscription. Will you think it presumptuous that I have attempted to write a short inscription [for John's gravestone]? I only send it in case you have none that pleases you better. You must not think for a moment of using it because I have written it. Can you not ask Gen. H[enry] R. Jackson to write one? He might do justice to the subject—it must be short and comprehensive and it should be written by a practised hand. My efforts are crude & imperfect—their sole recommendation is that they are the out–gushings of my heart. Thank God, for these late glorious victories! How can we praise Him enough for his mercy & loving kindness? My heart is too full to write more now. Only this Thank God! Ever, dear Lady, your sincere, & warm friend—

Lula Hansell

Sgt. Sanford Branch to Charlotte Branch

Winchester Sept. 15 62

Dear Mother

This is the first opportunity I have had of writing you since my last.

I left Orange C.H. the day after I wrote for the Rapidan, which was as far as the cars ran. Then I enlisted as a wagon driver & seperated from Eastmead, he having to walk, since which I have not heard from him. After breaking several wheels & shafts & killing 2 horses I arrived at Leesburg just 2 days after the regiment crossed the river and as the provost marshall would not allow straglers to follow the army, I was forced to join a division of sick & Barefooted men who were coming to this place, where I arrived yesterday. Our barefooted synod consists of Corporal [Ralph B.] Sandeford, Privates [Onesime] Danvergne, [John J.] Griffin, [S.T.] Islar, [William M.]

Patterson, [C.P.] Maroney & Sturdevant sick.

I met [John] Richardson & [John MacPherson] Berrien here. with those I am rooming over Reas Store. Mac & I called on Mrs. [James A.] Graham & Mrs. Meredith this morning.

I expect to leave here for Martinsburg as soon as the road is open which I hope will be very soon. If I stay here much longer, I shall be forced to draw on you again. I have not heard from you but onced since I left home, and now I do not know how to tell you to direct.

Your affectionate son
Sanford W. Branch

P.S. It is reported that Baldie [Samuel Hamilton Baldy] died yesterday at Warrenton from wounds received in the Battle of Manassas.

Sgt. Sanford Branch to Charlotte Branch

Camp near Martinsburg
Sept 23rd 1862
Dear Mother

I have at length found an opportunity of writing. I do hope you will not [be] uneasy about not hearing from me as it is impossible to send letters home. There is not a man in the company that has heard from home in a month. today there is a man from the ninth Ga. that is going home. Not a very safe transit but we are glad of any chance.

I arrived here yesterday after following the army round for about 3 weeks. We have only 10 men in the company. Thay are all well. Lieut. [Fred] Bliss, 2 Bacons [DeWitt Clinton and Albert S.], [G.H.] Mock, [H.J.] Mickler, Henry Davis, John Wright, Mell, [William B.] Dasher, [R.B.] Sandiford & 8 others are at Winchester barefooted with no prospect of getting any [shoes]. We had but one man badly wounded in Maryland. that was [Stephen] Barnwell, a very brave & honorable boy. He was shot in the knee, and had his leg amputated above the knee. Thay had to leave him in Maryland as he was too weak to be carried in an ambulance. Bliss had a bullet through his sleeve & Ganann [Joseph Gnann] a slight wound in his arm.

. . . All the boys desire to be remembered to you. As ever

your affectionate son
S.W. Branch

Sgt. Sanford Branch to Charlotte Branch

Camp near Winchester
Sept. 30, 1862

Dear Mother

I regret very much to say that since writing I have not heard from you. The only mail since the regiment left Richmond arrived today. I received 2 letters but neither from home. How do you direct—the best way is S.W.B., Co. B 8th Regt. (please forward). The mail facilities here very poor but better is promised.

Mr. [William H.] Gregory arrived this morning. He is in the 7th. He looks quite well & appeared very glad to see me. I certainly was to see him.

The company has increased considerable since the late battle [at Sharpsburg, Maryland, September 16–17]. The Provost Guard forcing the barefooted out of Winchester. [R.B.] Sandiford, [William] Marion Patterson & [Andrew J.] Carpenter are here barefooted and if made to march will suffer terrible.

I expect however that we will be in this neighborhood for some time yet as the enemy have not crossed the river in any force yet. Thay must of been terrible cut up. Tis said that our Brigade of not more than 3000 men killed a thousand & a lieut. of artillery told me 2000. Thay were evadently too badly crippled to renew the contest and we were to week to do so. If we had of had our 30 thousand stragglers engaged we would of been in Baltimore by this time. Hereafter stragglers are to be arrested, sick or well, and severely dealt with.

The only excitement in camp is the prospect of this Brigade being ordered to Savannah this winter. I hope that it may be so ordered. Do write soon & tell me all the news. Give my love to Grandma & all the other folks.

Your affectionate son
S.W. Branch

Sgt. Sanford Branch to Charlotte Branch

Camp near Winchester
Oct. 12th, 1862

Dear Mother

I have just received a letter from Hamilton per Goodwin who arrived in camp yesterday. It is the first from home for two long months. Why I do not get your letters I cannot imagine. The others get theirs.

Hammie says that you are very ancious about me. I am very sorry to hear it. I am in excellent health & spirits, only there is no prospect of a fight. I think the enemy were so badly crippled that it will take some time for them to regain. Our army is under excellent discipline but I think will fall back, probably to Gordonsville which is a much better base.

Mr. Gregory has just left me. I think I wrote you he was in the 7th, this brigade. He is quite well and very well satisfied. I believe he has not heard from Sava. since he left Georgia.

I am sorry to hear of Grandmother's illness and hope before this reaches you she will have recovered entirely.

Tell Hammie that I have selected two of his messmates Mickler & [William B.] Mell. I expect to leave the army tomorrow for Richmond but do not expect to be absent more than ten days. The boys can't imagine how I can get a leave of absence so I will be for explaining until my next.

We have just received a note from Davis A[lfred]. who was left with Barnwell, he says he is getting along finely.

Do sent me a paper occasionally, any date is news here.

With love to all I subscribe myself your affectionate son
S.W. Branch

Sgt. Sanford Branch to Charlotte Branch

Richmond Oct. 24

Dear Mother

I have at last heard from you but the letter was sad, sad indeed. I had received a letter from Hammie per Goodwin saying that Grandma was unwell but never dreamed that it was any thing more than usual. I should of liked to have seen her once more, but she is in a better world where I hope we may meet her again.

I am hear for a few days. Will leave for the Regt. next Tuesday with Col. [Lucius M.] Lamar. Shellman leaves for Savannah this evening to get cloths for the regiment. I hope he may be able to procure them, we want them bad enough. With love to all. I am your affect. son

S.W. Branch

Sgt. Sanford Branch to Charlotte Branch

Nov. 2, 1862

Dear Mother

I have just received your letter dated at Savannah and was very glad to hear from you. It has been snowing here all day with no probability of its stoping soon. Fortunately for us we have just reach this place were our flies were left so that we are quite comfortable. Joe Davis who was left as baggage guard here had quite a number of Blankets but as we had to march 13 miles to this camp he had to give away all but 3. there with 1 of mine make us very comfortable at night.

The Regiment arrived at Gordonsville on the 4th from Cedar Run, a distance of 107 miles which thay marched in six days pretty good for troops that have been in quarantine for Small Pox. I suppose you have heard of this. there was no truth in it. There has been no such disease in the Brigade. the health of the Regiment was never better, although we are suffering for clothing & shoes. When Shellman returns I wish you would send those knee boots if Hammie has no use for them. Also a pair of Pants, Drawers, undershirt & socks.

The order for the 1st Ga. Regulars to report to Macon created considerable excitement in this regiment. bets were freely offered of $100 to $50 that we would be in Georgia in 30 days. only on your account I wish it may be so. I think myself our chances are pretty good.

The day we arrived here I went over to the 7th to see Mr. G[regory] and was told that he had been sick for 3 weeks and had to be carried from Cedar Run to Gordonsville in an ambulance were he now is in the Hospital. I applied to General [George T.] Anderson for a pass. it was of course refused as we are 13 miles from there. I think we will be ordered to Richmond in a few days or at least to Gordonsville when I will be able to see him. Poor fellow I hope I will find him better.

The 1st Ga. will [be] susceeded by the 10 Ga. Bat. from Macon.

Col. Anderson received his appointmt. yesterday. we are all very glad of it he was serenaded by our band last night.

Lieut. Bliss, the Davis's & others send their respects to you.

Love to Hammie & all others

Your affect. son

S.W. Branch

Sgt. Sanford Branch to Charlotte Branch

Camp near Orange C.H.
Nov. 10. 62
Dear Mother

I have just rec'd yours of 6 inst. and was very glad to hear from you as I had not heard for sometime. You say that you would have preferred my coming home when I found out that I could not be exchanged. I never found it out, the commissioners kept promising to exchange me every week until I went to the Regiment. after being there some weeks and not hearing anything of an exchange, I went back to Richmond were I found I had been exchanged since the 21st Sept. I did not write you this before because I did not want to add to your troubles and anxieties.

[Charles C.] Hardwick arrived here yesterday. He looks very well.

I saw by the papers that Adj. Shellman would leave on the 15th of the month. I wrote you in time, as I thought, what I wanted and hope you will rec'd my letter in time.

Very sorry to hear of Hammie's accident [his wounded hand]. Hope he will recover soon. We are all anciously awaiting the next movmt of this Brigade, wether it will be to build winter quarters or move South.

I hardly think there will be another General engagement this winter.

Love to all
Your affect. son
S.W. Branch

At this time the Army of Northern Virginia was divided into two corps. The 8th Georgia belonged to Gen. George T. Anderson's Brigade of Hood's Division in the First Corps, which was under command of Gen. James Longstreet. November found them encamped near the Rappahannock River, with only thirty miles separating Confederate and Union lines.

Around November 18, Confederate forces learned that a division of 30,000 Yankees under command of Union general Charles Sumner was moving toward Fredericksburg. Fearing a surprise attack across the Rappahannock, Longstreet sent two divisions to Marye's Heights and the hills around Fredericksburg, including the 8th Georgia. Sumner accused the residents of harboring and providing materiel for "armed bodies in rebellion against the Government of the United States" and ordered the city to surrender or face shelling from his artillery.

Many of the residents fled, leaving behind a deserted town. The opposing armies sat and watched one another. By November 27 it was obvious that a battle was imminent. Union reinforcements and the rest of Longstreet's Corps had arrived as well as Stonewall Jackson's Army of the Valley, giving Lee 58,000 effective troops.[47]

Sgt. Sanford Branch to Charlotte Branch

Camp near Fredericksburg
Nov. 27th 1862
Dear Mother

Your letter of the 19th is just received. I am very sorry that I can not write with Ink but it is impossible to procure it. Since writing you last we have changed our locality considerable. We left Orange CH on last Wednesday and marched 3 days in the rain, a distance of 52 miles. I had just bought a new pair of shoes and walking in the water blistered my feet awful. by the second day I had to go barefooted. It was very cold and I suffered very much. on the 3rd day I cut my shoes so that I could wear them.

We have been here some days and I see no prospect of a fight. We have an excellent position and if the enemy attacked us it would be at a great disadvantage to them. It is reported that thay are leaving this morning in the direction of Petersburg.

I continue to enjoy excellent health although the duty is very heavy ~~I am very well satisfied~~ [sic] the men coming on duty every other day.

Since writing you last I have not heard anything of Mr. Gregory. He was sent to the Hospital from his company and thay have not heard from him since. This was about 4 weeks ago. I feel very uneasy about him and enquire every day.

I hope Shellman will leave our packages in Richmond as I think our next move will be in that direction. I do not think we will stay here long.

Please write me something about Capt. Butler [who had been wounded during the Seven Days' Battle on the Peninsula]. He wrote that he would be here a month ago. We are not very ancious about his coming.

If you have an opportunity to sent me a Blanket please do so as it is quite cool.

> Give my love to all
> Your affect. son
> Sanford W. Branch

During Capt. Butler's absence, Fred Bliss and Sanford were in command of the company.

Sgt. Sanford Branch to Charlotte Branch

Camp near Fredericksburg
Dec. 9, 1862
Dear Mother

I have just time at present to acknowledge the receipt of package of clothing which arrived on 4th, and were very acceptable. I am very much obliged to you for them.

I was shocked to hear of poor Gregorys death. since I wrote you of his sickness I havent been able to hear any thing of his case. I enquired almost every day of his comrades but they knew nothing more than I wrote you. We are about to change camp for better wood & water so I must close.

Your affect. son
S.W. Branch

Soon 147 Union cannon were in place on Stafford Heights and 100,000 infantry were assembled in the level plain below. On December 11 and 12 federal forces crossed the river on pontoon bridges under sniper fire from Confederate sharpshooters posted in buildings in the town.[48]

Sgt. Sanford Branch to Charlotte Branch

In line Battle near the River Dec. 12, 62
Dear Mother

As [Charles F.] Borchert leaves for home in a few hours I embrace the opportunity to write a few lines. The enemy's batteries opened this morning about 4 oclock, since which time there has been an incessant boom of artillery. No infantry has been engaged as yet except the pickets & sharpshooters.

Fredericksburg is reported in flames. There are a thousand reports about the progress of the fight. at one time we hear that the Yankees are falling back and then again we hear that we are allowing them to cross. I do not think that this regiment will engage them as we are in reserve. Hoping to hear soon

I am your affect. son, S.W. Branch

On the morning of December 13 the Union troops advanced under a blanket of fog; but around 10:00 A.M., when they were within range of Confederate troops on Marye's Heights, the fog lifted. As blue ranks advanced, deadly rifle fire from Georgians and South Carolinians posted behind a stone wall along a sunken road cut swaths into them. Ordered forward in relentless but unsuccessful attacks, wave after wave of blue-coated infantry fell. After six futile assaults, night halted the carnage.

The next day Gen. Burnside debated renewing the attack. Discouraged from further bloodshed by his staff, he declined. On December 15 the federal forces withdrew across the river, leaving the field, and a sound victory, in Confederate hands.[49]

2Lt. Sanford Branch to Charlotte Branch

Fredericksburg, Virginia
December 17, 1862
Dear Mother,

I expect you are blaming me now for not writing before, but this is the first opportunity that I have had since the battle began on Thursday last. We were not engaged at close column but had a pretty heavy skirmish on Saturday with a loss of three killed, three wounded and four prisoners. I do not know how many we killed and wounded, but we took 61 prisoners. I will begin and tell you what I know of the battle.

On Thursday morning at 3 o'clock, the signal guns were fired. Our brigade was formed and marched about one-half mile, where we lay in line of battle all day. The cannonading in the direction of Fredericksburg was very heavy all day but ceased entirely at night. The next morning we were marched about a mile nearer Fredericksburg and the river, where we were formed in line of battle. We stayed here about two hours, when we were relieved by the Tennessee brigade. This was the position where the battle raged hottest. This brigade was very badly cut up.

The next day we took position on the center in the advance line. This was Saturday. Our position was in an immense field. The woods was about a mile to our rear. In these woods the second line was formed. Our position was a very good one. The only advantage the enemy could gain over us would be to flank our right. Our regiment rested on the right flank. To prevent this a battery was placed on our right and about 200 yards to the rear. The enemy attempted this flank movement after the battle ceased on the right and left. There had been skirmishing all day with but little loss on either side. (I forgot to mention that about 150 yards in our front was a railroad embankment, running through a narrow swamp, the swamp extending down to the river [Deep Run]. The embankment was parallel with our line and the river. Our line was about one mile from the river.)

The enemy advanced up this swamp to the embankment. I t was a strong position. The only way to dislodge them was a charge directly in their front or to flank them on their right. We expected to charge every moment, but there we lay quietly receiving their fire, when I began to get impatient. I heard cheers to our right and rear. Looking in that direction, I saw a body of troops [Law's Brigade] emerging from the woods. They advanced steadily to the right of the embankment under heavy fire. Having flanked it, they charged the enemy, routing them completely. This was on the right of the swamp on the left. The left wing of our regiment charged with equal success, taking 31 prisoners. The other prisoners were taken by Companies H and B. Company A had two men shot dead. The men wounded were on the left.

Night put an end to any further fighting. At night I was sent out on picket in front of the embankment. Picketing with us were some of the 6th North Carolina who made so much noise as to draw the fire of the Yankee pickets, wounding two of these men. Whereupon they skedaddled, leaving nobody there but Henry Davis and I. After the firing ceased, the North Carolinians returned and there was no more firing during the night. We found everything belonging to a soldier's equipment, several hundred guns, knapsacks, canteens, &c. All night long I could hear the wounded Yankees lying in the swamps, crying, "Water, water" I was very anxious to assist them, but it was against positive orders to go into the swamp, so they had to lay there all night.

In the morning, the enemy shelled ours with grape and shrapnel, killing one of our regiment. There was very little skirmishing along the line, the enemy apparently preparing for a big battle at night. Our brigade was withdrawn to the woods, leaving only two companies from each regiment as skirmishers. This day passed off quietly. The next morning to our amazement the enemy had recrossed the river. I had no idea that they were so badly whipped. They left about 1000 prisoners in our hands besides what we took the day of the battle, which is variously estimated at from 1000 to 3000.

Last night we returned to our old encampment. How long we will stay here depends on the movements of the enemy. They can still be seen across the river. I do not think they will attack us again. All the better if they do. I think we can whip a million of them! This is one of the best positions in the world. We never had any doubts about our success.

Please write soon, as I have not heard from you in some time.

Your affectionate Son
Sanford W. Branch

2Lt. Sanford Branch to Charlotte Branch

Camp near Fredericksburg Dec. 25
Dear Mother

Wishing you a very merry Christmas I sit down to write you a long letter. Since my last we have had a very quiet time except the fourth day after the fight. On that day we lay all day in line of battle but it proved to be a false alarm. We are now encamped between the Railroad & River sending a strong picket to the River and a guard to the Railroad Station every day.

This is a very dull Christmas to us all. Most of the boys are at the station buying ginger cakes which sell at the remarkable price of 3 for a dollar, and scarce at that. I breakfasted with George Snider who is clerk for the Surgeon. We had big Homeny which was quite a treat.

I was very very sorry to hear of Miss Sallie Davis's marriage. I certainly had some hopes in that quarter myself, but alas, my hopes are born but to be blasted. I hope however now that the deed [is done] I will not be forgotten in the distrabusion of the cake.

. . . I saw McIntosh of the 4th Alabama on Saturday. He beged to be remembered to you. Rev. Mr. [David] Porter & Mr. Alcott of Sav. Hqts. Georgia Hospital & R. Assoc. are here. Thay gave me a fine pr. pants, I having sent all my cloths to Richmond and burnt the pair I had on.

The news from the North is generally believed here but I do not believe it. The Army would not submit to [John] Fremont and thay will not fight again under Burnside, so McClelland will have to be put in command again. I feel confident that we can whip any army that thay can put in the field under any Leader thay can produce. I consider the Confederate Army of the Potomac [later the Army of Northern Virginia] commanded by Lee, Jackson & Longstreet *invincible*.

Please tell Hammie that I should like to hear from him. I wrote him last from Richmond. Remember me to Miss Kennedy & Sarah.

Your affect. son
Sanford W. Branch

Hammie's company, Co. F, 54th Georgia, had been detached by order of Gen. Mercer on July 20, 1862, and ordered to report to Lt. Col. William S. Rockwell, provost marshal at the Chatham County jail. Federal prisoners of war were confined there, and the company served as guards and stood picket duty for the railroad depot.

CHAPTER EIGHT

We Will Stick Here in the Mud Until Spring

Life in camp near Fredericksburg in the winter of 1862-63 was much the same as the preceding one. Sickness plagued the 8th Georgia, and the Oglethorpes had their share of members sent to the Georgia hospitals in Richmond.

Sanford was elected second lieutenant of the company.

2Lt. Sanford Branch to Charlotte Branch

Camp Ida Jany. 1st, 63
Dear Mother

I rec d your letter dated 23rd this morning and was surprised to hear that you had not heard from me since the Battle. I wrote you 2 days after the battle. it was the first opportunity I had, as we lay in line of battle 2 days after the fight, the enemy not having recrossed the river until the 3rd day. The almost universal opinion here is that if we can whip them in a pitched Battle out west the war will be ended very soon. All accounts agree in representing the army which lately confronted us as being completly demoralised. I hardly think thay will fight again this winter and most sincerely wish thay would send our Corps to the assistance of our comrades in the west who I am afraid will be completely overpowered by [Maj. Gen. William S.] Rosencrans and [his] immense army. The New York Herald & other Yankee journals however seem to despond of there army of West accomplishing any thing as long as Johns[t]on confronts them. I think he is without equal on this continent.

Eastmead made his first appearance in camp yesterday he having been in Hospital for some time with Rheumatism. I havent heard wether Cole & friends have left Sav or not. A small box would be most acceptable if it could be sent safely but I can devise no way of getting it here.

Be pleased to present my regards to my Lady friends. Tell them I think of them very often.

Love to Hamie . . . & all friends

Your affect Son
S.W. Branch

2Lt. Sanford Branch to Charlotte Branch

Camp [Yeoby?] near Fredburg
Jany 7, 63
Dear Mother

Why do you not write. I have not heard from you for nearly 2 weeks and yet I know you must of written. I write you regularly about once a week. Wrote you on the 2nd day after the Battle on Christmas, New Years & now today.

I exchanged the musket of a sword yesterday and must say I am very much pleased with the change. I find it much lighter and more easily carried.

I was unanimously elected to fill the [second lieutenant] vacancy occasioned by the promosion of Lieut Hardwick. I felt very much flattered by the vote. I am in tempory command, Bliss being on the sicklist. I think he will get a furlough in a few days.

Remember me to all
Affectionately
S.W. Branch

2Lt. Sanford Branch to Charlotte Branch

[Undated]

Dear Mother

Your letter & package per [Hollie] Cole came to hand yesterday and both were very acceptable. I assure you I had on my last pr. socks and a handkerchief is something which although much needed I have not seen for a long time.

Fred left camp this morning for the Officers Hospital, Richmond. He is trying to get a furlough and I think he will succeed. don't mention this to anybody. if he gets to Savannah and a uniform can be made for a living price I should like to have one made. please write Hammie to enquire what one can be made for and let me know and I will try and send the money.

I am now in command of the company, no small responsibility, I assure you, but I will try and do my duty. I do hope Fred will be able to get enough conscripts to fill the company up it is now the smallest Co in the Regiment.

Tell Hamie I am now his equal in rank. Shellman having received his appointment I am second Lieut. Sr.

I hope you will excuse this letter. It is so cold I am writing in Shellman's tent, he having a stove. the tent being closed it is very dark.

Give my kindest regards to all the young ladies and Remember me particularly to the Lufs.

Your affct. Son
S.W. Branch

2Lt. Sanford Branch to Charlotte Branch

Camp 8th Ga.

Jany 22, 63

Dear Mother

Your letters of 10 & 13 inst. are just rec d. I am glad that you have at last heard from *me*. I cant imagine where my letters are. I must of written at least 8 since the Battle of Fredericksburg. This I will send by Mr. Ganan [Joseph H. Gnann] of this Corps and trust you will get it. He goes home recruiting. [William B.] Dasher of this camp leaves with him.

I have just rec d a letter from Fred. He is still in Richmond and does not know wether he will get a furlough or not. dont mention his being in

Richmond to his mother should you see her as he wants to take her by surprise should he get a furlough.

The clothes send for Mr. Gregory I distributed as follows Sargent Holmes Pants, M. Griffin 2 shirts, Pri. Davis H[enry]. 1 shirt. The gloves I kept. The letters sent also one found in his pocket I sent by mail to you. please return my thanks & those of my friends also to Aunt Lufburrow.

I am very well supplied with clothing now and think will have enugh for the winter.

There is news here. the news papers seem to think we will have another fight here soon but it will be impossible now as it has rained for two days. It is very unpleasant and so cold that I spend most of my time in the Hdqs. tent were I am now siting eating cakes made of musty flour and a very small quantity of molasses. on account of a break in the Rail Road the army is now on 1/2 rations, 1/4 lb. bacon & 1 lb. flour.

If a uniform can be made in Savannah for a price that I am able to pay I should like to have one. Bliss writes me the coat is worth over $100 in Richmond. I hope thay can be made for less in Savannah.

Ganan [Gnann], Dasher & probably Bliss will come to see you I expect. they are all my friends and I know you will be glad to see them. Thay will also call on Miss Iye [Ivy Felt]. don't let them take advantage of my absence.

With love to all, I am your affect Son
Sanford W. Branch

P.S. You wrote me that Hamie has written. I have never received his letter. SWB

2Lt. Sanford Branch to Charlotte Branch

[Jan. 23, 1863]

Dear Mother

It has been a long time since I have written you but I can hardly say it was my fault. About 10 days ago I wrote you and left the letter with the adjutant clerk. He forgot to mail it the night I gave it to him. The regiment went on picket. We staid on picket 2 days and were relieved to march to Richmond. commenced the march on Sunday morning at daylight in a terrible snow storm which continued all day. The next day it rained all day. I do not think any troops ever suffered more, the roads were in awful order.

The men positively stuck in the mud and had to be taken out. At night we were without tents and scarcely any axes to cut wood with. Continued the march 6 days and arrived here on the 20th. All well but [James E.] Sweat and [John J.] Griffin who were completely used up. My feet were so sore that I had to take the cars at Hanover Junction and join the Regt here. We are here awaiting orders some say to Charleston, Savannah, Blackwater & Vicksburg. I do not think we will stay here long.

My health was never better than at present. Dasher arrived here this morning. the cakes were very acceptable, that is what I got of them. He had to leave the trunk in Richmond, when some kind friend extracted all but 2 cakes. He brought some country made sausages from home. Thay were the best I ever ate. I haven't seen Mrs. Hines yet but understand she is in the city. Will probable go to the city with a guard after stragglers tomorrow and will try to call on her. Have seen Messrs. Bulkley & Branch thay are quite well. was very sorry to hear of Miss Davis's death and the probable stroke of John Symons. If you see Fred tell him I will write in a few days. he has written me 5 letters and I havent answered the first yet. Love to Hamie, the Luffs, Sarah & all friends.

Direct as usual to Richmond.

Your affect. Son
Sanford

P.S. I was forced to draw on Mr. Bulkley for $100 as the quarter master has not paid us for nearly 3 months and I had to have a loan &c. SWB

2Lt. Sanford Branch to Charlotte Branch

Camp Ida Mc.
Jany 25, 1863
Dear Mother

Your letter of 15th inst. is received. I am surprised to hear that you do not hear from me. I write every week regularly and cannot imagine why I received your letters and you do not rec d mine.

There is no news here, in fact it is awful dull. Being in command of the company [while Fred Bliss is in hospital in Richmond] I am relieved of picket & other duty and have to stay in camp all the time.

I was very much surprised at receiving a letter & package of candy from Aunt Lizzie. Both were very acceptable. I shall answer the letter in a few

days. Sandiford has just returned from a forage with an immence Rice
pudding and I must go and help him eat it. It is the first thing but Rasions
I have eating in a long time.

> Very affectionately
> Your Son
> Sanford

2Lt. Sanford Branch to Charlotte Branch

Camp near Fredericksburg
Jany 29, 1863
Dear Mother

I have just rec d your letter dated 25th. Sandiford was not a candidate
[for election to second lieutenant] nor were any of the others you
mensioned where did you hear it from? Has Neidlinger taken the house for
a year & at what rent. I hope Sherlock has paid the rent. [Charlotte owned
rental properties.]

It is snowing and very cold. there is not a particle of news and I am
beginning to get tired of this inactivity. I did think we would go to North
Carolina but now think we will stick here in the mud until Spring.
Longstreet hasent gone to the West. The only Troops that left this army
are 7 Brigades for North Carolina. We have still enough left to whip the
Whole Yankee nation even when they will.

Lt. Bliss has a furlough and left Richmond on yesterday for home.
[Sanford continued in command.]

Please write Hammie to see what [a uniform] can be made for and if you
think I can afford it have it made for me and send by first opportunity.
Please write soon & often, it is ten days since I rec d a letter from you.

> Your affectionate Son, Sanford

Charlotte was in Egypt, Georgia, in Effingham County. Many Savannahians
left the city in 1863 and 1864 because food prices were high and supplies short.

Charlotte Branch to 2Lt. Sanford Branch

undated

Trust in God my own dear child. Write to me as soon as you can and
tell me how to direct to you. When you take the cake out of the box put

your sugar in it. the sausages will not spoil if you hang them up. Your candy is in the bag just where you can get it, close to where the bag is laced up at the side. My own dear precious boy do take care of yourself for my sake.

Your Mother.

2Lt. Sanford Branch to Charlotte Branch

Camp near Richmond
Feb 24
Dear Mother

I wrote you yesterday but think it doubtful wether you will receive it as it went by the Regt Mail carrier. I went to the city yesterday and spent a very pleasant day. called on Mrs. Hines but she was not at Home. Saw Mr. J. Bailey. He has been very ill but is fast recovering and intends going home on furlough. The package of candy was very acceptable we have just ate. it was very nice. I believe a soldier would go farther for candy than anything else. I think the Division will leave its present camp in a day or two for Petersburg. The whole of Longstreets Corps will rendevous there as he (Longstreet) has been placed in command since [General Gustavus] Smith resigned.

I should like very much to have my uniform here as I could visit some nice young Ladies in this neighborhood. Please send it by first opportunity.

Your affect Son, Sanford

P.S. My most affectionate regards to Miss Gertie D[illon].

Fort McAllister, sixteen miles west of Savannah on the Ogeechee River, had been under attack frequently since February 28. On March 3 the federal forces attacked the fort with three monitors. McAllister held, and the attackers were distracted by the siege of Charleston Harbor and the Confederate batteries on Morris Island, South Carolina.

2Lt. Sanford Branch to Charlotte Branch

Camp 8th Ga. Vols.
March 5, 63
Dear Mother

I would of written you before but have been unwell for several days but have recovered without losing many pds. of flesh. There is no news to write about, still in camp about 5 miles from Richmond. Most of the men have built chimneys so that we are again comfortable. Lt. [Ebenezer Starke] Law & myself are messing with [Adjt. William] Shellman as we had to give our tent to the boys. We were all very ancious yesterday about Fort McAllister, the Richmond papers stated that at a late hour on Tuesday afternoon the firing still continued. This morning papers contain a telegram from Savannah that the vessels had drawn off. I hope, wile I can but doubt, that the Fort may be able to hold out against any force that may be brought against it.

I was disappointed in getting cloth from the Quartermaster but cloth enough for 3 suits to a Regt. were given this Brigade. The officers of this Regt. drew for this cloth and I of course lost. I know not how to thank you for your kind proposals to give me a uniform for my birthday present. My dear mother, you are entirely too liberal. I know you cannot afford it and yet you would deprive yourself and may be denying yourself to gratify you[r] undeserving child. I intend hereafter to try and save a part of my pay and yet I do not know how I will do it. My commissary bill is large as I am eating with one of the company messes and thay always buy as much as thay can. I haven't been able to draw a cent of my pay yet but expect to do so in a few days.

Lt. Law and all the boys desire to be remembered. Give my love to Aunt & Uncle Lufburrow & the rest of the family, Sarah & Miss Kennedy.

Could you not send a small box of eatables by Augusta, care 8 Ga. H.& R. Ass., thay paying expenses from Augusta to Richmond. You can not imagine how acceptable thay would be. Sweet potatoes are worth only $16 per bushel. Cornmeal $1 per 1/2 pd. Sausages 1 [?] pr lb in Richmond. Write soon, you do not know how glad I am to hear from you.

Affecty.
Sanford

The 8th Georgia, as part of Longstreet's First Corps, was detailed to the Peninsula to occupy defenses around Suffolk, Virginia, from March until May. Sanford and his companions did not participate in the Confederacy's greatest victory—the battle of Chancellorsville, which produced what was, perhaps, the Confederacy's greatest tragedy. Stonewall Jackson, wounded by his own men on May 3, died a week later of pneumonia. On May 9 Longstreet joined Gen. Lee at Fredericksburg. The army was reorganized with Lt. Gen. Richard S. Ewell replacing Jackson as commander of the Second Corps.

At this point the war in the west was not going well for the Confederates. Maj. Gen. Ulysses S. Grant had Vicksburg, Mississippi, under siege, and William Rosecrans was pressing Confederate general Braxton Bragg in Tennessee. A strategic move to alleviate the pressure on the Confederacy at those points was absolutely necessary.

As Sanford had suspected, Longstreet wanted to take his corps west against Rosecrans and march north to Cincinnati, Ohio. However, Gen. Lee decided to invade the North, which would draw federal troop strength out of the West.

Sarah L. Hine to Charlotte Branch

Richmond May 20th 1863
My dear Charlotte

I have been writing a letter to the children which I have duplicated for you & sister thinking you would be interested in it perhaps. I wrote you a long letter soon after I reached here with all the particulars in it about the Oglethorpes that I could glean from my husband who was there just from their midst. I directed it to Savannah, care of Mr. Chauncey Butler. I think you could not have received it for I have never had a line from you. I am going to direct this to Hamilton's care, I do not know your PO address. Your mind must have been spared much anxiety when you heard of the Fredericksburg fight by the knowledge that Hoods Division was too remote from Lee to be in the struggle. Since then the Division has passed through Richmond, but I am sorry to say I missed seeing the 8th. I went down to the Fredericksburg cars very early in the morning, and taking a very long walk to get there, the morning that I heard they were passing through but found when I reached the Depot that a part of them among whom the 8th had been sent on by a train the night before. Mr. Hine, who is still at the crossing and who comes down every Saturday evening and stays with me until Monday morning, says that he has not seen any of them but heard that they were at Orange Court House. I have had urgent and pressing invitations from the families with whom I boarded last summer both in Amelia Co. and in Albemarle to come into the country & visit them & eat cherries & strawberries. I may perhaps go for a short time. Please direct my letters to care James B. Hine, Gen. Hos. No. 4. I feel very *very* blue about our affairs in Miss[issippi, the siege of Vicksburg]. But the *Lord reigns*. I do try to be content. May he deliver us in his own time. I often think of you and wish you were with me, next best thing to that would be to hear from you. Do pray write to me. Very affec,

Your Friend
Sarah L. Hine

After its defeat at Chancellorsville, the Union army had pulled back north of the Rappahannock River, opposite Fredericksburg. Gen. Hooker occupied an advantageous position from which Gen. Lee was determined to draw him, while simultaneously forcing the withdrawal of Union forces under Maj. Gen. Robert H. Milroy from the lower Shenandoah Valley.

The decoys were the two army corps under lieutenant generals James Longstreet and Richard Ewell. Leaving the vicinity of Chancellorsville, both corps camped at Culpeper Court House on June 7. Hooker took the bait and threw a force across the Rappahannock two miles below Fredericksburg as an observation post. The Third Corps, under Lt. Gen. Ambrose P. Hill, was left to watch these troops, with orders to follow the rest of Lee's army northward once Hooker's troops retired across the river.

On June 9, 1863, Union cavalry attempted to cut Lee's line of communication with Richmond. They were met by Confederate cavalry under Maj. Gen. J.E.B. Stuart at Brandy Station, near the army's camp at Culpeper Court House. The result of this chance encounter, the largest cavalry engagement in North American history, the battle of Brandy Station, was important in two respects: for the first time Union cavalry held its own, and they successfully cut Lee off from his source of intelligence. The latter carried the graver consequences.

For Sanford and the common soldier in Lee's army, unaware of the strategies that governed their fate, the usual hardships of daily life were more noteworthy.

2Lt. Sanford Branch to Charlotte Branch

Camp near Culpepper
June 12, 1863
Dear Mother

I have rec d no letters from you for some time. why I fail to get your letters I cannot imagine. I know you write and yet others appear to get theres regularly. There is no news here. The calvary fight on Wednesday created a little excitement very little. Our division was under arms and march[ed] to within 3 miles of the Battle field were we lay in the sun all day and at night marched back to camp. You cannot imagine what a contemptable opinion the veteran infantry have of the calvary. This fight of Wednesday was the heavyest the calvary have ever had in Virginia. Our forces were completely surprised, the enemy having crossed the Rappahannock and nearly gained Genl Stewart [Stuart's] Hdqrs several miles from the river before thay were discovered. After our men recovered from there fight thay fought pretty well and finally drove the Yanks across the river. Our loss 70 killed 200 wounds, & about 150 prisoners. Enemy 100 dead on the field, 80 wounds, prisoners in our hands & 350 prisoners. A Georgia Regt also captured 3 pces. artillery.

As I have no ink to write with I must stop. Remember me to all

Affect. son
Sanford

Gen. Ewell left Culpeper Court House on June 10, crossed the Shenandoah River near Front Royal, and reached Cedarville on the 12th. After sending a division under Maj. Gen. Robert E. Rodes to dislodge Union forces at Berryville, Ewell continued with the rest of his command to Winchester. The Confederate Army of Northern Virginia was strung out along Valley roads and in mountain gaps on a long march northward.

The 8th Georgia, part of Longstreet's Corps, played its part in the center of the great move toward Pennsylvania. While Ewell moved his corps down the Valley, Longstreet was sent to guard Snickers's and Ashby's gaps, preventing Hooker from coming to the aid of Milroy in Winchester. Milroy's troops fled to Harpers Ferry.

Hill's Corps watched as Hooker's army withdrew once again to the north side of the Rappahannock. On June 14th Hill struck out to catch up with the rest of Lee's army. Passing behind John Bell Hood's and Lafayette McLaws's divisions and using the Blue Ridge as a screen, Hill crossed into Maryland, leaving the boys of the 8th and other regiments in Longstreet's Corps to bring up the rear of the Army of Northern Virginia. Another invasion had begun.[50]

2Lt. Sanford Branch to Charlotte Branch

Camp on Shenandoah
June 19, 1863
Dear Mother

As this is the first opportunity I have had of writing I take advantage of it. since writing last have been continually on the march. this is the fifth day from Culpepper and up to yesterday I have never experienced such warm oppressive weather. It seemed impossible to live. we have lost 20 out of 37 men, several of them are very sick. Fortunatelly for me, my nose bleeds almost every day which I think saved me. yesterday forded the river at Millwood and were resting, expecting to stop two or three hours when and order was sudingly given to fall in, that the enemy were near at hand. the brigade of Laws [Evander H. Law] with 2 batterys were sent off immediately to this point Snickers Gap. it is 12 miles from Millwood. it was about 2 o clock. had not marched more than 1 mile when about 50 men from the Regt. were compelled to fall out. fortunately it commenced raining [at] this time which saved us. I do not think I could of stood it 15 minutes longer when about 1/2 way to the gap a courier from Genl Anderson informed me that a Lady wanted to see me at a house near by. I went and found Mrs. Dr. [Elizabeth]Tucker [wife of a Berryville physician]. was very much pleased with her but could stay but a few minutes. She begs to be remembered to you. would like to write more about her but haven't time or space.

Arrived at Gap about dark tired & wet to the skin. made a shelter and slept all night. next morning crossed the river & took position in the Gap. Even 50 thousand Yankeys could not dislodge us.

This valley is the land of Milk & Honey. Butter & cheese at 15 cents per lb & eggs 10 ¢ doz. Since first crossing have been continually on the move crossing & recrossing, sometimes with cloths on & sometimes off. We thought we came here to do some desperate fighting but now think we have only to guard the Gaps of the Blue Ridge. if we do this, which is very easy, Hooker cannot get in the rear of Ewell I have never heard from [John R.]Richardson [Jr.]. is he in Savannah. I am very anxious about the pipe and tobacco bag.

Berryville
June 23, 1863

I started to write this epistle about a week ago.

Give my love to all, Hammie, Sarah the Lufs, Miss Iv & e&c. Have had but 1 mail in eight days and no letter in that. Write soon.

Your affect. son
Sanford

At home in Savannah, Charlotte and the others who held dear the men and boys in the O.L.I. anxiously waited to hear the consequences of Lee's decision. Two years after his death, John's many virtues were still being remembered by friends who missed him. Charlotte continued to receive letters of condolence even as the war threatened her remaining sons.

Mortie Davis to Charlotte Branch

Savannah June 24th 1863
My dear Aunt Charlotte
    Will you be kind enough to send by Cush the picture of my best of friend John, I will appreciate it I assure you, for there are few who knew his ways as I flatter myself I did. Kind at heart, generous to a fault, one could not know him but to love and admire his many manly qualities. . . . [W]e can but console our selves in but one way, he died the noblest death that is allotted to man, struggling in the defence of his country. . .
    I am aware my dear Aunt Charlotte how keen the blow is being felt by you, but remember you have two more, Sanford is as noble a man as ever breathed, and I am in hopes will be spared to do much to comfort his much afflicted mother. I wrote some verses when I knew no wrong, when my heart was unsullied. I know that I have in very many instances been guilty of much that was decidedly wrong, but henceforth my aim will be to try and recompense in a measure my kind parents. this is no resolve merely made to be broken, but with the aid of a higher power I am in hopes to succeed and prove to them I can and will be a man.

> What benefit can ever spring,
> From gloomy looks, and sight,
> Oh! a merry heart is a blessed thing
> And a cheerful face a prize.
> Then let us strive to love and smile
> Through life's short cloudy day;
> For tis at best but a little while
> That we together stay.
> Kind words and wishes when we meet,
> Should cheer our journey through;
> For there's nothing in this world so sweet,
> As love, and friendship true.
> Away with discord frowns or strife

Let us companions be,
Go hand in hand through the toils of life,
From guilt and envy free.
If love and kindness but prevail
And Faith our Helmsman be,
There will be music on the gale,
O'er life's tempestuous sea.
And though the rising cloud of fate
Their shadows o'er us fling,
We may with cheerfulness await
The changes time will bring.
For when the Heavens are o'ercast;
And angry surges roar;
We know that we shall reach at last,
A fairer, happier shore.

Your devoted friend and *nephew*
Mortie

On June 22 Gen. Ewell set off from Hagerstown, Maryland, marching through Chambersburg to Carlisle, Pennsylvania, where he arrived on the 27th. He was followed by Longstreet's and Hill's First and Third Corps, who camped outside Chambersburg the night of July 27.

Along the route of march, boys from the deep South were awestruck at the land of plenty—a land unscarred by two years of war. Fields were full of grain, and the luscious apples, cherries and pears were a real temptation to the hot, dusty marchers. Yet Gen. Lee had strictly forbidden any looting, stealing or destruction in his General Orders No. 72, which stated that private property would be respected and nothing taken except for commissary, quartermaster, ordnance and medical departmental use. His army would not mimic what had been done to the South and its civilians.

Sanford and his comrades had little knowledge of the military strategy, nor did they know the location of the rest of the army. They continued on in high spirits, naively joking of reaching New York unless orders arrived soon to stop them.

2Lt. Sanford Branch to Charlotte Branch

Camp near Chambersburg, Pa. June 28, 1863
Dear Mother:
     You will observe by the heading of this that we are in the Union again.

This Corps crossed the Potomac 3 days ago. The first day after crossing, marched across Maryland into Pennsylvania. Passed through Greencastel and Chambersburg. Where the other Corps are, I cannot tell. Rumor has it that Ewell is at Harrisburg and Hill between Longstreet and Ewell.

This is really the land of plentitude. the whole country appears to be one broad field of grain. Wheat, rye, barley and oats are the sold products of the soil. The people are all of Dutch descent, and of course, are mean and cowardly. Thus far, we have inflicted no damage to private property, except in foraging horses, cattle and commissary stores.

In passing through Chambersburg the women were right saucy, one saying that if I were our soldier boys I would not like to fight these fellows —they were too dark. I told her that her boys did not like to fight us, but I had never heard that reason assigned before. The sweet creature vanished, perfectly disgusted with Southern chivalry. At Greencastle, two wore small U.S. Flags, but when the boys enquired for Joe Hooker, as if they were really anxious to see him, they retired. One young lady sang the Bonnie Blue Flag very prettily and expressed a desire to have Old Abe's head on a pole. The Chaplain informs me that he found a secesh family in Chambersburg, that there was service in but one church. That was a Catholic. The sermon was a peace one. Love to all. . . .

The Division is resting here today and resuming the march tomorrow. I don't know when I will get an opportunity of sending this off but hope it will be soon. Love to all.

Your affect. son,
Sanford

At this point Lee, with no intelligence to the contrary, believed that the federal army under Hooker had not left the vicinity of Washington, D.C. His plan was to cut the railroad between Baltimore and Harrisburg and seize the Susquehanna Bridge at Wrightsville. However, the Army of the Potomac was looking for Lee in northern Maryland and was already approaching South Mountain. J.E.B. Stuart's Confederate cavalry had let Lee down and left him vulnerable, without knowledge of enemy troop movements or even the identity of his foe, for Hooker had been replaced. Lincoln had chosen his fifth commander of the Army of the Potomac—Maj. Gen. George G. Meade.

To intercept the Union advance, Hill's Corps was sent ahead on June 29, leaving Longstreet to follow the next day. Ewell received word to turn south and converge with Hill near Cashtown or Gettysburg. The Yankee intentions were unknown, and inclement weather made the march deleterious to the comfort of the troops. Henry Heth's Division of Hill's Corps had reached Cashtown on the 29th, and the next morning a brigade was sent to Gettysburg under command of Brig. Gen. J. Johnston Pettigrew in search of supplies. They encountered an enemy force, and being taken completely by surprise at the circumstances, Pettigrew withdrew to Cashtown and reported that Gettysburg was occupied. Around 2:00 P.M. on the afternoon of June 30, the 8th Georgia went into camp at Greenwood, about twenty miles from the bustling farm town of Gettysburg.

The next morning, July 1, a bright summer's day, Hill sent two divisions and two artillery battalions to Gettysburg to test the strength of the enemy force. About three miles west of town they clashed with Union cavalry under command of Maj. Gen. John Buford. Thus began the largest battle of the war—as a random encounter between the invading Southern boys and a small band of Union cavalry.[51]

CHAPTER NINE

This Government Has Taken a Fancy to Reb Officers

On July 1, 1863, the 8th Georgia was ordered to proceed to Gettysburg with the rest of Hood's Division; they arrived there on July 2. They and the rest of Longstreet's Corps would form the extreme right of Lee's line of battle.

The brigades of George T. Anderson and Jerome B. Robertson assembled on Warfield Ridge, an extension of Seminary Ridge. Before them lay a formidable formation of rocks called Devil's Den. They waited in a small line of trees, known as Biesecker Woods, for the arrival of Evander Law's brigade, which had been left behind at Chambersburg. These poor chaps joined the rest of the division around 11:30 A.M., after a grueling twenty-five mile march in the sultry July heat.

Gen. Longstreet sent wave after wave of Alabamians, Georgians and Texans against entrenched Union artillery and infantry on the slopes of Little Round Top and among the boulders of Devil's Den. The 8th Georgia and the rest of Anderson's Brigade waited in reserve. Their turn came when Anderson was ordered forward in support of Robertson's Brigade, which was engaged at Devil's Den and in the Rose Woods.[52]

They advanced to the left of Robertson toward the wheatfield of farmer John Rose. The Union brigade of Col. Regis P. DeTrobriand was posted along the southern edge of the field, connecting the Union line between Devil's Den and a peach orchard. As the 8th Georgia advanced across Plum Run, they came under artillery fire which played havoc in their ranks, driving them back to the streambed, which they used as a rifle pit. Its waters soon ran red with blood, but the Georgia boys held their line, eventually forcing Col. Charles Merrill's 17th Maine to abandon their position along a low stone wall and draw back through the wheatfield. These twenty-two acres quickly became a killing ground.

Among the boys from Savannah in Co. B, the carnage was devastating. Lt. Fred Bliss went down with a shattered knee. Capt. Alex Butler was severely wounded in the leg. Among the ten boys killed outright were close friends like privates Frank Goodwin and Richard Lewis. Many more fell wounded: James Sweat, John Griffin, and William Patterson, and even the brigade commander, Gen. George T. Anderson.

Sanford was thrust into command when Fred Bliss and Alex Butler fell. He was wounded while leading his company against the 17th Maine. The ball fractured his left wrist, tore through his ribs near the sternum, tumbled through his lung and exited beneath his left arm. He went down in excruciating pain, leaving the company without an officer as the battle raged around him.

At day's end, the wheatfield remained a no-man's land, the fire from both sides preventing the wounded from being removed until well after dark. Sanford was found alive and taken about two and a half miles behind Longstreet's line, to a farmhouse belonging to John Edward Plank. Here the surgeons of Hood's Division treated the harvest of the day's work.

Anderson's Brigade had sustained some of the heaviest losses of the day. The 8th filed no battle report, probably due to the high loss of officers. The devastation inflicted on the regiment was appalling, with 172 men killed, wounded or missing out of the 312 engaged—a 55.1% loss.[53]

Initial examinations of his wound provided little hope for Sanford's survival. The casualty reports listed him as "wounded, feared mortally," yet Dr. Thomas Alexander Means, the surgeon of the 11th Georgia, worked to save him.

The Plank farm became a house of pain. Many who had survived the assault on the battlefield were brought to the surgeon only to die later. Fred Bliss succumbed to shock and loss of blood after his leg was amputated at the thigh. He was among the sixty-four who were buried in the Plank yard beneath the bountiful fruit trees of the farm orchard.

When the Savannah paper ran the list of killed and wounded among the Oglethorpes, Charlotte endured a dreadful agony reminiscent of that July day two years earlier. But another tragic loss had been averted. Sanford was visited by friends who had emerged unscathed, and, at his request, they wrote home for him, assuring his mother of his survival.

Pvt. Addison R. Tinsley to Charlotte Branch

Near Gettysburg Pa.
July 4th 1863 (afternoon)
Dear Mrs. Branch,

You have ere this received I hope the list of casualties in the "O.L.I." which at Sandy's request was forwarded to Mr. Buckley [Bulkley], to be transmitted to you by telegraph, also a despatch from him in my name as follows, "Saw Sandy today, doing well, considered out of danger."

I left him about noon today, he was much better than yesterday & cheerful, seemed to feel no danger & requested that I should write you. The surgeon considers him a great deal better, & out of danger.

The wound is in the left breast, through the lung. It is of course a severe & dangerous one, but not considered by any means a fatal one & it is similar to the one recd by Capt. Butler around Richmond last summer.

Poor Fred Bliss died this morning about daylight. I saw him yesterday & was in hopes he would recover, & he appeared to think so; on returning to the "hospital camp" this morning I learned of his death. His right leg was amputated between the knee & body on the 3d or perhaps the night of the 2d. I think the former. I have a lock of his hair & a testiment which I will send by first opportunity; they were given to me for fear they might be lost. I requested Mr. Buckley to telegraph Alf. Bliss as follows "Fred died this morning about light," will you be pleased to mention the circumstances to one of the family. I would write Alfred myself, but have not time to write home. Will you be so kind as to send them word that I am well, & will write soon.

I can mention nothing of the army for fear that [this letter] may be captured. The wounded men of the Co. were doing well, and most of them (strange to say) very cheerful. No fear I think, need be entertained of their recovery. Capt. Edw. Stiles, Robt. Myers, & Wm. West are safe & well & beg me to mention it;

Very Respy & truly yrs.
Addison Tinsley

[P.S.] Capt. [John Couper] Fraser is severely wounded, though it is not thought dangerous.

Fraser died one week later. The Confederate army retreated from Gettysburg on July 4 in a torrential rainstorm. As many wounded as were thought could survive the trip back to Virginia were loaded into springless wagons and ambulances in a train that stretched seventeen miles. The men were soaked from the storm and suffered untold agony.

For those like Sanford, too critical to move, the only choice was to leave them in enemy hands. Dr. Means chose to stay behind and treat the men.

Charlotte left immediately for Richmond, intent on getting to Gettysburg to nurse her son. She applied for passes through military channels and even contacted Brig. Gen. John H. Winder and Gen. Robert E. Lee. On July 17 she was in Staunton, Virginia, and from there received permission to travel to Winchester. She arrived at Bunker Hill on the 19th, but was not allowed to continue into Pennsylvania, where she would have to cross federal lines. As the Confederate army was no longer in possession of the field, their authority meant little. She sought permission from federal authorities, but her request was denied.

Two years into the war the despair was felt deeply by the women, who kept their sadness confined within the lines of letters written to one another, all the while turning a brave face to the men who looked to them for emotional support.

Tallulah Hansell to Charlotte Branch

Oglethorpe July 6th, 1863
Dear Mrs. Branch

Accept my *warmest* thanks for your letter just received. It was doubly welcome, bearing assurances of your kind and continued interest in me after a silence so long and also for the little chaplet of flowers from the quiet, resting place of that dear friend whose place in my heart can never be filled by another. Nearly two years, crowded with events enough to fill an ordinary lifetime, have passed, since he fell weary of the life march, but my heart has not found that *Time* has any balm, nor any oblivious draught to offer to my heart. . . .

It was a *great pleasure* and at the same time a trial to me to meet your son Hamilton. I have more than an ordinary share of self control—having made it a *duty* to cultivate it—yet I could scarcely push back the tears when I met him. He reminded me so forcibly of the sweet days now gone forever. His manner and appearance were so much like John when I first knew him . . . and I appreciated his kindness *very highly*. My chief regret was that I was . . . unable to entertain him pleasantly. I was at the time just recovering from the most dangerous illness I have ever had, and in addition to it was "a stranger among strangers." . . .

. . . I have been *extremely* ill since I wrote you last, with *congestive chills*. For hours at a time I was thought to be beyond all hope and *twice, actually dying!* You cannot imagine the painful nature of the attacks—as the congestion was greatest about the lungs and throat. It was for hours a terrible struggle for breath, amounting almost to the death agony. Thank God! my trip to Augusta has cured me, I hope—and with care, I trust I shall soon be strong again.

. . . But I gladly leave it all in "my Father's" hands, and rejoice to know that I can do so. But I must not make you think I am sad or desponding. As soon as I saw Longstreets Corps again on the move, I knew you would feel anxious. I trust you will have frequent and cheering accounts from your dear boy. . . . And to Lt. Branch (who I was once very near asking to write to me now & then) please present my special regards and best wishes.

I did not receive an answer to my last letter, but if my health had been better I should have written to you without waiting. You must *never* think I am weary of the correspondence. I consider it a great compliment that you are willing to write to me, and am delighted whenever I see a letter with your writing. We are *not* "*strangers*", and the link which binds our hearts cannot be rusted by Time, nor severd by his rude touch. I believe it is too sacred for *Death* even to break. I have put the frail little flowers & the rosebud in my album, and prize them beyond expression. . . . I shall hope to hear from you soon & will try & be a better correspondent. May Heaven's choicest blessings rest on you and yours—prays your sincere & loving friend—

Lula Hansell.

[P.S.] You must not call me "Miss Hansell" but "Lula" or "Tallulah" my *home* names.

James Hine on behalf of Charlotte Branch

Gen. Hos. No. 4
Richmond Va.
July 14th 1863

Mrs. Charlotte S. Branch is a resident of Savannah Ga. She has already been bereft of one Son, Adjutant Branch of 8th Ga. Killed on the field of

the first Manassas. She now seeks a pass to Gettysburg Penn to attend
another Son dangerously wounded on the 2nd July and left in the hands
of the enemy. Her case is one well worthy of every consideration I will
vouch for her Loyalty to the South. To our cause she has cheerfully given
all of her sons at the beginning of this war as volunteers.

James B. Hine P.A.H.
in charge Gen Hosp No. 4

A July 14 appeal to Gen. John Winder from Julian Hartridge prompted the
following letters. James Seddon, secretary of war, was also contacted, but to no
avail.

Brig. Gen. John Henry Winder to Gen. Robert E. Lee

Richmond
July 15 1863
General
  Mrs. Branch of Savannah leaves here to endeavor to see her wounded
son at Gettesburg—under instructions to give papers to persons seeking
sick & wounded relatives. I have given her a pass to Winchester, if she
succeeds in reaching your Headquarters may I ask the favor of you to afford
her such facilities as may be in your power.

Respectfully, Your Obt. Svt.
J.H. Winder

Brig. Gen. Alexander R. Lawton to Gen. Robert E. Lee

Richmond Va.—
15th July 63
General
  I take the liberty of sending you this note by Mrs. Branch of Savannah
Geo, whose son was seriously wounded in the recent battle in Pennsylvania
—Mrs. Branch earnestly desires to reach and minister to her son; and her
case appeals strongly to every heart—Mrs. Branch has given three sons to
our service—one of them was killed at Manassas, another is now facing
the enemy at Charleston, and I trust she will be permitted to wait at the
couch of the third, who so much needs her services—
  I beg that any officer to whom this letter may be shown, will assist this

excellent lady and widowed mother in reaching her son.

I am, General, very respectfully

Yr. Obt. Servant, A.R. Lawton, Brig. Genl.

Eleanor Hull to Charlotte Branch

Suwannee Spring [Florida]
July 19th/62 [63]
My dear afflicted Aunt

I feel that I know not where or how to address you, but know that wherever you may be you are in affliction—I have seen by the papers that our darling Sanford is wounded, feared mortally. Oh! if it is true, God grant you support and strength to bear another deep sorrow. . . .

Sister [Carrie McIver] wrote me of meeting you in Savannah and of her visit with you to the Cemetery that dear beautiful spot. I am so much pleased to hear you have a photograph of our darling John for me for I have wished one so much and intended asking you to have me one taken for me when opportunity offered. I have wished to write you for a long time but ever since N. saw you in Savh I have found no leisure. On the day before he returned Sallie [Scarlett], [Francis D.] Scarlett and children came out and made us a visit, and then we decided to come here to be with her, as she came to Florida for her health. I was busy three weeks making summer clothing for the children and since I have been here I find little time for anything.

There are ten families here and seven of these are Presbyterian ministers of this church. [O]ne is a minister of the Baptist Church. Another prefect once attended the Episcopal while the third likes the Presbyterians best and is educating his two sons with a Presbyterian minister. . . . [Our own minister] preached for us thrice during his stay and held morning and evening prayers. Sallie had her three youngest children and I had Carrie baptised. It was a very interesting and solemn occasion. I know you would have enjoyed it so much. We have such a good, humble minister. Rev. Archibald Baker—formerly of North Carolina.

Every family here keeps house for the hotels have no proprietor. We have two rooms in the second story and have a little shanty for a kitchen, bring our provisions from home. There are two rows of cottages beside the Hotel. Bro. Joes family is also here. Sallie has returned home and we may go next week as we came only for a month. Since hearing of our reverses

I feel like going home. Yet there is nothing like gayety here. It is all at the Upper Spring twelve miles above here. There is great gloom pervading our country and I feel much dismayed, almost ready to give up. Yet I trust the Lord will bring us safely through the darkness. We feel very anxious about Charleston and Savannah—I hope dear Hammie is well. My love to him with a large share for yourself from

your ever affectionate
Nora

[P.S.] It is my constant and earnest prayer that you may be sustained and comforted in all your trials and grief—I tremble to hear from you and our dear Sanford.—E—

The fields of grain, and rich, lush pastures that surrounded Gettysburg produced the highest casualty rate of the war thus far—51,000 young lives were forever changed. More than 7,000 dead lay on the bloody field, and 6,800 Southern soldiers had become wounded prisoners in enemy hands.

Adams County, with its 11,000 residents, was overwhelmed by the presence of the 21,000 wounded who were left behind. The land for miles around the battlefield sprouted thousands of tents as hospital camps were hastily organized and laid out. The U.S. Sanitary Commission issued a plea for assistance and donations, which was answered within days. The Union wounded received preferential treatment, as was to be expected. Overworked Union surgeons and the lack of food, drugs, blankets and shelter left many Confederate wounded virtually neglected. Some men lay on the field, exposed to the elements, as long as July 6, their painful wounds becoming infested by maggots; yet the many reports of callous acts were, fortunately, equaled by those of kindness. Many boys like Sanford, helplessly wounded, far from home, and in a hostile territory, found unexpected friends in women sympathizers from Baltimore and New York who arrived to comfort their suffering. They flocked to Gettysburg bringing food and clothing for those who had no champions among the victors at whose mercy they had been left.

Miss Melissa Baker of Baltimore made her way out to the Plank Farm and, upon finding men scattered about the yard who needed nursing, set about helping any way she could. What she found there was heartwrenching: men lay in bloody pools, their wounds undressed. Most had not been fed since the battle ended. Sanford was among the patients in whom she took a special interest.

At first denied permission by Union authorities to tend "rebels," and turned away by townspeople who refused to house them, the women like Melissa persevered. " 'Our angels' as we used to call them," wrote one soldier. "And what they did, and what they told us, and what they passed through for us, what tongue can tell? . . . When our men were brought to the building, all of them being wounded, were more or less covered with blood and dirt, and the ladies from Baltimore made arrangements with a sympathizer, who lived near, to have all the washing done that would be needed at the hospital, and they would pay for it. As soon as the Yankees found out this was being done, they stopped it, making many of the men who were unable to obtain a change of under-clothing, lie for weeks in clothing covered with a mass of putrid blood. After our friends came, the majority of us got at least a part of a change of clothing."[54] Pails of milk were carried by hand and poured in cups held to thirsting lips. Fresh eggs and bread bought with the women's own money were distributed among the men at the Plank farm. They mailed letters home "per underground," permitting the prisoners to bypass the federal censorship.

The women arranged to have tents erected for quarters and stayed for several weeks on the battlefield caring for the wounded. Eventually, the Union surgeons came to realize their invaluable contributions and saw that whatever the Confederate wounded needed was provided, on the condition that these women also nurse the Yankee wounded.

By July 25, more than 16,000 wounded had been sent away from Gettysburg, leaving behind approximately 4,217 who were considered too delicate to travel. A consolidated field hospital was established on the Wolf farm, about a mile east of town on the York Pike, by Jonathan Letterman, the Medical Director of the Army of the Potomac. A large grove of hickory and oak trees provided both shade and fresh air, and a good spring ran nearby to provide clean water—a marked change from the contamination of the battlefield. It became the model of an efficient, well-run medical facility, one of the first of its kind in any war. Camp Letterman, under the command of Dr. Cyrus Chamberlain, consisted of some 500 tents set up in six double rows about ten feet apart, the rows divided into numbered wards. Each tent contained about ten patients, and a Sibley stove was installed when fall weather approached.

On August 21 the General Hospital boasted thirty surgeons for some 1,600 wounded, about half of whom were Confederate. The Southern surgeons continued to stay and treat their own wounded.[55]

Under the careful nursing of Melissa and dedicated friends and comrades like Pvt. James Garrett, Sanford was retrieved from death's door and began a long and slow recovery. His first letter home was a special event. Charlotte noted on it, "my son's first letter after the Battle of Gettysburg Aug 6 1863." His handwriting is weak. He obviously had difficulty writing it.

1Lt. Sanford Branch to Charlotte Branch.

Hospital near Gettysburg
Aug. 6, 63
Dear Mother,

I can write but few lines [as] Sergt. [Alexander K.] Wilson leaves in the morning early it is nearly dark now.

My wounds are nearly healed, fever gone, appetite excellent and if it was not for a discharge from the wound in my side I could walk all about. I am in good spirits & hope to see you soon.

Dear Mother God has indeed been very merciful. Do not worry yourself about me.

Your affect. son
Sanford

Pvt. James L. Garrett to Lt. Ebenezer Starke Law

General Hospital
near Gettysburg
August the 11 1863
Lt. Law
Dear Sir

I right you a few lines which leaves myself and Lt. J.J. Griffin geting along remarkabel well. the other boys was giting a long very well the last news we had of them Capten Butler was gitin a long very well. We are at the same plase and gets plenty to eat. Clothen plenty treatment very well much better than was expected. money plenty Greenbacks and Confederate very plenty. Lt. Branch says he hasnt nothing worth righting. Griffin is staing very well & wants to come to the Company very much. We got a letter from the boys. Thay said thay was all giting a long very well. Thay didnt say any thing about Little pat but I feer he is dead. Lt. Law I hav no news I will close. Due the best you can I will treet the boys the best I can. Col Brown is giting a long very well I will bring thes lines to a close fair well from

J.L. Garrett

Sgt. Alexander K. Wilson to Charlotte Branch

Richmond, Va.
Aug. 24th 1863
Mrs. C.S. Branch
Dear Madam

It has been but a short time since I left your son Sanford. I was with him up to the twelth of this month at which time he was doing well. I was there with him all the time and he always appeared to be in find spirits. at first he suffered when he talked much, but when I left he could talk with[out] hurting him. he was kindly treated. I left with him a young man who belongs to his company. He is a good nurse & that Sanford will receive kind treatment I have no doubt for all of our wounded that are in their hands has been treated very kindly, and again we all are indebted to the kind Ladys of Baltimore for their kindness to us while Prisoners. also from the City of New York they came & stayed with us all the time, these all were Southern Ladys in feeling. they thought a heap of Sanford.

I was indeed sorry in my arrival here to hear that you had been here and had gone. I sent to you the Letters that Sanford gave me to bring through and I am very sorry that you did not get the Letters that was sent to you by Flag of truce on the 1st and 3d of this month. Mrs. B. I am a nephew of Edward G. Wilson and am well acquainted with Mrs. Day a friend of yours. You will be kind enough to give my Respects to Mrs. Day. tell her that I am well and hearty. if you should wish to know anything else concerning Sanford I will be happy to inform you at any time if there is any Letters that comes by flag of truce, I will forward them to you. I am a paroled Prisoner now at Camp Lee two miles from this place, if you should wish to answer this please direct to A.K. Wilson, Hospital Steward 20th Ga. Regt.

Yours very respectfully
A.K. Wilson

Lt. Ebenezer Starke Law to Charlotte Branch

Camp near Fredericksburg
26th Aug [1863]
My dear Mrs. Branch

Enclosed you will find a letter which I have just received from Mr. Garrett—the nurse left with Sandford. I am truly rejoiced at the good tidings it brings of Sandford's improvement & the treatment they are receiving—this is the first tidings I have had of him save through your note of the 21st July, and I hasten to forward it to you—Mr. Sandiford received a letter a day or two ago from Mr. Buckley [Bulkley] in which he stated that you were about starting for Savannah. I therefore direct this to that place—I fear from that letter that you never received my note in answer to yours—Sandfords valise was sent to Richmond together with the Baggage of the other wounded officers to the Georgia Hosp. & Relief Assn. his key & sword I have here waiting an opportunity to get them to Mr. Buckley.

Trusting that Sandford will soon be able to travel & that he may be speedily restored to you I remain

Yrs. very sincerely
E. Starke Law

1Lt. Sanford Branch to Charlotte Branch

Aug 27. 63
Dear Mother

I have just received your letter dated Aug 13th. O the joy it caused, the first word from you since I was wounded. But I was very sorry to hear that you were trying to come to me. My wound is 2/3 healed, and I have been out of danger for weeks unless some unforseen accident occurs. I have written several letters and sent a dozen messages to you since 15th July. Direct at General Hospital. DO WRITE

Your loving son
Sanford

Tallulah Hansell to Charlotte Branch

Oglethorpe Ga. Sept 1st/63
My Dear Friend,

Words are inadequate to tell you how very much my heart was gladdened by your letter, brought me by the last mail, but one Deeply thankful to "Our Father" am I, for this new evidence of His great mercy. To me, it was almost like the raising of him [Sanford] from the dead, and I am sure none rejoice more sincerely with you over his deliverance from the very jaws of death as it were, than I do. It is true, I have never met him, but as I wrote you before for his unselfish and wonderful devotion to his brother and my friend, and for your love for him as well as for the sake of the brother I have recently had the pleasure of meeting, I felt a deep and abiding interest in him. I could not keep back the tears when I read your letter. . . .

I noticed in yesterday's paper that all prisoners—*officers,* are to be removed from Gettysburg to Johnson's Island, Lake Erie, as soon as they are able to travel. I have a friend from Alabama wounded and captured near Shelbyville in June last, now a prisoner in Ft. Johnson. He is a very dear friend and as true and gallant a man as ever drew a sword for the defence of all most dear to us. Can you communicate with Lt. Branch? If so, as a *great* favor to me, ask him if he is sent to Johnson's Island to await exchange, to find out *Lt. William Pelham* of Ala. and let him know that our thoughts & prayers are with him in his galling captivity. For *my* sake, they will know each other—for their own, after becoming acquainted they must love each other. If I could, I would be delighted to get a note through to Lt. P. who has been a correspondent for three years, but have no friend who is acquainted with the agents of the "underground railroad."

I was very much pleased to hear of the impression I had made on Lt. Hamilton B. I assure you the pleasure was mutual and I cherish the hope of renewing our acquaintances at no very distant day. . . .

I am glad to report Father's health as still improving, though he is very feeble. He is seventy three years old, and it is hard for him to recuperate in this debilitating climate. He was in Marietta a few weeks, but he is never so well contented as when at home. I am busily engaged now in "Society" work for our soldiers, and have my hands full. Since the *novelty* of the thing has worn off, we have very few to work, so those who sew at all, have our extra share to perform. I can assist in this great struggle for our rights only with my needle, and in *little* things, so I am always willing and anxious to do my full share. Do you know the family of the Rev. Mr. [Charles H.] Daniell—a Baptist minister? He has a son a friend of mine, who I understand is on furlough in Savh.—if you meet him, remember me very kindly to him. I hope he will come & see me—he does usually when in Ga. My very kindest regards to your son, Hamilton when you see him, and to his brother also if you have an opportunity of writing to him. I always shall feel interested in them. . . . May "Our Father" give his angels charge over you and your dear ones and keep them safe from all harm. I know He did it on that battle field of Gettysburg. Good–bye—with sincerest affection,

Your true friend, *Lula Hansell*

1Lt. Sanford Branch to Charlotte Branch

[directed care of Mr. Thomas Bulkley in Richmond]
Genl Hospital near
Gettysburg Sept 11.63
Dear Mother

I have been expecting to hear from you the last week but have been dissapointed. do write as often as you can you cannot imagine how much pleasure your letters give me. My health continues to improve slowly. Our treatment here is excellent the fare for a sick man is very good, but if I could only get some good Homeny & Rice I think I could fatten on it. Give my love to Hammie Sarah, & the Luffs & all friends. Remember me in your prayers dear Mother I feel as if that will do more good than all the medicine in the world.

Your affect. Son
Sanford

1Lt. Sanford Branch to Charlotte Branch

Genl Hosp. Sept 18
Dear Mother

Your letter of Aug 26 rec'd was glad to hear that you had arived safely home. I continue to improve very fast thank God and hope to be exchanged or paroled soon. It is raining very hard today making it so dark I can scarcely see how to write. When you write again tell me something about Hammie [who was still near home with the Savannah Cadets]. I am very much pleased with this Hospital the diet is very good and the medical attension excellent. Remember me to Sarah the Lufburrows & Butlers. Write soon to

Your affect. son, Sanford W. Branch

1Lt. Sanford Branch to Charlotte Branch

General Hospital Gettysburg Sept. 21st

As I have an opportunity to write pr underground Rail Road I hasten to adopt it. In your letters you have never acknowledged the receipt of any of my letters thay were all sent by Flag of truce I do hope you will get this it will go by Harpers Ferry to Smithfield where the bearer lives. there it will

The Branch brothers on the eve of war, c. 1861. From left, John, Hamilton and Sanford. *(Atlanta History Center)*

Charlotte Branch, date unknown. (*Atlanta History Center*)

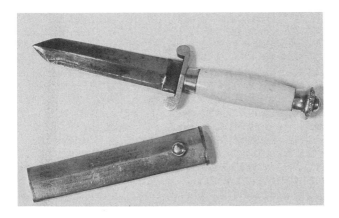

Presentation dagger engraved "Presented to Pvt. John L. Branch by his Comrades of the Oglethorpe Light Infantry as a mark of their esteem for his faithful and soldierly conduct as Brevet 2nd Lieutenant of the Corps during the year 1856 & 7. By resolution of the Corps Savannah June 1857." (*Atlanta History Center*)

Lieutenant John Branch in the service uniform of the Oglethorpe Light Infantry in 1861. (*Atlanta History Center*)

This handsome dress uniform of the Oglethorpe Light Infantry belonging to John Branch was carefully packed away after his death. (*Atlanta History Center*)

Hamilton McDevit Branch in his Oglethorpe Light Infantry uniform shortly after he joined the unit in April 1861. *(Atlanta History Center)*

Hamilton Branch and an unidentified young lady, possibly Georgia Elkins or Sarah Allen, both of whom served as apprentices in his mother's millinery shop. *(Atlanta History Center)*

Hamilton Branch referred to this "likeness" in his letter of March 7, 1862. (*Atlanta History Center*)

Matured by war, First Lieutenant Hamilton Branch of Company F, 54th Georgia Infantry, was photographed in 1863. (*Atlanta History Center*)

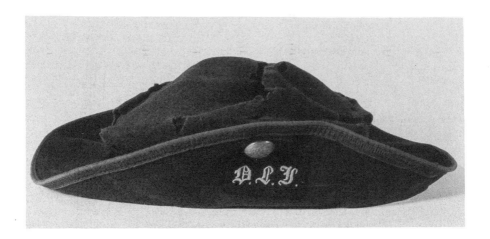

Hamilton Branch's hat bears a Georgia state seal button and a ribbon embroidered with the Oglethorpe Light Infantry insignia. He wore it when he posed for the sculptor who executed the Confederate monument in Forsyth Park, Savannah. (*Atlanta History Center*)

Hamilton Branch wore this coat through the Tennessee Campaign of 1864 and probably finished the war in it. Years later a fishing line with hook and sinker was found in the breast pocket. (*Atlanta History Center*)

A remarkable photograph of the hospital tent at Letterman Hospital in Gettysburg. Sanford Branch is on the right, lying in bed. The soldier behind him is believed to be Pvt. James Garrett, who later died of smallpox. The invalid on crutches may be Capt. Benton Miller of Hancock County, Georgia. The others are unidentified. (*Atlanta History Center*)

Prison stockade on Morris Island, South Carolina, where Sanford was confined from September 7 until October 21, 1864. The prisoners were used as a human shield to protect the Union batteries. Although squarely in the line of fire, none were harmed in the bombardments, thus earning them the designation "Immortal 600." *(Library of Congress)*

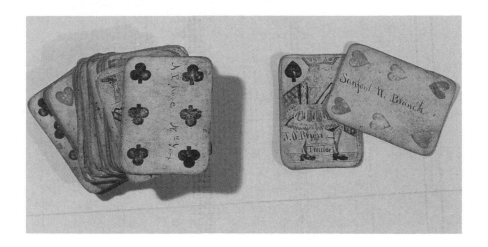

A deck of cards carried by Sanford early in the war. On them he collected the autographs of fellow prisoners at Old Capitol Prison, Washington, D.C., in 1861. Most likely the cards were left at home when he went there on parole, as no later signatures were added. *(Atlanta History Center)*

In 1905 Major John Ogden Murray, a survivor of the Morris Island prison, formed the Society of the Immortal Six Hundred to honor his fellow former prisoners. Medals were struck, and Margaret Branch purchased one for her uncle Sanford. His name is engraved on the back. *(Atlanta History Center)*

William Pelham and Tallulah Hansell Pelham in their wedding photograph, 1868. Most of Lula's letters to Charlotte were written from the Hansell home in Oglethorpe, Georgia. *(Dan Sullivan)*

Francis Stebbins Bartow of Savannah, Georgia, photographed as
president of the Georgia Historical Society in 1860. Under his
capable command, the Oglethorpe Light Infantry was
recognized as one of the best drilled of the city militia companies
to enter Confederate service. (*Atlanta History Center*)

The Confederate monument in Forsyth Park, Savannah. Hamilton
Branch suggested the stance for the figure of the soldier atop the
monolith and posed for the sculptor. (*Hargrett Rare Book and
Manuscript Library, University of Georgia*)

be giving to some scouting party of our cavalry. So you see it is very doubtful whether you ever get it or not.

My health is much better I am fattening fast have an enormous appetite and if I was only home I would weigh 200 in a very short time. I am in hopes of geting exchanged or paroled soon. the Yankee papers speak of a new cartel having been agreed upon I hope it may be so for am tired of this country. I have been so fortunate in having the attendance of a talented & very suscessful surgeon, Dr. Means of our Brigade. There are now about 600 Confederates & 400 Yankees at this Hospital, a great meny of them very badly wounded, mostly amputasions of the Leg & Arm. Tomorrow will be a grand gala day here. there is to be a grand picnic. preparasions have been going on for a week or more. Strange ideas is it not to have a picnic among the dieing & the dead.

. . . You have no ideas how meny friends we have here any thing we want is supplied.

> Your affect. son
> Sanford

A banquet was given on September 23 by the Christian Commission and the ladies of the town. According to the *Star and Sentinel*, the Gettysburg newspaper, four to five hundred chickens, twenty to thirty hams, and fifty tongues were donated, along with oysters, pies and ice cream. Amusements were held that evening with foot races, minstrel shows, and greased pole climbing, all accompanied by a band from York.[56]

1Lt. Sanford Branch to Charlotte Branch

Genl. Hosp Gettysburg
Sept 24th
Dear Mother

I have been expecting a letter from you for several days but have been disappointed do write as often as posible. My wound improves fast and now discharges very little. My general health is also much improved and I am fattening very fast. Still I have to be very careful not to take cold. We hear there that officers are being exchanged I hope it may be true as I am a little anxious to see you. Hoping with the help of God to see you soon. I am your aff. Son

> Sanford W. Branch

On July 3, 1863, United States Secretary of War Stanton had issued General Orders No. 207, prohibiting exchange of any Confederate officers.

Lt. Ebenezer Starke Law to Charlotte Branch

James Island, 28th Sept 63
My dear Mrs. Branch
    I have just seen Corpl [John J.] Eubank[s] of Co. G of this Regt. who was left at hospital near Gettysburg with our wounded. He has been for some time assisting the man I left in waiting upon Sanford, and left him on the night of the 14th Sept. He reports him as getting along very well indeed —being able to sit up in bed—says that his appetite was good and that he was supplied with everything he wanted. Ladies from Baltimore visit the hospital frequently supplying all the wants of our wounded. To use his own language "they could not have been treated better at home"—Dr. Means was still with him at the hospital.

                                    Very truly yrs. in haste, E. Starke Law

1Lt. Sanford Branch to Charlotte Branch

Genl Hosp Gettysburg
Sept 30th
Dear Mother
    You cannot imagine how much disappointed I am as day after day I fail to hear from you. I write very often and hope you are more fortunate I have received but 3 letters from you since my captivity. I had my photograph taken today. how much pleasure it would give me to send it to you. I also walked today for the first time and now hope to recover rapidly. Remember me to all friends. Hamie & Sarah. Write often.

                                    Your affect. son, Sanford W. Branch

1Lt. Sanford Branch to Charlotte Branch

Genl Hosp Gettysburg Friday evening Oct.2
Dear Mother
    As an opportunity offers pr Underground to write I embrace it although I wrote yesterday pr Flag of Truce. I am told that this will certainly go through. I hope it may, I am very anxious to hear from you, I have recd but

3 letters from you. do write often. I am improveing in health & spirits, in fact I feel better today than ever since wounded, although it is a very unpleasant day it having rained all day. I was just thinking how pleasant this rainy day would be at home. O how I long to see you. I hope the day is not distant when we may be either paroled or exchanged. This government has taken a great fancy to Reb Officers.

Tell Hamie I should like very much to hear from him. I intended to write a long letter but haven't time. Give love to Sarah & Hamie and Remember me to Aunt & Uncle Luf. tell them I dreamed I was with them last night. May God protect you.

Your son, Sanford

1Lt. Sanford Branch to Charlotte Branch

Genl Hosp
Oct 13, 63
Dear Mother

Your long expected letters of 23 & 26 insts were received last night. I had almost despaired of hearing from you. My wounds are almost healed up and my cough has left me entirely. it has always been a source of great uneasiness to me. I was afraid I never would get over it but now thank God I have recovered of it entirely. I don't think I can call on Mr. G. I am not in want of money. Love to all.

Your affect. Son
Sanford W. Branch

1Lt. Sanford Branch to 1Lt. Hamilton Branch

Gettysburg
Oct 17, 63
Dear Brother,

I have just a half an hour before dinner and dont think I can spend it more profitably than by leting you hear from me. My wound continues to improve but I have had a tedious time of it 75 days without geting off my back. If I live I never want to go near a hospital again. I am perfectly disgusted with hospital life, a day seems like a week. Hoping to meet you and our dear Mother soon. With love to all

I am your affect Brother, Sanford W. Branch

Tallulah Hansell to Charlotte Branch

Oglethorpe
Oct. 20th, 1863.
My Kind, Dear Friend,

It was with the truest joy I received your letter by the last mail. I had for many days been hoping for its appearance, for your letters, so full of true kindness, and affection, are *always* very dear to me. I hasten my reply in order to enclose you a letter to my friend Lt. Pelham, to whom I have never written a line since last June. He is *only* a friend, but you know my friendships are as strong as the *loves* of most women, and he has often in his bouyancy of spirit and frankness, very much reminded me of my friend who laid down his bright young life at Manassas. How can I help being attached to him, for himself, and with these associations clustering around him?

I enclose you a letter of one page—(the very *largest* page I could find,) and tried in vain to procure a U.S. stamp to put on it. I must ask you to fill up any blanks in the address. I am so much obliged to you for your consideration and kindness in thus thinking of me, while your heart is so burdened with love and anxiety for your dear, brave boys—Lt. Sanford must have had a very anxious time, and a long suffering one too, from July until now. I do most sincerely hope he will be soon exchanged, and restored to your loving watchfulness. I am sure with a dear Mother's tender care, he would soon grow strong again. *You* indeed have felt this war heavily, and deeply—and it is an honor to you to have implanted those true principles in the hearts of your sons, which have led them on in the path of duty, and the *path of glory!*

. . . Is your youngest son still on James Island? I have seen Col. [Charleton H.] Way's Regt very highly complimented recently. I always feel so much interest in your boys, and want them under all circumstances to regard me as a true friend.

I thank you cordially for the kind invitation to visit you in your woodland home [in Effingham County], and though it is impossible for me *now* to say when I can do so, as my Father's health is *extremely* feeble, I will look forward with pleasure to the Spring time, when I may possibly see you. . . . Our home is in a poor little country village, where we have but few congenial friends, and we live just as quietly as you can do. I love the fields and woods, and would *enjoy* it with *you* anywhere. Your society and that of those dear to the loved friend of my girlhood, would be all I desire.

We have much serious sickness in and around my family, indeed through the whole of South Western Georgia the sickness is unprecedented. My sister, Mrs. Fish has a little son, now extremely ill & we have several ill servants. I have been having "dumb chills" nearly two weeks, but I have not given up yet, so many are so much sicker than I am. A thousand thanks my dear friend, for your kindness about my little poems. I wrote some weeks since a little poem, published in the Macon Telegraph—which has been most kindlly and generously noticed by competent judges of writing—among others, Judge Nisbet of Macon who is excellent authority. I enclose it to you, knowing you are a partial critic of my "waifs." I have written a more finished & better poem this week, entitled "Chicamauga". It will appear in the "Baptist Banner" this or next week I think, The Editor—Mr. Ells—formerly of the "Field & Fireside" has urged me to write something for a long, time, but I have never yet sent him a piece. Mr. Gardner, wrote a very complimentary leter inviting me to write regularly for the "F & F" and I have occasionally sent a piece, but he pays some of his writers—and *said* he would pay me at some *future time*—In the meantime I cannot afford time, stationary or *trains gratis*, when Mr. G. is a man of such wealth. If he was *poor*, it would be a different matter. I think of writing regularly now. I have received such kind encouragement from the press. But my sheet is full & as I enclose my letter & a poem, I will not trespass longer—Write soon, I am *always* so glad to hear from you. Kindest remembrances to your sons—God bless you Good-bye—

Truly Yours
Lula

[P.S.] Please read the enclosed letter to see if it contains anything *contraband*.

1Lt. Sanford Branch to Thomas A. Bulkley

Genl Hosp Gettysburg
Oct 21
Messr. Bulkley & Co.
Gents

The body of Lieut. Bliss of my company was disenterred & shiped to Fortress Monroe to be sent to Richmond per Flag of Truce. It is marked to your care. Please take charge of it and ship it to Savannah by express. I am improveing slowly but it will be months before I can be moved unless I recover faster than I am at present. Please acknowledge receipt of this.

Your friend, Sanford W. Branch

Gen. Alexander R. Lawton to Charlotte Branch

Richmond Oct 23, 1863
Mrs. Branch
Savannah
Dear Madam

Your letter of the 5 inst. asking that if possible a special exchange of your son might be effected enlisted my warmest sympathies and has had my earnest attention. The seeming delay has been caused by difficulties preventing an interview with Judge [Robert] Ould. Yesterday I presented the case to him; and whilst I am sorry to inform you that he reports that no further special exchanges of officers will be allowed, yet I can cheer you by the hopes espressed by him that there will very soon be a general exchange of *all* officers . . . of this he seemed *quite* confident. Our Govt is unwilling to make special exchanges of officers because the Yankees have nearly double as many of our officers as we have of theirs. By special exchanges they could release *all* their officers and thus leave a remnant of our officers subject to any cruelties they might choose to inflict. I will bear your case in mind and if at any time anything should become possible, will not fail to do what I can in behalf of your son.

Very Truly Yours, A.R. Lawton

1Lt. Sanford Branch to Charlotte Branch

Gettysburg
Oct 28 1863
Dear Mother

Another flag of true mail and no letter. You can imagine the disappointment. my friend Capt. [Benton H.] Miller from Sandersville received five. I shall probably be moved to Baltimore the last of this week or first of next. My address will be Wests Building Hospital. I am very glad of this change as I will be more comfortable there. . . .

Your affect Son, Sanford W. Branch

1Lt. Sanford Branch to Charlotte Branch

Gettysburg Oct 29
Dear Mother
   Yours of 3rd 9th & 1st were received yesterday, also Hammies of 5th making a total of 8 since my sojourn here.
   I have anticipated Mrs. B[liss's] desire to have Freds body and through the kindness of a friend [Melissa Baker] have had it disenterred and shipt to Richmond per Flag of Truce care T.A. Bulkley & co. I wrote to Messrs B. & Co. on the subject but thay may not get my letter. you had better correspond with them on the subject. Hoping it may arrive safe & with love to all I am

your affect Son
Sanford W. Branch

1Lt. Sanford Branch to Charlotte Branch

[Undated—end Oct. 1863]
Dear Mother
   Your second letter dated 22nd was received day before yesterday. I have nothing interesting to write except that I continue to improve not only in health but spirits. my tentmates say that I ought to be discharged. if the commissioners arrange a cartel, which I think they will, I think I shall avail myself of the opportunity to travel South. You did not mension where Hammie was. at Savannah I hope. How are the Lufburrows & other friends, particularly Mrs. Bliss. Poor lady how I do sympathys with her. Fred was her darling boy, she almost worshiped him. he was a great loss to us, all ways kind & oblidging. he had meny meny friends but not a single enemy. Please remember me to Hammie, Sarah & all others. Tell the former I would be glad to hear from him.

Your affect Son
Sanford W. Branch

Hammie's company was then stationed on Rose Dew Island, Georgia, a few miles from Savannah, where they stood picket at a battery on the Little Ogeechee River.

1Lt. Sanford Branch to 1Lt. Hamilton Branch

Gettysburg Oct 30th

Dear Brother

Your long expected letter dated 5th was recd yesterday. Many thanks for it. Was very glad to hear that Mr. Tiger [or Ziegler] was so near home. Will leave this 'burg for Balt. in a few days. My address will be Wests Building Hospital. Have heard from Mr. [James L.] Vallotton & Sec [or Lee] Stout and of Bob Leabury but not a word of our dear relatives. Capts. Jackson & [Benton H.] Miller desire to be remembered to there "Old friend Branch." Love to all the Zoozous & Zoozays. Write as soon as you rec d this.

Your Affect
Sanford W. Branch

I enclose U.S. Stamp

1Lt. Sanford Branch to Charlotte Branch

[Undated—after Oct. 29, 1863]

Dear Mother

As I have an opportunity pr blockade this morning I of course embrace it, although I have nothing to write about. I continue to improve slowly. Have received 5 letters from you, written something less than a hundred. Do write to Mr. Bulkley about my uniform pants & vest. thay are in my trunk. I fear the moths will ruin them.

I have sent Fred's remains through and do hope it may arrive. mension this to Mr. Bulkley. it is marked to his care, he had better forward it to Savannah. I of course will write him but it is very doubtful wether he ever receives it. Dear, Dear Fred, how I should like to take charge of his body. I am so afraid something will happen to it. it would be dreadful if it should be lost. do write to Mr. B. immediately on the recepsion of this. when you hear that the remains have arrived in Richmond let Alfred Bliss know of it. Love to Hammie, Sarah, the Lufs, Miss Iv. & Miss Gerty. I am in a mighty good humor this morning, but have had the blues for 2 weeks.

Your affectionate Son
Sanford W. Branch

1Lt. Sanford Branch to Charlotte Branch

Gettysburg Oct 31st
Dear Mother
    This will probablly be the last letter you will receive from this place, as I will be sent to Balt. next week. I am very anxious to get there as it is very cold now and I don't improve as fast in a tent as I would in a house. Thank God I am still improveing and just as home sick as it is possible to be. I hear there is a chance of exchanging being resumed. again hope it may be so, as I have no ideas of spending the winter in a Fort. much prefer the Sunny South, but I may not be allowed a preference. Love to all. Good bye.

Your affect. Son
Sanford W. Branch

1Lt. Sanford Branch to 1Lt. Hamilton Branch

Gettysburg Nov 2nd
address Baltimore
Dear Brother
    As we all feel very dull to day I amuse myself by writtin letters, writing to almost every body I know. I should like to have you read some of my letters received since my sojourn here. My lung wound is healing. the splint was taken off my arm 3 days ago, the scab droped last night. I had thought it never would get well. I broke it over 2 months after being wounded. I think of spending Christmas with you the weather permitting. Love to Mother. Remember me to all.
    Is Tom Rolland married.

Your affect. Brother
Sanford W. Branch

CHAPTER TEN

I Will Not Be Able to Enter the Army Again

On November 4, 1863, Sanford was transferred to the West's Building Hospital in Baltimore, an old cotton warehouse at the end of Concord Street near Union Dock, across the basin from Fort Federal Hill. According to Lt. Henry E. Shepherd, also wounded at Gettysburg and taken to the West's Hospital, the structure was "dark, gloomy, without adequate ventilation, devoid of sanitary or hygienic appliances or conveniences, and pervaded at all times by the pestilential exhalations which arose from the neighboring docks."[57]

Reports of the quality of care provided at the hospital are mixed. Capt. Robert Park of the 12th Alabama, who was confined to bed with a badly infected wound in the leg, found the treatment callous and even cruel. When he arrived, the surgeon in charge of Officer's Ward B demanded that Park remove the bandage so he could see the wound. "Without uttering a word in reply, he took hold of my leg, and began to roughly press the flesh surrounding the wound . . . until it began to bleed, and jets of arterial blood flowed from it. . . . I saw he had unnecessarily and designedly produced hemorrhage, and for the first time in my life, I cursed."

Park had every right to claim mistreatment. The surgeon disallowed meals to be sent up to him, although other wounded officers in the third-floor ward enjoyed that privilege. He was ordered to report to the mess hall on the ground floor, despite the fact that he could not negotiate the stairs. After three days of missing meals, he crawled down the stairs to claim his meager officer's allowance of "some cabbage, and two slices of loaf bread, three-quarters of an inch in thickness. . . . Near by was a tin cup of soup . . . [and] in a very few minutes, I might say seconds, all the tables were cleared of their contents." He reported that his "food was mush and molasses with hard bread served three times a day."[2]

It was characteristic of Sanford to keep information from his mother if he thought it would upset her, so perhaps he purposely did not report negative conditions. Nevertheless, he did improve.

1Lt. Sanford Branch to Charlotte Branch

Wests Building Hosp.
Baltimore Nov 6. 1863
Dear Mother

I arrived here 2 days ago & dont think I was at all injured by the trip. Was glad to get away from Gettysburg as I did not think I ought to be in a tent this cold weather. I am pleased with the management of this hospital. The officers are very strict, no noise is allowed, the persons & beds of the pasients are kept very clean & the food is very good. I am pleased with the prospects both of recovering & exchange. I rec d a letter from Capt Butler last week he was quite well.

Your affect Son
Sanford W. Branch

Thomas A. Bulkley to Charlotte Branch

Richmond Nov. 6 1863
My Good Friend

I enclose you a letter from Sandford to me which you will perceive is of very late date. I am sorry to hear he does not improve faster. I write to Mrs. Bliss yesterday stating that the body of her son had been forwarded to me, our care. it is to be hoped that the enemy will suffer it to come. I tried to get you some U.S. Stamps, but have not as yet succeeded. the Twenty dollar bill came safe to hand. My wife & children are well. Also sister & Husband the fam sends love to you. we are having delightful weather now. every thing in the way of provisions are very scarce & high the prospect of the coming winter is not a pleasant one.

In haste, Yours Truly
Thos. A. Bulkley

1Lt. Sanford Branch to Charlotte Branch

Wests Building Hospital Baltimore Nov 15. 63
Dear Mother

I have been disapponted again & again in not hearing from you. the last letter I received from you was at Gettysburg Oct 20th. I am much pleased with the Hospital & improve faster than I would of at Gettysburg & am walking about. The only objection I have is that smoking is not allowed. from the time I was wounded until about a month ago, I had no desire to smoke. dispised tobacco & the taste of liquor but now I would like to smoke, although it is better that I should not & think the taste of liquor rather pleasant.

Love to all, Your affectionate Son
Sanford W. Branch

J.W. Laird to 1Lt. Hamilton Branch

Richmond Va.
Nov. 17th 1863
Dear Sir

At the request of your brother Lieut. Branch, I avail myself of this, my first opportunity to advise you of his condition. I left him on Thursday last, at the West's Hospital Balt. Md. where he arrived from Gettysburg on the 3rd inst. His wound in the breast opened after his removal, but was not such as to cause any uneasiness—it being much better the last few days before I left. The arm which was broken, is entirely well. His condition is much better than when I first saw him, some two months since—Now he can walk about without assistance, & is quite fleshy. I have nursed him since the 1st Sept. ult.

He has been very kindly treated, particularly by the ladies; & has won to himself many warm friends. His spirits are *very good*—Hoping he may soon be with you—I am

your obt. Servt., J.W. Laird

Thomas A. Bulkley to Charlotte Branch

Richmond
Nov. 17, 1863
My Good Friend

I avail myself of the first opportunity to inform you that several paroled prisoners called at the store yesterday who have just arrived by Flag of Truce Boat. they all report that Sandford was doing very well and in good spirits having left him last Thursday the 12th inst. he had been removed to Baltimore at Wests Hospital Building. the Hospitals at Gettysburg had all been broken up. Sandford's wound had not quite closed but his cough had nearly left him. he told these men to call and see me and inform me how he was. Lieut Bliss' body has not yet been received. I had a letter from his mother a few days since. all are well with us and send kind remembrance to you.

Yours truly
Thos. A. Bulkley

1Lt. Sanford Branch to Charlotte Branch

West Building Hospital Baltimore Nov. 19th
Dear Mother

I received a letter from you a few days ago, the first since my arrival in Balt. I am improveing very rapidly, for the last week have been up nearly all day. A piece of bone came from my lung wound this morning making *No. 40.* I am geting home sick. when confined to bed I was more contented than now. We continue to hope for a exchange however, although there appears to be but poor prospects at present. There are but 2 officers left here now from Georgia. Lt. [Tomlinson F.] Newell of Millidgeville & myself. Love to all

Your affect. son
Sanford W. Branch

While events in 1863 had wrought irreparable changes in Sanford's life, Hamilton had seen little danger in service with the Savannah Cadets. Shortly after enlisting, Co. F was detached from the 54th Georgia and assigned to guard federal prisoners at the Savannah jail. On August 9, 1862, the company rejoined the 54th and reported to a battery at Camp Anderson on Beaulieu plantation, twelve miles from Savannah on the Vernon River, owned by Benjamin Cole, father of Hammie's friend Hollie. There the cadets guarded earthworks, provided picket posts at all approachable points, and for the first time were forced to subsist on scanty government rations instead of delicacies from home. It was a monotonous job lightened with harmless mischief, yet soon the novelty of soldiering wore off and the younger boys left the company. The winter of 1863 saw the cadets fighting the cold more than the Yankees. They were stationed on the right of the 54th on Ship Yard Creek at Beaulieu. Several times vessels of the blockading fleet ventured up the river to throw a few shells, but no damage was ever done.

The cadets rejoined the 54th in May 1863 and on the 21st received orders to report to Rose Dew Island, to the command of Maj. Alfred L. Hartridge. The two-mile move was accomplished with a small boat that took many trips back and forth to convey baggage, tents, equipment and men. The batteries on Rose Dew were designed to prevent Yankee gunboats from ascending the Little Ogeechee River. None of the troops assigned there were experienced with heavy ordnance. Through drilling, however, they soon became quite proficient. Log cabins were built for winter quarters, slow work not completed until January 1864.

Located close to Savannah and near outlying plantations, duty was easy for Hammie, and a little diversion could be found now and then.

1Lt. Hamilton Branch to Charlotte Branch

Rosedew Post
Nov 29/63
My Dear Mother
    Yours of the 26th was received last night and I was very glad to hear from you, especially as I had not heard a word from you since my departure from Camp Liberty. I would have liked very much indeed to have been able to be at the examination but could not. I went up to the Country to a little dance on last Monday evening. I enjoyed myself very much. Miss Cone *was there* also Miss Reeves, Miss Hovenstein, Vic; Miss Towers, Ester; Miss Dasher, Fannie; Miss Krenson, Mary; Miss Hines, Phemie; and others. Miss Cone is a very nice young lady but she can't come up to Miss Elvira. By the By it is reported down here that Mr. Curry [John Carry?] has bought a place near Mr. [William] Brewers and that Miss Florence is soon to become Mrs. C . . . , is this so. Mother you must be sure and take good care of Miss Elvira for me. Tell her that I say if she had of seen me swallow a whole partridge

yesterday she would not have thought the mouthful of candy was so awful. Tell her also that I hope she will get over her fear of me by the time I come back. Tell her also that I am coming up Christmas to see *that young man* and that she had better keep a good watch on him for if I get a chance I intend to shoot him. Take good care of her Mother. And with much love to all I remain as ever your caring son.

Hammie

For Sanford, Christmas and New Years passed with no change in his imprisonment. He received an 1864 pocket calendar, probably from Melissa Baker. In it he collected autographs of fellow officers, a popular pastime among prisoners, and its pages were used to keep score for games.

1Lt. Sanford Branch to Charlotte Branch

Wests Building
Dec 20th
Dear Mother

I have just reseived yours of the 4th inst. your advice im regard to the use of Tobacco will be strictly adherred to while an inmate of this Hospl. at least as the rules forbid its use. I do not think I will ever use enough liquor to be injurious. Hammie writes that you are very uneasy about me & the conditon of my wound. the wound is one that heals very slowly, I had almost dispaired of its ever closeing, but about 2 weeks ago the opening where the ball entered closed, I think permanently. it had scabed over & opened several times, now I do not think it will open again.

Your affectionate Son, Sanford W. Branch
Love to all.

1Lt. Sanford Branch to Charlotte Branch

Wests Building
Jany 22nd
Dear Mother

I was very much disappointed in not hearing from you yesterday. it was the first mail from Dixie for several weeks & I thought certain I would get at least one letter. I know it is not your fault.

My wound is nearly well & my health is excellent. My lung is not as badly injured as was at first thought. We still have some faint hopes of exchange. Love to Hammie & Sarah.

Your Affect Son
Sanford W. Branch

1Lt. Sanford Branch to Charlotte Branch

Wests Building Hospl. Baltimore Feb 1st 64
Dear Mother

Your letter Dec 8th recd. Was very very glad to hear from you. Had not recd a letter from home for six weeks. Was pleased to learn that Hammie was enjoying himself. Would be glad to hear from him. Tell Mortie [Davis] I am anxious to get the letter mentioned in your last. I regret to have to announce the death of Mr. J.E. [James L.] Garrett of my company. He was left with me by order Col. Towers and from the night of my removal from the field to the time he was taken sick was my constant companion, administering to my every want. I feel that I am more indebted to him than to any other human being for my recovery. [John] Griffin can tell you all about him. He was so kind & attentive. Remember me to the Lufburrows, Sarah & all friends.

Your affect Son
S.W. Branch

[P.S.] There are rumors that we will be sent away in a few days, but do not wait to hear from me again. Write immediately.

1Lt. Sanford Branch to Charlotte Branch

Wests building Hospl. Balto Feb 10th.
Dear Mother

I have received your letters of Jany 8th & 27th, the only ones recd this year. Was very sorry to hear of Mrs. [Elizabeth or Eliza] Champions illness but hope she may recover. Have not recd Morties letter. Tell Hammie the last 4 or 5 he wrote have failed to reach me. I am almost well. My wound troubles me very little. I was surprised at my weighing 155 lbs a few days ago, 159 being the most I ever weighed. I have not heard from Capt. Butler since I wrote you last. Love to Hammie, Sarah & the Lufburrows.

Your affect Son, Sanford W. Branch

As his wound improved, it was deemed unnecessary to keep Sanford in a hospital. He was transferred from West's Building Hospital to Fort McHenry as a regular prisoner of war on March 2, 1864.

1Lt. Sanford Branch to Charlotte Branch

Fort McHenry
Mch 19th
Dear Mother
     Your letter of 2nd inst recd this morning. I write every week and as I get most of your letters cannot imagine why you do not get mine. Was very sorry to hear of Miss N's marriage as I had serious intensions in that direction myself. Please get Hammie to inquire of Mr. Philip Minis & Mr. Price as I have recd letters requesting information please attend to this as these people have been very kind. There appears to be some prospect of an exchange if we were only at Point Lookout. there are only 40 officers here mostly badly wounded men. Let us hope for the best.
                                                          Affect Son
                                                     Sanford W. Branch

1Lt. Sanford Branch to Charlotte Branch

Fort McHenry
April 13, 64
Dear Mother
     I have been waiting several days hoping to hear from home before writing again but as I have made it a rule to write very often I shall do so now. Hoping to get your long expected letter before writting again I need not tell you how much disappointed we have all been about the cartel which the papers stated the commissioners had agreed upon & which we have been ansiously expecting the 2 governments to acept. it was the first time that I have been really deceived. I must acknowledge that I was very confident last week that ere many days I would be with you. Has Lt. Law sent my coat home. I hope he has not lost it. I charged him to send it home when he left me at the hospital. Love to Hammie & all others.
                                               Your Affect Son, S.W. Branch

[P.S.] Do not imagine I am despairing.

1Lt. Sanford Branch to 1Lt. Hamilton Branch

Fort McHenry
May 1, 64.
Dear Brother
    Your letter of 28th was recd on 26th. was surprised to hear from you as about a dozen of my letters are still unanswered. I was foolish enough last week to believe that we poor dilapitated fellows were about to be exchanged, but have just heard from Point Lookout that the boat carried about 40 officers (just the number here) from there. Well I suppose our turn will come one of these days. Dont you think that Job was very lucky never to have been a prisoner. Say to Waudell [Hugh Waddell, Jr.] that I regret that the fortunes or rather misfortunes of war prevented my being present at his wedding. please tender my congratulasions. Tell [Mortie] Davis that I have been expecting a letter from him ever since the war began. [Alex F.] Butler is still at Johnsons Island. Love to Mother, Sarah & all friends.

Your affect. Brother, Sanford W. Branch

1Lt. Sanford Branch to Charlotte Branch

Fort McHenry May 1, 64.
Dear Mother
    I have recd but one letter from you since my arrival here but am glad that you get so meny of mine. I ought not to complain as I get more letters from home than any of my friends here. I am very much dissapointed that no cartel has been agreed on as we were very confident but will try to be patient. My wounds are entirely well and my health is excellent for which I ought to be very thankful, for while I will not be able to enter the army again, still I will not be the helpless invalid that I thought I would be last winter. I am much better than I ever expected to be. Hoping still to see you soon I am

your affect Son
S W Branch

Charlotte Branch to 1Lt. Sanford Branch

Bellheim
May 17th 64
My Dearly beloved Child

Hope defered maketh the heart sick. I have been looking for you by every flag of truce boat since the resumption of exchange. I do long most earnestly to see you. You and Hammie are on my mind day and night. May the good Lord take care of both of you, and spare you to me. I have visitors for Sara with me, Mrs. Freemand [the former Sarah E. Davis] and Miss Ellen Axson. Morty sent me word that he would postpone his visit untill you came home, so you see you may expect one visitor. All our friends are well, Many very manny are constantly asking about you. The lady I mentioned to you was about to be married is still unmarried so you may stand a chance yet. Marrying is the order of the day. Miss Magie [Margaret] Roberts was married last Wednesday evening to Mr. Robert Guerrard. Maria Blois is to be married to Lieut. [James] Hunter [Jr.] next Wednesday.

With renewed trust in God who does all things well I am your devoted
Mother
S. Branch

Charlotte Branch to 1Lt. Sanford Branch

Bellheim
May 20th, 64
My Darling Child

It is but a fiew days since I wrote to you, still hopeing that you will soon be with me. I have not heard one word from you since the letter of the 19th March. I am sure you write and would be so very glad if I could get them. I trust to see you very soon. I sit and think of what we will do and where we will go when you get here, even your Horse is looking for you and the Servants *all* express themselves as so impatient at the long delay there is in your exchange; Let us continue to beg Gods blessing on us as a little family and suplicate him to be Mercifull and reunite us very soon. Could I see you and Hammie together again in our quiet home, I should be so happy. With devoted love I [am]

your Mother
C.S. Branch

Charlotte Branch to 1Lt. Sanford Branch

Atlanta
June 1. 64
My Dear Child.

Do not be surprised that I am at this place. you know I have been planning for years to visit Mrs. [H.C.] Hathaway and so have made it convenient to do so at this time, that I might get tidings of Hammie sooner than if I were at home. He is well at this time, I shall (perhaps) go to Marietta in a day or two. all our friends are well and very desirous of seeing you. I am very hopefull and trust we shall all be together in our house ere long. I have been in Atlanta before but would hardly recognize it as the same place, it is so much larger than it was. citties may be larger and more flourishing, but still they cant rival our beautifull Savannah, that Eden of our Nation. There are a number of Savannahians here, among them Mr. [Heman] Crane. [his son] Horrace is in Savannah, Charlton Way is at Marietta, and so is Charlie Olmsted. Miss N. is not yet married. You my darling must continue to put your trust in God.

I dayly and hourly pray for you. with a yearning heart I am hurting for you. as ever

your Mother
C.S. Branch

Charlotte's motivation to visit Mrs. Hathaway likely sprang from the fact that Hammie and the Savannah Cadets had been thrown into the defenses around Atlanta.

1Lt. Sanford Branch to Charlotte Branch

Fort McHenry
June 6, 64.
Dear Mother

I was very disappointed in not hearing from you yesterday as it was the first Flag Truce mail for six weeks, but still hope to hear as it sometimes takes several days to get the whole mail. the last letter I recd was from Hammie directed to Point Lookout. please direct here as I expect to stay at this place until winter. I recd a letter from Capt. [Alex] Butler yesterday. he was well & had heard from Lieut [Hollie] Cole May 12. My health is very good & friend[s] are well but most ansious to get home once more. One of our number left yesterday for Fortress Monroe, he having been exchanged. he promised to write you I think he will do so. If possible I would be obliged if you could send me some money as I am unwilling to apply to persons here. Mr Joseph Jackson (father of my friend and fellow prisoner [Thomas G. Jackson]) Box 731 Richmond can forward package of money safely to me, he having sent several packages to his son. dont send more than $25 or $50.

love to Hammie & Sarah
Your affect Son
Sanford W Branch

Sanford did not remain at Fort McHenry. Just nine days after writing this letter, on June 15, he was transferred to Fort Delaware, called "the Andersonville of the North."

CHAPTER ELEVEN

I Am One of the Fortunate, or Unfortunate, Six Hundred

Fort Delaware prison, on Peapatch Island in the Delaware River, was one of the most infamous prisons of the war. In June 1864, when Sanford Branch arrived, 10,000 Confederate prisoners were confined there. Sanford was assigned to the officer's compound outside the fort itself, wooden barracks surrounded by a stockade wall and parapet that was patrolled day and night by guards. One of 1,500 officers, he was assigned a bunk in Division 22.

The complex was poorly drained, and food was inferior in both quantity and quality. A drainage ditch ran through the barracks area, and every conceivable activity was conducted there, from bathing to laundry to cooking. The lack of adequate sanitary conditions fostered an outbreak of smallpox in July, taking many lives.[59] Its death rate of 13% rivaled Andersonville's 12%.

About the time Sanford arrived at Fort Delaware, Maj. Gen. Sam Jones, the Confederate commander in Charleston, South Carolina, was upset because the Federals who were bombarding his city were targeting civilian areas while military installations sustained little damage. When Jones was told he needed to confine fifty Union officers in Charleston, he quartered them in a house in the residential district, then notified Union major general John G. Foster, who was conducting the bombardment, of their presence.

Gen. Foster, frustrated at the length of time Charleston had held out against his bombardment, warned Jones that if he did not cease firing at his batteries, he, too, would soon be firing on friends. When Jones refused to be bullied, Foster sent for fifty Confederate officers, prisoners from Fort Delaware, to be placed under fire at Fort Gregg and Fort Wagner on Morris Island. Among them were several of Sanford's new friends.

Melissa Baker to 1Lt. Sanford Branch

Friendsbury July 15th 1864
My dear Lieut. Branch
     Your letter of the 6th of July, I did not receive until yesterday, more than a week in coming, a longer time than any yet;—before yours came, it had been nearly two weeks since I had heard from any of our friends, that indeed I began to think, some of the Rebels might have cut off all communication —you know they are very daring at times, so much so, as to frighten even our *brave* Baltimoreans—and I believe a visit from them was really expected as some of the more fearful of our citizens, caused the fall of one of our trees across the road, near the front gate, to delay if possible their approach from the country. (Though I regret the loss of the tree, a Weeping Willow, I should have been only too sorry had it have been one of our oaks.) This formidable barrier together with the recent deep excavations and embankments across the streets and alleys of our City (in view of the Tobacco hogsheads of last year) must have so alarmed men who had been accustomed to cross the mountains of Virginia that they never made their appearance in our midst,—but retired with additional company after creating intense excitement throughout the land.

[On July 11 Confederate major Harry Gilmore raided Towsontown, near Baltimore, and burned the home of Governor Bradford in retaliation for the earlier burning of Governor Letcher's house in Lexington, Virginia.][60]

     The heat of Midsummer and other causes, has occasioned the sudden departure of many for the North, where I hope they will find rest for the weary "and a panacea for their fears."—I had an invitation to visit friends on the Hudson but preferred remaining at home, as we now have frequently to receive some not very welcome visitors. What beautiful moonlight nights we have, last night one of the bands was playing "Home" very sweetly and I could not help wishing—it was only your friends and that I could see you all on your joyful journey home. May this happy time soon come. I was very glad to hear that you had received the pants, Oil and box of provisions all safely. The fruit I should think did not keep very well. I suppose Lieut. [William N.] Ledyard received my letter soon after yours, as I wrote to him the day after and to Lieut. [James H.] Robinson & [John Penn] Breedlove on the fourth and hope to hear from them all soon.

Your sincere friend Melissa Baker

[P.S.] You did not say how your health was at present. I hope it is better. Remember me to all of our friends. I wish we could hear from Capt. [Thomas G.] Jackson and Col. [William Henry] Forney, they must suffer from the heat. [Both were among the fifty prisoners held in Charleston.]

Lt. Hollie Cole to 1Lt. Sanford Branch

Point Lookout Md
July 21st 1864
Dear Sandy,
    Some time has elapsed since I recd your letter. I answered it immediately —but you have not responded— I addressed you at Fort McHenry but have since learned that you had been removed to Ft. D. there are various rumors afloat relative to a speedy exchange—God grant that it may be true —I am enjoying pretty good health but have been quite unwell. a large Dixie Mail came through on the 18th. No letters for me. my respects to Capt. [James H.] Fields, [O.] Boler and Henry Davis— I recd a letter from Capt B[utler] today Lt. Cye [Cyrus B.] Carter of Tatnall Guards was killed —nothing from Hammie—write soon to yours truly Care of Pro. Marshall

R. Holly Cole
Co. "C" 6th Division

1Lt. Sanford Branch to Charlotte Branch

Fort Delaware, Division 22
July 24. 64
Dear Mother
    I have just recd your letters May 17th & June 1st. the only ones for 2 months. You cant imagine how shocked I was at receiving your letter from

Atlanta. it was some time before I could gain courage to open it and O what a relief when I learned that all that I hold dear on earth were well. Have been here about a month. it is very pleasant here in summer but very cold in winter I am told. have almost made up my mind to stay here another year. Hollie Cole is at Point Lookout, also [John H.] Bogart, [Nicholas] Pendergrast & [Luncy or Lancy]. I have written this short note so that you may be certain to get it as I put my last stamp on this & thay are very scarce here. Capt.[Harris Kollock] Harrison & Lt. [Gordon K.] Fort are here, also Lt. Zipro [Samuel H. Zipporer].

Your affect Son
Sanford W. Branch

Melissa Baker to 1Lt. Sanford Branch

Friendsbury July 29th 1864
My dear Lieut. Branch

Since Tea I have received your letter of the 24th and it made me feel so sorry for you—that I could not but leave the friends on the porch and come into the parlour, and write you a few lines—though the evening is so very close and warm, and plenty of moths flying around the light. Prayer is over, and Father has retired—Mother being still in her sick room, The party on the porch, my sister, Mrs. Jones and her daughter Mary, who are spending the summer with us, Lillie G. Miss E. ——, a daughter of your friend of last summer and a nephew of ours—all enjoying themselves quietly—it being too warm for very much talking even. Sometimes we have music . . . .

I have heard of your sweet singing and wish you were here at times to accompany the young ladies as they play on the melodion or Piano, but I expect your thoughts are oftener homeward and nothing would please you as well as the voice of your own dear Mother welcoming you home again. I do indeed feel for the disappointment of both. Do not feel discouraged, perhaps another arrangement will be made. What will not the untiring efforts of a Mother effect. May you soon hear the joyful news of your release is my earnest wish.

I am very sorry that your health does not improve more rapidly, and that you feel the change of climate so keenly. I sent or rather ordered to be sent to you on Tuesday last a pr. of blankets, drawers, socks, a flannel and cotton shirt—I hope they have gone and have reached you; as I have not been in town myself since, though I am now well again and will go to inquire, I hope they will be such as will suit though I could not choose them. Excuse this rambling letter and let me assure you that yours are never a bore to me. I often recall the scenes of this time last year.

Ever your attached friend
[Melissa Baker]

[P.S.] Tell Lieut. Ledyard that I received his letter also tonight, I am very sorry that the box was exposed to the rain, of course the contents would not be in as good condition.—though the rain to us was most acceptable—and hope we soon shall have more. I have written to Lieut. Robinson and Breedlove this week.

[P.P.S.] I hope you are one of the good Dr. [Isaac W.] Handy's attentive hearers—some ladies in Balt. are trying to get a large Tent to send to Fort Delaware to be used for religious services.

Rev. Isaac W. Handy was a Presbyterian minister from Portsmouth, Virginia, who was arrested for voicing pro-Southern sentiment at a dinner party in Baltimore. He was well known at Fort Delaware for his religious services among the prisoners and later wrote a book about his imprisonment entitled *U.S. Bonds*.

On August 3, just a few weeks after their departure from Fort Delaware, the fifty prisoners sent as human shields were exchanged for the fifty federal officers in Charleston. Both commanders had agreed the threat of placing prisoners in jeopardy was uncivilized as well as a direct violation of the ethical laws of war.[61]

The incident renewed hopes among those at Fort Delaware that the Union might have reconsidered its stand against exchanging prisoners and that perhaps the cartel would be reinstated.

Mrs. Charles Baker to 1Lt. Sanford Branch

"Athol" August 8th '64
Lieut. Branch

Dear friend, You will perhaps be surprised at receiving a letter from me, but as I wished to send you a "box" I think I shall write to you, and thus "break the ice" for further correspondence should you wish it. I send the box tomorrow. in it you'll find ham, cheese, tomatoes, coffee & sugar. In your box I send a package for Lieut. Alfred Rowland, I do not know his Division. Imagine our pleasure this morning at reading in the paper that all those sent to Charleston had been *exchanged!* Write me if we could be permitted to send the daily papers to prisoners, if so, I will send you some if you would like to have them.

When you write, please send me the number of your Division. I cannot write a very long letter to-night. That I may hear from you soon is the hope of Your friend,

Mrs. Chas. Baker

The letter was written by Melissa's sister-in-law, Elizabeth Bosseman Baker. Charles J. Baker, her husband, was a prominent Baltimore citizen and president of the Franklin Bank.[62]

Alice Minis to 1Lt. Sanford Branch

176 Hoffman St.
August 11th/64.
Lt. Branch

I have just received your letter & hasten with pleasure to answer telling you to expect by Saturdays Express the three bottles of Cod Liver oil. I send *this number* thinking it best to send again should you require more, trusting you will not hesitate to ask for anything you may wish. Last Flag of Truce brought us letters from Sav. all were well & your Mother's fears much lessened since the news of your whereabouts & safety but anxious for your exchange which I trust will come soon to all on both sides—Our friends Col.[Marshall J.] Smith & the "saucy Major" [two of the fifty in Charleston] have been exchanged & are at home ere this. Let me know when the package reaches you & dont hesitate to make known your wants. I send a can of peeches to take after the oil.

Yours truly
Alice Minis

1Lt. Sanford Branch to Charlotte Branch

August 16.64.
Dear Mother

I have recd your letters of 17 & 20 May & 1st June. was surprised to hear of you being in Atlanta. Hopeing the flag of truce may not be interrupted again it was nearly three months since I had heard from you. Lts. Fort &

Zippro & Capt Harrison are here & well, also Capt. [James H.] Fields of my regiment. Still have strong hopes of getting home soon. My health is much better than when at Fort McHenry, indeed I am almost as well as before Gettysburg. Has Lt. [Thomas G.] Jackson written you. he has been the kindest of friends. we were together until he was sent to Charleston. I miss him very much. He will probably advise you to send me money. I shall not need it.

Your affect Son
S.W. Branch
Direct Division 22 Officers Barracks Fort Delaware

By August 1864 the Andersonville prison in Georgia, designed to hold 10,000 prisoners temporarily, housed a population of 32,000. The North was screaming for something to be done to alleviate the suffering and instigated a policy of retaliation against Confederate prisoners of war. Under this "eye-for-an-eye" measure, innocent men were deprived of food, clothing, and personal articles of comfort sent to them by family and friends; boxes and letters containing money were confiscated. The war had bestowed a new kind of deprivation which its captives were helpless to alleviate.

Early in August Confederate authorities sent six hundred Union soldiers from the disease-infested stockade at Andersonville to the Roper Hospital in Charleston. The men were to be held there only until a new facility under construction at Columbia could be finished. Jones protested the move, saying he had neither guards nor suitable quarters for more prisoners, but his complaint was overruled by sheer necessity.[5]

When Foster received word that more Union prisoners were in Charleston, he threatened Jones with a repeat of the previous episode. Jones replied that he intended to move the men as soon as possible, even though they were in much better circumstances than they had been at Andersonville or would be in Columbia. They had a good diet at Roper, and the accommodations were clean and spacious. Foster refused to wait. He requested that six hundred Confederate officers, of all grades, be sent from Fort Delaware.[6]

The prison lists were checked at Fort Delaware on August 11, and six hundred men were chosen. On August 13, their names were called. Among the ecstatic young men, who surely thought they were being chosen for exchange, was Sanford Branch.

1Lt. Sanford Branch to Charlotte Branch

Fort Delaware Aug. 20—64 [actually the 19th]
Dear Mother

I wrote you a few days ago, but as there will probably be a flag of truce in a few days will write a few lines well knowing how welcome my careless letters are to you. I am in excellent health & *spirits* I am one of the fortunate ones selected to be sent somewhere and as a change is always acceptable to a prisoner have concluded not to let anyone go in my place, although have had several aplicasions. Have just finished my evening repast. Find Ham & onions. Sweet Potatoes & tomatoes prepared by myself. I am prepareing myself to take charge of your culinary affairs. I can promise greater economy in fuel & material than any artist you have ever had in your kitchen. I can bring satisfactory references. in writing be particular to address to Division 22 as there are several others of our illustrious name here.

Your affect. Son, S.W. Branch

Capt. Thomas G. Jackson to Charlotte Branch

Richmond
August 20th. 1864
Mrs. Branch,

Mr. W[illiam] B. Sturtevant of Co. B 8th Regt. Ga Vols. informed me that you had not heard from your son Lieut. Sanford W. Branch for a long time, also that a letter which I took the liberty to write you from Charleston SC had not reached you. I was separated from the Lieut on the 20th of June last and have had no information of him since. At that time his wounds were healed, his general health was improving, his spirits were good and he was pleasantly situated as to his mess arrangements. I shall write to him on Monday and shall endeavor to make arrangements which will contribute to his comfort. All of us are very hopeful that a general exchange will soon be effected. I shall in the meantime see what can be done in the way of a special exchange, but our Authorities are so much opposed to them that I can scarcely hope,

With the wish that Sanford may be soon restored to you

I am very respectfully
Your Obt. Svt., Thos. G. Jackson

It was a hot, sultry Saturday morning on August 20, when the six hundred left Fort Delaware for their journey South. Spirits were high—Dixie was just days away. As they boarded an old steamship, the *Crescent City*, the boys each found a berth in the rows built three tiers high around the boiler of the freighter. It was stuffy and crowded, but that couldn't mar the enthusiasm of men who thought they were bound for home. The ship headed toward Fortress Monroe in Virginia, where they expected to be exchanged. But exchange was not to be their fate, and the floating prison sailed on.

1Lt. Sanford Branch to Charlotte Branch

On board *The Cresent*
Port Royal Harbor
Aug 29. 64
Dear Mother

    As I wrote you from Fort D. I was one of the fortunate or unfortunate six hundred sent here from Fort Delaware. Arrived here on last Thursday after a passage of four days. Strange to say I was not sick & now consider myself a first rate sailer. Most of the officers aboard are confident of an early exchange but I am not so sanguine, having been disappointed so often. Still I think we stand a better chance of exchange than other prisoners of war confined in the U.S. I am very tired of being on Shipboard and hope we may soon be landed. You remember how tired I used to get of the cabin. I am equally so of the forecastle, I think the next two weeks will decide our fate whether exchange or imprisonment for the war. God grant it may be the former. We get more news here than when at the Fort. We have submarine grapevine & other telegraph lines. From the last reliable telegram by grape I think you may look for me an hour after the recepsion of this.

    Capt. Harrison is aboard.

Your affect. Son
Sanford W. Branch

Love to Hammie & friends

Sanford was being facetious. "Grape" was gossip, and wild rumors abounded. On the night of August 24 the *Crescent City* ran aground at Cape Romain, forty miles north of Charleston. A desperate attempt by the Confederates to take the ship was foiled and, after anchoring at Port Royal, Hilton Head, South

Carolina, for several days, the *Crescent City* sailed into Charleston Harbor on September 1.

Life aboard the crowded ship had been miserable. During the eighteen days many of the prisoners were seasick, and the amputees among them could not climb the ladder to the water closet on deck. Consequently, the hold was filthy. Thanks to the ship's boiler and the August heat, temperatures rose above a hundred degrees, and water was scarce. For two days they were without water altogether, and the torture of the suffering threatened the sanity of the feverish men. When it seemed they could endure no more, they reached the wharf on the southern end of Morris Island.

The men scrambled out and, too weak to walk, fell upon the beach. Prodded by bayonets, they were induced to march three miles up the shore to Battery Wagner, the largest of the Union forts, where they were herded into a fifteen foot high palmetto-log stockade that held rows of tents. It took only a moment for them to realize their predicament. The stockade was squarely in the line of fire between the Confederate forces at forts Sumter and Moultrie, and the Union batteries under Gregg and Wagner. The awesome truth struck like a thunderbolt—they were to serve as a human shield for the Union forces assembled against Charleston, under fire from friend and foe alike.

Forty of the seriously wounded prisoners were allowed to go to the U.S. Hospital at Beaufort, South Carolina, but not Sanford. Instead, a test of extreme physical endurance awaited him. Sanford put on a brave show in his letters, not disclosing how dangerous the situation really was.

Charlotte Branch to 1Lt. Sanford Branch

Bellheim Sept. 19th. 64
My Darling Child

I have been looking for a letter from you for many days past, I rec your letter of the 20th of August, and as in that you mentioned you were about being moved from Fort Delaware I hoped to learn where you had been sent before I wrote to you. I have rec. a letter from your friend Lieut. Jackson. Allso one from his Father acknowledging the receipt of a letter of credit which I had sent to him to forward to you. I find myself murmuring at the long delay there is in your return to your home and often think why was it not you instead of your friend who was exchanged. but this is very selfish. My heart is very bitter to those at the North who have professed *to love you* so much, and yet have never raised a finger to aid you in your necesaties.

thay well know that you are a prisoner, and allso that I would repay them for anything they might do for you. This leves us all well. H[ammie] is still with us. he went up to the front [near Atlanta] and reported for duty but his arm was not yet entirely healed so he was sent back with a 30 day furlough. God bless you and keep you my Precious Child is the ardent prayer of your Mother

C.S. Branch

Melissa Baker to 1Lt. Sanford Branch

Friendsbury Sept. 24th 1864
My dear Lieut. Branch

If I had known where to direct a letter I should certainly have written before this—and have been wishing so much to know how you were getting along. I . . . waited to reply [to your last] untill I had a box ready—and I was so disappointed when my boxes were returned to me from town—the order prohibiting them and also letters, having just been issued. I had a box for Major [William Worth] Goldsborough, and for Lieuts. [David A.] Coon and [John C.] Cowper. . . . I only wish I could send where you are at present. George [Baker, Melissa's nephew] received a letter from Lieut. Cowper this week and I was very glad to know where you were to be found and take the earliest opportunity of writing.

I received a letter from Lieut. Ledyard last week, from Beaufort. he said he was very comfortable but regretted that you were not with him—his account of the suffering on the boat was indeed distressing to us—and we could not but feel that you must be more pleasantly situated now that you are removed to Morris Island—though danger attends you there, yet I have no fear but what you will again see your Mother—and hope to hear very soon of your exchange.

Is your health as good as when you left Fort D. the warmer climate may suit you better,—How very anxious you must be to get home, now that you are so near. Do you hear from your Mother still—I received a letter from Capt. Jackson just before he left the Harbour. Said he had not heard from Balt. since June. I had written three letters but he never received them, and I have written since. I was delighted to hear he had returned to Dixie and also Col. Forney, may you soon follow—will you all forget to write to us after you reach home? I must hope better things, though we have never received one yet from Dixie. All your friends at Athol are well —Mrs. Baker goes still to see after Lieuts. Ferguson and Campbell, they have been sick all summer, and very little hope for the recovery of the latter. Remember me very kindly to all of our friends—tell Lieut. Breedlove he never replied to my last. . . . We never hear now from Fort D. Do write before you leave and believe me your constant Friend

M. Baker

1Lt. Sanford Branch to 1Lt. Hamilton Branch

Morris Island
[Sept] 28, 64
Dear Brother

I have just learned by letter from Mortie Davis of your safety & whereabouts. I hope you will excuse my paper when I tell you tis the last sheet in the mess & to borrow here is out of the question. We have nothing to lend nor is there any thing to borrow. I have had but two chews of tobacco in five days & nary a smoke. I have written Mother several times since my arrival here, in each of which I made touching appeals for something to eat. the trouble is I have had no appetite for several months & the change of climate here has affected my health & appetite so favorable that the rations dont begin to satisfy me. Besides you know we were sent here for retaliatory purposes & when thay retaliate on prisoners thay dont git more than thay ought to eat. Can not greenbacks be bought at Augusta or Savannah. if you can get them send me a small amt. as soon as possible. I am afraid brother dear there must be some particular attracsion for you in Augusta, as almost every letter from home speaks of you being on a visit to the gay city. Remember me particularly to Mother & my friends & write soon to

Your affect. Brother
Sanford W. Branch

1Lt. Sanford Branch to Charlotte Branch

Morris Island
Sept. 28. 64
Dear Mother

I have just recd a letter from Mortie. was delighted to hear that all were well. I have written you three times since arrival here. My health has improved very much since last transfer. I think Fort Delaware the coldest place on this continent. the climate here is delightful. My appetite is also very good. I wrote you in former letters that a box of provisions would be most acceptable. I hope you will excuse me for repeating it again. Anything will do if only a box of Pilot Bread & it will be difficult to get things cooked here as wood is scarce. If you could procure a small amt. of Greenbacks please send them, care some officer in Charleston. I am very much [in] need of money to replenish my wardrobe. Love to Hammie & Sarah. Do write soon & often. I will receive letters of two pages. Direct to Prisoner of War Morris Island a U.S. stamp is not required.

Your affect Son
Sanford W. Branch

1Lt. Sanford Branch to 1Lt. Hamilton Branch

Morris Island
Oct. 2 64
Dear Brother

I wrote you several days ago but as it was a long one presume it will not go as all letters longer than one page are to be returned. This I regret very much as I was in hopes of receiving answers by next flag. I am very much in want of money (the old cry) if you could procure Greenbacks please send me some. I have written Mother respecting a special exchange. I am very ansious to get home before winter as it is very important that I should remain in this climate if I would live. I think Mr. Hartridge could effect an exchange in my case. I cannot tell you what I have suffered since being wounded. I lay seven months on my back & was in hospital 9 months. Write as soon as you get this.

Your affect. Brother
S.W. Branch

1Lt. Sanford Branch to Charlotte Branch

Morris Island
Oct 2nd 64.
Dear Mother

I have just learned that all letters covering more than one page are returned so presume that you have not recd mine (some six in number). I have long been advised by friends, some of them medical men, to apply for a special exchange but hoping that this detachment would be exchanged have delayed doing so until now. Mine is an urgent case. should I be sent north I would not probably live the winter. Four exchanges have been expected since our landing here, Capt. [Henry] Buist captured about 4 months since & Lt. [Edmund Irby] Mastin. I think Mr. Hartridge or anyone having influence at War Dept or with Genls. [Sam] Jones or [J.F.] Gilmer could arrange in my case. I dislike very much to trouble you & would write Mr. H but for the scarcity of paper. Hoping to hear from you soon & often

I am your affect Son
Sanford W. Branch
My rank is 1st Lt.

In October Sanford received the following letter from Lt. Col. Frederick Warley, who was one of the original fifty officers sent from Fort Delaware.

Lt. Col. Frederick Fraser Warley to Sanford Branch

Florence SC
Oct 7th 1864
Dear Branch

Yours of the 21st ult reached me yesterday. I write by this mail to Mr. Wagner, who will send you the oil by next flag of truce, it it can be obtained. I am sorry your letter was so long delayed & hope you have not suffered by reason of this. I will be glad to aid you or any of the officers in any way possible.

I have never seen a list of our officers on Morris Island & do not know how many of my acquaintance are now there. Remember me kindly to all of them. Ask any correspondent of Miss Alice [Minis]'s to present my respects when they write. I have written her since my return home. My health is very good, my wound has given me much trouble.

I hope you are very comfortable and that our shells do not disturb your slumbers.

Write me frequently
Your friend
F. F. Warley

1Lt. Sanford Branch to Charlotte Branch

Morris Island
Oct 9, 1864
Dear Mother

Yours & Hammies letters of Sept. 28th were recd per last flag. I was surprised that you had not recd my letters written from this point. I have written 7 or 8, some of them may have been destroyed on a/c of length. Am sorry that I did [not] recd yours enclosing letter of credit. will write to commdg. officer at Fort Delaware and have it forward to this point. O I am so anxious to see you. until now I have never dispaired, but I can see no hope of a general exchange so unless a special can be effected in my case, I fear it will be a long time before I see you. We have a great change in the weather today, it being very cold. I am pretty well supplied with blankets but some poor fellows are without any and suffered very much. Dont forget to send me something to eat. I am very hungry. Love to all

Your affect.Son

1Lt. Sanford Branch to 1Lt. Hamilton Branch

Oct 9. 64
Dear Brother

Your welcome letter of 28th inst is recd. You are strangely taciturn. You say your wound is healing but do not tell when where or how you are wounded. I am of course very ansious but hope it is nothing serious. I am also a little curious to know who Mortie Davis married. You beg me to make known my wants. I assure you I have done so at length in former letters. My wants are a little more pressing than ever before. I am an object of charity. When any one comes to me to borrow I tell them I am the sole owner of a suit of underclothing (generally dirty for we have to do our own washing here) which cant be borrowed. The people of Charleston, God bless them, have sent a bountiful supply of tobacco & provisions enough for several days. Cooked Potatoes will not keep but the raw are excellent for scurvy. Boxes sent by last flag reached here two days after.

Your affect Brother
Sanford W. Branch
Write soon

Melissa Baker to 1Lt. Sanford Branch

Friendsbury
Oct. 19th 1864
My dear Lieut. Branch,

Your letter of Sept. 15th was a long long time in coming as I did not receive it untill last week—yet it was most welcome, being the first that I have received of yours since some time before you left Fort D. The one you wrote from Hilton Head has not yet arrived so I hope you will write again your "Home address"—and also that before many days you can direct your letters from that place, that you would have above all others to write from, and with those around you who have ever been near and dear to you. I wrote to you a month ago, as soon as I knew from letters received by others, where to direct a letter—let me know if you received it. Since then I have heard from Capt. J[ackson] he was at home and delighted to be there, and wished me to inform you that he had written to your Mother.

Lieut. Robinson writes that he is now alone, every one of his old friends having left. he complains that you have neglected or forgotten him, but that others of the Charleston party have written frequently. he does not express the wish to be of your number but seems to bear his disappointments about an exchange better than formerly—and is trying to be submissive to his fate. I wish so much that you were with Lieut. Ledyard, he has written to all of his friends here. I replied some weeks ago and have been expecting another from him. Your friends inquire after you. . . . [I send kindest remembrances] to Lieuts. Cowper, Breedlove, Major Goldsborough &c. His mother has gone to Fort D. to see her son. Write very soon again, and believe me, ever your friend. Remember me to your friend Griffin when you meet.

Melissa Baker

Charlotte Branch to 1Lt. Sanford Branch

Bellheim Oct 23.64
My Dear Child,

I am anxiously expecting a letter from you. Your last (rec by me] was dated the 23 Sept. Hamilton left last night. he regreted much to go without hearing again from you. No doubt you are as much disappointed in geting letters as we are. I write once a week and why you do not get them I cant imagine. All things are about as usual with us. our family is very small. Mrs. Warner made us a visit last week, she says that Mary and all of them want you to come up and see them when you come home, which we all trust will be soon. All your friends send love. Henry Davis is at home and so is Joe. God bless you my own precious child and may you soon be restored to your

Devoted Mother
C.S. Branch

The unfortunate six hundred suffered grievously in their rough prison on the beach of Morris Island under the watchful guard of the 54th Massachusetts Colored Infantry. The monotonous sound of the surf was occasionally interrupted by shelling from forts Moultrie and Sumter, but it was the nights, when the Union batteries diligently shelled Charleston and Sumter, that were most terrifying, filled with exploding shells and mortar rounds. Eighteen shells fell among the tents in the unprotected stockade and exploded into deadly shrapnel. Amazingly, none of the men sustained injury.

Col. Edward N. Hallowell, commanding officer of the 54th Massachusetts, was vindictive in his position of authority. Rations issued to the six hundred were supposed to be identical to those received by Union prisoners, yet Hallowell allowed them only a cup of soup and a few wormy crackers a day. The men suffered serious weight loss, up to sixty pounds, and their resistance to disease was lowered.[7] Lt. John C. Cowper of North Carolina, one of Sanford's friends who had been with him since their wounding at Gettysburg, contracted pneumonia and died on October 14.

The Union prisoners left Charleston around October 13, yet Foster retained the survivors of the six hundred under fire until the 23rd, when Union authorities ordered him to cease his offensive against Charleston. Now saddled with 555 officers who had become a liability, he arranged to send them to Fort Pulaski, Georgia, with the 157th New York Infantry as guards.

On October 24, Sanford arrived at the sallyport of Fort Pulaski. So near home, he must have had mixed emotions at coming full circle to the place where he had begun his service nearly four years earlier. The fort was crowded, but Col. Philip P. Brown of the 157th New York promised better treatment, and rations were issued. They hoped for exchange as news of an agreement to release ten thousand sick and wounded ran like wildfire through the casemate cells. But once again the six hundred were exempt from conventional treatment; only a few lucky men received special exchanges, and those were arranged through political connections.[66]

Life in the fort settled into a routine. The men divided into teams to cook and do laundry. Sanford served on these details with three comrades, whose names he duly noted in the little, well-used book he had carried with him from Fort Delaware.

1Lt. Sanford Branch to Charlotte Branch

Fort Pulaski
Oct 25 64
Dear Mother

At last I am again on the soil of my native state, although still a long way from home. We arrived here yesterday after having been on board Schooner three days. I cannot say I enjoyed the trip as much as former visits to this post nor do I like being domiciled here. If one can judge from appearances I should say we will winter here. Immediately after landing, a large Southern mail was distributed. I was very much disappointed in not hearing from home, Do write by every flag. For fear you may not have recd my many letters I will mention that prisoners are allowed to receive boxs & money both of which your humble servant stands in need of. Love to Hammie & Sarah & friends

Your affect. Son
Sanford W. Branch

1Lt. Sanford Branch to Charlotte Branch

Fort Pulaski Ga.
Casemate 30, 2nd Division Nov 2, 64.
Dear Mother

I have just learned that there will be a flag in the river tomorrow & after a great deal of trouble have suceeded in procuring material to write these few lines. Speculations are rife as to the object of this flag, some asserting that it relates to our case & others to the ten thousand sick & wounded. in either case I should hope to be selected. We are very much pleased with the change from M. Island. I think I have increased ten lbs. since removal. nevertheless I am the most ansious boy to recieve a box that you ever saw. Love to all

Your affect. Son
S.W. Branch

None of the six hundred were exchanged.

1Lt. Sanford Branch to Charlotte Branch

Fort Pulaski
Casemate 30 Nov 2 [64]
Dear Mother
    I have been greviously disappointed in not receiving letters from you per
last flag. it seemed to me that I was the only one forgotten, nearly all the
prisoners recd at least one. Our quarters have been much improved by the
addision of 4 very large cooking stoves, so you can send me as meny
potatoes & as much grits & butter as you please, anything that a human
being could eat would be most acceptable. Tis said that there will probably
be flags in the Sav River regularly. if this is so I presume you will see it
announced in the papers. I do not think we will be sent North to winter
and as I shall require clothing would like my pay, if it can be drawn, inverted
in greenbacks which if sent by mail to this post will be delivered.

Affect
S.W. Branch

Charlotte Branch to 1Lt. Sanford Branch

Savannah
Nov. 2 [1864]
My Darling Child,
    It is with a nervous hand and with much excitement I write. I feel that
you are very near your home and I long to fly to you. Oh how I long to clasp
you to my heart. all your friends are hopeing you will be exchanged very
soon. I send you by the boat a package of Tobacco. we sent a box with
eatables to you while you were at Morris Island which we learned you did
not get. I regret much that I did not know in time that there would be an
opportunity of sending eatables to you, but trust I will see you so soon that
there will be no need of sending. God bless you my son, and Oh may we
soon meet and savor the joy of being again together in this life.

Most devotedly your Mother
C.S. Branch

1Lt. Sanford Branch to Charlotte Branch

Fort Pulaski
Casemate 30
Nov 3rd
Dear Mother

I was pained to learn yesterday from Col. Benet [William T. Bennett, the Union exchange agent for the Department of the South] that you were on board the flag of truce boat & had not heard from me. this is most unaccountable as I have written no less than fifteen letters since landing on Morris Island. I am happy to say that this will not occur again as Col. Benet has kindly offered to take charge of my letters. We are very much pleased with the change of quarters. We are now as comfortable as prisoners could expect to be. have large cooking stoves so you can send as meny potatoes, grits, butter &c. as you please for I have the appetite of an Ox. Anything will be most acceptable. I would also like some Greenbacks if thay can be procured. You know how I have always opposed special exchanges except in extreme cases but as several exchanges have been effected since our arrival in this dept. & as my health is not as good as I could wish, I would like one of it made in my case if not too much trouble. And now my dear Mother I think I have troubled you enough for this time. With love to Hammie & Sarah I am

Your affect Son
S.W. Branch
1st Lt.

[P.S.] I have recd tobacco. the boxes are being delivered

1Lt. Sanford Branch to Charlotte Branch

Fort Pulaski
Casemate 30
Nov 4th
Dear Mother

I was very sorry to hear from Col. Benet that I was the cause of so much uneasiness. I assure you I have written often I fear too often. in future I will write but one letter pr week on this size paper. There were about seventy–five boxes delivered this morning. you cannot imagine how disapointed I was. better luck next time. I get very good rations here, but want something from home. do send me syrup (in keg). Eggs, Ham grits potatoes Butter. or anything that a human being would eat. We do or will do our own cooking here so you need not send me any thing cooked except crackers or bread. Anything sent I will certainly get

Your affect Son
S.W. Branch

Charlotte Branch to 1Lt. Sanford Branch

Savannah Nov 5th 64
My Dear Son

Yours of the 23 is just recieved. I hope you have rec the few lines I sent by last Flag of Truce boat.

You must indeed feel strangely at Fort Pulasky, that place where you have spent so many pleasant hours and where you enjoyed the society of some of the noblest men that ever lived.

I send by the Beauregard [the flag of truce ship] a box of tobacco. our friends thought it would be better to send it than to send money as you could dispose of it and purchase what you wanted. I allso send a box of eatables which I trust will reach you safely.

We are all hopeing that you may soon be brought safely to your home. How thankfull I am to Our Heavenly Father who has spared your life through so many dangers.

May Gods blessing be and abide with you is the prayer of

Your Mother
C.S. Branch

Elizabeth Baker to 1Lt. Sanford Branch

Athol.
Mon. Nov. 7th 1864
Lieut Branch,
Dear Friend,

Thinking a few words this morning from "Athol" may prove acceptable, & serve as a reminder that you are not forgotten, even if they bring no ray of sunshine to your new prison-home, I have decided to write. I have heard through Major Goldsborough of your removal from Morris Island. I hope your present quarters may be found more comfortable, & hopes of exchange more cheering—We were quite shocked & pained to hear of Lieut. Cowper's sad death, & would like to hear some of the particulars. Whether he was resigned & calm in that last sad trying hour & if the Saviors Presence & Love was with him as he went down into the dark valley. How sad for him to be so near his home & not to reach it after all.

But I do not wish to make you sad or gloomy & hoped to have some bright word to cheer & comfort you. I know how you must be feeling now that you are so near your own beloved home & even *see* the "Promised Land," & how intense the Longing must be to be at "home" once more. I trust & pray your longings may soon be fully met & satisfied.

Do you know where Capt. [James R.] McCallum is & why he does not write? I fear he is sick. If not with you can you find out if he is at the hospital at Beaufort. Miss Anna D. wishes to be remembered, & trusts she has not been forgotten during these long months that have pased since you met. Praying you may ever be watched & guarded by the Loving Father—

Your sincere friend
E. Baker

Capt. Jacquelin Smith to Charlotte Branch.

Savannah Nov. 7th 1864
Dear Madame
    I have the honor to inform you that on yesterday I met Col. Bennett the Agt. of U.S. for exchange of Prisoners. he informed me that he saw your son on Thursday last at Ft. Pulaski—that he was very well & in want of nothing & that he, Col. Bennett, would do all in his power for him— Thinking this news would be agreeable I thus transmit it

I am Madam
Respty Your Obt Svt.
L. Jacquelin Smith
Capt. actg.

[P.S.] I will send any letters for you to Mr. [Walter] Chisolm as you requested Capt. Lamar to do—& will forward any you may wish with pleasure to your son.

Capt. Jacquelin Smith to Charlotte Branch

Savannah Nov 9th 64
Dr Madame.

Your note just recrd. I have the honor to inform you that the boat goes down tomorrow morning at 10 [A].M. & also that any packages you send to Capt. Neely A.Q.M. will be taken charge of & sent to your son. Hoping that he may be exchanged at an early day—

I remain
Your Very Obt. Svt.
La R. Jaquelin Smith

[P.S.] Col. Waddy will ask the Yankee agt. to deliver the pakcages as soon as possible to your son. any letters you wish sent send to my office & they will be forwarded. The mail will close tonight.

1Lt. Sanford Branch to Charlotte Branch

Nov 10, 64
Dear Mother

Your letter of 8th inst. was handed to me by the gentlemanly Provost Marshall on the afternoon of the sixth. The boxs were delivered early next morning. The eatibles were in good condision & were highly appreciated by a number of friends including several sick comrades with whom I shared the chickens & delicasies. Le Beouf was excellent. We have very good facilities for cooking & you know I am very fond of baked potatoes. The tobacco is a very fine article and I think I can dispose of it at a very fair price. The health of our officers is very good, there are very few sick. Gordon Fort has been quite sick but is much better. Remember me kindly to Mortie Davis. please say to him that I have authorized several friends here to have packages sent to his care. if he will give these his attention I will feel obliged. All letters & packages if not contraband are promply delivered do write often. Love to Hammie & Sarah

Your affect. Son
Sanford Branch

Melissa Baker to 1Lt. Sanford Branch

Friendsbury
Nov 13th 1864
My dear Lieut. Branch

I received your letter about ten days ago and I wrote to Lieut. Breedlove last Monday, but as I directed it to Morris Island, he may not get it now that you have all been removed from there. I hope you are much more comfortable or at least not exposed to the same danger. I wanted to write to you all last week but other duties prevented, though at the same time I felt as if you would not receive a letter, expecting that you were already on your homeward way. I am still of the same opinion though I am writing now and will rather risk the loss of a letter than give up the hope that you are even at this present moment seated by your mother's side, enjoying the bliss of that reunion which only those can appreciate, who have endured a like painful seperation. . . . Lieut. B. gave us the sad information of the death of Lieut. Cowper, were you with him at the time —was he conscious of his situation? and did he express any readiness and willingness to die. He is the first one gone of all those that were in the tent together when we last visited Gettysburg. May all the others be ready when their summons shall come. It is very painful to hear of the death of any of those that we have become interested in—and on this account I dread their return to military duty. May God protect and preserve you, my dear friend.

From your Friend
M. Baker

Do write even as you recieve this, as the letters are so long in coming. Mrs. B[aker] wrote to you last week. Lieut. Ledyard writes that he never hears from any of his friends of the Charleston party.

The winter of 1864–1865 blew into the casemates of Fort Pulaski on a cold seawind, with a cruel and chilling vengeance. The temperatures fell to below freezing, and the four stoves allowed were not sufficient to keep 313 men warm. The blankets that had been confiscated on Morris Island had not been returned, and the officers paced the floor all night to keep from freezing.

Retaliation rations were reinstated for the remnants of the six hundred, but Sanford's fortunes finally changed. On December 5 he and five others left Fort Pulaski. According to Capt. Henry C. Dickinson, who watched the men as they left, their physical condition was so deteriorated that "all together would not make a good soldier."[67]

Sanford had received his special exchange. He was sent to Charleston and, on a flag of truce ship in the harbor, was freed after seventeen months of confinement and severe treatment. He was handed a piece of paper, signed by the Confederate agent of exchange, identifying him as "a paroled prisoner of war, not yet exchanged and under Genl Orders is entitled to transportation from this point to his home."[68]

Broken both physically and emotionally, Sanford came home to Savannah after an absence of nearly three years. Time and hardship had taken its toll, and Charlotte was distressed at her son's weak and emaciated appearance. Yet it brought some relief. For him, the war was over.

CHAPTER TWELVE

We Cannot Afford to Lose Atlanta

While Sanford spent the winter of 1863–64 as a prisoner of war, Hammie and the cadets of Co. F of the 54th Georgia were stationed at the batteries and fortifications around Savannah. On February 7, 1864, they marched to Savannah and boarded a steamer for Scriven's Ferry, and on February 8 they marched to within two miles of Red Bluff, South Carolina, where they were assigned to guard river batteries and man a picket post. This uneventful duty continued until April 5, when they were ordered to proceed immediately to Pocataligo, Georgia, via the Savannah & Charleston Railroad.

They were encamped at Frazier's farm near Beaufort Island, Georgia, when they received their new marching orders—reinforcements were urgently needed by the Army of Tennessee at Dalton, Georgia, to defend the state from a full-scale Union invasion.

The Confederate victory at Chickamauga, Georgia, in September 1863 had been followed by a disasterous defeat at Missionary Ridge, Tennessee, in November. Gen. Braxton Bragg, commanding the Army of Tennessee, had retreated to Dalton to reorganize the army. Instead, he resigned his position.

On December 27, 1863, Gen. Joseph E. Johnston took command of a demoralized and neglected army of 40,000. They faced 110,000 well-equipped and confident Federals commanded by Maj. Gen. William T. Sherman. Johnston, who possessed an aptitude for administration, began an energetic program to restore the army's damaged morale. He furloughed men who had not been home in years, improved the rations and supply needs, and readied the line of defenders for what he knew would be a difficult spring campaign. Although the president was unsure of him, he enjoyed wide popularity among his men.

Johnston objected to Jefferson Davis's proposals to mount an offensive and recapture lost territory in Tennessee. Instead, Johnston decided to concentrate all available Confederate forces in northern Georgia, await the enemy invasion, defeat it, and then deliver a counterattack and pursue the routed Federals northward. To execute his plan, Johnston needed three corps: one was led by Savannah native Lt. Gen. William J. Hardee, another by Lt. Gen. John Bell Hood. To supply the third, President Davis ordered the 15,000-man Army of Mississippi under Gen. Leonidas K. Polk to join Johnston in May 1864. Once they were assembled, Johnston would have nearly 75,000 men.

Johnston's strategy was to withdraw deeper into Georgia, stretching the Union supply lines and tying up valuable troops as guards at depots, bridges, and occupied towns as well as establishing formidable defensive positions of trenches and forts to protect Sherman's goal—Atlanta, the rail hub of the state and heart of the Confederacy. On May 1, 1864, Grant telegraphed Sherman that he was moving against Lee; a coordinated movement against Johnston was put into motion.

The 54th Georgia was brigaded with the 57th and 63rd Georgia, all three regiments under the command of Brig. Gen. Hugh W. Mercer, himself a Savannahian. On April 29 they left for Dalton, and on May 3 they were assigned to Maj. Gen. W.H.T. Walker's Division, Gen. William J. Hardee's Corps. They participated in an evening dress parade witnessed by generals Johnston, Walker, and others, all of whom were impressed with the drill and appearance of the command. The young cadets found themselves the subject of amusement for the veterans in Johnston's Army of Tennessee, who dubbed them "Silver Forks," "Boiled Shirts," and "New Issue" because of their inexperience.

Lt. Hamilton Branch to Charlotte Branch

Dalton Ga
May 3 / 64
My Dear Mother

I arrived here this forenoon after a series of adventures safe and sound. the train I came on collided with a freight train and bruised one man pretty

badly and smashed the cars pretty badly. We are in Genl Walkers Division
and Genl Hardees Corps. I met Bill Dueberry [William Dewberry]] here
today. he was very kind to me and begs to be remembered to you. I am
writting in his office now. we are encamped about 3 miles from here in the
direction of Cleaveland [Cleveland, Tennessee]. I will write to you again
soon. All the boys are well. I also met Capt. Willie Reed who was very kind
to me. I had quite a pleasant time in Macon. Excuse brevity but I am in a
great hurry and now praying that God will bless and watch over you and
yours I remain your loving son

Hammie

[P.S.] John and Bob [Robert M. Butler] are well. Sam Douse [Samuel
Dowse] and Charlie [Charles W.] Davis also. I will write soon and give you
an account of my travels.

1Lt. Hamilton Branch to Charlotte Branch

Bivouac Mercers Brigade Dalton May 4/64
My Dear Dear Mother

I arrived here safely and wrote to you yesterday but directed your letter
to Savannah and therefore write again. We are about 3 Miles from Dalton
in the direction of Cleaveland we are in Walker W H T Division and in
Genl Hardees Corps. there was a dispute in reference to which Division
we belonged to Walkers or Pat Cleburns, but it has been decided in favor
of Walker I believe. The country here is more hilly than the portion of
Virginia through which I passed, it is very cold up here at nights, we had a
very heavy frost night before last. The train on which I came from Marietta
backed into a freight train near Frankfort and a general smash up was the
consequence, one man about the middle of the train was pretty badly hurt
but that was all. the cars though were broken pretty badly. I was in the back
car and strange to say it was the least hurt of them all. I met Bill Duebery,
who is now a Major on Genl. Johnston's Staff, in Dalton yesterday. He was
very kind to me indeed. I also met Willie Reed who was very kind also. I
am agoing over to see Capt. Darry Lamar and Lady this afternoon. I was
left over all day Sunday in Macon but had quite a nice time, for Willie
[William J.] Marshall who was there found me out and we went up to Dr.
Branhams to see Miss Jennie McLaughlin and Miss Emmie Branham. Miss
Emmie is very pleasant and is a very nice young lady and I believe if I were
a *young* man I would fall desperately in love with her. The army up here

are in fine spirits and confident of victory in the coming fight and if the people at home will only do there duty and keep the disasters away from home there is no doubt but we will whip them.

Direct to Co. F 54th Ga. Reg. Mercers Brigade, Dalton Geo. Remember me to all my friends. all the boys are well. God bless you my dear mother as ever

your loving son
Hammie

Mercer's Brigade had arrived none too soon. On May 6 Gen. Sherman's 100,000-man army advanced in two columns on Tunnel Hill, north of Dalton, and occupied it the following day. On this spot, the battle for Atlanta began in earnest.

Sherman personally commanded the larger force, which met Johnston's Confederates on May 8–9 at Rocky Face Ridge, two miles northwest of Dalton, but this encounter was only a Union deception. A second Union column was dispatched on a flanking movement toward Resaca, Georgia, twelve miles to the south on the Western & Atlantic Railroad. Johnston reacted quickly when the feint was discovered, and the Confederates were firmly entrenched before Sherman could unite his two columns.

1Lt. Hamilton Branch to Charlotte Branch

Bivouac Mercers Brigade
in line of battle between Dalton and Tunnel Hill Ga
May 8 / 64
My Dear Mother

I have wanted to write to you for the last two days but have not had a chance as we have been marching and counter marching all the time. the enemy are advancing and we expect the big fight tomorrow and we intend to give them a good whipping and try and end the war. they have been skirmishing all day. we have just returned from a tramp to help Genl Hood but after marching about two miles he sent us back. But I must stop as the enemy have begun the attack and our long roll is beating again.

All the boys are well and in fine spirits, Good bye my darling mother and do not forget to pray for your boy, God bless you and preserve you is the prayer of your loving and devoted son

Hammie

The "long roll" refers to the drum call beating the men to assemble to arms. It signified that a battle was imminent.

On May 13–15, part of Sherman's army under Maj. Gen. James B. McPherson met Confederate resistance at Resaca. Additional troops under Lt. Gen. Leonidas Polk bolstered Johnston's larger army, well protected behind a double row of trenches extending in a three-mile long crescent along low wooded hills west and north of the town. After some initial skirmishing, the artillery batteries dueled away the first day. One major Union attack ended unsuccessfully, and Sherman ordered another flanking movement.[70]

Although Sherman had lost a chance to destroy Johnston's outnumbered forces, his troops crossed the Oostanaula River, and Johnston was compelled to withdraw to meet the threat. The Southerners retreated through Calhoun, fighting delaying actions against the Union pursuit. Walker's Division was employed as a mobile reserve force, rushing between Calhoun and the battlefield to counter Union threats. They also covered the army's retreat to Calhoun and checked the pursuing foe on May 16 with a surprise attack at the Rome crossroads, which fell for lack of troops to protect it.

Falling back through Adairsville to Cassville, Gen. Johnston issued a confident message to his army anticipating victory in an attempt to draw Sherman. McPherson was drawn into an ambush, but Gen. Hood failed to attack, and the opportunity was lost. The Confederate army retreated across the Etowah River to Alatoona. Despite the giving of ground, Johnston's men never lost faith in him, nor in their chance of success.

1Lt. Hamilton Branch to Charlotte Branch

Bivouac Mercer's Brigade 3 miles from Resaca, Geo
May 10th /64
My Very Dear Mother

I wrote to you on the evening of the 8th just as the long roll was beating. After falling into line we marched about three miles from our position, and about five miles from Dalton. Here on the top of a high hill we were put into the trenches and made to stay there all night. Our trenches were on the two sides of a battery of eight guns which commanded the Valley below us. Col. [George W.] Gordon was in the trenches in the left and Col. [Charelton H.] Way in those on the right. above the center of Col. Way's line the pioneer corps then built us a small battery for two guns and the next day Capt. [R.T.] Beauregard was sent there with two 10 lb. Parrot guns. We stayed in the trenches all of the 9th and about 3 oclock a.m. our large battery were attacked by a few of the enemy and were repulsed. Before this attack there was skirmishing from early dawn and about 2 p.m. oclock Lt. [William E.] Reddick, a very nice young man and gallant officer, was killed whilst standing on the parapet. He was killed by a sharpshooter from a great distance. the enemy threw quite a number of shell over us and a few minnie balls.

Our boys all behaved very well. We were under fire about two hours. Capt. [George Anderson] Mercer and Capt. [Edward W.] Drummond both had narrow escapes. We were kept in the trenches untill about 1 oclock a.m. of the tenth when we were taken out and marched to this place which is 11 miles from Dalton. We arrived here about 10 oclock but as there is no chance of a fight here now, the enemy having fallen back, I suppose we will go back to Dalton tomorrow. We had an awful time marching to this place. We had to come down a very steep side of the mountain in the dark. I do not know when the big fight will come off but suspect before long. we had four or five men wounded in our regiment, nine in our co.

As ever your devoted
Hammie

1Lt. Hamilton Branch to Charlotte Branch

Bivouac Walkers Division near Calhoun, Geo.
May 13th 1864
My Very Dear Mother

I have recieved your letter encloseing Mr. Butlers memorandum. I am very glad that it has been paid although I did not intend that you should pay it, and therefore I will remit you the amt. as soon as I can draw my pay. they owe me now from the 1st of Feb/64.

I wrote to you on the 10th and imediatelly after writting we were marched out and formed into line of battle, we then stacked our arms and went to sleep. About 10 oclock it commenced raining and I have never seen it rain harder than it did. I was awakened by slipping down the hillside on which I was sleeping it was a very steep one and the water running under me caused me to slide. I was sleeping on and covering with one blanket viz Sam Douses who was sleeping with me or rather I with him as I have not seen my blanket since we started to march as I put it in Genl Mercers waggon and that has not been seen since. the rest of my baggage was put into the officers waggon also and that has not been seen since, so that I now only carry my sword, sash, haversack and canteen. My cloths are very dirty as we have been marching for the last week on very dusty roads and I have not been able to change my cloths.

I arose the morning after the rain and dried my cloths, after which we fell in and were marched to Resaka which was about 3 miles. But we were too late, for the enemy had gone back. After staying there about two hours we were marched back and bivouacked at the old place. The next day the 12th, about 4 oclock p.m. we fell in and were marched through Rasacka and across the Ostanula to this place where we arrived about 9 oclock p.m. Here we have been ever since, and do not know when we will move but have been expecting to go every minute.

Genl Walker has just gone out and is shelling a party of the enemy who are putting a battery up on the river in front of us. Genls Johns[t]on and Sherman are playing a large game of Chess but Johns[t]ons boys are sure to carry him through. We do not know why we have been moved away down here but we know that it is all right.

Mother, I do not know but that you had better send me some cloths, that is send them to Mrs. [M.E.] Robinson. I mean under cloths. you might also send my dark uniform and then if I get where I can wear them I can send to her for them. We do not know when the big fight will come off, but we are certain of victory if the lord is willing. Remember me to all my friends. Ask Sarah Brigham if she can not write to her dear little cousin at Dalton, that is you can give her the directions. All the boys are well so far. I believe the mail is not allowed to leave here now. Anyhow I write and you will get it some time, but I must stop now as the long roll is beating. Write to me often

as ever your devoted son
Hammie

In line of battle below Calhoun Ga near the lines May 15/64

The long roll was beaten to send us on picket. we went on picket on the river about 1/4 mile from Calhoun. we remained on picket all night and the next morning we were ordered to rejoin our regiment which has been ordered to reinforce the forces at Resaca.

We marched about two miles and met our regiment. we then marched down and crossed the Oustanula at Resaca on a pontoon bridge just above the Rail Road bridges. In doing this we were subjected to the fire of a yankey battery about 1/2 mile off but we crossed with only the loss of 2 men killed and 4 wounded, all of the 63rd Ga. We then marched through Resacka and about two miles above on the rail road where we formed a line of battle and stayed about 1 hour and a half during which time we were occasionaly favored with a S[hrapnel] shell, round shot or minnie ball. but fortunatelly no one was hurt. We then marched on about a mile and were put into the trenches where we stayed untill about 10 oclock when we were ordered to this place, which is about 12 miles from Resaca by the road. In recrossing the river last night we crossed on the rail road bridge and were not troubled at all. in going into the trenches we were subjected to a fire of minnie rifles and had three or four wounded, viz 1st Lt. [James H.] Griffin shot through the left lung and 1st Lt. [Grigsby E.] Thomas [Sr.] shot in the face and one or two men.

We are now in line of battle away down on the flank, for what purpose we know not. You must excuse bad writting as I am lying down and Johnnie is asleep with his head resting on me, and also as I have been up two nights now and have been marching all of one night and day. I must close now as I want to try and get a little sleep before going into the fight.

as ever your devoted son
Hammie

1Lt. Hamilton Branch to Charlotte Branch

Calhoun Geo
May 16/64
My Very Dear Mother

I wrote to you yesterday but as Dr Knox is a going to Savannah and has kindly offered to carry letters for us I write to let you know that we are all still quite well, but dirty. Genl [John K.] Jackson attacked the enemy yesterday and drove them to there breastworks when he very foolishly charged them without having a support and was repulsed. so last night about 10 Oclock we fell back to this place. Why we fell back I know not for the enemy were not troubling us at all. it may be though that the enemy are moving his forces to Rome and if so we will go there too.

last night was the third night during which we have been on the march. but last night we rested half the night and therefore feel quite fresh this morning. We have not been into a fight yet. it is reported that after our forces fell back from Resaca that the enemy captured two of our hospitals and killed all the wounded. Also that they fired into our ambulances and killed the wounded. I do not know that this is true but it is reported so. Bob Butler is well and in fact all the boys are well. Remember me to all my friends. Write to me soon and often. We have whipped the enemy on all sides thus far. we are falling back gradualy, that is fall back 8 or 10 miles and then stay three or four days. I do not know how far back we will go but it is all right. Genl Johns[t]on knows what to do, and he will come out all right.

as ever your devoted son
Hammie

1Lt. Hamilton Branch to Charlotte Branch

Bivouac Co F 54th Ga.
Mercers Brigade, Walkers Division
Hardee's Corps, Army of Tenn
on line of battle near Bartow Geo May 18th 1864
My very dear Mother
     After writting to you on the 16th we, our brigade, were marched about 7 miles down towards the river for the purpose of cutting off a party of yanks, but when we arrived there we found that they had gone. we then had the pleasure of marching back over the same ground to reinforce Genl Walker whose skirmishers were engaged with the enemy. we went back in a hurry as we were liable to be cut off. when we arrived back we found the Gallant Major [Arthur] Schaaf with his brave battalion engaged with the enemy near Calhoun. There were other skirmisers but they did not act as well as they ought to have done. the enemy were driven back two miles, the Sharp Shooters suffered severely. Maj Schaaf escaped unhurt, although he led two charges on the enemy. The brave Capt [Horace D.] T[w]yman, than whom no more gallant officer lives, had his right leg broken and recieved a flesh wound in his left. they also lost severely in men. we formed a reserve line of battle here and waited until night when we fell back to [Adairsville]. Here we staid all day and the enemy appearing in the evening [General Benjamin F.] Cheatham was sent out to drive them back, which he did. we lay in line of battle here until 1 AM when we started to fall back again and have now reached this place, which is about two miles from Bartow. we expect to fall back again to night and do not know where the

General intends to stop, but this we do know—that when he stops he is agoing to fight *the* battle of the war and that God helping he is agoing to give them the worst whipping they have had. My boys are all well but nearly worn out and we, Walkers Foot Cavalry, have been doing all the strategy for Genl Johnston and have marched night and day for the last 10 days with very little rest. It is now about 10 [a]m and as I want a little sleep before we start again, which I suppose will be about dark, I must close. Remember me to all my friends and write soon. Send me some envelopes in your letters. Good bye my darling mother and hopeing that God will protect you and watch over you I remain your devoted and loving son

Hammie

[Bartow County, originally Cass County, Georgia, was renamed for Col. Francis Bartow in 1861, the first Georgia officer killed in the war.]

in line Battle,
Mercers Brigade Bartow, Ga
May 19th, 1864

After writing to you yesterday, for a wonder, we did not move, but had one good nights rest, although I was awakened about one Oclock by fire, it being near my head. It was caused by some large rails being put on the fire and they burned to the ends and set the leaves on fire and they burned to my bed which was about eight feet from the fire. My bed fellow, Sam Dowse, had his hat and haversack burned. I awoke just in time to save his cartridge box, although the strap was burned. I got through with a small hole burned in the side of my hat, and the silk and velvet burned off one part.

This morning we were sent to the front to relieve General [Lucius E.] Polk's Brigade who were acting as rear guards. We then threw out skirmishers and fought them for awhile, then we fell back drawing them after us. We fell back about a mile to where our army was in line of battle and took our place in line on the top of a hill in an open field. Here the enemy commenced shelling us and shelled us for about two hours, killing one man and wounding several. My company lost none. This line was formed for the purpose of checking the enemy, which we did. Here Colonel Way read an order from General Johns[t]on, praising our army for the soldierly qualities they had shown during the falling back. General Mercer then said to us 'Silver Forks show what metal you are made of.'

That the good Lord will be with you is the prayer of your loving son

Hammie

The brigade casualties to this date were four killed, forty-two wounded, and twenty-three missing, although only one man of Co. F was a casualty.[71] The Cadets earned the respect of the veterans.

Sherman was impatient as his advance on Atlanta ground to a standstill in front of Confederate gun pits. On May 23 he ordered a feint toward Dallas, but Johnston blocked him. On May 25 Hooker's Corps attacked Hood's Corps at New Hope Church, but they were decimated by the concentrated Confederate fire from entrenched positions. Johnston, believing McPherson was withdrawing to reinforce Hooker, attacked a strongly held Union position at Dallas and was repulsed. Then Sherman's attempt to attack Johnston's right flank at Pickett's Mill on May 27 became such a disaster for Union forces that Sherman deemed it his "worst defeat" in his memoirs.

With Johnston firmly blocking his forward movement, Sherman shifted to the left to regain contact with the Western & Atlantic railroad at Acworth, but he finally gave up and shifted his focus to the railroad at Big Shanty.[72]

The other three divisions of Hardee's Corps actively participated in the week of fighting around Dallas, but Walker's Division continued to serve as a mobile reserve. Hammie and his company were shifted about until finally assigned a front-line position atop Ray Mountain.

Mrs. Elizabeth Schaaf to 1Lt. Hamilton Branch

Savannah Ga.
May 25th, 1864.
Dear Hammie:

A friend of mine has just sent me over the Republican to read a letter from you! How can I thank you sufficiently for thoughts so kindly expressed for my dear Husband! I cannot express my thanks dear Hammie, but pray that God may bless and give you a safe and speedy return home. I can never forget this kindness and you can have the happy conciousness of knowing you have made one sad and anxious heart the happiest to-night in the Confederacy.

May Heaven's choicest blessings descend upon you, is the prayer of your warmly attached friend

Lizzie Schaaff.

The following letter of Hammie's describing the action ran in the May 25 edition of the *Republican*.

1Lt. Hamilton Branch to Charlotte Branch

Bivouac Co. F 54th Ga. Reg Inft Mercers Brigade Walkers Division
Hardees Corps
Army of Tennessee
May 21st / 1864
My very dear mother

I have not heard from you for some time. the last letter I recieved from you was dated the 13th and I was very glad to hear that you were well, and I hope that you may continue to enjoy good health and that the time may not be far distant when we may all be together again. Mother if you ever get an opportunity do send me something good to eat. Never let an opportunity pass, and mother could you not send some little thing up to Cousin Maria and ask her to send it to me by the first opportunity.

We are now only 43 miles from Atlanta. we are between Etowa station and Altoona. we laid down behind our stacks after my last letter was written and slept until 1 O'clock when we were ordered to move which we did and marched through Cass Station and Cartersville. About good daylight—we arrived at Etowa Station where we staid until about 12 Oclock to allow our army and waggons to cross the river. there were four bridges across the river, viz the railroad, dirt road, and two pontoon bridges. I went into the river and had a good bath but had to put my same dirty cloths on. I then sat down and saw a greater portion of the army cross the river. I counted 105 regiments of infantry, crossing and I know there were two brigades, Jackson and [States Rights] Gists, behind me.

After crossing the river we marched to this place where we have slept all night. I have been in and taken another wash and feel quite well this morning although hungry. Genl Johns[t]on thinking that the enemy were about to stop following him, determined to advance from Cassville, Bartow, upon them, but finding that they intended following him, he has commenced falling back again, and no one knows where he will stop. My company are all well. God has protected us and we have not lost a man out of the company. Johnny sends his love to you. Do send me something to eat as soon as you get a chance. there is no use sending it except by some one. Today is the 21st May, just three years since we left Savannah for

Virginia. Remember me to all my friends and write to me often, and with the prayer that God will continue to watch over you I remain as ever

your loving and devoted son

Hammie

1Lt. Hamilton Branch to Charlotte Branch

Bivouac Mercers Brigade

Near Powder Springs Ga

May 24 / 64

My Very Dear Mother

I have been so worn out that I did not feel at all like doing anything but resting whilst we were in Bivouac near Altoona, from which place I wrote you on the 20th. We stayed at that bivouac nearly three days and therefore had quite a good rest. We left that bivouac on Monday the 23rd at 10 AM Oclock. The sun was shining very brightly and it was very warm indeed. we marched very slowly until 4 1/2 Oclock PM when we went into bivouac having marched but 6 miles, although as it was so warm it appeared to be about 12. We stayed at this bivouac until about 4 1/2 AM when we were awakened and fell in ranks and marched until about 5 PM when we were halted and marched into our present bivouac. we have not the prospect of a pleasant night, for as the boys say there are rain seeds on all sides.

I am still quite well although I have chafed today for the first time. as we have stopped near a creek I have just been down and taken a wash and have received from Buck [William B.] Hassett the bottle of camphor which you sent to me, and have used some of it and I think it has helped me. All the boys are well. there are some of the countrymen who have been sent off sick and Jas [J.] Keane was lost from the company on the 11th and has not been heard of since. we think he has been taken prisoner.

Mother do you not think that Mrs. Robinson could now and then send me a little bundle of eatables. if so please send her a small box, say about 50 or 100 lbs. We are now only 22 miles from Atlanta by the dirt-road. Good bye and my God bless you, as ever

your devoted and loving son

Hammie

May 25th 1864

Bivouac I dont know where Co F 54th Ga Mercers Brigade

After writting yesterday we were presented by Buck Hassett & Co with a goose, which I had killed and then proceeded to clean and divide, after which I fried the Capt[John W. Anderson, Jr.] & mine and having a piece of corn bread we fried that and sat down to supper. Just as we had finished eating, which occupied some time as the goose was quite tough, it commenced raining. we then layed down and went to sleep. it rained until 12 O'clock. at 1 AM we were called and found ourselves ringing wet. we got up and put on our trappings and started back over the same road on which we marched yesterday. we marched I do not know how far but think about 3 miles, and then went into the woods about 1/2 mile where we stopped and stacked arms. we had just got to sleep when we were made to get up and fall in and marched about 1/4 of a mile where we now are. thus you see we have marched back towards the enemy but for what purpose unless for strategy I do not know.

The stoper was knocked out of my ink bottle yesterday and all the ink emptied into my haversack. I put the bottle and my pomade divine which was covered with ink down by my haversack to dry out and in leaving last night forgot them.

My boys all looked badly this morning, having marched, fasted and been wet. they have had nothing to eat now in two days. Ed[ward E.] Foy and Judge [Williamson T.] Brewer are as well as any. Mother when you write send me one or two sheets of paper and envelopes in you letter especially the envelopes as I have none. I have not heard from you now since the 13th, what is the matter with the mailes I know not. do you get my letters. they are all connected. Remember me to all. tell the folks that I would like to have some of their milk clabber. God bless you my darling mother

as ever your loving son, Hammie

PS If you see Aunt Lizzie [Elizabeth Butler] try and get her to write to Bob about his being so slow. the Capt has threatened to reduce him and was about doing it the other day but I talked with him about it and he did not do it. but I cannot say anything again for the Capt has brought his neglect to my notice several times and I have been obliged to acnoledge his neglect. he has been fooled so often is the only excuse that he gives. when we are in line of battle near the enemy and have been called to retreat at midnight in a hurry, he has always been about the last to get up and fixed when he ought to be the first, as it is his duty to call the men and fall the company in, and the Capt says that he can hardly find him when he is needed. he is also late always in going after the rations. Orderly Sergeant is the most important officer out here in a company and must be filled by a quick energetic man. I should hate to see Bob reduced but still I can say nothing as I can make no excuse. Write to Aunt Lizzie if you cannot [rest of letter missing]

1Lt. Hamilton Branch to Charlotte Branch

Mercers Brigade, May 26th 1864
On the march to the Front
My Very Dear Mother

After writting to you on yesterday I laid down and went to sleep, and slept about two hours. I then got up and felt quite refreshed. we staid at that bivouac until about 4 PM when we fell in and were marched 1/2 mile to the right through the woods. here we formed line of battle and rested. from that place we could hear quite a heavy skirmish going on a little to our right and front. we staid in line of battle until about 7 PM when we were marched through the woods on byroads until 10 Oclock PM when we were halted and allowed to go to sleep.

Just at this place quite an amusing incident occured. we had stopped in the road sometime and some of us were resting ourselves on the ground. all were not down because it had been raining the whole time that we were on the march and they were afraid to be on the wet ground. I was at the head of my company and Judge B[rewer] and Joe Ganaan were at the foot of theres, therefore we were together. I was laying down on the ground Judge was sitting on his blanket roll at my head and Joe was half lying down by Judge. I had just dosed off when some one hit me on the knee and I heard a noise as if the horses of an ambulance were running away with it down the road. so I just rolled over into the woods and jumped up, and looking around not a man was to be seen on the road which just a moment before was crowded. they had all taken to the woods, Judge says that he thought the thing was upon him and that he was a going to be run over and therefore he closed his eyes to recieve it. just then Joe whispered yanks and judge says have they gone by and opened his eyes. this noise was heard by the whole division and they all jumped into the woods. as yet no one has been able to account for the noise as nothing has been seen, but it is thought that some horses in the rear must have run away but were stopped suddenly. We laid down at this place until 2 AM when we were called and marched into a big road and up to where we now are. we have stacked arms and are about 1 1/2 miles from the enemy and are awaiting orders. Ed Foy was sent off to the hospital yesterday, nothing serious I think.

In line of battle
near Dallas GA
May 27th / 64

After writting yesterday we were marched to near New Hope Church and formed into line of battle. here we were kept all day and until 1 AM this morning. heavy skirmishing was kept up during this time in our front. we were then formed and marched to this place where we now lie in line acting as a reserve to our line of battle which is about 50 yards to the front and as covered by breastworks. we have been moved once or twice to the right and left, as the skirmishing indicated the point to be attacked. My boys are all well so far. If you have not spoken to Aunt Lizzie you need not, as Bob is attending to his business better now. We all think there will be a fight here in a day or two. Genl Johns[t]on has been offering the enemy battle for two days now but he has not accepted yet.
as ever your loving and devoted son

Hammie
God bless and protect you my darling Mother

In line of battle as Reserve to Cheathams Division near New Hope Church
May 28 / 64

After writting on yesterday we were marched a mile and half to the right over two very high hills and up on to the top of another one, when we formed line of battle and sent out skirmishers. I do not think the army had ever been on these hills as there was no signs of them. the sides of the hills were as near perpendicular as it is possible for a man to climb up. we built small stone works here and staid until 1 Oclock AM when we were ordered to this place to report to Genl Johnston. we arrived here at 5 AM. whilst at our stone works we were subjected to the fire of the sharp shooters, but lost no one out of my company. Our skirmisers charged the enemy at that place and drove them in. There was quite an engagement on our right yesterday. we drove the enemy back two miles I believe, and captured a number of prisoners. We are expecting a fight here every day now. On the march last night I was so sleepy that I was dozing off all the time. Judge Brewer is still well. Remember me to all my friends. I have been living high for the last day. our boys were so starved that they asked General Mercer to let them kill some hogs and he gave them permission so that we have been living on fresh pork. You do not know how much I want to hear from you. your last letter was dated the 13th.

as ever your loving son
Hammie

[P.S.] Bob B is well

1Lt. Hamilton Branch to Charlotte Branch

In the trenches near New Hope Church
Walkers Division
May 29 / 64
My Dear Mother

I gave my letter of yesterday to our waggoner and begged him to send it off as soon as possible. after writting it we were moved about 1/4 of a mile to the left, and put into the trenches. we were near the bottom of a very steep and high hill and in a very bad position. we were for a wonder allowed to stay in this position all night, but half the men could not sleep as the hill was so steep that they would slide down as soon as they went to sleep. Sam [Dowse] and I managed to get a good nights sleep by placing a log against a tree and resting our feet against it. this morning about ten oclock we were moved to the position we now occupy which is about a mile to the left of the one we had yesterday. we are on a very high hill and have a splendid view both in front and rear for a great many miles.

The 1st Vol Reg Ga arrived this morning and have been put into our brigade. I received the letters and envelopes from Lt [Charles C.] H[unter] and Fred Hull has told me that he has the bundle for me. the under cloths are much needed as I have not changed mine in three weeks.

On Skirmish line
May 31 / 64

We remained the whole of yesterday in the same position that we were the day before until about 2 PM when we were sent out on picket where we now are. for a wonder our brigade has been allowed three nights sleep, that is the three last nights. We were allowed two but of course as we, that is my company, was on picket last night we could not sleep at all. every thing has been very quiet here for the last two days. scarcely a gun has been fired. I went down this morning and washed all over and put on my clean cloths and you do not know how proud I feel. I wish you could see the cloths that I took off. they are as dirty as dirty can be. All the boys are well. the Capt [Fred Hull] has had a chill and some fiver. do not tell anyone as he has not been very sick. The O L I are on picket with us. Harmon and Paul [Elkins] are well, also Judge B. Remember me to all. I am in hopes of hearing from you today. In your next tell me the dates of the letters you have received from me and whether they are connected.

as ever your loving son

Hammie

Tell Mr B that he must make a good crop of sugar cane as I want to be in at the boiling. Tell Mrs B that I am very glad that she has gotten entirely well and that the next time I come that I will steal another waffle. Tell all the others to take good care of the things at home and my darling mother you must take good care of your health and live to bless your loving and devoted sons

Hammie

1Lt. Hamilton Branch to Charlotte Branch

Hd Qrs Co F 54th Ga, Infty Mercers Brigade
Walkers Division
Hardees Corps Army of Tenn
In the trenches near New Hope
June 2nd 1864
My very dear Mother

After writting to you on the 31st we remained on picket until 5 PM when we were relieved by Co H 54th. I had persuaded Capt Anderson in the mean time to go to the rear and he went about 2 PM leaving me in command of the company. after being relieved from picket I brought my company back to this place where we remained all yesterday the 1st, although we were expecting to move every minute as Genl Johns[t]on was up on this hill looking at the enemy who were evacuating the left of their line, our men occupying their breastworks as soon as they left them. In Dallas they left an envelope on which they had written off for Chatanooga will be back in a few days with something to eat. they left a number of our wounded in Dallas.

On the 31st I went on the top of Edwards Mountain which is just to our left and upon which Col [George W.] Gordon is stationed. from that place I had a magnificient view of the country in our front. I could see two lines of the enemys fortifications and also their waggon trains and cavalry passing. our battery on the top of this hill fired six shots at a house in the valley from which the enemys sharp shooters were annoying our men. at this signal the skirmishers from Genl JK Jacksons Brigade advanced and set the house on fire and burned it to the ground.

In line of battle
4 miles to right of New Hope
June 3, 1864

After writting yesterday it commenced raining and rained very hard for about an hour. I having nothing to protect me got quite wet but by going to a fire and taking off my cloths and holding them to the fire I got them dry. by this time it commenced raining again but not very hard. after raining awhile we were ordered into line and started to march at 4 PM and marched over very boggy roads until 12 Oclock midnight when we were halted in the woods and laid down on the wet ground and went to sleep and slept until this morning when we formed line of battle and are now supporting Genl [Carter L.] Stevenson but there is no telling where we will be tonight. I am not bothered with anything on a march now as since we left Dalton the only things I carry are my sword, haversack and canteen. I sleep on the ground and cover with nothing. The boys are all well, that is all of my boys that you know. a great many have been sent off to the hospitals but none but [George W.] Brownell and [William H.] Bradl[e]y from Savh. Judge, Harmon and Paul are all well. Bob is well. We do not know when we will have a fight but are expecting one every day. I received your letter of the 26th with copys of Santys. I am very glad to hear from him but am sorry that the poor fellow has suffered so much. I hope that he will soon be exchanged and be at home with you. Mother do write to me often. Hoping that God will bless you and yours

I am your loving and devoted son
Hammie

[P.S.] Send me some stamps and one or two envelopes in each letter. I have not a stamp. Remember me to all my friends. I am just agoing to have my supper cooked. it consists of hardtack and a piece of bacon. Our army is still in fine spirits and confident, God helping us, of victory. The enemy are on short rations and not in fine spirits, for they have found us not demoralized but only drawing them into a trap.

With Hammie again exposed to death and danger at the front, Charlotte became more and more anxious about his safety. When the Savannah Relief Committee went to Marietta to establish a supply depot for the troops from that city, Charlotte accompanied them and became a nurse there.

Located on the Western & Atlantic Railroad, the city had been a hospital center since June 1863. A large hospital complex grew in the town square, filled by the steady flow of wounded and sick who arrived daily as the fighting moved southward, ever closer. Once again the "Mother of the Oglethorpes" took special care of the Savannah boys. She saw Hammie on the few occasions he could leave the front, yet he wrote to her daily, under the most adverse conditions imaginable, his battle accounts chronicling the fighting record of the Savannah Cadets.

1Lt. Hamilton Branch to Charlotte Branch

8 PM
In line of battle 3 miles left of Altoona
June 3 1864
My Very Dear Mother

I wrote you a letter today and gave it to Dr. [I.E.] Godfrey to mail for me, but since then I have seen Mort Ferres who tells me that you are in Atlanta. Mother if you have brought anything for me from home do not send too much at once as I cannot carry it. if you send to Savh Committee at Marrietta care of Mr [John] Reil[l]y, Forage Master, Mercers Brigade he says that he will bring anything for me. he goes every second day. he will be in Marrietta tomorrow afternoon, the 4th, at 3 or 4 Oclock. and every other day as long as we are around about this country here which I hope will not be long as I want to advance. he will be in Marrietta on Monday again. something to eat will go right well. All here are well. Capt A[nderson] is at the infirmary about two miles from here. I received your letter of the 24 this afternoon but have never recd yours of the 3rd. I am very glad to hear from Hollie and Santy. Yours of the 26 has also been received. Hoping to hear from you soon I remain

your loving son
Hammie

[P.S.] Send me some stamps

1Lt. Hamilton Branch to Charlotte Branch

In line of battle between
Altoona and Acworth
June 4th 1864
My Very Dear Mother

We remained in the place from which I wrote to you yesterday until last night at eleven oclock when we started for this place, where we arrived this morning at 4 Oclock.it rained almost the whole of yesterday and therefore the roads were in an awful state. last night we were formed into line at 8 PM and kept in line until we started on the march. this morning after building breastworks we were moved from them about 300 yards to this place where we again built breastworks. I am glad to hear that you are taking care of Capt T[w]yman. if you come across Capt [Lewis A.] Piquett of the 63 Ga look after him also. Charlie Davis of my company has been sick sometime and today I have sent him to the rear. if he gets to Atlanta take care of him.

In line of battle somewhere around Marietta
June 5 / 64

We stayed at our old line of battle all day yesterday and until 11 PM when we were formed and marched over the worst road I have ever marched on to this place. we arrived here about 7 Oclock this morning. it rained all day yesterday and almost all night. I am covered from head to foot with mud as I fell down seven times on the march and the mud was from 6 to 18 inches deep. I do not know exactly where we are but think not more than 5 miles from Marietta. Capt Bailey of the Savh Comm was with us yesterday. Good news from Lee is it not [the repulse of the Yankees at Cold Harbor, Va.]. our men are very anxious to turn around upon the enemy and give them a good thrashing and with the help of the Almighty if Genl Johns[t]on will put us upon them we will annihilate them. Old Joe is all right and will give us the word. Write to me and tell me where you are. I sent gave Cousin M some letters please get them and put them away with my private papers.

as ever your devoted and loving son
Hammie

1Lt. Hamilton Branch to Charlotte Branch

In line of battle near Marietta Geo
June 6th 1864
My very dear mother
We have only moved fifty yards to the rear of our position of yesterday, and therefore have had another nights sleep, which has greatly refreshed us and today we are already to go it again. our front line have built breastworks but we do not know that this is to be our permanent line of battle and therefore we are expecting to be moved every moment.

Mother I will now give you a few of my wants. I want some paper and envelopes as the sutlers ask entierly too much for it. also some stamps. also a five dollar bill as I owe a man three and a quarter, and if you have an opportunity do send me about a canteen full of molasses. could you not send home and get a little good syrup from Mrs. Brewer or Aunt Luff and send me a little now and then as long as I am near Marietta.

Mr Reily left here for Marietta again today he says that he has told the Savannah Commitee to save any they get from me and that he would bring it to me. do not send to much as I do not stay long enough at one place to eat much and cannot carry much on a march as there is only Sam Dowse and myself now to carry it.

My friend Captain Piquetts mother is with him in Marietta I believe. I am very sorry for him poor fellow as he has lost a leg. Remember me to Capt T[w]yman. How is he getting along. I recieved your letter of the 1st this morning. if you would send your letters by mail I would get them a great deal sooner as we have a mail every day. if you do not hear from me for several days now and then you must not imagine that I am hurt for I may not be able to write sometimes or that is to send the letters off, especialy if we commence fighting, for Genl Joe J makes everyone go into a fight even to postmasters. if you do not promise me this I will write only once a week or now and then instead of every second or third day as I have been doing, ever since we have been in danger.

Remember me to Cousin M and all the others. also to the folks in Scriven when you write. Did you ever receive my letter with the messages to all the folks around home. let me know the dates of my letter recieved or whether they are connected or not. Praying Gods choicest blessings on you, and that you and we may soon have the pleasure of being together once more. I mean you my darling mother and your two boys who love you with there whole heart.

> I am as ever your loving and devoted son
> Hammie

June 6th 1864

Wonder of wonders we have had another whole nights sleep and have not moved for a whole day. I have spent the day with the Oglethorpes, 1st Ga. they are all quite well. we had quite a nice dinner, viz fried cornbread and bacon for the first course and fried bacon and cornbread for the second course and for desert we had bacon and cornbread fried. you know that I enjoyed the dinner in fact could not help it. strawberries and cream, marmalade, custard, curds, clabber sweet milk, waffles and scrambled eggs are know wheres. I have some letters from my sweetheart that I will send to you in my next. please put them with the letters and papers which I gave you to keep and destroy for me. I have some more letters from some other of my sweehearts and if I have time I will send them to you also. I send one from Mrs. Shaaff read it and put it away with the others and if you desire to *you can read all the others*, although I believe in these times young ladys letters are considered private. what were they in your time. No signs of a fight at present. We are all ready though, the enemy are reported fortifying at the Altoona Heights. With my prayers for Gods blessings on you my darling good mother I remain

> your devoted and loving son
> Hammie

PS I have resolved mother to say my prayers every night and ask Gods help in making me a better boy

1Lt. Hamilton Branch to Charlotte Branch

In the front trenches
near Lost Mountain
June 8 / 64
My Very Dear Mother

After having eaten an exceedingly large dinner, I sit down on a rail with my paper and ink on another rail (the one serving as my stool, and the other as my desk. I have managed this by throwing one end of the third rail of a fence down on the ground for the seat and then using the top one which is flat for a desk. what do you think of the idea.) for the purpose of writing to you. We did not move at all yesterday and therefore had another good nights sleep.

this morning about 7 Oclock Maj [Nathaniel O.] Tilton our Divison Qr Mr called to tell me that he had seen McF[arland?] and that he had told him to tell me that you were well and that he also was to have given him a bundle for me but they had missed one another. about 10 Oclock Fred Hull called and told me that he had a basket for me and so I went over with him and recieved it. just after opening it and takeing the things out we were ordered to fall in and so after giving Lts H[unter] & [Phillip R.] F[alligant]something, Sam [Dowse] and I put the rest into our haversacks and started off. we marched about 1 1/2 miles to this place, after getting my company fixed in the trenches I started to find Sam who had been sent off on guard. I found him at a farm house guarding a garden, he had had the ham boiled and so we sat down under a nice oak and eat our dinner. and we are both now suffering from having eaten too much. the things came safely. the rye bread was a little mouldy, the cake was splendid, also the butter. the biscuits were a little hard, and the ham will do us more good than all. I am very very much obliged to you for the treat and Sam says that he is also.

June 9th 1864

We have not moved since yesterday. I recieved your letters of the 2nd & 3rd last night. I am very glad that you have met with so many friends. Tell Miss Alice Gordon that I should like very much to meet her, as she was always a favorite of mine. ask her if she remembers the hard names that Mrs Roberts called me one afternoon when I was sitting with them on her steps because I thought more of her than I did of Georgia [Elkins].

Remember me to all my friends. tell Mrs [H.C.] H[athaway] that I shall call for the biscuit as soon as this campaign has ended.

as ever your loving son
Hammie

On June 10, when Sherman resumed his advance, Johnston ordered his troops to block the move. Rugged terrain, reinforced by strong fighting trenches and combined with a change in the weather, slowed enemy progress. It rained nearly every day, making the red Georgia clay almost impassable for men and wagons. The Yankees modified their fighting tactics. Instead of massed attacks, they crept forward in small groups of riflemen to pepper the Confederate lines with skirmish and sniper fire, holding the Southerners in one place while Sherman with greater numbers was free to maneuver elsewhere—usually around Johnston's flanks. Every day saw shooting someplace on the line, and sometimes everywhere at once. The casualties mounted.

Johnston fortified three high points north of Marietta—Brushy Mountain, Pine Mountain and Lost Mountain. Mercer's Brigade occupied a forward line of trenches ahead of the left center designed to stall Union advances toward that sector. Sherman's threats beyond the left flank at Lost Mountain caused Johnston to reposition on June 15. He moved his left wing behind Mud Creek, which created some hot moments for Hammie and the Cadets.[73]

1Lt. Hamilton Branch to Charlotte Branch

Skirmish Line of Troops
In front trenches
near Lost Mountain
June 10th 1864
My very dear mother

After writting to you on yesterday the enemy were reported advancing and therefore we were moved to the right about 300 yards to fill up a gap in the lines. this we did, but the enemy observing us, after we had taken our position, opened on us with their cannon and did some very pretty firing, exploding some of their shell just in front of us and striking our battery four of five times. they fired fourteen shots when they found that we had a battery on our left, and they accordingly ceased firing. just before they began with their artilery, we saw their skirmishers make a charge to our left, and retire and then make another charge and take position behind a rail fence. they were about a mile and a quarter from us. after their artilery had fired on us we saw no more of them until this morning, although we were expecting them all night and we were ready for them. this morning about 10 AM we saw their skirmishers make another charge, over the same ground as in yesterday, and pass over the fence which they occupied on yesterday and go into the woods. then a body of troops advanced, and halting at the edge of the woods near a barn on the field through which their skirmishers had charged, they carried the rail fence alluded to and made a breastwork along their line. they then moved back and forward in the old field and drove some cows into their lines. about this time it commenced raining and we were ordered on picket, where we now are. the enemy fired on us as we came here, and their balls are now whizzing all around me but my men are protected by piles of rails and rocks and are safe, unless struck by cannon balls. my head quarters are on the right of my company which is on the top of a good little hill in the middle of and old field, so that I have a good view but have to keep my head down pretty close. their pickets are about 300 yards from me, and are throwing their balls pretty near to me. All the boys here are well. Dr [I.E.] Godfrey told me this morning that Capt A[nderson] was quite sick and that he thought he had pneumonia and that he thought he would send him to a hospital. lookout for him. if he goes I think he will go to the Empire Hospital. Remember me to all my friends especially Miss Alice. Praying that our Heavenly Father will bless you and preserve you I am your devoted and loving son

                                                                        Hammie

On skirmish line
June 11th 1864

The enemys skirmishers continued to fire on us during the whole of yesterday but ceased at dark and did not commence again until this morning. one of their sharpshooters made a very pretty shot at me just now, as I was changing my position from my Hd Qrs to this picket post which is shaded, being covered with brush. he fired at me but I happened to be just passing in the rear of a rail pile and his ball hit that instead of me. I saw a sight yesterday which I do think would make the greatest coward fight, vis just in front of my line and between me and the enemy there is a house inhabited by a man, his wife and six little children with a negro man his wife and four little children. Lt H J [was] put at this house with a squad of men to act as videttes. the enemy fired two shell at this house yesterday which of course scared the inmates and made them take to their cave. J. and we all advised him to move to the rear as there may be a fight here any moment and so after passing the night in great suspense he sent his family off this morning. they past along our line and a ball from the enemy came very near hitting them. I did feel awfuly to see them leaving their home thus. I expect to be relieved from picket this afternoon and will return to the trenches. I forgot to state that our battery shelled the enemy yesterday doing excellent firing. My last letters from you are dated the 2 & 5. Do write. send paper and envelopes as I am out. I have not seen McF yet—With much love

your devoted son, Hammie

P.S. no one hurt on my side yet

1Lt. Hamilton Branch to Charlotte Branch

In front Trenches
near Lost Mountain Geo
June 12th 1864
My Very Dear Mother

We were relieved from picket yesterday about 4 Oclock and sent back into the trenches. whilst the pickets were being relieved, I was standing by a tree with the Lieut who relieved me and two of the men were standing by me. I was showing the men where they were to go when a yankey took a shot at me. his furlough giver struck the tree and fell at my feet—I picked it up. it was pretty well mashed. I got my men all off safely. one of the Lieuts who relieved the company on my left was wounded in the neck just after relieving the company. I am in hopes of recieving a letter from you today as I have not heard from you since the 5th. Do you recieve my letters. they are accounts of my doings every day. Remember me to all my friends at home and where you now are. And hopeing that our heavenly father will continue to bless you I remain

your loving and devoted son
Hammie

Tell Maum Sallie [Sarah, a servant] to take good care of the garden and chickens as I expect to be home next winter and will want a plenty to eat.

Tell Fannie to take good care of all the young ladys for me. Tell Cousin Carrie [McIver] to remember me when she is eating all the good things. Tell Aunt Lufburrow that I would like to have some of her pumpkin or potatoe pies or some clabber and biscuit. Tell Miss Joe that I would like to know how her nose is or weather she has shot any more crows lately. Tell Miss Florence that I would like to know how *he* is for I have not seen him in some time. Tell Elvira that I say that *he* is well but that the first chance I get that I intend to to have him shot to put him out the way. Tell Jennie to be a good girl and not get sick any more. Tell Sallie that Mr Branch has douted and stopped. Tell Willie [another servant] that he need not be afraid of Mr Branch now, for that he is scared himself. Tell Sallie A that she must take good care of you and have my cloths ready for me when I come.

Tallulah Hansell to Charlotte Branch

Oglethorpe
June 13th 1864
My Very Dear Friend

Many thanks for your most welcome letter received a week ago. My engagements are such that I am obliged to write in "odd minutes" or not at all. This warm weather the fatigue is beginning to depress us and I fear that six weeks longer of hard work will make us sick. I was surprized to learn that you were in Atlanta though it is exceedingly kind in you to be nursing our dear brave boys. God bless them! I would like so much to be your assistant. I heard that a dear young friend of mine was in one of the Macon Hospitals quite sick. I wrote a most urgent appeal to the Surgeon in Charge promising to do all I could to cure my friend and then to send him back as soon as he was able to go. I tried all my persuasive powers on the Surgeon but to no purpose as he refuses to let Capt. [William] Spencer come. Don't you think it right hard to refuse me. I have written to him again, hoping that my importunity may avail, but I fear it will be in vain. I was so glad to hear that Lt. Hamilton was still unhurt. May his life and health be very precious in the sight of God. Are you not proving that "hope deferred maketh the heart sick." I am in the *exchange* business. But I have heard twice recently from my friend Lt. [William] Pelham. An intimate friend of his Dr. [Charles] Force [a physician from Washington, D.C.], has been recently exchanged and Lt P sent by him a beautiful little ring to me. The

Yankees are exchanging now *alphabetically*, and it will be a long long time even with *regular* exchanges before his name is reached. I congratulate you that Sanford's turn will come soon. I do so long to hear that he has been restored to you.

We are feeling sad to think how our beloved Georgia is suffering, but try to look on the bright side and hope soon that Sherman will regret his temerity, or that the Yanks will, for I trust Sherman will never live to reach the boundary of the State he has sullied by his vile presence. My brother's daughters are with us as refugees from Marietta. My sister-in-law, despite all entreaties has decided to remain even if it falls into Yankee lines, of which there seems no doubt. I am afraid you will over-work yourself for I have often heard of your self-sacrificing spirit. You must remember your boys and remember *me* too—almost your daughter, am I not? *I* feel so, at all events and hope you do. . . . You must pardon the hasty manner in which I have written, it is late and I do not know when I may have another opportunity. How long do you expect to remain in Atlanta! I have a brother, my eldest brother [Andrew Jackson Hansell], now on Gov Brown's staff. also a nephew in the Corps of Engineers. It will afford me pleasure to have you meet them. Please find time to write to me soon. I am always interested in all that concerns yourself and your family. My Parents and sister Fannie write in love to you. May God preserve and bless you in the constant prayer of your sincere and loving.

Lula H

Sanford was a prisoner at Fort McHenry at this time. Lula was mistaken about the alphabetical order of exchange; there is no evidence that this was ever implemented anywhere except perhaps at Johnson's Island for a short time.

1Lt. Hamilton Branch to Charlotte Branch

In Front Trenches
near Lost Mountain Geo
June 14th 1864
My very dear Mother
Still in front. I do not know why we have not been relieved from this duty yet, our men are fully well worn out. we have one or two men wounded out of the brigade everyday, but have had no one killed. the balls of the enemy are continualy falling about where I now sit—I suppose they fire at

our pickets and fire too high and the balls come to where we are. the enemys breastworks are in full view of us and are distant about 1200 yards. we have not been expecting a general engagement around here. Sherman is not agoing to fight if he can help it, but will flank us as long as he can, and Genl Johns[t]on cannot afford to lose the men that he would if he were to attack the enemy in his works Genls Lee and J. Johns[t]on have got to take care of their men. the army here are confidant that we can whip Sherman in an open fight. we cannot afford to lose Atlanta and the people there may rest assured that this army will have to be whipped before the enemy can have Atlanta.

It has just been reported that Lt. Genl [Leonidas K.] Polk was killed today whilst riding up the lines with Genl Johns[t]on. we are all very sorry for he was a good man. I have seen neither Mc or Mr Stevens who is Mr S. I had to borrow this paper and envelope. I sent you a letter yesterday by Mr Reily. If you should come to Marietta before we fall back from there I will try and get Dr Godfrey to give me a pass as soon as we are relieved from here and come and see you. Keep my cloths. don't send the valise up here for it would be lost without doubt. Remember me to all my friends. As to being engaged I am not and do not intend to be until the war is over. And now my darling mother praying that our heavenly father will protect you and bring us all together again, I remain as ever

your loving and devoted son
Hammie. B

June 15th 1864.

Still in the advance. Private H[enry] Ettinger of my company deserted to the enemy last night. he was a jew, and is no loss to the company. his father and mother went from Petersburg to the enemy about a month ago. a yankey deserter was brought in last night. he is a young Kentuckian, was formerly in our army. he says that he knows nothing. the army are confidant he says of success. You say you recieved my note of the 3rd. did you recieve my letter of the 3rd. How is Miss Alice. Give my kind regards to Capt T[wyman]. I do not see any chance of our being relieved from here at present. All are quite well here. Write soon to your loving son

Hammie

CHAPTER THIRTEEN

Our Loss Has Been Quite Severe

Sherman's advance was halted temporarily, but flanking moves forced Johnston to pull all his forces back. The Confederate defense formed a ragged triangle on the high ground at Lost Mountain, Pine Mountain, and Kennesaw Mountain. Pine Mountain, at the apex, was the first to go in the Union assault, and the Confederate center lay vulnerable before Gen. George Thomas's Union troops. Lost Mountain was abandoned on June 15, as Johnston concentrated all his strength in holding the solidly entrenched Kennesaw line, with the Chattahoochee River to his rear.

1Lt. Hamilton Branch to Charlotte Branch

In main line of trenches
in between Lost & Kenesaw Mountain
June 16th 1864
My Very Dear Mother
    Just after I had finished writting to you on the 15th the enemy commenced shelling our line and after shelling for about an hour when they began to advance and were met by our skirmishers who fought them

bravely, until our line fell back which we did because Genl [M.P.] Lowrey who was on our right had fallen back. it appears that Genl [William B.] Bates who was on the right fell back from some cause or other which exposed Genl L to an enfilading fire and caused him to fall back which he did, first sending a notice to Genl M[ercer] that he was preparing to do so, but before Genl M could order us to fall back he recieved an order from Genl Cleburn to fall back imediately and also a notice from Genl L that he had fallen back and was in the main line. this of course left our right exposed and the enemy took advantage of this, therefore we had to go away around by the left which we did without loss, and took our position at the foot of Lost Mt and in the main trenches here.

we staid until 12 Oclock at night when we were ordered to rejoin our division which was about 1 mile to our right, but we had to go around about way which took us until this morning day break. we are now in the trenches and expect to have a fight but do not know. the enemy are right in our front. We lost several men from our brigade wounded, some killed and about 20 taken prisoner. amongst the killed was 1st Sgt [Harrison] Clay Elkins of the Georgia Rangers, and no man would be missed more than he. a shell came through the breastwork and exploded, breaking his thigh and also striking him in the back. as he was struck, he raised up and cried, They have killed me boys but dont give it up, hold your own, and he continued to tell us to do this until he was carried off. he was taken to the division hospital where he died about 1/2 4 Oclock.

In line of battle 3 miles from Kenesaw Mt and 4 from Marietta June 19th

We remained on the main trenches until 10 Oclock PM when we fell back about 2 miles to this place. I do not think that our right fell back any but only Genl Hardee who was commanding the left. the enemy could have done us a great deal of damage last night, for it was a very still night and their sharpshooters were only 50 and 100 yds from our breastworks in some places. and if they had notified their General and he had opened on us with his artilery which he had in position he could have hurt us greatly for we [were] in range of his guns for an hour after we left the breastworks.

The 1st Ga lost quite a number yesterday in a skirmish Lt Cyrus Carter was mortaly wounded. If you were in Marietta today I could get to you as there is no chance of a fight here today. I think that we will fall back to the Chattahoochee in a few days. Your last letter recieved was dated the 10th. I hope you recieve my letters. I have not seen Mr. Stevens or Mc. yet.

Remember me to all my friends. tell Cousin Maria Mrs. H. that I will try and see them when we get near Atlanta, tell them not to be scared. Have you my shoes and cap, if so keep them for me. I am the dirtiest boy you have ever seen. Praying Gods blessing on you I am your loving and devoted son

Hammie

1Lt. Hamilton Branch to Charlotte Branch

In main line of trenches
near Lost Mountain
Dear Mother
    The enemy attacked us this morning in our front lines and the brigade on our right falling back caused us to fall back, which we did in good order. We were exposed to a heavy fire of shell and minnie balls. None of my boys were hurt. Clay Elkins of Co. I was hit on the leg with a shell, the Dr. says Mortaly. he was a noble boy. he cried they have killed me boys but dont give it up, hold your own. Cpl [James A.] Kesler of the same Co. lost part of a finger and was struck in the face. A Mercifull Father has protected us. Clay is Georgias brother. Praying Gods blessing and protection of you and yours I am your loving son

In line of battle, foot of Kenesaw Mountain
June 19th 1864
My Very Dear Mother
    After writting to you on the 17th we were moved about 3/4 mile to the right and put into the front trenches near the Marietta road. my company was then ordered out on picket but Genl Hardee considering it dangerous for us to go out in the day ordered us to wait until night fall and so we stacked our arms and eat our dinner. the enemy then commenced shelling us and shelled us very heavyly for about 1 hour. at dark we went out in front of our breastworks, that is four of our companys with mine on the right. we were then deployed on the left file of the left company and advanced to form a new line of pickets, as the pickets from Genl Cheathams division whom we were to relieve had been driven in. my company was the only one that herd the order and advanced. we advanced about 500 yards when we met Genl C[heatham's] pickets and I relieved them and found that there was no one on my left, and I imediately went back to try and

find them which I did and was bringing them up when the enemy charged my company and were driven back. I then joined my left to the right of the other companies and prepared to fortify a picket line in the rear of the pickets. we worked all night but did not finish fortifying. the enemy attempted to make another advance but faded during the night. a little before day I put my men into the pits and made ready for the enemy, it then commenced raining and rained hard until about 9 oclock. I made my boys fire as often as they could during the rain so as to try and keep their loads dry. the pit that I was in (the second from the right) became halffull of water and I suppose the others were the same, and about 1/4 8 I found that not a gun in my pit would fire. a Lt. and 30 men from Co. A had been put on my right and between me and Genl [William Henry] Carrolls pickets.

About 1/4 9 it stopped raining and the enemy advanced to my right and extended down just past the left of my company. when they arrived about 40 yds from me I gave the order to rise and fire. the men then got up and told me that the men on my right had fallen back. the men tried to fire but not a gun would fire. seeing then that the men on my right had fallen away back, I gave the order to fall back which we did, the enemy advancing with two lines of skirmishers supported by lines of battle. they advanced until within sight of our batteryes, when they opened on them and the men with the stars and stripes fell back. our men, all but my company and Cos. A & C, were then ordered to advance and three Cos of the 1st Ga to assist them, they advanced and skirmished with the enemy untill night. the skirmishing was very heavy.

I will now give you an account of my self. I sat in the pit until I was cramped all over and chilled. I could not stand up because the breastworks was not high enough and the enemy were fireing the whole time. when I got up I could hardly move. after getting out of the pit, I stoped to look back after my company to see if they were all right. I found that two of the men in my pit were not out. I then told them to get out which they did. I then fell back and got behind the breastworks. as soon as the enemy were driven back by our cannon I was ordered out again, and I reported that not a gun in my company would fire and he ordered me to go and have the loads drawn. I had already ordered Lt. [Charles C.] Hunter to take what men I had with me and carry them out, which he started to do but was shot before he got over the breastworks. he was shot high up in the hip, severe but not dangerous. in the mean time I was looking up the rest of my company who were around the fires in the brigade trying to dry themselves. Lt. [Phillip R.] Falligant then came up and informed me that Lt. H was wounded and I then told him to carry them, the men, around to the brigade ordnance train and I would meet him there. we went there and was informed that the loads could not be drawn and that I had better see Capt Harden who was a mile and half off. I then told Lt. F to take the company back to the breastworks and that I would try and see Capt H. Lt. F did this and was shot very slightly in the calf of the leg. he is here.

I and Sam Dowse went to look after Capt. H but could not find him. I then went into a house and tried to dry myself and then went to sleep and slept until dusk. I then found that we were preparing to fall back and as I was barefooted thought I had better go ahead which Sam and I did. we went until we arrived in Marietta where we found that the army was not coming back that far, but was agoing to stop about 1 1/2 miles from Marietta. we then went to bed upstairs in the Marietta Hotel and slept until morning. hearing here that Lt. F. was wounded I thought that I had best go back which I did but found that Lt. F. did not have to go to the rear. if I had known this I would have stayed and tryed to get me a pair of shoes in Marietta. I have been barefooted two days and it is pretty hard although by the time you get this I will have recieved a pair. if it were not for the rocks I could get along better.

I recieved your note of the 17th today. I could not have gone to see you even if I had recieved it before. if we do not have a big fight in a day or two I could see you if you were here. or if you were here now I might get to see you. Do you recieve my letters regularly, you do not tell me. I write about every other day.

I lost two men killed yesterday, viz P.D. Phealan [Phelan] and Jas Weldon, three wounded, viz Lt. Hunter, Priv. L Bragg and Cpl Thos [H.] Hinely, and four missing, viz Sgt. [Charles F.] Bailey and Priv [James Samuel] Spear, [William T.] Coleman, and [Ira] Payne. I am afraid that some of the missing are killed. I am as well as could be expected but when I first started to retreat from picket I thought sure that they would take me as I could hardly move being cramped and chilled so. Bob Butler is well and all the boys but those I have mentioned. that is they are as well as they can be. I do not know whether they will fight here or not, the enemy followes pretty closelly they are now in our front.

I recieved the paper and envelopes, also the syrup which was splendid. Sam and I have feasted off of it for two days. you do not know how nice it

is. if John Reily goes to Atlanta you can send me a little more of the same
sort. Remember me to all friends everywhere and when you write let me
know how they are getting along in Effingham Co. and Savannah. tell
Cousin Maria that she has not answered my last letter yet. Remember me
to her and Mrs. H. also to Capt T[w]yman. tell him that his battalion [1st
Battalion Georgia Sharpshooters] has only 30 for duty today. Praying that
our heavenly father will in his great goodness protect you and yours. I
remain your devoted and loving son

                                                                    Hammie

1Lt. Hamilton Branch to Charlotte Branch

In trenches left foot of Kenesaw Mountain
June 22nd 1864
My Very Dear Mother

We have remained at this place ever since I last wrote to you, viz on the
19th. we have been busy building the trenches which we now occupy. their
has been constant rains. both of water and minnie balls, for the last three
days, and on the 20th there was a very heavy artilery fire from the anemy.
I recieved your note on the 20th and started imediately to see you. Dr Elliott
of the 1st Ga very kindly gave me a seat in a ambulance, but after riding
100 yds I found that the ambulance would not reach Marietta until
morning with the load it had in it, viz two wounded men and myself, and
I therefore got out and walked to the division hospital, where I arrived
about 10 PM. the roads were in very bad order and my feet were hurt quite
badly by the stones, as I was still barefooted, and my socks were worn out.
I slept with Charlie [Charles W.] Godfrey at the hospital and started next
morning to find you which I did about 10 AM. I felt a great deal better. after
washing and putting on my cloths I felt a great deal better, and the Capt
and I both felt a great deal better after eating the two nice meals that we
did.

after leaving you we went to the Griffin Relief Association and the Capt
getting his things we started for this place, where after wadeing through
the mud we arrived about 7 PM. my company then went on picket and are
still there. they are held in reserve about two hundred yards from the enemy
and about fifty from our picket line. the enemy have been shelling our
trenches, one of their shells exploded in the top of the tree against which
I am leaning and the limbs and leaves fell all around me. it would make

you laugh to see Bill [William Pender], the negro boy, hug the ground. every ball that goes anywheres around us makes him lie close.

We are all and ready for the fight. it is thought that the big fight will come off here as we have no good position to fall back from here on. as we can be flanked behind this better than we can here. Charlie G's shoes fit me pretty well. On the road a man told me I had better fall down and waller as my socks would have to be dirtied anyhow. Remember me to all at Mrs. F tell Miss F. that the corncake was splendid and that I am now agoing to again enjoy some of the molasses. Write to me mother and praying Gods blessings on you I am with much love

your devoted son
Hammie

1Lt. Hamilton Branch to Charlotte Branch

In the trenches
left foot Kennesaw Mt
June 25th 1864
My Very Dear Mother

There is nothing new up here, everything is exceedingly quiet, even the sharpshooters have almost ceased firing. the old saying of there always being a storm after a calm may be proved true up here. some think that we are agoing to fall back whilst others think that we will have the big fight. will take place here. Our guns on Kennesaw have just opened, on what I know not. the enemy are reported moving this morning, I do not know in which direction.

We arrived here safely last night and all the boys are quite well this morning. I met Isaac Cohen [of the Savannah Relief Committee] yesterday as I was coming out. he appeared to be very glad to see me and invited me to come over and see him at the hospital. he said that he would try and give me something to eat. the enemy are shelling us in return for our complements to them from the mountain this morning. I have not seen Capt [William H.] Ross yet, as he has been absent all day. I will see him this evening I expect. Have you heard from home lately. if so how are they all. Bob has not recieved the bundle yet. Charles Miller is still in the hospital. Tell Miss Rebecca that I was so much worried about the provost guard that I did not interupt her talk with the Doctor. Remember me to Cousin Maria and Mrs. H. Also Give my love to Miss Alice Gordon and tell her that I will try and get to see her if I ever come to Atlanta. tell Cousin M. that she has not answered my last letter yet.

Have the Savannah Commitee decided where they will locate yet. You must be ready to leave Marietta and get some of the commitees to let you know when they are ordered off as I do not want you to fall into the enemys hands. When you write to Savannah and up home Remember me to all my friends. if you write to Cousin Mary or Kate tell them to say to Sarah B. that she must remember me when she is having such good times at White Bluff. Praying Gods blessing on you I am

your devoted son
Hammie B.

The threat of Sherman's advance caused the evacuation of Marietta, necessitating the move of thousands of wounded, who were dispersed to makeshift hospital sites around the state. An estimated 12,000 men were in hospitals in and around Marietta during the June 1864 battles.[74]

1Lt. Hamilton Branch to Charlotte Branch

Near Kennesaw Mt.
June 28/64
Dear Mother

I am very well indeed as are all the boys. Capt. Anderson is not very well this morning in fact he ought not to be here in the front. do see Mr. Wynn and try and get some wheat bread from him for the captain as he is not able to eat the cornbread and bacon which they give us out here. if you can send anything out to him that he would relish you will be confering a great favor on this gallant soldier as well as obliging

Your devoted son
Hammie

The Capt will not go to the rear but keeps about here. Remember me to all. Pat Cleburn and Cheatham gave them fits yesterday and Genl Cottrell of Missouri just piled them on top of one another. this was on our right and left. we were not engaged. It is said here that Col. [George W.] Gordons men were surprised yesterday and that they did not act very well.

I will write to you tomorrow. if you can send me a mornings edition please do so. Write me also if you have time. Bill will be in town until about 1 O clock

Hammie

1Lt. Hamilton Branch to Charlotte Branch

Near Kennesaw Mt
June 29/64
My Dear Mother

We recieved the things yesterday evening for which the Capt and I are much obliged. the Capt is looking better this morning and I think that with a little good food and the fresh air of these hills that he will soon be well again. the boys are all well today. everything was quiet around us yesterday I went on the mountain yesterday. I will write to you in a day or two. what was the date of my last letter to you. have you seen little [Albert R.] Hunt of my company. he shot himself accidentaly yesterday. he is at the Infirmary I think. have you recieved my letters since the 10th. have you heard from Cousin Maria, how was she. I am sorry about the potatoes. if I had the ground moles I would give them to the Yanks. I am glad that they are all well at home. I have a pair of shoes, they are new now Miss Jessee W. wrote that she was very glad to hear the report of my capture contradicted. I send you a bag, you can use it for something. With much love
your devoted son

Hammie

1Lt. Hamilton Branch to Charlotte Branch

In the trenches
Kennesaw Mt.
July 2nd 1864
My Dear Mother

Since writting to you last there has nothing of interest transpired. the enemy shelled us almost everyday, and on the 27 after shelling pretty heavyly, they advanced on Genls Cleburn & Cheatham (who are to the left of us) in from three to seven lines of battle, and were repulsed losing about 4000 men. they also charged Genl [Samuel G.] French (who is on our right and occupys Kennesaw Mt) and were repulsed, losing about the same number. amongst the enemys killed were two generals, and one colonel that we knew of, viz Genls [Daniel] McCook & [Charles G.] Harker.

on the 28th Sgt. [William A.] Shaw and myself climbed to the top of Kennesaw, a few of the enemys shell passed over the Mt and exploded near us. a few minie balls also fell around us, but by getting under the rocks when we heard them coming, we excaped unhurt. On arriving at the top we went into one of batterys, and I borrowed a glass from the man on duty there, but was told not to expose myself as the enemy would fire at me from their battery in front of the mt. I looked out of the embrasure and had just fixed my glass when seeing a smoke arise from the battery below, I jumped behind the parapet and the shell exploded just over us. I then went to look again and they fired at the same place, the shell exploding about the same place. the men then told me that their 1st Lt had been killed right where I was standing and so I concluded to move. I then went about ten feet to the left and getting behind some bushes I had a fine view of the country around and of our and the enemys trenches, also of their waggons, a large number of which were parked in two old fields about three miles off. I then started down and arrived at the trenches safe and sound.

I forgot to state that the enemy came on 6 companies of the 63 Ga. who were on picket, before they knew it and killed and captured quite a number of them. they left their dead and wounded on the field. the next day whilst the 54 Ga. were on picket on the line established after this surprise, a wounded man was heard in front of our line, crying for water. Capt. [James N.] Shinholter of the 57 got up, and ran out to him with a canteen of water and telling him to try and crawl into our lines, ran back to his post, the enemy fireing at him all the time. after getting back one of the men said that if anyone would go with him that he would go out and bring the man in. so Capt. S goes out again and with the help of this man brought the wounded man in. the skirmish lines were about 200 yds apart and the man was in the middle of them.

We went on picket on the . . . [letter is torn] anyone being hurt. the enemy commenced earlly this morning to shell us, and shelled very heavyily for about three hours, and in fact they have been shelling us all day but have not advanced. We expect the big fight to come off in a day or two, and if it does we will give the enemy a good whipping, but Genl Johnston may fall back from here, for the purpose of drawing the enemy down to the river. if he does it will be for the best and you may be sure that it will be all right. All the boys are well. Hoping that our Heavenly Father will continue to protect you and yours, and praying that he will give unto your boys new hearts and make them followers of Jesus, I am as ever

your loving and devoted son
Hammie

In line of battle 6 miles from Marietta and 7 from the river
building trenches
July 3rd 1864

As I inferred yesterday we fell back from our posetion, near Kennesaw Mt. At 11 Oclock last night we got off very nicely, the enemy did not bother us at all. we passed through the [Georgia Military] Institute grounds, also through Mr. [Roswell] Kings place. he has a very nice place indeed. We arrived here about 6 Oclock this morning pretty tired as we had been resting such a long time that we were stiff. I mean by resting that we had not been marching. we staid at Kennesaw . . . [letter torn] for all the time and did not have any one at all hurt by the enemy whilst at Kennesaw nor have we had anyone hurt on our march from there. the enemy are now 1 1/2 miles from here. Col. [Robert H.] Anderson is bringing up the rear with his brigade of cavalry.

[John] Mac[Pherson Berrien] has just passed here, he is quite well. they [the Oglethorpe Light Infantry] have had 6 or 7 wounded already to day. I do not know how long we will stay here but expect for a few days anyhow, as long as old Joe sees fit. Anyhow the country here is quite level and neither army will have much the advantage of the other except that we will have our breastworks and they will have to charge them and if they do that we will ruin them, as troops behind breastworks always have a great advantage over those charging them.

Bill will cary this to Atlanta. he comes back on Tuesday. You ought to see me now. I have my head, I mean hair, cut just the heighth of the comb, viz about 1/4 or 1/8 of an inch. also my side whiskers shaved off. All the boys here are quite well and in good spirits. Give my love to Cousin M. Mrs. H and Miss Alice [Gordon]. tell Cousin M. to answer my last letter. And praying Gods blessing on you I remain

your devoted son
Hammie

The Atlanta Campaign became a running battle, a race for life or death as Johnston's army defended against Sherman's blows.

Even with his youth, Hammie was a capable and conscientious officer. His dependability earned him greater responsibilities, which he unquestioningly accepted. The deprivations inherent in the army at this stage of the war were patiently borne, while the smallest diversion was a grateful pleasure. The company spent most of its duty as pickets or digging rifle pits, the deadliness of a sharpshooter's ball ever present.

Johnston ordered Brig. Gen. Francis A. Shoup, his chief military engineer, to prepare two lines of field fortifications between Kennesaw and the Chattahoochee, one at Smyrna, where the 54th's right rested on the railroad, and another at the river, to prevent the Confederate army from being trapped.

The next letter was sent "By Bill" and addressed to Mrs. M.E. Robinson, corner Washington and Peters Strs., Atlanta.

1Lt. Hamilton Branch to Charlotte Branch

In the trenches of Co. F 54th Ga
Smyrna Church
July 4th 1864
My Very Dear Mother
     After writting by Bill we finished building our breastworks and are now pretty well fixed. we had not quite finished a battery that was being built just to our left, when the enemy having driven in the skirmishers, opened on us. they shelled pretty heavyly for a while but our batterys opening on them they stopped. quite a number of our skirmishers have been killed and wounded in the last two days. Lt. Robt [Henry] Lewis of the 1st Ga was dangerously wounded yesterday and Lt. [J.T.] Mann of the 54th Ga dangerously this morning. the enemy brought their artilery up very near our picket line and as they, the picket, only had rail breastworks they were slaughtered in one pit. 5 were killed and the rest (4) wounded, the slightest wound being a leg shot off.
     I have not had any hurt thus far. We are now building a stockade and I expect we will stay here a day or two anyhow. Sherman did not eat dinner in Atlanta on this the 4th of July, nor will he eat there at all unless we send him there, and then he will not be able to stay very long.

In line of battle
1 mile from the Chattahoochee River,
July 5/64

We remained at Smyrna Church until 11 Oclock last night when we fell back to this place. we are near the Atlanta road and are 8 miles from Atlanta. it is thought that we will not cross the river but fight here, but I do not think so. anyhow we are fortifying here. the enemy did not follow us very closely to day, in fact we have not had a gun fired at us today. As soon as we stopped here I heard that there was some potatoes to be bought about a mile from here and therefore I went down and grubbed about two quarts up out of the ground they were very nice indeed. I also got a splendid mess of blackberries and some apples. Last night the enemy had a band playing in front of us and were huzzaying for about three hours as if some one was making them a speech they were evidently drunk. Lt. Mann died yesterday. We are all well. Give my love to all, I have never recieved the paper you gave Charlie G[odfrey]. I recieved a note from him today about it. Praying Gods choicest blessings upon you I am

your loving and devoted son
Hammie

1Lt. Hamilton Branch to Charlotte Branch

In Reserve of Walkers Division 1/2 mile of
Chattahoochee River
July 6th 1864
My Very Dear Mother

After writting to you on yesterday we were moved one mile to the left and placed in position behind a portion of the stockade erected by Genl [Francis A.] Shoup, Genl Johnston's Chief of Artillery. this was the strangest sight we have seen since we have been here. it put me in mind of the fortifications I have read of in the account of the first American settlers lives. It was made thus—on every little rise and commanding every little valey there were built redouts and block houses and all between these there were rails and logs about 12 feet in length stuck up in the ground close together, the whole forming (as some of the men remarked) a wall between the Cornfeds and Wheatfeds, and I would have liked it better if the wall had been 1/2 mile in heighth and had been built farther north. we remained at that place doing nothing until dark when Bill arrived and we went to work with a good will. after eating we were ordered to pull down the stockade and build a breastwork instead. this we did working all night and until 9 Oclock this morning when we were ordered to stop work and fall in. this we did and were moved back into the woods about 200 yds where we dined. immediately after dinner, or in fact before, Capt. Anderson had finished for he had to eat as he was marching. we were ordered off and marched about 1 mile to this place and were put on reserve of our division. as soon as we stopped I put for the river and took a nice bath and put on my clean cloths. I then went back and just as I had arrived and was sitting down writting to you, we were ordered off again and are now (after having marched 1/2 mile to the left) in the trenches, and ready for a fight. we do not know how long we will stay here, and would not be at all surprised if we were moved in five minutes. thus it is we work all night and march all day and rest all the other time. therefore we soldiers have plenty of rest and time to spare. We have not had a gun fired at us now for thirty–six hours in fact there is very little fireing along the lines now. the enemy are shelling our pontoon bridges both on the right and left, and we are now putting some in the center. I do not know whether we will cross the river or not. Old Joe knows what he is at and will take care of us and do what is the best. Praying Gods blessings on you I remain

your devoted son
Hammie

1Lt. Hamilton Branch to Charlotte Branch

In the trenches
2 minutes later
July 6/64
Dear Mother,

Capt. Anderson desires you to get him 1 lb pure coffee and also try and get him 1 lb Charleston coffee (substitute) and have the coffee parched, and then run them through the mill together and then put the rest of the $20 coffee in sugar. Please cover my canteen. have it scoured out and make a new strap out of a piece of one of those Joe Brown shirts and then beg a cork and run the piece of iron through it and send it back by Bill. also try and get my sword scabbard mended and send it back to me as soon as you can. mother please have my cloths washed and then mend them. I recieved three sheets of this paper to day. the young man Charlie G. gave it to thought that [it] was his and used it all up. do try and get my knapsack from our waggons and send me my toothbrush. you can get some of the Q M to get it for you or Mr. Reily will do it. Give my love to Cousin M. and tell her to write to me, and also the next time that she sends me a note by Bill to put her name to it. Also give my love to Miss Alice Gordon and to Mrs. Hathaway. Write to me often and by Bill this time. I wrote to you yesterday. as soon as there is a chance of no fighting I will try and get in to see you. I will have to carry the sick to the infirmary which is about three miles from here in a day or two. send the letter to Lt. Jas Hunter by Express. With much love

your devoted son
Hammie

1Lt. Hamilton Branch to Charlotte Branch

In the trenches
1/2 mile from the Chattahoochee River
July 7th 1864
My Very Dear Mother

As you see by this we have not moved since yesterday, nor have we had more than a half ours work to do. the enemy have given us quite a rest. they are very quiet in the front of us, and the hill's running down into a branch and then going up on there side. they cannot see us, and on account of the bush being cut down in front of us and the hill's being pretty steep, they would have a hard time getting to us. therefore we are let alone. I am very glad of it, for we have been exposed to their fire, and consequently under the necessity of keeping down in our holes, for such a length of time.

If Sherman would only charge Johnston, where he now is, the Yankey Army of Tenn would only exist in name, but Old Joe will have to attack him I am afraid. afraid because we will lose so many of our precious mens lives doing it. We are all quite well and in good spirits, although we do want this falling back to stop. Why do you not write to me. Send me a few envelopes whenever you have a chance as I cannot buy any here.

On Picket Line
July 8/64

After writting on yesterday we were ordered on picket and went out about three hundred yards in front of our trenches, to relieve the 1st Ga.

we arrived there safely and have had quite an easy time of it. We are in a thick woods and have a strong line of videttes about 200 hundred yards in front of us, the enemy are firing all the time and our men reply occasionaly. the balls fired at our videttes pass all around us, we have not had but one man hurt and he was shot by a stray ball a few minutes ago. his name is John Pierce. he was struck in the hand and also in the leg. We will be relieved in a bout an hour. There were two dispatches recieved by the grape vine today, viz that we are to man the heavy guns around Atlanta and also that we are to be sent to Charleston. We are all quite well. Give my love to Cousin M. Mrs. Hathaway and Miss Alice. I have not heard from you since you left Marietta. I do not know what Old Joe intends doing but it will be all right. Praying that God will protect you and yours I am as ever

your loving and devoted son
Hammie

Charlotte left Marietta and went to Bellheim, a house in Effingham County.

1Lt. Hamilton Branch to Charlotte Branch

Bivouac on banks of
Chattahoochee River
July 9th 1864
My Very Dear Mother

We were relieved from picket about 1 hour after I wrote to you on yesterday and returned to our place in the trenches, where we arrived about 8 Oclock PM. We remained there all night and were called at daylight this morning and fell in. we were then marched across the river and on to within about a mile of the railroad where the Savh Comm now are. here we were stopped and I was sent to the division hospital with the sick. after turning over the sick I went on about a half mile father to the Commitee. here Mr. Solomon gave me some bread, butter and honey. I then went back to the hospital and taking the men that were to go back to the front started for my command. I found them about two hundred yards from where I left them, and engaged in building a battery. I then eat supper, and after eating the Capt and myself went down to the river and took a nice bath, from which we have just returned. (I had proceeded thus far when the fire by which I was writting went out.) We found that the brigade had moved about three hundred yards to the right and were lying down in an old field awaiting orders. we staid there until about 11 Oclock, when we were moved back into the woods where we are now agoing to sleep.

July 10th 1864

We had quite a nice sleep last night. Our army crossed over the river during the night and we have taken up the pontoons, and burned the bridge. (about the bridge, I have only heard) we are now in bivouac about 400 yards from the river and the enemy are in plain view on the other side. some of our pickets and some of theirs were in swimming together this morning, but they are now firing on each other. We have been left here as rear guard to keep them from crossing for awhile. our brigade is here and Polks and another. It has been raining for the last hour or two. Much to our surprise the enemy have not planted their batterys opposite to us, nor have they fired a shell at us yet. You ought to see my head now since I have had my hair cut so short. it is about 1/4 inch in length. We are all well and anxious to meet our enemy and not give any more ground up. Praying Gods blessing on you, I am

your devoted son
Hammie

1Lt. Hamilton Branch to Charlotte Branch

On rear guard south bank of the Chattahoochee River July 11th 1864
My very dear mother

I send all my extra clothing to you by William. do not send me any more, until you recieve a request for them from me, as I cannot carry them with me, and on a push one suit will do me for a week or two. The cake from home was very nice although a little mouldy. How about the ham. Where is it? Is it boiled, we have no way of boiling it up here. You had better send the things up for Judge [Brewer], by William. Send me something, never mind what, to eat. if you have the preserves you had better keep them two or three days as I may get to see you, and can bring them out with me.

The Capt. says that if the relief committee have more potatoes or peas or rice than they need that a little would be quite acceptable just now. If you can get a small vial with a tight fitting cork send it to me to carry my ink in. I wish you could see me now that my hair is so short, since my [hair] has been cut it has become quite fashionable to wear the hair short and it is said that on account of the scarcity of finetooth combs in the

Confederacy, Jeff [Davis] is agoing to have all the mens hair cut short. . . .
Mr. Solomon gave me some cloth for handkerchiefs which I am now using.
Write to me by Bill as that is the quickest way. also send an answer to my
request of the 4th. Praying Gods blessings on you I remain as ever

your loving and devoted son
Hammie

1Lt. Hamilton Branch to Charlotte Branch

On rear guard south bank
of the Chattahoochee River
July 11th 1864
My Very Dear Mother
Nothing new turned up after I wrote to you on the 10th. we remained
at the same bivouac in line, until this morning about 12 Oclock when we
fell in and were marched back about 100 yds. so as to be covered by a ridge
of hills. this was done so as to protect us in case we were shelled. About 10
this morning a body of the enemy were seen sitting down under a oak tree
about 1/2 mile off. Capt [Hiram M.] Bledsoe [commander of the Missoui
Battery] imediately threw a shell which, exploding just in front of them,
made them skedaddle for protection. It has been raining for the last two
hours and I am afraid that we will have a bad night of it. I and all the boys
are well. I had a tooth extracted on day before yesterday. it was much
decayed.

On Picket on the river bank of the Chattahoochee near RR Bridge
July 12th 1864
We were ordered on picket soon after I had written to you on yesterday
and came down here to relieve the 1st Ga. We are in pits about ten yards
from the river. this morning we made an agreement with the enemy not to
fire on one another, and so our boys have been amusing themselves all day
talking with the enemy. the troops imediately opposed to us belong to the
20th Army Corps Genl Hooker and are detachments from the 123 NY,
5th Conn & 141 NY & 46 Penn which compose Genl. Knipes Brigade. the
yanks are very anxious to trade for tobacco. they say that they will give
Indian rubber cloths, knifes, coffee or anything for tobacco. For the first
time since we have been out here our whole regiment is on picket together.
All the boys are well and in good spirits. How is Sgt. [Robert] Butler getting.

Remember me to Cousin M. & Mrs. H, also to Miss Alice. And praying
our heavenly father to bless you and protect you I remain

> your loving and devoted son, Hammie

The river was only seventy yards wide, making it easy to call out to one another.
After this incident fraternization was discouraged by orders not to let the enemy
go swimming and to stay on the banks.[75]

1Lt. Hamilton Branch to Charlotte Branch

Bivouac in line
two miles south of Chattahoochee River,
July 17/64
My Very Dear Mother

Since writting to you on the 12th our regiment has been relieved from
picket and is now in the rear enjoying a rest we were relieved by a regiment
from Genl Cheathams Division after being relieved which was about 9 P.M.
we were marched 1 mile to the rear and went to sleep. we [were] called at
daylight 13th and marched to our brigade which had been relieved on the
morning of the 12th. after joining the brigade I was sent off with the sick
to division hospital. after finding it, which I did about 8 Oclock P.M., I went
to Atlanta where I remained until the 16th when I returned to bivouac
and found the regiment still in the woods resting. I went to see Mrs. Gordon
on the 15th. Whilst in Atlanta I dressed in a borrowed biled shirt, calico
jacket and blue pants.

We have no idea up here what Genl Johnston is agoing to do. a great
many think that he will attempt to cut Sherman's Army in two and fight
it by detail. others think that he intends to fall back from here. the army
have vastlly improved by their rest and are being got ready for the next
move, whatever that may be. try and get me a little vial with a tight fitting
cork for an ink stand. Give my love to Cousin M. and Mrs. Hathaway also
remember me to Capt Elliot and tell him that I arrived here safe and sound.
I wrote to you on the 4th about Miss Jennie. did you recieve it. if so please
answer it. With much love and praying gods choicest blessings on you I
remain as ever

> Your devoted son, Hammie

The next letter is addressed to Charlotte at Robinson's in Atlanta, "per James."

1 Lt. Hamilton Branch to Charlotte Branch

In trenches 1 1/2 miles right from RR and 4 from Atlanta
July 19th 1864
My Very Dear Mother

I recieved your letters of the 17th on yesterday whilst on the march from our bivouac, (where we were when I wrote to you on the 17th) to this place. we remained at our bivouac after my last leter was written until yesterday morning at 12 Oclock when we fell in and marched to this, where we arrived at dark. we have built breastworks here but it is thought that they are only to be used in an emergency and that we are to advance on the enemy.

We learned yesterday to our great surprise and sorrow that our beloved gallant commander [Joseph E. Johnston] had been relieved from the command of this army. I never have seen or heard of an army so wrapped up in a commander as this army proved itself to be on yesterday. when it was announced everyone seemed to feel as if they had lost their best friend and the general remark was, well this army is lost, and everyone seemed to be whipped. as for myself I have never felt so downhearted in my life as I did on yesterday, and if we had not have been ordered off, I know that I could not have helped from crying. Genl Johnston had the love and confidence of every man in his army, and not one doubted but that he would annihilate Sherman before he had finished the campaign.

Gnel Hood the present commander of this army is a fighting man and no doubt a fine officer and under him we will gain the victory, but he is not Genl Johnston. On passing Genl Johnston's headqrs. yesterday every company regiment and brigade gave three cheers as they passed, and each marched by with cullors [sic] unfurled. We expect a general engagement soon. All are well. I am

your loving and devoted son
Hammie

Replacing Johnston with Hood proved to be beneficial for the Union. An aggressive, combative man, Hood's strategy was to defend Atlanta by attacking—a mistake for a commander soundly outnumbered and outsupplied.

1Lt. Hamilton Branch to Charlotte Branch

In reserve of troops
in trenches in front of Atlanta
July 21st 1864
My Very Dear Mother

We were sent on picket after I wrote to you on the 19th and went out and built rifle pits on the picket–line. we remained on this line until about 10 Oclock on the 20th when we were ordered to move to the right along the picket line so as [to] be in front of our division. (Hardees Corps had been moved to the right about a mile preparatory to being advanced on the enemy) we marched to the right about a half mile then halted and prepared to advance as skirmishers. we were then moved still farther to the right, and prepared again to advance. but before doing so we were moved still farther to the right. we then found that a line of battle from our division, composed of [Gen. C.H.] Steven's and a part of Mercers Brigades had already advanced and was charging the enemy. in this charge Genl Stevens was shot in the head, supposed to be mortaly wounded. as we were not needed now we were ordered to fall in on the right of Genl [S.R.] Gist who was held up in reserve. this we did and found that the line in front had fallen back thus leaving us in the front.

Capt Anderson was then sent out with Co. A, C & F to act as skirmishers in front of Gist Brigade. just after we were deployed I found that about 300 yds of me and just on the top of the hill a body of men were fortifying. As I did not know whether they were friends or foes, I went and reported the fact to Genl G who ordered scouts sent out to find who they were but the scouts not liking to go I went myself and got within fifty yds of a sharpshooter before I knew it. but he did not fire on me and there I stood looking at him and he at me for a full minute. I then jumped behind a tree and comenced to fall back to the skirmishers. the sharpshooters then opened and we fired on one another until we were relieved which was at 8 Oclock P.M.

We then fell back with Gists brigade to the breastworks, about a mile from where our brigade was in the morning. we stopped behind the breastworks where they passed through some gentlemans place, and a beautifull place it had been, but now alas nearly ruined. we slept here all night, and at daybreak were awakened and marched about two miles to the right along the breastworks. we were then stopped and put in the trenches. we remained here about one hour and a half and were then marched about a half mile to the left, and put in reserve about 50 yards from the trenches and at the foot of a hill.

we are now lying down here and trying to rest. we do not know what the next move will be. I have not heard officialy the result of the fight on yesterday, but it is reported that Genl [George] Maney commanding Cheathams Division forced the enemy back on the left a mile and into the Peachtree Creek, and Genl [William B.] Bates with his division did the same thing on the right. Genl [C.H.] Stevens had to charge up a hill about a quarter of a mile in length. the right of his brigade drove the enemy back to the creek also, but owing to the formation of the ground and the strength of the enemys position the left (where Genl Stevens commanded in person and where he was wounded) was not able to dislodge the enemy and consequently the right had to fall back.

we lost quite a number but I understand the enemy sufered a great deal more. I did not have any one hurt in my company and only one or two were wounded in the regiment I believe. We are all well. Sam Dowse has gone to the division hospital, he is quite sick. Why have you not written to me. I have not heard from you since the 17th. How is Bob. Remember me to Aunt Lizzie and Bob, also to Cousin M when you write. Praying our heavenly father to give you strength to bear up under all your trials I am as ever

your loving devoted son
Hammie

This action became known as the battle of Peachtree Creek. Confederate losses were reported as 4,796 to a Union loss of 1,710.[76]

1Lt. Hamilton Branch to Charlotte Branch

In trenches 2 1/2 miles S/E from Atlanta
July 23rd 1864
My Darling Mother
    After writting on the 21st we were moved from reserve into the trenches about a mile to the left. we remained here until dark when we fell in again and were marched through Atlanta and about 6 miles beyond and in the direction of the East Point. we arrived at the 6 miles about 2 Oclock A.M. We were then halted and went to sleep. We slept until daybreak when we

were formed and marched on about 6 miles. this brought us in the rear of
the enemy. we then formed line of battle. Cheatham on the left next
Cleburn then Walker and Bates on the right. one half of each division was
in the front line and the other in the rear. in this way they forwarded
through the woods and charged the enemy. we did not charge but were
kept under a heavy shelling. here a shell killed Charlie Davis and wounded
John Breen [and] J.E. [James Elkin] Dennard. After staying here about 1
hour we were ordered to charge the enemy in our front so as to relieve Genl
Cleburn who had charged and taken two lines of the enemys breastworks,
and Gist and Stevens having been repulsed left him liable to be flanked
and cut off. we advanced on the enemy who were formed in this shape
[here he has drawn a trench at angles showing Mercer's position and the
Union position] and had their artilery posted all along the front line.

we advanced about 200 yds when it was found that it was madness to
advance our little brigade and therefore we ordered to halt and after awhile
to fall back. we fell back to our old position and were then ordered to join
with Cleburn on our left. this we did and were then marched to the right
a little ways and formed line of battle in an old field. Gnel Lowrey then
came gallaping up to us and told us that we now had the yanks where we
wanted them, and that now we would charge them and not leave one to
tell the tale, and says he, I know that you are just the boys to do it.

we then advanced about a quarter of a mile through the woods and then
with Lowreys Brigade on our right we charged one line and drove them
from it. we then jumped over this line and charged the second and drove
them from that also. here the big mistake was made, for we were ordered
to halt. the enemy were now behind another line about ten yards in front
of us and pouring a galling fire into us, for the line that we had taken had
three gaps in it and through these they fired on us. it was here that Lt. Col.
[Morgan] Rawls was wounded and Maj. [William H.] Mann, Lt. [Joseph
H.] Gnann Co. I, and [William] Neyle Habersham and A.M. Wood Co.
F, besides others killed. Pvt. Geo. Waters, R.E. Brantley, A.L. Sammons
were wounded in the charge and M[artin] Henges was wounded by a stray
ball. in the morning Ike [Isaac] Barren was also slightly wounded. Tom
Mell is missing. the other boys are all well. If we had not been halted in the
second line we could have taken the third line and thus cut two corps of
the enemy off, but as it was we had to remain behind the second line and
keep firing at the enemy and they at us, both behind breastworks and only
20 yds apart.

We remained in this position until 12 Oclock, when we were ordered to establish a picket line and then fall back. this we did to the lines that Cleburn had taken and we have now fortifyed ourselves, and are awaiting the next move.

We have punished the enemy severely, killing a great number and taking a quantity of prisoners and a number of guns. Our loss has been quite severe. Genl Walker is killed and Genl Gist wounded. the gallant Lt. Joe Clay Habersham is also killed. Several Colonels in our division are killed. Poor Mrs. Habersham. The Yankey General [James B.] McPherson is reported killed and Genl Blair captured. whilst behind the breastworks one of Cleburns men gave me a sword which he had captured I have sent it to the Relief Commitee to be forwarded to you. also I have sent you some stamps given me by George Patten for you. With thanksgiving to our heavenly father and prayers that he will guard you I remain

your devoted son
Hammie

[P.S.] Capt [John] Scriven Turner and Lt. Oneal [Henry T. O'Neill] of the 1st are killed.

On the Battlefield
July 23/64 My Darling Mother

We charged and captured the enemys works on yesterday. Habersham, Davis, and Wood are all that I know off being killed in my company. John, Charlie, and myself, thanks to our heavenly father, are safe. Maj [William H.] Mann and Capt Scriven Turner and Lt. Habersham are killed. Col. [Morgan] Rawls and Col. Olmstead are wounded. Return thanks to God and pray for me

Your devoted son
Hammie

The daylight hours of July 23 were spent in a cautious truce, as the dead of both sides were buried by comrades. After writing to his mother, Hammie was ordered into the trenches on the Confederate right around 8:00 P.M. that evening, with his company and Co. I as pickets. The morning of July 24, his post was attacked by a Union force, which was successfully driven back. On moving down the trench to reform his line, Hammie was hit in the shoulder by a random ball. Upon examination and treatment, the damage was determined to be severe enough to warrant a thirty-day furlough. He and his mother, who was then near Atlanta, went to Effingham County, their temporary home. He would not return to the army for two months.

While home in Savannah, Hammie paid a visit to the brother of Charlie Davis, the friend who had been killed at Atlanta. The visit prompted the following reply from Charlie's brother, who was in the Savannah Volunteer Guard as a signal man and telegraph operator.

P.D. Davis to Hamilton Branch

Whitmarsh Island
Turners Rock [Battery]
Aug 2h /64
My Dear Friend.
I have received several letters from *Father* since the *death* of my *dear, beloved*, and *idolized Brother*. Oh my God how it *pains* my *poor broken heart* to use that word in connection with the *dear, gone one's name*—*gone from earth forever*—yes *never, never*, will I (one who *loved* & held him ever dear to his sick heart) see his *bright* & sunny face again, upon this earth—Hammy I have always *wished* & *hoped* if either of us were to be sacrificed for our countrys good—It should be me. But alas! the next thing I hear, he is *dead*, yes *gone from me forever*, and I left behind—to mourn the *dear ones death*—You knoweth not my dear friend—the *pain*, & *suffering* of my *poor, broken heart*—I am wandering from the subject I commenced to write you on it is this—I have heard from Father frequently since I last saw you And he says, he has not heard a word from *John Anderson* —Do Hammy if you can possiblely do so send me a description of the ground & place, where our dear *beloved*, & *noble Charley,* was buried. I am exceedingly anxious to see you again. The morning you were here I felt so *sad*, & *badly*, I hardly know what you *told me* about the dear one. If you can not come (but I truly hope you can) write of the description, and give it to my Boy or leave it at Dr. Harris' house.

I can *think of nothing* all *day*, & *dream of nothing* at *night*, but the *dear, gone one*. My heart is full of revenge and when I can get among the *vile, low*, & *degraded poltroons I shall have revenge. And my revenge will be great.* come out if you can possible do so . I would come in and see you but as I am the only one at my post, that will be impossible—

Your aff, sad & bereaved friend P.D. Davis

CHAPTER FOURTEEN

I Think It the Most Gallant Fight of the War

The shoulder wound that sent Hammie home in August 1864 probably saved his life. Gen. Hood ordered another reckless assault on the Union lines at Ezra Church, Georgia, on July 28 that cost the South 5,000 lives. After losing nearly 20,000 men in a little over a week, Hood was forced to withdraw into the last ditch fortifications in Atlanta.[77]

August dragged by under seige. While Hammie was recovering at home, the Savannah Cadets suffered the fate of the 54th Georgia at the battle of Jonesboro on August 31, the last battle for Atlanta. With his arm still in a sling, Hammie left Egypt on September 3 and reported back to his company around September 7. He found the 54th temporarily under the command of his old friend, Col. Charles Olmstead of the 1st Georgia, but many familiar faces were missing, claimed by the war.

1Lt. Hamilton Branch to Charlotte Branch

On the Road
Sept 4 1864
My Very Dear Mother

I met Mary [Marie Eugenia] Dickerson [age 15] on the cars Saturday night. she was alone and on her way to school. she begged me to stop over Sunday with her at her fathers and then excort her to school. she would have to go by herself if I did not go with her and therefore after seeing Genl Cumming and Derry Lamar at Millen and hearing from them that there would be no more fighting for a week or so I determined to stop with her, and here I am. Mother please send one of the best of my photographs to Mrs. Shaaff as soon as you can. just enclose it in an envelope and direct to Mrs. Arthur Shaaff care Capt H.J. Dickerson Savh. I am still in good health and fine spirits.

I met Cousin Lans Co. on its way to the front this morning [Co. E, 1st Regiment Local Troops, Forest City Guards of Augusta]. I expect to be in Griffin tuesday. Write to me often directing Co. F. 54 Ga. Mercers Brigade, Cleburns Division, Hardees Corps, Army Tenn. With much love I am as ever

your devoted son
Hammie

The next two letters from Hammie to Sanford were written while the latter was held prisoner on Morris Island.

1Lt. Hamilton Branch to 1Lt. Sanford Branch

Bivouac Cleburns Division
Sept. 7th 1864
My Dear Brother

As you see by this my arm has healed enough for me to return to duty. I left Mother on the third. she was very well, only anxious to hear from you. your last letter was dated the 24th July, the very day on which I was wounded. Joe [Josiah Law] Holcombe was killed on the 31st Aug. all the other boys are well. Mother has heard from Capt. Jackson. When you write remember me to Hollie Cole and Willie White, also to [George Norris] Saussy. Mort Davis is to be married on the 8th. Have you ever heard from your *dear uncle* and *aunts*. Write to me at Savannah. Hoping that this will find you well and that we may soon meet again.

I am as ever your loving brother
H. M. Branch

On September 10 the generals agreed on an armistice to last ten days. While it was in effect, Hood allowed his men to go home. The army was reorganized, and the 54th Georgia was placed in Cleburne's Division, Gen. Walker having been killed. The army was readied for a new strategy—a march into Tennessee to confront the Union army under Maj. Gen. George H. Thomas at Nashville. Their mission was to cut the Union supply lines and pull Sherman back into Tennessee.

On September 18 the rested Army of Tennessee marched toward Newnan, Georgia, following the West Point railroad. Brig. Gen. James Argyle Smith was given command of the brigade. Phillip R. Falligant, captain of Co. F, 54th Georgia, who had been furloughed for illness, suffered a relapse as he hastened to rejoin the Cadets. He died on the road, leaving the company without an officer.[78]

Hood and Sherman faced each other warily; neither hastened to act. On September 26 Hardee's Corps was reviewed by President Jefferson Davis who was "greeted by vociferous cheers along the entire line."[79]

On September 24 Hammie was wounded again, this time in the thigh, and once more he was furloughed home.

1Lt. Hamilton Branch to 1Lt. Sanford Branch

At Home
Sept 28/64
My Dear Brother
Yours of the 29 was recieved this morning and I was very glad to hear that you were well and I hope that you may soon be with us. My wound has healed up splendidly and I am enjoying splendid health. Mort Davis was married about the first of the month. All your friends are well as are also all at home. There has been church up home every day for the last week. All the ducks were there and I enjoyed myself very much. My dear brother if you need any thing write to me and let me know and I will send it to you. When you write remember me to all the boys at Point Lookout. With much love and hoping to see you soon I remain

                                    Your affectionate brother, Hammie

Gen. Hardee requested a transfer to Savannah and was put in command of the coastal defenses and city. His replacement was Maj. Gen. Benjamin Cheatham, the last corps commander the Savannah Cadets would have.

The Confederates crossed the Chattahoochee River on September 30 on a miserable march northward that took them within sight of Lost Mountain and the Kennesaw defenses, through Big Shanty, Cedar Town and Calhoun. A shortage of rations and water complemented the discomfort of cold mountain nights. On October 13 Cleburne's Division hit the railroad several miles below Dalton, then crossed the Alabama line west of Alpine, Georgia, on the 18th. On the 20th they were in Gadsden, Alabama, where they were joined by several members back from furloughs. They crossed the summit of Sand Mountain, a ridge running the length of northern Alabama, a thirty-five mile march, with no water, on October 24–25. When they arrived on the outskirts of Decatur, Alabama, on October 28, they were issued rations—two ears of corn per man. Reduced to half this amount, they marched twenty miles on October 30, arriving at Tuscumbia, Alabama, on All Hallows' Eve.

About this time Charlotte received a letter of appreciation from one of the soldiers she had nursed near Atlanta.

Capt. Horace D. Twyman to Charlotte Branch

Oak Hill Madison Co. Va.
Oct. 22nd 1864
My Dear Madame,

   I have long contemplated writing you but being ignorant of your post office I determined to delay until I could hear but all of my correspondents have failed to give me the desired information and this morning I have resolved to write one, send it to Savannah, with the hope that some of your numerous friends will forward it to you. I have no doubt you have heard through Mr. Crane & others of my secure arrival home. and I am glad to be able to report myself still improving, though comparatively speaking, helpless as yet. I am wedded to two crutches with but little prospect of escaping them very soon. My health with the exception of my wound is all that I could ask, and without exaggeration I suppose I have fattened thirty pounds since reaching home. Pieces of the fractured bones are still coming from my wound and every symptom of continuing for some time. I have high hopes of being able to rejoin my command by the coming Spring campaign but very much fear I will not be fit for Infantry service again.

   Much to the disappointment of us all Atlanta fell and I hope is about to fall again. We can get no authentic news here from Gen. Hood. I have heard that he was last seen at Dalton. I would give my all to be with him now but impossible. I regretted to see the old and tried veteran Johnston removed, for he was my first choice in the Confederacy, excepting Gen. Lee, and his being removed from command does not cause me to appreciate him less. His every act displays signs of Generalship of the first magnitude, but as the change has been made it becomes us all as loyal Confederates to give Gen Hood, his succcessor, a united and earnest support.

I received a letter from Lieut. Bryan of our Batt. a week or ten days ago and he gave me the melancholy news of the fall of many gallant and good officers in the Batt. and Brig. Every fight that I hear of in Georgia I think of your anxiety for your son, but I hope earnestly and sincerely he has escaped with a wound no worse than the one received at Atlanta before I left. Lt. B [Hammie] wrote me in the fight at Jonesboro we lost three of the most popular officers in our Batt. Lt. [Josiah Law] Holcombe, Lt. [S.W.] Lawrence, & Lt. [Henry] Herrmann. I wrote to Mrs. [Isaac] Cohen not long ago but have not heard from her since. she was then grieving and regretting the fall of Atlanta—Give her my kindest regards when you see her. Did Mrs. Robinson get out of Atlanta before its fall? That was an infamous order of Sherman banishing the inhabitants of the place and requiring them to move either North or South.

I notice in the papers that Savannah has become a point for the exchange of prisoners, which will tend to revive the spirits of the place, in the absence of a threatening Army. I thought when there it was the safest position I knew of any where in the Confederacy and my opinion has not been changed since reaching this section, for there has not been scarcely a week since I reached home that I have not been annoyed and threatened by small Yankee Raiding parties. Winter is now about here and I hope that will keep them quiet and let me remain in peace what time I have to remain.

My family desires to be remembered to you and my mother wishes me to say she feels peculiarlly indebted to you for your kind and unceasing efforts in protecting and taking care of me during my sickness in a land of strangers, and hopes yet she may have an opportunity to return it, that she may show by action as well as by word the great appreciation she has for you as the preserver of my life. It is useless for me to repeat my appreciation of your invaluable and kind service to me, as I have reiterated it to you over and again. the more I meditate over my critical condition the more deeply indebted do I feel to you, Mr. & Mrs. Cohen & Mr. Crane. I must beg of you to excuse my delay in writing, but ignorance of your Post Office is what produced it. Hoping this directed to Savannah will reach you safely, I remain

With high respect
Yours, most truly
H.D. Twyman
Somerset P.O., Orange Co. Va.

P.S. Remember me to Mr. Crane & family, & also your son Lt. B.

While his comrades marched overland to confront Gen. Thomas in Tennessee, Hammie struck out to rejoin them, travelling west by train to Griffin, then south to Mobile, Alabama, where he spent a few pleasant days in female company before returning to the hardships of army life.

1Lt. Hamilton Branch to Charlotte Branch

Battle House, Mobile Ala
Oct 30/64

We remained in Montgomery until the afternoon of the 28th when took the train on the Ala & Fla Rail Road to Pollard and then the train on the Mobile and Great Northern RailRoad to the Ala River and then took the [steamer] Senator and went 20 miles down the river to Mobile. from the Senator we had a fine view of the enemys fleet as well as our own and land batteries. Mr. May took Willie and myself out to ride. we went to Mr. Mays place 5 miles from Montgomery and then on the way back we stopped to see the Miss Shaws of Washington N.C. I also called on Miss Beasely three times and enjoyed myself very much. Miss Bettie is a very nice young lady. she sewed bars on my collar for me. We leave here this afternoon for Corinth. Mobile is quite a city. it is very much like New York. I am of the opinion that Mobile can be taken if the enemy try very hard. Bob Grant is here and will leave with us. I do not know when you will hear from me again. . . . And praying that God will bless you I am as ever

your devoted son, Hammie

1Lt. Hamilton Branch to Charlotte Branch

Okalone Miss
Nov 1st 1864
My Dear Dear Mother

   I left Mobile Ala at 4 P.M. of the 30th, the day on which I last wrote to you, and traveling all that night arrived at Artesia 215 miles on the Mobile and Ohio RR at 12 M on the 31st. there learning that we would have to be over at this place all night, we determined to visit Columbus Miss which we did arriving there at 2 P.M. We remained there until 9 1/2 this morning when we left and at 12 took the Mobile and Ohio again and arrived at this place at 4 P.M. we have secured a house to sleep in and have had a very nice supper and will have a beakfast before we leave here, which will be at 10 1/2 to morrow morning. we will then leave for Corinth Miss, Tuscumbia, Ala and Pulaski Tenn. I have passed through Enterprise, Meridian, and Columbus. also pass Macon and Egypt. Egypt is just 7 miles from here. I passed there at 3 P.M. and wished very much that it was Egypt, Ga. At Columbus Miss I met Mrs. E.B. Waddell a sister in law of Hugh Waddell. she is a very nice young lady or that is lady for she is about 30 years of age. I do not know when you will hear from me again as this is the end of the mail route. And now praying that God will bless and protect you and yours I am as ever

                                    your loving and devoted son
                                                      Hammie

[P.S.] I bought two very nice watermellons in Columbus Miss one of which I have now. God bless you my darling mother. Hammie. Give my love to all enquiring friends.

1Lt. Hamilton Branch to Charlotte Branch

Corinth Miss
Nov 3 1864
My Very Dear Mother

   I have just met Charlie Hunter who is here on his way to Savannah quite sick and as I promised to write to you by the first opportunity, I now do so. I arrived here last night, after having passed through Verina, Tupelo, Baldwin and Rienzie, and am now quartered on the floor in what was once the Tishomingo Hotel, but expect to leave in a few minutes for Cherokee Ala. and from there for the army. I am in find health and good spirits. my leg though is just the same, still running, although I have not felt much inconvenienced by it yet. You need not be surprised if you hear that Hood is at this place for I think he will come back here before long, although no one knows. Give my love to all my friends. I wrote to you from Mobile and Okalona. God bless you my darling mother. May he protect and bless you is ever the prayer of

your devoted son
Hammie

1Lt. Hamilton Branch to Charlotte Branch

Bivouac Cleburns Div Tuscumbia Ala
Nov 7th 1864
My Dear Dear Mother

After writting to you from Corinth Miss, I got on board the train for Cherokee Ala. after going about three miles the engine stalled and we all had to get out and push her up the hill. we then got in and went about 1/2 mile when she stopped again. we had the same luck all day, and suceeded in getting 14 miles during the day. at night the wood gave out and we had to lie over all night. this was at Byrnesville, Miss. the next morning we ran down about a mile and had some wood hauled to us by waggons. we then went about 4 miles, when the engine again stopped and also one of the cars ran off the track. the engine then took the first five cars and carried them about 3 miles to Iuka Miss and leaving them there went back after the ballance of the cars of the train. returning with them, she then hitched on to the whole of the train and going on her way arrived at Cherokee Ala at 3 Oclock P.M. having been 28 hours going from Corinth to Cherokee, a distance of 30 miles. I left Cherokee at 4 and marching along the railroad about 5 miles stopped all night in a church. the next morning I marched to Tuscumbia Ala, a distance of 10 miles.

After remaining in this place three or four hours I went out to camp which is about 1 1/2 miles from Tuscumbia and about 300 yds from the river. here I found all the boys looking very well after their rest. [James Potter] Williamson and [William F.] May, Capt. [James J.] Lachlison, Lt. [John K.] Bedell and myself came together and are all well. Judge and Tom [Thomas A.] Brewer are both here and are quite well. also Lt. George

Brewer a cousin of Miss Joes is here and is quite well. tell Miss Joe that I had a talk with him yesterday in regard to my being married, but as he is a fine looking young man and did not mean me but Lt. M. Branch of Co. B, I have concluded not to kill him but to let him off.

Harmon Elkins is all so here quite well. Doctor Godfrey examined me yesterday and says that if I will let him cut that place again and put costik in it that he will warrant to cure me in two weeks but as it does not inconvenience me very much I have concluded to let it go on as it wants to until it either gets better or worse.

Remember me to all the people around home and in Savannah. Tell Sarah Brigham that I shall expect a letter from her. I do not know where we will go or what we will do but I would not be surprised if we went back somewhere between here and Corinth and spent the winter. I think that it is almost too late to go into Tennessee. We do not know anything about Sherman. [Major General Nathan B.] Forrest has brought up the four transports that he captured and they are now being unloaded at Florence [Alabama] four miles from here. the two gunboats he captured are now patrolling the river. God bless you my darling mother.

as ever your devoted son

Hammie

In early November, having caught up on the news from his comrades, Hammie wrote a summary of the unit's activities the previous August and September, when he was furloughed home with his wound.

1Lt. Hamilton Branch to Charlotte Branch

Hd Qrs Co. F 54th Ga Reg
Smith's Brigade, Cleburne's Division
Cheatham's Corps, Army of Tenn
near Tuscumbia Ala
Nov 8th 1864
My Very Dear Mother

Since writting to you on yesterday we have not moved, and there is nothing new here. I will try and give you an account of the moves of my company during my absence. After I had written to you on the 23 of July we were moved about 1/2 mile to the right and put in the trenches at 8 PM, I having at the request of the men been put in Command of Co. I, was sent out with Co.'s I and F to relieve the pickets of [R.C.] Tylers Brigade, this I did. the next morning the enemy advanced on my line and I drove them back, and was going over my line when I was wounded in the arm and went home with you. my company the next day was moved back to where we were on the 20th and a day or two afterwards were moved to Peachtree St. Atlanta where they remained a day or two and were then moved farther to the left near East Point where they remained about two weeks when they were moved farther to the left and down the M & W RR two miles. here they remained about a week when they were moved down the road about two miles and built rifle pits. the next day they were moved along the works to within 10 miles of Jonesboro and that night the[y] marched to Jonesboro where they arrived on the morning of the 31 Aug. They then charged with the division and ran the Cavalry under [Brigadier General Hugh J.] Kilpatrick about 1 1/2 miles when they learned that [General Stephen Dill] Lee's Corps had fallen back, and they then fell back to their breastworks. The next day the enemy made a feint in front of our boys and massed their troops in front of [Brigadier General Daniel C.] Govans Brigade. They then charged Govan three times and were repulsed each time. they then massed a solid body of men 75 feet deep and walked over Govans Brigade capturing Govan and a large number of his men (about 300).

that night our Corps fell back to Lovejoy where they were joined by the rest of the army. here they remained about a week when the enemy having fallen back, they were moved back to near Jonesboro here. an armistice having been granted they remained about two weeks when they were moved to Palmetto. here they remained until the 29th Sept (whilst here they were reviewed by the President) when they went to within two miles of the Chattahoochee and the next morning they crossed the river and marched to within 8 miles of Powder Springs, having crossed Dog River, where they remained 4 days when they marched in a heavy rain 9 miles and remained all night in the woods. the next morning they crossed the Coosa River and remained all night 1 mile from the river. the next morning marched to within 8 miles of Rome. they then went to Cedartown, Cave Springs and several other little places. they then went to Dalton and destroyed the rail road from their to Tilton. the next day they marched 19 miles from Dalton. they then marched through those valleys and went to Blue Pond. they then marched to Gadsden where they remained two days and then went to the top of Sand Mt. where they remained three nights, or that is they were that time crossing it. they then marched to near Summerville. they then marched to Decatur where they remained two days. they then marched three days when they arrived at this place where they have now been 7 days. This is as near as can gather from the boys memory. Your devoted son

Hammie

Nov 9th 1864

We have not been moved yet although we expect to go every hour. no one knows where we will go although most people think that we will make a big raid into Tennessee and then go into winter quarters somewheres around here. we were ordered to march this morning at sunrise but the order was countermanded. The river is very high today, and may possible keep us here a day or two longer. Was it not a pity that we could not save Forrests last capture, I mean at Johnsonville. just to think what a help it would have been to us, 4 Gunboats 11 steamers, and 17 barges loaded with supplys, besides the houses and wharves filled with supplys. it was too bad that he had to burn them all. I think that 75,000 to 120,000 tons is a pretty large amount of stores for the yanks even to lose, and I think it will tell on Sherman.

If we cross the river you must not expect to hear from me until we come back, for I will not have any way of sending a letter off. Give my love to all my friends. Tell Miss Joe that I have not seen her sweetheart yet. Have you heard from my poor dear brother lately. I have not recieved a letter from you yet. Harmon Elkins, Judge and Tom Brewer are here and are quite well. My leg is about the same, no better or worse. We have been having rain ever since I have been here. God bless and protect you my darling mother. Write soon and often to

your devoted and loving son, Hammie

1Lt. Hamilton Branch to Charlotte Branch

Hd Qrs Co. F, Smith's Brigade
Cleburnes Division, Cheathams Corps
Army of Tenn near Tuscumbia Ala
Nov 12 1864
My Dear Dear Mother

I recieved your leter of the 30th Oct this morning, and was very glad to hear that you were quite well, but sorry that you had not heard from me as I have written 5 times to you, and I hope that you have recieved some of them before now.

Genl Hood disclosed his plans to the army today. he intends to strike at some point before the winter sets in. this point is on the Nashville and Chattanooga RailRoad, and he expects to strike it and then open communications south. then he will go into winter quarters. Forrest will have command of our cavalry. Genl H expects to be successfull and do great things. he does not intend to fight over his number, but will fight Sherman wherever he meets him. Sherman has now one corps at Huntsville, one at Stevenson, one at Chattanooga, two at Marrieta and one at Atlanta. our corps are all in the right place.

we are having fine weather now, pretty cold, as the men most of them are without blankets. the river is rising and has been for a week. we would have been on our way now but for our pontoon being too short, but it will all be right tomorrow, and then we will go. I do not know when you will hear from me again, but you must not be anxious about me, for I hope it will all be well. I hope my dear brother may soon be exchanged, and that he may remain with you. [James] Williamson is still here. Bob [Grant], Harmon [Elkins], Judge and Tom [Brewer] are all well. And now my darling Mother hoping that Our Heavenly Father will watch over you and bless you, and that he will guard your boys and make them followers of his, I remain your loving and devoted son

Hammie B.
Love to all.

Despite Hood's optimism that Sherman would break off his assault on Georgia and pursue the Army of Tennessee if they threatened the Union supply lines, his own supply system had all but broken down. Many men were barefooted and short of blankets and clothing, and morale was beginning to decline. The Confederate commander, Gen. Beauregard, was concerned, yet Hood's close relationship with Jefferson Davis prevented Beauregard from challenging the plan.

Long and hard marches in the incessant, chilling rain took a physical toll on the exhausted men. At night they shivered under thin blankets; during the day they slipped and stumbled on roads either muddy or frozen. "We had to walk in the middle of the road," wrote J.M. Miller, a Mississippi soldier. "In some places the mud and water would be knee deep."[80]

1Lt. Hamilton Branch to Charlotte Branch

Bivouac Cleburne's Division near Florence Ala
Nov 13th 1864
My very dear mother

We left the bivouac from which I wrote you on yesterday at 8 Oclock this morning and marched to the Tennessee river opposite Florence. we then crossed the river on a pontoon bridge. (the river here is very wide and there is a great strain on the bridge). we then marched through the town which is a very pretty little place, and where there were plenty of young ladys. we then marched about a mile where we are now bivouacing. I have sent Bill to town with two pr of socks to have darned for me. I think we will leave here tomorrow morning, although we have just heard that the pontoon bridge has broken. if this is so we may stay here a day or two. We are now 45 miles from Savannah, Tenn but we will not go there as it is out of the way.

Nov 15th 1864

Contrary to expectation we did not move yesterday but remained in camp bivouac until 8 Oclock A.M. when we were formed without arms and marched to within a mile of Florence, where we were put to work fortifying. we worked all day and went back to camp about 5 Oclock P.M. It rained almost all night, and this morning we are again at work with our fortifications. we will finish them today, and then I expect if everything is ready that we will move on. we are fortifying here so that in cas[e] we fall back we can cross the river under the cover of these fortifications. We are all well and in good spirits but anxious to move forward. Williamson was at work all day yesterday. Harmon, Judge and Tom are all well. This will be my last I expect for some time. Love to all I hope Santy is with [you]. God bless you both.

Your loving son
Hammie

Sanford was confined at Fort Pulaski at this time. He would not be exchanged for another month.

1Lt. Hamilton Branch to Charlotte Branch

Bivouac Cleburnes Division, near Florence Ala
November 19th 1864
My Very Dear Mother

After I had written to you on the 17th we were ordered to go out and strengthen our works which we did, and they are now cannon ball proof. and on yesterday there was a detail sent out to build rifle pits in front of the works, which they did, and we are now strongly fortified at this place and are only waiting for fair weather and more supplys before we advance into Tennessee. We have been having rainy weather for the last two weeks. I do not know at what point we will strike the N & C RR, but I wish that we would hurry up, for after this rain we are agoing to have very cold weather. some persons think that we will go by Huntsville and take the garrison there and then go on. I have only recieved one letter from you. why do you not write to me. Has my dear brother been exchanged yet and if so how is he.

Nov 20th 1864

The weather is a little better this morning. the clouds are breaking and it is quite cool. if this continues I think we will move forward in a day or two, and then I do not know when you will hear from me again. [William B.] Hassett has applied for a detail and if he gets it, he will leave here in a few days for Savannah. I will send some letters to you by him. please put them in my desk. Harmon, Judge & Tom are quite well. All my boys here are well.

I have with me Lt. [William A.] Shaw, Sgt. Robinson [George R. Robertson], Cpls [Hugh H.] Harrigan and [W.G.] Solomon and Privates Barren [J.J. Barron], [George W.] Brownell, [William H.] Bradley, Bryand [D.J. Bryant], [William S.] Gavan [Albert R.] Hunt, [William B.] Hassett, [Ben J.] Helmy, [J.D.] Jarrall, Lacklison [Robert or K. Lachlison], [William F.] May, [E.] Nease, [William B.] Puder, [Joel P.] Rackley, [Alexander J.] Raymur, [James Potter] Williamson, and Cook Bill Pender. besides these there are up here detailed [J.O.] Andrews, [Andrew J.] Coleman, [T.A.] Miller, [John] McCormick & [A.L.] Sammons J., 28 in all. Give my Love to all my friends. I shall write whenever I have an opportunity. I write every other day, do you get my letters. I pray that God will watch over and protect you and yours. Good bye until I write again, my darling mother.

your devoted and loving son, Hammie

1Lt. Hamilton Branch to Charlotte Branch

Hd Qrs Co F 54th Ga Reg Infty Brig Genl J.A. Smiths Brigade
Maj Genl P.R. Cleburnes Division
Lt. Genl F. Cheathams Corps
Bt. General J.B. Hoods
Army of Tenn
General P.G. Beauregard's Dept.
near Florence Ala
Nov 21st 1864
My Very Dear Mother

I wrote you on yesterday by mail, but as Hassett is about leaving for Savannah and will be more certain of delivering a letter to you, I write again. The weather did not clear up as I thought it would on yesterday, but still remains cloudy and rainy. notwithstanding this we leave in a few moments for the first march of the new campaign. our destination is unknown, but we march in the direction of the Nashville and Chattanooga Rail Road. a part of our army has already gone. We have just heard of Shermans move in the direction of Macon, and we expect the people down there to take care of his three corps whilst we take care of the remaining four under Thomas. We expect to have a hard time and to have some fighting to do, but we intend with Gods help to ruin Thomas' Army. God Bless you my darling mother and help you to bear up under your many trials. I intend to say my prayers every night and to live so that if I am taken from this world I will be carried to that better and brighter world. Harmon, Judge and Tom are all well. Remember me to all my friends and with much love I remain your devoted son

Hammie

Later Nov 21/64

Our division started this morning our brigade has been left here until tomorrow when we will bring up the rear of the army. It has been snowing right lively for the last two hours. the snow melts as fast as it falls.

On November 21, the Confederates entered Tennessee without Gen. Smith's brigade, which was detailed to convoy the supply train. Thereby the 54th Georgia missed one of the greatest bloodbaths of the war—the battle of Franklin. Once again Hammie's life was spared by a fluke in timing.

1Lt. Hamilton Branch to Charlotte Branch

Bivouac Smiths Brigade
near the Tennessee line
Nov 28th 1864
My Very Dear Mother
　　We left bivouac at Cheathams Ferry this morning and marched to this place, which is 18 miles from the ferry. Our regiment marched in the rear of the train of 140 waggons that we were to convoy to the army. the roads were very bad and the marching very hard on the men. I was compeled to ride the last two miles on account of my leg. We went into bivouac at 9 1/2 P.M.

Nov 30th 1864
　　We again marched in the centre and made 10 miles going into bivouac at 5 P.M.

Near Henryville Tenn
Dec 1st 1864
　　After marching 3 miles this morning we came into the Waynesboro & Columbia Turnpike but it was not much better than the Natchez Trace road on which we have been marching. We made 15 miles today and bivouaced about 5 1/2 P.M.

Bivouac 2 miles beyond Mt. Pleasant Tenn
Dec 2nd 1864
　　Yesterday we marched in front of the train and to day in the rear, my company being the rear guard for the brigade. after marching 9 miles the turnpike became a great deal better. We marched through Mt. Pleasant a very pretty little place and bivouaced at 7 P.M. 2 miles beyond the village. Today we heard for the first time of the Battle of Franklin and the death of Generals Cleburne and [Hiram G.] Grandbury of our division.

Bivouac near Spring Hill Tenn
Dec 3rd 1864

We marched 20 miles today passing through Columbia a very pretty place. Genl Cleburne was buried here yesterday. we also passed through Spring Hill. there are a great many of the wounded from Franklin in these places. Genl Smith was born in this county. he will command our division it is thought.

Dec 4th 1864

We marched through the battlefield of Franklin today, also through the town. it is a very pretty town. all of our badly wounded are here. I think the charge of our Corps at this place was the grandest charge of the war. we made 24 miles to day and bivouaced 5 miles from Nashville Tenn.

Smith's Brigade, with the 54th Georgia, was ordered to proceed to Nashville on December 4. They stopped six miles from the city and took a position in trenches while awaiting further orders.

Dec 5th 1864

We marched to this [unidentified] place this morning and threw up rail fortifications. here we rejoined our gallant old division, but there are few of them left.

Dec 6th

On yesterday some negro troops [probably the 14th or 44th U.S. Colored Troops] advanced and drove in our division pickets. last night and today we have been fortifying in our front.

Dec 7th 1864

Today the negro troops advanced on our brigade pickets but were driven back. we, our brigade, held the position from which our division men were driven on yesterday.

Bivouac Smiths Brigade
18 miles Nashville
Dec 8th 1864

I was sent out this morning in charge of the pickets from our regiment. as soon as we were posted we were relieved by the pickets of some other brigade and on returning to our bivouac we found the brigade just starting for Murfreesboro. we marched 16 miles and bivouaced on the turnpike, having made a very good march.

Hood had ordered Forrest and the division of Gen. William Bates to lead an offensive on nearby Murfreesboro. Forrest, realizing Murfreesboro was also heavily fortified, took his 6,000-man force and entrenched around the city, cutting off supplies, in an attempt to force the enemy to attack him. The stategy appeared to be working, but, unfortunately, Bates's Division was recalled on December 8. Forrest, deprived of the manpower he needed to be of effective service, was then ordered to Lavergne Station with his two small brigades of infantry—Smith's and Joseph B. Palmer's brigades. They could do little more than create a diversion while Hood fought Thomas at Nashville.

1Lt. Hamilton Branch to Charlotte Branch (continued)

On the Nashville and Chattanooga RR 3 P.M. Dec 10th.
We have been employed for the last two days destroying this Rail Road. Genl Forrest says that he intends to feed us well, and that he wants us to destroy this road totaly and then he wants us to fight well (and not do like Bates Division) for he intends to capture Murfreesboro, the garrison and all their supplies and if they have any clothing he intends to fit us out before he gives any to the army. It sleeted all day yesterday and it is very cold today. this is the hardest road to take up that I have ever seen.

During this period Hammie found time to write a long entry about the battle of Franklin.

Dec 12th 1864
As we had nothing to eat yesterday we did not work, nor have we worked today, but have been in bivouac about 1/2 mile from the rail road. We have been hearing heavy fireing the last two days in the direction of Nashville. As I have just taken a good wash and put on good clean cloths and am therefore free from lice, I will tell you all I have learned about Hoods fights.
Hood sent two of his corps to make a feint against Columbia whilst Cheathams corps was to try and [get] between Columbia and Nashville. if he had done this, Hood would have bagged the whole of Thomas' forces. Cleburnes Division arrived in their rear at Spring hill in time and drove the

enemy into the town, but he was not met by Bates Division and therefore the whole of Thomas army escaped from Columbia and arrived at Franklin with the loss of only a few men. Hood then pursued him and came upon him fortifying at Franklin. he also caught a courier with a despatch from Thomas saying that as F[ranklin] was the key to all East Tennessee that he intended to hold it. Hood imediately ordered the attack on the reception of this news and right Gallantly the attack was made.

Cheathams Corps made the principal charge with Cleburnes Division in the centre, [John C.] Browns on the [he leaves a blank] and Bates on the L. In front of Bates there was an open place of about [blank] yards. he was to charge into this and flanking the enemy sweep down their lines, whilst the others charged the breastworks. where the turnpike enters the town their is at the second line of works about 50 yds to the right a gin house or barn (at this place on the works the gallant Genl P.R. Cleburne was killed) and on the left about 75 yds there is a thorny locust thicket. the enemy had cut a part of this down for a abatte. it was to the right and left of the turnpike that Cleburnes Div charged and gallantly they charged too, although they paid dearly for it. they came against the first line of works in column of regiments by brigades and driving the enemy from them swept around by regiments into line and followed the flying foe. this they did so closely that the enemy could not fire on them until they were in 40 yds of the second line. they then opened from their works but Cleburnes men did not stop until they had reached the works and a great many going into the works were captured. the division then fought over the works but as the enemy had the advantage they could not get them out. they laid down in front of the works and the enemy would take and stick their guns over the works and shoot our men. this our men could not do as the slant was on our side our men laid there until night when the enemy left. the charge was made at three P.M. Bates division as usual failed. if they had done their part as well as Cleburne and Brown, we would have ruined the army of Thomas. our total loss in this fight was 3300. our division lost 1650, almost one half of the number they carried in. our brigade was with the salt train, therefore we can say that we have been saved by salt.

Maj. Genl Cleburne and Brig Genls [Hiram] Granbury, [Otho F.] Strahl, Gist and [John] Adams were killed and Maj Genl [John C.] Brown and Brig Genls [George W.] Gordon, [John C.] Carter and [Thomas M.] Scott were wounded. Gordon was also captured. In Browns Div every General and Staff officer was killed or wounded. the ground over which this charge was made was as open as your hand. the distance between the first and second line was 300 yds and there was not a bush or stump even to protect them. I think it the most gallant fight of the war.

Genl H[ood] says that if he had had more daylight or if the enemy had staid until next day that he would have had them all. he did not use any artilery on account of our women and children being in the town, but he intended to surround the town and open next morning from 108 pieces of artilery and to fire 100 rounds from each piece.

After the fight at Franklin Genl Hood sent Bates over here to Murfreesboro. after waiting a day or two Hood, finding that Bates was doing nothing, sent Genl Forrest here. he imediately went to work. Bates Division was ordered to advance on the town and draw the enemy out, then to keep them engaged whilst Forrest went around in the rear and captured their works. Bates went out and the enemy came to meet him and advanced a skirmish line. Bates men, seeing the skirmish line advancing, ran like a scared dog. Forrest, seeing this galloped in the midst of them and failing to rally them cursed them and knocked several of them down. in the mean time Forrest had sent his cavalry to the rear and they charged into the town and fought the enemy there but finding that Bates had failed they fell back. Genl F. says that if Bates had held his ground 30 minutes, that he would have taken the whole force of the enemy. I do not know whether he will attack them again or not but anyhow we are here waiting on him.

Lavergne Tenn
Dec 13th 1864

We marched from our bivouac to this place (4 miles) this morning and have been engaged tearing up the tracks. I had to destroy the tank. while doing it Genl Forrest came up to me and said that he wanted it destroyed totaly. Col. Olmstead told him that he had put a man there that would do it. we then had a little talk and Genl Forrest took from his pockets and gave Col. O and myself each a fine large apple.

In bivouac Dec 14/64

At Dr. [R.T.] Coleman's request Capt [George W.] Moody and myself accompanied him to a little sociable at Mr. Goodmans, about 2 miles from here. We had quite a nice time. there were 8 ladies and 8 gentleman. we danced until 1 Oclock, and also eat a very find supper. We had an inspection today. one of the ladies at the frolic last night was a Nashville girl. The sleet which has been on the ground for the last 5 days thawed this morning.

Near Lebanon Turnpike
5 miles from Murfreesboro
Dec 15th 1864

We left bivouac this morning and marched to within 8 miles of M[urfreesboro] when we turned to the left and marched to this place. Genl Forrest is in command of the party. We have been hearing the report of heavy artilery in the direction of Nashvile all day. it is very quick and heavy. We had to ford a creek this morning. it was about half thigh deep. consequently the water ran all down my boot legs.

Nashville was a Union victory. On the evening of December 16, Hood began the long retreat South, pursued cautiously by Thomas. It was a difficult and severe night march, reminiscent of Napoleon's retreat from Moscow. The icy wind and snow caused suffering for soldiers dressed in rags, with no blankets or shoes. So brutal was the cold that men could hardly keep up the pace on the frozen ground. Many limped with unhealed wounds. Forrest's troopers dismounted and gave their horses to the barefooted plagued by frostbite. Horses and mules, worn out by the gruelling campaign, fell dead in their traces. As Forrest was the rear guard, his men were harassed by enemy cavalry all the way through Tennessee.

1Lt. Hamilton Branch to Charlotte Branch (continued)

Columbia Tenn
Dec 19th/64

We were called at 4 A.M. on the 16th and marched all day. recrossed the creek and marched until 8 P.M., when we went into bivouac and slept until 12 when we were called and marched all night and all day and bivouaced for two hours the next night, when we again got up and put. and marched all night and day and all the next night and bivouaced two miles from this city. in the 3 days we made 60 miles and over the worst roads I have ever seen. about 200 of our brigade were barefooted. Genl Forrest made his escort take up barefooted men behind them. Our army is now on the retreat. it has been driven from its works at Nashville. I have not learned any particulars yet.

Columbia Dec 20th

On the morning of the 19th we marched through Columbia (having crossed Duck River on a pontoon Bridge) and bivouaced just on the skirts and on the Pulaski turnpike. Our army left here this morning for the Tennessee river. our brigade and 6 others together with the cavalry will hold the enemy in check and allow Hood to retreat. as soon as he gets out of the way we will follow him. Our brigade has lost 3 or 400 men. they could not keep up with us and have been captured by the enemy. my company arrived here with 2 Lts, 1 Cpl and 1 man, but I expect 2 or 3 more of my men have crossed but are not with us. The enemy charges our corps yesterday and Old Frank drove them back and captured their battery.

From all that I can learn our men did not fight well at Nashville. a part of Bate's division and some other brigades formed a line of skirmishers. on the 15th they charged Stewarts Corps (on the left) 4 times. the first 3 times they were driven back, but the 4th time they flanked him and made him fall back a quarter and also capturing from him 16 pieces of artilery and several hundred prisoners. on the 17th they charged Lee and Cheatham 6 times. the first 5 times they were repulsed but the 6th time they broke through Bates division, [J.J.] Finleys, and [R.C.] Tylers Brigades running, but H.R. Jackson's Georgia Brigade fought until they were captured. Genl Hood says they fought well, and Genl Smith (whose division Cleburnes was in reserve) who saw the fight says that they fought splendidly. after this our army fell back. we lost several thousand prisoners but not many killed or wounded. the enemy put their negroes in front. Genl Lee was shot in the foot and Genls Ed Johnston [Edward "Allegheny" Johnson]and H.R. Jackson were taken prisoners. George and Willie Patten are missing from our brigade. Isaac Cohen carried me in town to day and introduced me to the Longs. they treated us well and gave us a nice dinner.

Dec 21st

Our brigade and Genl Browns together with 6 others have been left here by Hood with Genl Forrest and his cavalry to hold the enemy in check until he gets out of the way with his army and men. Genl F[orrest] has taken a great fancy to our brigade and Genl Browns. he made a special request for us to be left here at the post of honor with him. the other 6 brigades volunteered to stay. this I consider the highest compliment that can be paid a brigade. Genl F. told Genl Hood that col. Olmstead had a brigade of men. Genl H replied that he was glad for that, he had a great many children with him. I do not know when we will leave here as the enemy are not pressing us. Poor Frank [Francis Edward] Bourquin was killed last night by a tree falling on him. the tree was cut down by some of our cooks. Frank was in bed, he is burried near the cemetery here. It has been snowing all day.

14 miles from Columbia, on turnpike
Dec 23/1864

We remained here all last night and all to day until this afternoon when we moved 1/2 mile towards Columbia and forward line of battle. we remained here until dark when we went into bivouac.

14 miles from Columbia
Dec 23/64

We left Columbia yesterday and marched to this place. we formed line of battle twice but the enemy did not come up to us. Genl Forrest drew them on until he got them where he wanted them. this was about 5 miles from Pulaski. he then stopped and formed line of fight. we then built rail breastworks and waited for the enemy to charge us. this they would not do. therefore Genl F. told us that when he sounded the charge that he wanted us to go forward with a vim. we had 3 brigades of infantry, [Winfield S.] Featherstones, [John C.] Browns, and [James A.] Smiths and two of Cavalry. as soon as the bugle was blown we charged and drove the enemy back capturing 1 piece of artillery, about 40 horses, 50 carbines, and 15 prisoners. we had two wounded on our side. Raymus [Alexander J. Raymur] of my company (who with [William S.] Gavan and Barren [J.J. Barron] had joined us at Pulaski) captured a horse and sold it for $1000.

Pulaski Tenn Dec 24

We left our bivouac of yesterday this morning and marched to within three miles of this place, when we stopped and formed line of fight. We remained in line until 7 P.M. when we moved to this place and took position in the enemys old works 6 miles south of Pulaski.

Dec 25/64

We marched through Pulaski this morning and leaving the turnpike turned into a very muddy road. the enemy followed us very closely, in fact they charged our men who were left to burn the bridge at Pulaski.

Stegar [Sugar] Creek
20 miles from Pulaski
Dec 26/64

We remained at our fighting ground yesterday an hour or two after the fight and then at 3 1/2 Oclock P.M. we commenced to fall back again. we marched all the afternoon and until 11 at night. we crossed, that is waded, about 20 creeks and went into bivouac in a mud hole at this place. it had been raining for the last two days but as I had captured a rubber cloth on Christmas I managed to keep pretty dry. I also captured a shirt and testament off of the gun we captured. this morning we found the enemy had not been satisfied with their drubbing of yesterday, but were upon us again. Genl F. therefore made his rear consisting of two brigades of Inft and 1 of Cavalry charge them again. they drove the enemy back killing a number of horses and taking some prisoners. we then fell back during the rest of the day, and bivouaced at night near Lexington.

Dec 27th

We left bivouac at daylight and fell back to Shoal Creek where we bivouaced at night.

Bainbridge Ala Dec 28

We were called at 1 A.M. and marched to the pontoon (about 2 miles) when we crossed over the Tennessee and are now safe again on this side of the river, at Shoal creek. [Joel P.] Rackley and [D.J.] Bryant joined me. I left the brigade this morning and have started for the rear.

Dec 29th Corinth Miss

I arrived at this place this morning, dirty, lousey and hungry.

On New Year's Day 1865, Forrest's command caught up with the Army of Tennessee near Corinth, Mississippi, and the Savannah Cadets rejoined Cleburne's old division, now commanded by Gen. Smith. The blood-soaked remnants of what had been the largest Confederate army in the West sought refuge in friendly territory.

John Bell Hood resigned his command on January 23, and was replaced by Gen. Beauregard. Six months earlier, Hood had taken command of an army of 50,000; after the Tennessee campaign only 18,000 remained. Brig. Gen. Richard Taylor was given command of Leonidas Polk's old corps and left in the

Trans-Mississippi. Cheatham's Corps was sent to Augusta, Georgia, the headquarters of the Western army.

To add insult to injuries already sustained by the brave young men of Savannah, Fort McAllister had been attacked and overrun on the 13th, its entire garrison having fought to the last man. There was no choice but to evacuate the city. Sherman had entered Savannah unchallenged on Christmas Day.

Hammie was furloughed, too broken down to continue with his comrades in the Cadets to their final fate in North Carolina. On February 1, 1865, he was a patient at the 3rd Georgia Hospital in Augusta, under the care of friend and surgeon Joseph C. Habersham. He was given permission to remain in private quarters and report every other day. His mother was able to visit him, travelling up on the train from Egypt.

Sanford, of course, was exchanged in December. Charlotte's boys had come home, but their trials were not over.

CHAPTER FIFTEEN

We Lost Everything but Honor

Savannah, with a number of New England-born residents, had always been a town of Unionist sentiment. It was the question of constitutional rights that had galvanized her Confederate stance during the war. Now defeated, she had no choice but to capitulate, and to do it as painlessly as possible was the decision of city officials. Still, Charlotte Branch had no intention of collaborating with a government against whom her oldest son had given his life, and a great many families agreed with her.[81]

Thirty-two thousand victorious Union soldiers entered Savannah, a quiet and cautious city, in December 1864. They built shanties on the once graceful squares and confiscated all of the available wood, depriving the citizens of fuel to ward off the cold.

Early in January 1865 Sherman permitted some residents to leave the city. At the same time Secretary of War Edwin M. Stanton and Gen. Henry Halleck directed that families of Confederate officers be removed, "and share the fortunes of their husbands and fathers." Even the Union newspaper, which had been established for propaganda purposes, agreed that the order "bears heavily upon many who are comparatively blameless." The directives continued for weeks.[82]

On February 4 a notice ran in the *Savannah Republican:* "All citizens now residents of this city are requested to call at this office and register themselves as such. Heads of families will report the persons composing their households." Maj. Gen. Cuvier Grover, the Union commander in charge of Savannah, thus identified the families of Confederate officers. Another notice appeared in short order, requiring all families of "rebel officers" to be ready to leave the city in twenty-four hours.

Charlotte and Sanford were among those exiled. On February 20, she received a pass from the U.S. provost marshal's office "to go outside the lines and remain." They left for Halcyondale, Georgia, in Scriven County, with a wagonload of household necessities. It was a humiliating act of submission, further adding to Sanford's depression.

Melissa Baker to Charlotte Branch

Friendsbury Feb. 18th 1865
My dear Mrs. Branch

It was an unlooked for pleasure, receiving your letter last week, and I appreciate your kindness in writing, as I scarcely expected to hear so soon, judging from my previous disappointments, in regard to friends that left months ago, whose letters have as yet remained unwritten or have been mislaid on the way. Though I felt confident at the same time that Lieut. Branch would be the last one that I could accuse of forgetfulness or neglect. The last letter that I received from him, of date Dec. 6th says he expected to be with you in a few hours. . . . I am so glad to hear that he is really again with you. Disease and the depressing influence attendant upon long confinement must have made sad change since I saw him, and how much more perceptible to a Mother's eye.

But now that you have him all to yourself to watch over, nurse, and to cheer, and the balmy air to invigorate, I am very sanguine that he will soon recover his health & spirits. . . . Give him my warmest regards. I shall expect his promised letter and hope to hear from you also, and of his entire recovery from his last attack. Tell him Binnie got a letter from his friend Capt. [Henry R.] J[ackson] a few weeks ago, it was written in November.

I remain your friend
Melissa Baker

Col. Joseph F. Waring to Charlotte Branch

Near Goldsboro, N.C.
Butler's Cav. Div., Gen. Johnston's Army
March 30, 1865
My dear Mrs. Branch:

     I am truly grateful to you for your kindness in sending me news of my dear mother and family. Your letter has just reached me. I congratulate you on getting back your gallant boy, but am sorry to hear that his health is so bad. Tell him, he has my best wishes for his speedy recovery. I hope he may soon be able to strike another blow at our foes. I am glad to hear that our people are still defiant. If every Southern mother were like you, desertion would be unknown in the army, and the War would soon end.

     The short sightedness and folly of our women are the causes of our present difficulties. The people of S. Carolina have paid dearly for it. Sherman has devastated the country to such an extent, that in the line of his march, people have been forced to go to the old Yankee camps to pick up the grains of corn left by the horses. One of my men visited a house in S. Carolina, in which he found a young woman & three children in bed. They had not tasted a *particle* of *food* for two days. There are many instances of equal suffering. I passed a house yesterday inhabited by a lonelly widow. She had not a dust of flour. These things cannot conquer us. Poverty & suffering will but harden our people. I am as confident as ever that we shall win our independence. It is not written that we are to bend beneath the yoke of the Yankees. God is scourging us for our sins. He will yet bless us. Nations as well as individuals must suffer the pangs of maternity.

     . . . I have escaped without serious hurt, by the blessing of God. I have had two horses wounded four different times, but have had to abandon only one of them. I got a scratch on my left shin about a month ago but it did not disable me.

With great respect I remain
Very truly your friend
J.F. Waring

P.S. . . . Capt Twyman is still suffering from his wound. He walks with a stick. His address is Capt. Horace Twyman, Care of Davis Twyman Esq., Madison C.H. Va. At least that address will answer. J.F.W.

Although he had been declared unfit for the field, Hamilton was still in the army. He reported to army headquarters in Augusta where he was assigned to collect deserters and men who were separated from their commands. He forwarded 509 officers and men to Augusta while on this assignment.

Then came the news of Gen. Joseph Johnston's surrender on April 26, 1865. All Confederate soldiers were urged to surrender, but Hamilton instead attempted to join the Army of the Trans-Mississippi under Gen. Kirby Smith. Before he could leave, however, that army also surrendered. The war was over.

The Branch family returned to Savannah sometime in May. Sanford's old lung wound caused an occasional attack of an asthma-like condition, and he coughed up blood frequently. At age twenty-five, physical debility and the emotional drain of all he had endured left him severely depressed. Hamilton began to court Marie Dickerson, the girl he had met on the train. Her father, who had retained his shipping business with the Central Railroad, hired Hammie as a stevedore, hard work that earned a bare wage. He boarded in town while Sanford and Charlotte returned to Effingham County, to the vicinity of Brewer.

Melissa Baker to Charlotte Branch

Friendsbury
June 30th 1865
My dear Mrs. Branch

It has now been more than three weeks since I recieved your kind and unexpected letter. . . . I so often think of your son and it has been a great relief to hear that he has improved so much in health and appearance and to know that he was no longer a prisoner, particularly when I heard how those suffered who were still at Fort Pulaski when he left.

I received his letter about the middle of May and replied to it, a few days afterwards . . . and hope has received it, . . . as his came quite quickly.

The fall of Richmond and surrender of Gen Lee, was as unexpected as it was sad to us, all came in such quick succession, we were entirely unprepared for it, and then such conflicting accounts of sufferings in the army, desertions, &c. All added to make more painful the calamitous result of a four years effort for freedom. It is mysterious to us and if we attempt to attribute the failure to the love of gain on one side, how much more guilty is the other, of the same sin and thus more hateful. The South no doubt needs purifying and the innocent must need suffer with the guilty, yet I cannot believe that all that is past will be in vain. The South will yet raise to do battle for the Lord, "for the truth as it is in Jesus." Though humiliated, she is not degraded. . . . My love and prayer is that the South, collectively and individually may become more and more the truely and dearest follower of Him, who hath promised to be a guide to the meek & holy and jealous God, the govenor among the nations. It has been a pleasure to me, "My dear Mrs. Branch" to think I could have administered in any little way to the sufferings of your son, but what I did was so small, not worth mentioning, that I hope you will not refer to it again, nor feel any weight of obligation for I am sure I shall never be the loser—my regret is that I could not have done, or still not do, more for the many who were suffering and helpless. There have been those whose self sacrificing spirit, and devotion to the cause, has been truly noble.

Tell Lieut. Branch that I heard quite frequently this Spring from his friend Capt. Jackson, untill within the month past. He promised to come on and see us and we do not know why he delays so long. His brother William was in Fort Delaware but we did not know it untill a short time before his release, with most of the prisoners. Mrs. Baker has had several of her correspondents from there to see her, on their way home. The authorities here are a little more lenient than they were two months ago, to the returned prisoners—perhaps they find it a better poling, as they were losing ground in a pecuniary point of view—and that would have more influence than any feelings of humanity, I might say, without being invidious.

Lieut James Robinson stopped in Balt. on his return from Johnson's Island. he came out and staid all night with us, and I have received a long letter from him this week. After speaking of the pleasure of being once more at home and among friends, he gives a sad account of affairs in Portsmouth, not a business firm with whom he is familiar—all Yankees or Jews and the young men as they return home, stand at the corners of the streets having nothing to do—this is the most deplorable part. I do feel so sorry for them, but so helpless to aid. There are many in our own city in a like condition. Lieut R. is very anxious to get something to do, and would be willing to go anywhere's—as he thinks there is no opening at present in his own city.

My sister's two sons, William and Harry Graves, returned lately, one from Vir. after Lee's surrender, and Harry last week from Johnson's Island. He was captured in April at Dinwiddie Court House. He has been most of the time the past four years engineering which was his occupation before he went South—and he would like to resume it—if there is a situation to be found anywhere, except North. He was highly thought of, for his ability and character while in the service & was not withdrawn, to enter the army proper, untill that Fall. William has been trying but has not succeeded as yet in getting a situation in our City. I hope a change may come soon—whereby the young men may get employment and I trust your son will improve in health so much more, as to be able to attend to whatever he may see fit.

Remember me very affectionately to him and also to your youngest son. I would like to hear from him in reference to the remains of his friend [Fred Bliss] that we had removed from Gettysburg. Would his Mother, Mrs. Bliss prefer to have them removed to Savannah or interred here. He can let me know when he writes again. Lieut Parsons a friend of his wrote to me from Fort Delaware early in June and sent a Receipt for some clothing—I received the letter, the 6th of June and sent all the articles he wrote for the same day, as I knew he might be leaving soon, but not hearing from him since, I do not know whether he would have left before they could reach him. I should like to know really if he received them.

. . . Hoping to hear from you soon again, and also to see you & your children at our home as soon as you can arrange to make us a visit, I remain
Your Friend as ever,
Melissa

Melissa Baker to Charlotte Branch

Friendsbury
July 23rd 1865
My dear Mrs. Branch

It has been nearly a month since I wrote to you last, and . . . I should like so much to hear from you again, and how all are getting along around you these sad days. I daresay there are some who can take a more cheerful view of the state of affairs at present, and can look forward with some degree of hope to the future of what they would claim as their own nation. It would be well if all could feel thus—. . . though it must be very hard to say "all's for the best," and the want of employment for the young men as the[y] return home after enduring what they have done, must indeed be very disheartening. . . . I am very glad that numbers [of former Confederate soldiers] who intended leaving for some other land, have now determined to remain. The South cannot spare her sons, though I do not wonder at the desire to be far removed from what must so continually remind them of their state and condition.

Tell Lieut Branch I received a long letter from Lieut Robinson after his return home, he had stopped to see us on his way from Johnson's Island—he says in his letter that now that he is at home he has nothing to do—all the business firms in Portsmouth and Norfolk are either Jews or Yankees, not a familiar one among them, and their best buildings taken by the Yankees or Negroes. It must be a gloomy sight for him. He would like very much to get a Southern Agency—I wish I could hear of a situation for him here, but it seems in vain at present.

Capt. Jackson intended making us a visit but I heard from him lately and his mother has been very ill and he was worn out from nursing and anxiety —she was better when he wrote, but he was still anxious about her. I hope he will be able to come and see us soon, I shall always be glad to meet with our Gettysburg friends. When you return to Savannah, I want you to please send me your Photograph and also one of your sons. I shall prize them highly. Col. Brown sent me his photograph from Macon, Ga. He had it taken while in New York. It is very good, and I am very glad to be remembered by him. I suppose he has concluded to remain in Georgia. Does Lieut Branch ever hear from Capt. [Benton] Miller. None of his friends here have ever had a line from him since he was exchanged.

Tell your son that Mrs. [Helen Brademeyer] Mason whom he may remember as visiting him while he was at Plank's farm was married lately to Dr. [F.W.] Patterson, who had charge of the hospital at Barksdale's Division. She was there for some time with Mrs. Harman Brown [who nursed at Antietam and Gettysburg] and Miss [Matilda] Saunders, and has been devoted ever since to the Confederate cause. She visited Richmond after the surrender of Lee, and the Dr. returned home with her. They have now gone to Saratoga and will afterward take up their abode at her farm near Baltimore.

. . . Capt. J[ohn R.] Johnson from Savannah called to see me lately with a note from Mrs. Bliss. She wishes the body of her son to be sent to Savannah and will send word at what time. As Capt. J. leaves Balt. for New York tomorrow night I will send this by him and also a book which I hope you will accept, it may give you a little pleasure. . . . Capt. J.'s daughters have been to see us, they are very pleasant young ladies. one of them went with us to the Fort today to inquire about Mr. J.D. Howell, Mrs. Jefferson

Davis's brother—and found that he had just been released. I only wish we could hear the same of her husband.

Remember me very affectionately to your son—and tell him he has not replied to my last letter. I hope to hear from you both very soon.

May God bless you

Melissa

In the fall of 1865 Charlotte returned to Savannah. Her business had suffered from neglect in the later years of the war and was virtually shut down in 1865 by the poverty of her former customers. She joined the Needle Woman's Friend Society, an organization formed to give work to widows and orphans. The articles they made were sold and the funds distributed among the members.

Sanford remained at either Brewer or Halcyondale. He obtained permission from federal authorities to keep a shotgun and only occasionally returned to the city to collect his mail. He needed the quiet, healing solitude of country life.

Melissa Baker to Sanford Branch

Friendsbury
Nov. 8th 1865
My dear Lieut. Branch

Why is it that I do not hear from you now? I have been expecting again and again to receive a letter in your handwriting but have as yet been disappointed. . . . I feel that I cannot wait any longer but conclude according to your mother's proposed arrangements that you have now returned to Savannah as she expected to be there this Fall. . . .

My first and most natural question will be, how is your health? How have you been all summer, were you able to attend to anything, or do you feel any stronger? Have your wounds entirely healed or do you still raise blood. I hope I shall hear of your improved condition let me know all about yourself and if you are better reconciled to the present state of affairs and what do you think of the future prospects of the South. It is wonderful the accounts we recieve from many places, of the resignation of the people and the cheerfulness with which they have gone to work again, to repair their broken fortunes. . . .

Do you ever hear from Capt. Jackson now? I hear occasionally. he is still in Richmond engaged in his profession we have been told repeatedly by friends who came of his intention of visiting Balt. but he has not yet arrived.

His Mother was very sick this summer and also his brother. Major Turner has been here. he is better and the Dr. thinks will recover the use of his limbs, he still suffers very much at times. Capt. Wheeler passed through Balt. he was out at Athol, to see Mrs. Baker. he has an artificial arm and can make some use of it. Lieut. Robinson has been in our city about two months, has a situation in the office of the Balt. & Ohio Railroad—he was out to see us last week and seems pleased, though he would prefer a more lucrative place. I hope he will be promoted as he is capable of filling a more important situation. But there are so many applicants at present that many are glad to get any place at all. Do you know Capt. John Johnson, now in business in Savannah. he was here this summer. I wrote to your mother by him but have not heard whether she received the letter and book sent.

Mrs. Bliss wrote to me and also sent me a Photograph of her son for which I am very much indebted to her. She wished the remains of her son sent on this fall—will you please see her and let me know to whose care in Savannah to send them—as the steamers and other vessels go from here now to that place, we can send direct. Write soon so that I can attend to it before the very cold weather. Have you seen Lieut Parsons yet, and do you know if he received the clothing sent him just before he left Fort Delaware? they were exchanged—I think they might write. Nor have we heard from Col. Forney since his return home. I wonder when we shall ever meet again with our old Gettysburg friends. I wish you and your Mother could come on to see us. give much love to her and my kindest regards to Mrs. Bliss. Do write very soon, I shall be anxiously expecting a reply, and do not feel satisfied with only thinking of you.

Your ever sincere friend
Melissa

Tallulah Hansell to Charlotte Branch

At Home. Feb 1st 1866.
My very dear Friend.

When your most truly welcome letter came I was so delighted to hear from you, and to know that you still loved me, I wanted to write to you immediately. . . . On Monday, my head ached so that I could not write, and it was but the beginning of a violent attack of inflammation of the bowels &c, and now I can hardly write legibly, nor as long a letter as usual. . . .

As I wrote you of my aversion to leaving home this winter, and my petition to have my marriage deferred a few months, at least, you will not be surprized to hear that I am still Lula *Hansell*. Lt. Pelham is now with his elder brother Charles, in Talladega. He had not been admitted to the bar before he went with the army, and wanted to go into some business which would be immediately remunerative. His Father was anxious to have him a Lawyer, and as his talent is for speaking & his mind bright & peculiarly adapted for that profession, I was also anxius to have him resume his studies & be admitted. He will not apply for a license to practice law until May, and we have not fixed upon any time for our marriage. As much as I desire to be with him, I know it will be very hard for him to struggle along for a while, and cannot & will not fetter him. He writes often & is as true and devoted as any one could possibly be. . . . If I chose to indulge my heart, I could tell you many things about him which remind me often of your dear John—the same fearless daring, the same noble & frank nature, scorning deceptions. . . .

You & your sons feel like relations to me, and I do hope you look upon me as a child. You have no daughter yet—and I feel like asking the place until a more worthy one shall claim it. . . .

I have never heard any particulars of Capt. Wm. Spencer's death, though the family have made many inquiries. I think if I were a man, I should never rest, until I had gone to Franklin & heard something definite.

. . . My Parents desire me to send their kindest regards to you, and so does Fannie. She calls this postponement a "joyful reprieve." I am afraid I felt so too. It is hard to know that the Yankees have made us too *poor* even to *marry*, is it not? "Willie" will never forgive them I think. He says we have been so long parted now. . . Give my sisterly love to your boys, & tell them if they can arrange it at *any time* to come here, we will always give to them a cordial welcome. . . . Please let me hear soon. I am so weak & need your letters. With sincere love believe me Yours affectionately—

Lula H.

Melissa Baker to Sanford Branch

Friendsbury
Feb 1st 1866
My dear Lieut Branch

You will think me very neglectful I know, in not having replied before this to your letter received in December and to your Mother's a few days before Christmas. . . . Mother was sick at the time and continued ill for several weeks—and I was expecting also a visit from our mutual friend Capt. Jackson and wished to tell you something about him, but he did not make his appearance untill about two weeks ago. . . . He was at Friendsbury part of the time but staid mostly at Athol, as that is the gathering place for the young people, and more cheerful at the dreary season . . . [as the] mud of the streets made the walking almost impossible, and he could not see as much of our City on that account. . . . He had his Photograph taken for me, but we have had nothing but clouds since untill today and it could not be finished, so I have deferred a little my letter to you, that I might send you a copy—he is thinner than when in prison and having removed his moustache and beard, makes a difference in his appearance. Do not neglect sending me yours and your mother's also, I shall prize them much. Capt. J. wanted to know when you were coming on to make a visit. . . .

We hear of so much suffering in various parts of the South that we scarcely know where it is the greatest, how I wish it all could be relieved, and there are those who could help but do not. A minister from Richmond is now in our City to recieve contributions for the poor of that place —whose sufferings have been intense during the past cold weather, many without shelter and without food and fuel, having had to give place in many instances to the negroes in their little shanties.

I hope your health is still improving and that you will have no more return of those attacks, and if you could only have some occupation that would suit you, your mind would not feel so depressed at times—we must try and take a brighter view of the future, though all may look dark at present.

I gave your message to Lieut Robinson, he said he would write to you, though as he left our City the day after Christmas, to go to Norfolk to assist in a paper there, and writes that he is occupied day and night, he may not have had the time. I wrote and reminded him of his promise, he is very much attached, so he tells me to a young lady from Vir. who is now at school in our City—and his present seperation is very painful to him, but he has promised to return in March on a visit. Lieut. Whitaker has been on here, came to place his sisters at school—both he and they were out to see us. We were quite surprised to hear of his marriage, which took place last summer to a young lady of South Carolina and they left afterwards for Texas, he driving a carriage drawn by mules and preparing their meals by the way, quite an undertaking I should think for the young lady.

. . . The vessel will leave Balt. this week that will convey the remains of Lieut Bliss to Savannah. I have written to his mother and also to Mr. Johnson to whose care they are directed. I hope all will arrive in safety. I expect to hear from you again soon and remain your true friend

As ever
Melissa

Lt. Frederick Bliss was reinterred in Laurel Grove Cemetery in Savannah on February 9, 1866. Family and friends attended.

Sarah Hine to Charlotte Branch

Solitaire
Feb. 10th 1866
My dear Charlotte

Your letter of Dec 5th mailed the 20th reached me three days ago. You cannot think what a welcome it recieved. It had been just about a year since I had had a letter from you before, & I had so yearned to hear of your welfare & your childrens, & to tell you of our plans & prospects. I will not say hopes, for myself I have none, they are buried in the grave of my country.

I have written you several times in the last year, & to Hamilton also. I wrote him two or three letters to Augusta after I heard that Hoods army was there naked & barefooted, begging him to let me know where he was that I might send him some money & be to him a mother, for I thought Sherman had cut you off from him, but I suppose the letters never reached their destination.

dear Charlotte how can we ever give up the Confederacy. One thing I shall glory in to the latest hour of my life, We never yielded in the struggle until we were bound hand & foot & the heel of the despot was on our throats. Bankrupt in men, in money, & in provisions, the wail of the bereaved & the cry of hunger rising all over the land, Our cities burned with fire and our pleasant things laid waste, the best & bravest of our sons in captivity, and the entire resources of the country exhausted—what could we do but give up. Our people certainly struggled as becomes free men who felt that every thing that was dear to man was at stake. Well may you say we lost every thing but honor & I am sure you echo the sentiments of every heart in this land when you say "I detest the United States."

I do not see a spark of love for the Union exhibited in the speeches of any of our public men neither governors messages nor any thing else. I am glad there is not, if they expressed it I should think it was duplicity. During the existence of the Confederacy my anxiety about my sons & others whom I loved in the army, & my intense yearnings for the triumph of our cause kept me in a state of continual unrest & discomfort to say the least, often times it amounted to distress, yet I would cheerfully accept the situation again if I could, with all its disturbing & distressing influences to live once more under the government of my choice.—We have nothing on earth to look forward to, we have no future, no country, we are slaves to the will of others, & must do their bidding & obey their behests. May God forgive me for there are times when my heart rebels against *His* government & I feel as if I could not accept His will in the matter.

The war has left us penniless. We had a little pile of money laid up towards buying us a house when the war broke out, a good part of it was in specie. James felt & so did I that if it was put into Confederate bonds it would help sustain the government & be perhaps equally secure, & it was converted into eight per cent bonds. It is all gone of course, but I do not grieve about it I am glad we did what we could. All that James made during the war was also in Confederate money & bonds, & what little State money we had & still have is not much better than the other.

We are keeping house now about 8 miles from Lotie & a little farther than that from James B. My husband has rented a plantation & hired some hands & expects to plant five or six hundred acres of land this year. The house is an old framed one, two stories, guiltless of paint & dilapidated but still it looks quite cozy & comfortable since we have got it fixed. We have the use of the cows with the place. I am milking seven now & making more butter than I can use, sell the surplus in Thomasville for fifty cents a pound. I also have eggs for sale, I get from twelve to fifteen a day & there are only three of us to eat. We shall probably milk fifteen or twenty cows in the summer. I have a very competent servant who does all our milking, cooking, washing & ironing.

Cornelia & I do the housework ourselves. My furniture all went up in Sav. as I suppose you know. Sister Mary sold the whole of it for less than a *hundred dollars.* I could not replace it here for less than fifteen hundred or two thousand. I had some things here, the piano, one silver & plate, most of my carpets & curtains, all my bedding, one bed & mattress, eighteen or twenty pillows &c. I have had to buy some necessary things & am very comfortable in a plain way, have more than most of my neighbors & much more than I deserve. I have not a bureau in the house. Mary writes me that she left one at Mrs. Frierson's & believed that there was one left at your store. Please write me whether there was or not & whether there was anything else left there. I have so little, that almost anything would be useful. I thought I would try & get my bureau from Mrs. F's shipped to me to Thomasville when the road was open if Frank could get time to do it which I doubt. Mary thinks she left a stove of mine at Mrs. Lathrops, which I want very much if it is to be found.

Henry [Lathrop] has about twenty hands hired & is trying to make cotton with free labor, James B. has rather more than this. He is working the plantation of his wife's fathers estate on shares, is very much pleased with country life, as are we all, particularly now when our cities are all under Yankee rule, we are more removed from it here. I shall be obliged to direct this to Hamilton for you did not give me your address. Our post office is Thomasville, we are seven miles from there. I saved one sofa from the general wreck too, & three or four big chairs, the quartelle tables & three bowls of china & glass. I had four but one was stolen from me.

Maria Elizabeth & her mother are in Atlanta at their old home. Their house was not destroyed but they had nothing else left. Maria writes me that she has all the work she can do. I have three books ready for publication but don't know where to look for a publisher. The idea of trying to issue at the North is perfectly repugnant to me, & our publishers are all broken. I had a novel (not the Commoners) in the hands of E[?] & Cogswell Columbia So. Ca. when Sherman burnt them out. They prepared to issue the book & give me half the profits. The copy they had was destroyed of course, but I have rewritten it from the old notes. The other work is Christian counsels to my son. They are all there, or at any rate two of them, so intensely Southern that I doubt if any northern publisher would issue them. I suppose the Commoner would hang one for treason if it were out.

Dear Charlotte I wish you would come & see me, come & spent some weeks & make me a good visit. I have a thousand things I would like to talk about. We would be glad to have the boys come too, & I think they would enjoy it. It would be dull for them to stay with us very long as we have no young folks about us, but James B has, his wife has four sisters all younger than herself, three of them grown & very lovely young ladies. They are entire orphans & have no brother. His wife is a very sweet woman, he could not have suited me better in his choice. Young ladies will be no inducement to Sanford I suppose, but there we will try & amuse him too if we can, & change may benefit him. It is sad to have his health sacrified so early in life, but then it is a blessing that he is spared to you. I shed many tears over his supposed death once.

Cornelia is almost grown & has made very good progress in her studies in the last two years, she has been taking lessons in household duties lately. I was without any servant at all Christmas week & she milked all the cows night & morning. James brought the water & wood & made fires & I cooked.

. . . I dread to see the day when Cornelia will be old enough to be marriageable. Frankie has just been spending a week or two with us, his home is with Lottie, she cannot bear to give him up & I know she is better fitted to train him than I am. I am expecting Miss Poolie Stewart here to live with us. I promised her years ago that I would always find room for her in my home, that was when she was able to pay board. I feel equally bound to give it to her now that she is not. She is a sweet woman & homeless & not a relative on earth. I should not be surprised to see Mary any day. She is miserable at the North. Love from James & myself to you & yours

Affec.
Sarah Hine

[P.S.] Is Sarah Allen with you. I dont know how any family could live any where for five hundred dollars a year, but I guess provisions are cheaper here than with you. They will probably rise as soon as the road is open. Corn can be had for a dollar, bacon & ham twenty cents, when there was any, & the new will soon be in now. Sugar twenty five cents, Eggs twenty five, Syrup fifty, flour about twenty five dollars a barrel. Do not say any thing about my having written books, It will be time enough when they are published, if they ever are, to make it known. I want to write another, if I only had the statistics I would, the prison life of Confederate prisoners.

Charlotte Branch to Tallulah Hansell

Brewer June 11th, 1866
My Dear Young Friend

I am really longing to hear from you and yet have no right to expect a letter from you, for I suppose you are so much engaged that you will hardly have time to write to me. I find myself constantly thinking of you and wondering if you are yet Miss Hansell or if you have changed it. My heart's desire is Dear Precious Friend, that you may be very very happy, that God will make you and yours imminently useful in this life and blessed in Eternity. A very Dear Young Friend of Mine (My pastor, Dr. Axson's Daughter [Ellen]) was married last week. They (the family) was very anxious for me to come to the wedding. I could not make up my mind to go. They were married in Church and stood or would stand just on the spot where I had seen the Coffin which contained the frame of my slain child [at] rest. it would have been too painful for me. . . .

I have not yet had my picture taken but will go to the city in July (I like to spend the 21st at the cemetery) then I will have it and Sanford's and Hammie's done to send to you. I have a fork I will send to you, you must not think it mean in me to send you such a trifle but it is out of my power to send you such a gift as my heart [desires] me to send, but which circumstances forbid. This fork was My Dear John's and I know you will value it for his sake. Will you write me if there is any way that I can send it to you. Do if possible. Write soon to me. Present my love to your Father and Mother and to Mr. Pelham and to all of your brother's family. My Dear Father be ever near to you is the Prayer of your loving friend.

C.S. Branch

[P.S.] Direct to me at Savannah. There is not anyone loyal enough to ask or [illegible] in the neighborhood I am happy to say;

Tallulah Hansell to Charlotte Branch

At Home. June 25th /66.

My very dear Friend,

After long waiting and watching, I have again been cheered by a letter from your dear hand. Accept my most sincere thanks for your continued love and kindness to me. . . . I feel that *here* is the love of a true mother's heart, the purest, truest love on earth, and had I nothing else to thank our dear John for, I should feel that I could never feel sufficiently grateful for your love, bestowed on me for his sake. He & I had talked of you many a time, and he had so often said to me, "If I live & can arrange it, you & my mother shall know each other, I'm sure you would love her."

. . . I have been perplexed and troubled very much since my last letter to you, and I have often felt that it would be a great pleasure and assistance to me, if I could only tell you all my perplexities, and secure your advice as I should feel sure of your sympathy. When I read of the gift you had for me, the tears crept up into my eyes, and the words ere hardly discernable through them. I have no words with which to thank you, but my heart does *most truly* thank you. My dear friend, *no* gift with which *he* is unconnected could ever be as highly prized by me, as I would value any little thing which had been his. A glove, a book, anything that had been his would be prized, as around it would cluster sweet memories of my girlhood's friend. . . . Several persons from here will be in Savannah & returning this week, among them Col. Wm. Willis late of the 4th Ga. Reg't, Dr. Leggitt, Mr. Graddy, either of them would take pleasure in bringing it, if you should receive this in time to hand it to them. . . . I shall be very glad to have your picture & those of your sons, and shall put them with those of my own family. I wish I could be with you in Savh on the 21st but with so many ties at home, I have no idea whatever of leaving home soon.

Last week my friend, Dr. [Charles] Force (whose visits during the latter part of the war I mentioned probably) was here on his way from Washington City. He left there to fight for us, and is now living in Selma, Ala. . . .

I'm afraid Mr. Pelham is living in Tuscaloosa, but I am hoping to induce him to come nearer home. His family are very kind to me, and I hope they may find something in me they can love. He has a good many peculiarities & is decidedly eccentric in many things, but "his faults all lean to virtue's side"—and he is warm-hearted, true & constant. Last month he was to have "come for me," but a week or two before it was quite settled, circumstances arose in which he was concerned and by which he was constrained to wait longer. He frets at it, while as much as I love him, I am rather glad than otherwise to be left still at home. This he thinks *unkind* in me, but he is annoyed now, and will see things right after a time.

So you see, dearest friend, my life lately has had a good many discords to disturb its harmony. . . . I am interrupted by company & must close my letter. Love to yourself & your household, dear lady, from us all. . . .

With sincere affection
Your true friend
Lula

Tallulah Hansell to Charlotte Branch

Home. July 21st. 1866
Kindest, best Friend

Where shall I find words which will speak to you one half of the gratitude that is swelling in my heart? How shall I form into words all the deep sympathy which floods my very soul on this anniversary day, which opened the door of the heavenly home to our dear John, but closed before we too could enter. . . . On this day, I have a fresh memorial of his and your love for me. When I saw his name and mine on the fork which had been his, I felt anew the pain of his death, but with it, I also realized afresh, the affection you have given me. How can I thank you? I am a very beggar in words when I try to express myself to you. . . .

It was my intention and desire to have written to you, so that my letter would have reached you by today, but my eyes have been troubling me this week, and I have not dared to write to any one. The prescription made for me by Dr. Force has done me a great deal of good, and indeed I think I could hardly have borne this enervating, intensely hot weather unless I had gained strength previously. Do you know how very near I was to seeing you a short time ago, while so many went to Savannah on the Excursion trip? If I had had time to have written, and found out exactly your depot, & if it would have been convenient to you to have had me with you, I should have come for two or three days. . . .

How much pleasure it would be to have you here in my own country home. . . . We are poor, it is true, but we have a very comfortable home, and . . . I can safely say I think we could make your visit pleasant. Can you not come?

. . . I have been much troubled in mind & heart for several days past. "Will" wrote to me on the 21st June, that he would certainly be with me in a short time, and gave as the outside limit *three* weeks, but seemed assured that it would be much sooner. He was on his way when he wrote, and said he would breakfast at home the next morning & with me in a few days. It has now been a month, and I have grown heart-sick with waiting, and still I am without any news whatever! He expressly said, "If I fail to be with you within the appointed time, you may be sure that it is from some unexpected & *very serious* cause." This onlly adds to my uneasiness. I do trust I shall have good news from him today.

I try to be patient & hopeful & true, but this suspense is very wearing. I look as though I have been very ill—am as pale as a very ill person now. Mental anxiety shows on me much sooner than bodily sickness or pain—It makes me droop at once.

Monday. July 23rd./66
My dear, dear Friend.

On Saturday, I was interrupted before I could finish my letter, and by the delay I have additional thanks to give you for your precious letter with its enclosure—your photograph. . . . I prize it greatly, and feel that it is the face of a very dear and highly esteemed friend. I have been wanting it a long time, and am truly rejoiced to get it. I shall esteem it among my *most valued* treasures. How much dear John looked like you—I felt the tears dimming my eyes so that I could hardly see your face at first. You are something like my own mother—The eyes very much alike. . . . Just the first opportunity I have, I will have my photograph taken for you, and hope I may succeed in securing a good, lifelike picture for you.

Saturday's mail brought me letters from Will & his sister [Bettie]. He is well, but one of his brothers has been so ill, he has not felt right to leave him. Bettie has just returned home after seven months absence, and Will of course, could not leave immediately. He hopes to come by the first of August, but really, I have been disappointed so often lately that I shall not allow myself to anticipate his coming, or even to think much about it, for fear of another disappointment. His sister & mother seem disposed to love me and give me a most cordial welcome, and should I marry him, I shall try to be worthy of all their kindness and affection, but I grow more averse to leaving home, with every day that comes, and it seems harder to conquer this feeling than it did a year ago. I wish I could see you & talk to you all about it. . . .

Who is "Hamilton" with in Savannah? Our merchants sometimes visit S. and as they are good & true Southern men who have been heart & hand with us for the past five years, I would like Mr. Branch to meet them.

. . . Sometime ago, you asked for a copy of lines on the death of my [nephew and] darling pet. "Little Cliffy"—as we called him. Clifford Stockton, his real name. Hoping to procure a printed copy, I did not send them, but I have failed to get those, and now send a written copy. . . .

My letters to Franklin [Tenn.] in regard to my dear friend, Capt. Wm. Spencer, have never been answered satisfactorily. I have never been able to learn if he has even a grave, or if his bones are bleaching on the far off hills of Tennessee. His poor widowed mother is going down broken-hearted to the grave. I shall never, never rest until I can learn something definite about him.

Please give my very kindest remembrances to your dear ones, and for yourself dearest Lady, accept the warmest love and constant prayers of your truly grateful & devoted

Lula H.

Tallulah Hansell to Charlotte Branch

Oglethorpe, Nov 26th./66
My dear kind Friend

When your truly welcome letter came, I was just rallying from a Congestive chill, and was better only a few days before I was again sick, & was obliged to deny myself the pleasure of writing to you. . . . Please accept . . . my true thanks, and convey also to both my kind friends, your sons, my thanks, & high appreciation of their goodness in sending their pictures. I . . . assure you that theirs with yours, have honored places among my dearest & truest friends. . . . An old acquaintance was looking over my Album a few nights ago, and started with pleasure & surprize, saying "Where on earth did you get Sanford's picture—I didn't think he had ever heard of you." I told him of our friendship & the link which bound us, & he then said many kind & cordial things of Lt. B. The gentleman was Mr. Rowland Hall, lately of Macon. Since his marriage he resides in this county, near a little station called Marshallville. He was a "rebel" soldier, with Hampton for some time. . . .

Whom do you think was with me when I received your letter? Ah! I know you have guessed already—& need not I shall tell you it was my "Will, o'the Wisp"—my Alabama boy with his clear blue eyes and bright smile. He came the latter part of September, *on his way to Texas*, and had been here but a week when I had the chill, he remained with me, nursing me as tenderly & delicately as a mother could have done. Poor fellow, he was terribly alarmed about his "little woman." After vainly trying to secure a *travelling companion*, not only for Texas, but for a longer & more important journey, he left about the middle of Oct. My last news from him is not very cheerful, he likes the State & country very well, says he thinks however it is a good place for rough, adventurous men, but he does not think he could ever feel satisfied with it as a home for *me*. For several reasons, I thought it best for him to go out this time alone, but particularly on account of the feeble health of my dear parents, and fearing I might only prove an additional care & burden to him while in an unsettled state. If he could get into business nearer home, I should be delighted, but it is *exceedingly* trying & painful to me to think of a home in that afar land, so distant from all who love me. . . . I think sometimes, that I have no right to marry. . . . If I would be the only one to suffer I would give up my own happiness *joyfully* for my dear Parents. but "Will" will not listen to the proposition to release me, unless I can say I desire it because I do not love him. *Unfortunately*, I cannot truthfully say this, so I am still under the promise. Please don't imagine my dear friend, that I have not proper affection for him. God knows my heart clings to him with such love that it is a bitter trial to be thus severed, but my path seemed so hedged about & narrow, I could go but one way. . . . May God pity me!

Lt. P.'s sister has written urging me to go & assist at her marriage, Dec 5th—She will live in Ga. but not within visiting distance of me, I'm sorry to know. She is a most lovely person, & is sincerely attached to me—his family all write to me, but are hurt now that I did not go to Texas with him. Really, he was not able to afford it & I couldn't increase his cares. But I can't go to Bettie's wedding though I long to do so. I have been in O[glethorpe] now for more than three years. Bettie is very anxious to know me personally & so are all the family, but I can't afford a suitable wardrobe, nor the other expenses & must decline. . . . Ever sincerely, dear Mother of my unforgotten, dear friend—your

Lula

I had a most touchingly beautiful letter last week, from [John Esten Cooke] the author of "Surry, of the Eagle's Nest." I would like to have you read it. Of my little notes to him, he speaks so kindly.

. . . I have no congenial society here, as the villagers are almost without exception uncultivated, unrefined people. They are kind & friendly, . . . but, to be candid, they are different from those to whom I have been accustomed. . . . Fannie & I are trying to get up a school, but there are very few children here, most of them very poor & there are several teachers here already. We are not sanguine of success, but *must* work, or be dependent entirely on our brothers & sisters, & that I cannot consent to be as long as I can possibly work. Father went to Marietta for six weeks, but came home before frost & has been very, very ill; he is still feeble. Fannie had fever, &

went to the Indian Springs [spa]. She only grew worse there, & came back
looking wretchedly, & her health has been miserable until within a few
weeks. I have never had so much nursing to do in my life as during the past
five months. . . . Our village has been one large hospital, and is but little
better yet. I have had to *cook* & *milk* often, and am quite an accomplished
"Bridget." I don't pretend to prefer it to reading & music & those modes
of passing my life to which I was reared, but I certainly very much prefer
it, to having my dear ones do it. . . . Among the poor negroes, we have a
missionary work, & I have been constantly called upon by them in sickenss
& death—once in the absence & illness of all ministers, I had to conduct
the burial srvice of one who had been a most faithful, trusty house servant.
I felt embarrassed, *at first*, while I thought of my singular position—the only
white person grieving and several hundred negroes—but this passed away,
& I a white woman, young enough to feel timid—felt no shame nor fear
when I saw the glistening tears on those dusky cheeks, & heard the earnest,
hearty ejaculating prayers for blessings on the "dear young mistress." It was
only a "cup of cold water" to the "little ones," but I tried to do it for *Christ's*
sake.

Lt. Pelham became quite anxious to "take charge" when he saw how
much his "little woman" had to do. He is now with his uncle, Gen. Wm.
Pelham, near Austin. I have no idea when he can return, but know God
will bring it all right in His own time. . . .

I'm afraid my long letters tire you, dear lady, but I have so much to say
to you. I never know when to stop. I feel that it would be a very great
pleasure to be near enough to sit by you with my hands in yours, my head
on your lap, & feel your kind kiss on my brow—then I could talk to you
"heart to heart." There are troubles heavy on my heart of which I cannot
write. I must bear them, & in His good time, they will be removed if it shall
be best for me.

The hardest now is this, a gentleman in the fullest, most beautiful sense
of the word, loves me devotedly, has loved me long. He was a very gallant
soldier, . . . is doing well in his profession, & as kind now as he was before
I told him that which was unpleasant to hear, painful to speak. He . . . left
one of the large cities (Washington), giving up home, friends, & a very
large fortune to fight for us—suffered wounds & in prison, & now, he writes
that he is sorry God spared his life—that it is worse than all to think of my
marriage to another. . . . I thought he had crushed the feeling more than
a year ago, & now it suddenly starts up again like a death's head at a feast!

He has *everything* to attract & is a noble man. I have no possible objection to him (though he is a *little old* for me, but has a fresh *young heart.*)—but I belonged to another before I met him. He . . . usually has controlled himself admirabley—indeed I thought he had ceased to care for me except as a *sister*—. . . [He] makes me unhappy at this bitter avowal of his wretchedness. It seems so strange for a man to love *me* thus, I in poverty, homeliness & no longer young! I can't understand it at all.

But I must stop, begging you to keep my counsel & advise me if you can & *sympathize.* I know you will. My Parents, & Fannie send their sincere love to you & your sons. . . . "Will" asked to be remembered. Pray for me, for him—for that other dear *brother* friend. It is sad—sad. I am not worth the pain I give such hearts. Write soon to your true & loving

Lula

Even as Lula bemoaned her new role as housemaid and farmhand, so, too, did Savannahians learn to live their lives with new rules and restraints. In the years immediately following the war, they slowly restored bits of the antebellum era, yet many homes were forever changed by the loss of sons, brothers, fathers and husbands.

EPILOGUE

Benevolence, Drill and Business

The commercial life of Savannah slowly rebuilt itself in the wake of military occupation by federal forces. There was an uneasy coexistence between citizens who were suppressed and stripped of their rights and Union troops who did little to endear themselves to the population.

When the Reconstruction government took hold in March 1867 under the Congressional Reconstruction Act, Georgia's citizens were plunged into oppression. The invaders brought more unrest and deprivation than the war had. Known as the Force Bill or the Military Bill, the preamble stated that the state governments of the former Confederate states had been set up without the consent of Congress. It also stated that these "said pretended governments afford no adequate protection for life or property, but countenance and encourage lawlessness and crime." To establish "peace," the South was divided into five military jurisdictions with a military tribunal in each. The abuse of power was assured, and the plan contradicted its alleged purpose by practicing unconstitutional acts upon its jurisdictions. It was pure and simply a punishment.[83]

Further practices included suspension of the writ of *habeas corpus,* and the denial of presidential authority to challenge any decisions the tribunals made.

Confederate veterans were displaced and barred from holding political office or voting. They had no voice in civic affairs, when in many cases these men were the most qualified for the job.

Despite the troubled times, Hamilton Branch and Marie Eugenia Dickerson were married in Savannah on January 9, 1867, in a modest but proper ceremony at her father's home at 81 York Street. The young couple moved next door to No. 83, facing Oglethorpe Square. Within weeks Marie was expecting their first child, another mouth to feed in the struggling household.

Their Confederate service had put its indelible mark on the lives of Southern men—proud of the role they had played, and seeking to find acceptance of that identity, they were determined that their comrades who had died should be forever remembered. Soldiers buried in unmarked graves hundreds of miles from home were disinterred and brought back to Georgia. The ladies of the South joined the effort.

Charlotte was one of the founding members of the Ladies Memorial Association, organized at Independent Presbyterian Church on February 16, 1867, which undertook to have the dead removed from the Pennsylvania battlefield where her son had been wounded.

Sanford worked as a clerk at the dry goods store of Henry Lathrop & Company, at the corner of Congress and Whitaker. He longed to have some business of his own, but for now, in a time when it was difficult for former Confederate officers to secure any kind of position, a salary was a success story. For a time he boarded on Jones Street with his mother, who continued to work for the Needle Woman's Friend Society.

Hamilton volunteered as a local firefighter with the Metropolitan Fire Steam Engine Company and was elected vice-president of the organization.

When the conduct of "scalawags and carpetbaggers" became too much to bear, the citizens felt compelled to reassert their rights. On March 7, 1868, the radical government denied the Supreme Court jurisdiction over the Reconstruction acts. The military tribunals reserved the right to try and court-martial citizens for whatever it deemed an offense. Its mission of grinding the feelings of defeat into Southerners went unchallenged.[84]

Northern sympathizers pleaded with their government to allow aid from Boston and New York to reach friends and relatives in Savannah, a goodwill gesture to repay the Savannahians of 1774 who had sent donations of rice to Boston in its dark days. After much diplomatic negotiation the provisions were allowed to arrive.[85]

Tallulah Hansell to Charlotte Branch

At Home [Oglethorpe, Ga.].
April 23rd. 1867.
My very dear Friend,

For a long time my pen has been almost idle, as my fingers, have been too weak to guide it. This . . . has been the cause of my remissness in writing to you [to acknowledge your] remembrance of me shown by my cards of invitation to your son's marriage.

I overexerted myself in getting up a little Entertainment for the "Hollywood" [Cemetery] fund, and while exhausted almost with fatigue, was drenched by being in a storm. During . . . February, I was very ill. . . . Mental anxiety, I think, has been so great and so long-continued, that it has seriously affected my health. The path of duty seems so hedged about with difficulties, that it is impossible for me to tell which is duty, the greatest duty, I mean. When my engagement was entered into, it was *cordially* approved by both families; and then the war ended so disastrously, that my duty to my parents seemed to require my presence and aid at home. Mr. P. tried to establish himself in business . . . but without capital could not succeed. He had a most liberal offer in Texas, and it is to his interest to go there. Of course, I cannot ask him to return—but how can I go so far from home, and leave these dear ones feeble and old, and so much reduced?

. . . My parents & family wish me to follow my own heart, "Will" pleads our "long, unnatural separation," and I know not what to say or do. If the Military bill [the Congressional Reconstruction Act, implemented on March 2, 1867] had been defeated there was a good opening for him in Southern Ga, he has had to give up the law, and is planting with his Uncle in Texas.

Of your new daughter, I have had most favorable accounts, and do offer to her and her noble husband my sincere congratulations, even at this late day. . . . Of your son's (Sanford's) returning health, I was *truly delighted* to learn. How many, many times I have thought of his beautiful, touching devotion to his dying brother, *my friend*. . . . It would be a mournful satisfaction to me to stand at the grave of our dear John, and place on it a garland of fragrant flowers bedewed with the tears of loving friendship. . . . I can but believe that should his spirit be permitted to hover near that place, my little offering would not be quite unnoticed by him—my dear friend. . . .

You ask if I am writing. I am having . . . some pieces republished, and have promised to write for . . . the "Cuthbert Appeal," edited by Col. Henry Jones, formerly of Liberty county, and Rev. Theodore Smith a Presbyterian minister. They are just re-publishing some humorous sketches, called "Meddleton Soldier's Aid Association." My health is not sufficiently restored to allow me to write much. . . . I must beg your indulgence for any dull letter. and also ask another from you at your earliest convenience. My warmest regards to Lt. Sanford, and also to Lt. Hammie and his wife. For yourself, my dearly valued friend, accept the sincere love of

your true & loving
Lula

More than 18,000 Confederate soldiers were buried at Hollywood Cemetery in Richmond, Virginia, during the war, most in graves with wooden headmarkers. The Ladies Memorial Association launched a campaign to raise money for a monument to the dead, and a pyramid built of fieldstones was erected in 1869.

Melissa Baker to Charlotte Branch

[On black bordered stationery, directed c/o William H. Davis, Savannah]
Friendsbury June 16th 1867
My dear Mrs. Branch

Your welcome letter was received about a week ago. I with yourself have wondered at our long silence and regret that weeks and months should go by without a line passing between us. . . . I wrote to your son Sanford after the receipt of that grass which was beautiful and which you so kindly sent me—but as I directed my letter only to Savannah (expecting him to be there at that time) I suppose he never received it. I should have acknowledged the "Reception Panel" of your son Hamilton, but the letter you mention as having written after his wedding I am sorry to say I never recieved. . . . I have written but very few letters all through the Winter and Spring. We have had sickness and sorrow, watching by the bedside of dying friends. Our Father passed away from us, went to rest on the tenth of March, as quietly and gently as a child falling asleep upon its mother's bosom. His strength had been failing for the last two years. . . . [H]e had no pain and slept well untill near the last, when he had frequent nervous paroxisms, which were painful to us, but the Dr. said he did not suffer. He enjoyed the singing and prayer in his room and when no longer able to articulate would respond by raising his hand. . . . His children and grandchildren were around him to catch the last glimpse of intelligence & to bid him goodbye. He was in his eighty-sixth year and had nearly completed the sixty third year of his married life. . . . Mother bore up wonderfully, she is now eighty three years of age and still very active though suffering at times. She says all her recollections of Father's death is pleasant, she looks back with thankfulness to the chamber consecrated by prayer and praise and for the many blessings that surrounded her.

More painful was it to us, to watch the decline of our sister Anne Jones (the mother of Cousin Jane, whom your son will remember.) She had been a sufferer for more than a year past. Being in the prime of life and having always enjoyed good health, her disease was a great affliction to her, and the trial great to leave her children without a parent—but she was enabled through grace to give up all, to desire to depart, and to be resigned to her Heavenly Father's will. . . .

But you will think me selfish, too much engrossed with what relates to home, to have a care for others—let me say, I have frequently thought of you and Sanford—and if he was in any business in Savannah as he expected last Fall. I was very glad to hear by your letter that his health had so much improved. I hope he will write to me. I hope you are pleased with your son Hamilton's marriage and that you find his wife all that you would have a daughter to be. Remember me kindly to them.

It would give me a great deal of pleasure to visit you, but I would not like to leave home to go so far away from Mother at her widowed age for she always says she thinks she will die suddenly—her health has been pretty good this summer, yet she is feeble and has to be down every day she suffers at times from dyspepsia. . . . She expects to go to Sing Sing, this week to visit my brother [William Baker] there, as he is anxious for her to come. I hope the change will be of service to her, if she will stay long enough.

Tell your son I received a letter in April from Geo. Forney, I had not heard from him for a year previous and was too glad to get his letter, he writes in good spirits as regards himself, says he is practicing law in Jacksonville, Ala. and makes a support for his family but he speaks of the desolation around and the effects of Yankee misrule. . . . I have not heard from Capt. Jackson since last Fall. I cannot think why he does not write, Does your son ever hear from him? I know he is not fond of letter writing —but I shall regret if there is any cause for his silence, as I feel an attachment for those friends with whom we were particularly associated at Gettysburg, that time cannot obliterate. I have not heard from Lieut

Robinson for a long time and not from any other of our prison friends since the surrender.

Some of the ladies of the Southern Relief Association have established a Depository in Balt. to receive work done by the needy, to help those who wish to help themselves. They also give out work, their sales have been profitable and they feel encouraged with the result so far. Mrs. Baker and Mrs. Brown are very active there.

There is another association formed here to assist in educating the young girls of the South, those whose friends are most destitute. They appointed me a manager, though I have only been able to attend the meetings of late. I think it will be conducive of good if we can use the proper discrimination. It is yet in its infancy but there is nearly twenty now in charge at schools here and elsewhere, and others under consideration but we wish to be prudent and not promise untill we can arrange about the expenditure. I send you an appeal—perhaps you can aid us sometimes in reference to those applying for this assistance from their children.

Mrs. Baker and her family are well, her son Charles was married last Winter. George is still at Washington college. Mrs. Davidson was very ill last winter, she is better at present, the young ladies are well. I hope this will find you in good health and your son improved. Give him my most affectionate regards and write soon again.

Your sincere friend
Melissa

The Ladies' Depository of the Southern Relief Association, formed in 1867, was similar to Savannah's Needle Woman's Friend Society. Melissa and her brother Charles were active in many organizations formed to benefit the war-stricken South. As president of the Franklin Bank in Baltimore, Charles served as vice-president of the Baltimore Agricultural Aid Society, which supplied destitute Virginia farmers with tools, seed, and stock. The Southern Relief Association, another charity founded by the Baker family, raised $106,623.65 to be sent directly to "the relief of the destitute people in the States wasted by civil war."

Melissa Baker's letters end in 1869. Whether the correspondence continued is unknown; perhaps the letters were not kept. Melissa never married, but continued her life of charitable work in Baltimore. In the *History of Baltimore, Maryland,* she is mentioned as vice-president and manager of the Home for the Friendless in 1898. She remained at Friendsbury, where she died March 27, 1899, after suffering for four days with pneumonia. She is buried in Loudon Park Cemetery in Baltimore.[86]

In the South, the problems of Reconstruction were exacerbated by race riots incited by outside Union agitators. Military authorites had to be called out to break up such a meeting in Chippewa square on September 30, 1867. While most black citizens paid little attention to these agitators, white citizens felt uneasy, fearing the consequences of not being allowed to bear arms for protection. The situation was volatile.[87]

Amid the turmoil, Hammie and Marie became the parents of a daughter, Charlotte Hamilton, born on November 18, 1867.

Tallulah Hansell to Charlotte Branch

Home. Nov 22nd 1867.
My precious Friend.

In these long weary weeks & months of illness & bereavement, my sore sad heart has many times turned towards you with inexpressible longing. . . . You knew of my illness during the Spring. The middle of May, I was attacked by violent Bilious Fever, & one disease succeeded another, until the present time when I have got into a low, weak state from which nothing seems to be able to bring me. The doctors have ceased to give me medicine except by absorption through blisters & say they can do no more. The simplest tonics give me fevers & I have been in bed for *six months*, except for about two weeks!

This is but a light affliction compared to the great, the irreparable loss we have recently sustained in the death of the best, most unselfish & generous of fathers. Yes, dear friend, God has written me *"Fatherless,"* and for days last week, we thought that our darling Mother would leave us also. . . . You will rejoice with me when I tell you that in all my affliction, God has comforted & sustained me—until I can indeed say "His loving kindness—oh! how great."

I must soon follow him—my Father unless I have a speedy change—pray that I may be faithful to the end, & that Satan may not be suffered to tempt me to a fall. Pray for me, dear friend, that I may do & suffer the will of God *cheerfully & meekly.*

I expect Mr. P. very soon, we were to have been married in December, but now it seems doubtful if I shall live to see him. He has not known until very lately of my illness—says God cannot . . . part us now after all our trouble & love. Poor fellow! he makes it hard for me to give up life.

Fannie has been ill also. O[glethorpe] has been worse, comparatively than [the yellow fever epidemic in] N. Orleans this year—whole families are down at a time. I have no fever this afternoon—have had thirteen chills in 13 days—sometimes have two in the day. Tell me of yourself & sons, & daughter & remember me most kindly to them. Dear lady I had prayed to see you—it may never be allowed us on earth—but *up there* may we meet! Write soon—If I change, I will let you know—if I go home you will hear it in some way. God bless you. God be with you & yours—For dear John's sake, remember his old friend kindly. I *hope* I may get well, but "God's will be done." believe me to be in deepest affliction as in brighter hours, ever sincerely your loving friend

Lula H.

The unrest in Savannah contined. Hamilton, who now had a wife and baby to protect, and others who had served in the army felt it necessary to prepare for the worst. He called a meeting of the former members of the Savannah Cadets on July 29, 1868, at the office of Capt. Henry J. Dickerson. The United States government had forbidden the antebellum militia companies to reorganize, so the company was secretly reorganized as a "club," and Hamilton Branch was elected captain. The Oglethorpe Light Infantry followed the Cadets' lead, and Sanford was elected as its lieutenant. William Harden of the Cadets wrote, "of course, strong efforts were made to break up our activities, but we so managed our affairs that we were not suspected of being members of military organizations."[88]

Each man was responsible for acquiring his own arms, and they met once a week, at night, to drill. It was agreed that they would muster at the south gate of Chatham Academy on Hull Street if the bell at the City Exchange signaled an alarm.[89]

Tallulah Hansell to Charlotte Branch

Oglethorpe
Jan. 16th 1868.
My dear kind Friend,

Since your last letter I have not been able to write to you until now, and must beg your indulgence for the hasty, poor messenger. I was so glad to hear from you, dear friend. . . . I thank God for what you are, and what you have been to me. . . . My health is improving a great deal, but while I have regained flesh, I have neither strength nor color yet, but have reason to hope for recovery. I can take a weak tonic occasionally & sometimes escape fever for several days, at a time. The chills cling to me in spite of all I can do. I have them often, two & even *three* in a day!

My friend Mr. P, came on New Year's Day from Texas, and declared he would never leave me again, particularly while my health is poor. I expect to give up my name with my maiden freedom on the 29th inst. In our deep mourning, ill health, and other circumstances, there will be no party, & no cards. His brother may come, perhaps his sister, who lives at Mt. Zion, Hancock Co. I wish he could have waited until Spring—but he said it would be impracticable. I had made up only two calico dresses—black—and from my long illness my wardrobe was sadly out of order. I am very much hurried, of course, and so cramped by lack of means that it is very hard to prepare. I can get nothing here, and am considerably annoyed by the haste, but shall try to do my best. My mourning I shall not lighten yet, and will only lay aside my sad garb for that one evening for pure white. Will does not like black, but will not say anything against my wishes. Crape, I cannot use, much as it sickens me, but I wear very deep mourning otherwise.

I am about to ask a very great favor of you, that I would not trouble you with if I had faith in any one else to whom I could send. I want a bonnet, and living out of the world pretend no dictation to you, but only say that I am almost brunette, hair & eyes dark brown, & my head *large* with large features. I don't fancy the helmet fronts to the bonnets, but like best the "Fanchon" & similar shapes. Please, if quite convenient, look at them & let me know prices &c. Being in close mourning, it would be black, but as bride might admit *a little* ornament. I leave it *entirely* to your good taste & judgment, only stipulating that it shall not be expensive. I have bought very little, & at any other time would have said that a marriage was an *impossibility*, but Mr. P. *needs* me, & I should be silly to refuse when I can by a sacrifice of pride, go with him now.

The world may sneer at my plain wardrobe, but if he is not ashamed of his little "brown-eyed wife"—I shall be contented. You know that leaving home is a very great trial to me, but I can't trust myself to write a word of this painful parting that shakes my resolution so terribly. We shall leave early in Feb. for Ala. and spend a few weeks at his Father's in Calhoun Co., where we shall then turn our steps is yet undecided, but I trust, *not* to Texas.

Congratulate the young parents for me. I should so much like to have them with you & "Sanford" at my marriage. Pray for me dear friend, as you have never prayed before, that I may be a true, loving, *good* wife & "helpmate" to my chosen one. He is brave & true, but wayward now, & has strayed from the fold. God ever, ever, ever more bless you & yours, & With increasing love,

I am, gratefully & devotedly
your loving
Lula.

This is the last letter from Tallulah Hansell. She and Will were married January 29, 1868, in Oglethorpe, Georgia. They settled in Jacksonville, Alabama, where Will worked as a contractor. Theirs was a tumultuous marriage. Will had been severely beaten in the head by Yankee captors during the war, and this may have exacerbated his unpredictable and often violent behavior. They had five children, but the couple lived apart for the last years of their marriage. Lula and the children were living in Atlanta in 1889 while Will worked for the railroad in Anniston, Alabama. On July 9 of that year he was killed in a shootout with two Anniston police officers, captains Stallings and Parsons. The local papers stated that it caused little excitement, "as everybody had thought for some time that Mr. Pelham would die that way," since he had been shot in a duel the previous year.[90]

A second child, Margaret, was born to Hammie and Marie in 1869, and the Dickerson family continued to support the young household. Sanford worked for Lathrop & Co. until around 1870, when he was hired as a bank clerk. For the present both brothers were concerned with putting food on the table, and they hoped that the future would hold more. At some point in the late 1870s Sanford and Charlotte moved in with Hamilton's family at 81 York Street. The extended family was devoted to one another, and to the memory of John.

Each July 21, on the anniversary of that fateful day when John and the others fell at Manassas, the Oglethorpes, who included Hamilton as an honorary member, honored their fallen comrades. They commemorated their baptism of fire with shooting matches and drill contests held beneath the summer sun in the Park Extension. Sanford, as the high scorer for two years in a row, won the cherished prize medal. He had his name engraved on it along with every winner since the award was bestowed in 1859.

The day began with the color guard arriving at Charlotte's residence. Once known as the Mother of the Oglethorpe Light Infantry, Charlotte had been designated custodian of the colors. Hamilton's children gathered around her for the exciting occasion. "I remember as a child, the thrill when there was a parade and the color guard would come with fife and drum early in the morning," wrote Margaret, years later. "My grandmother would bring the flag to the porch and they would salute and receive the flag, repeating the ceremony after the parade ended."[91]

The company would then march to the Confederate monument and fire three volleys in honor of those who had spilled their blood and sacrificed their youth in the first battle of the war. A day of public celebration ended somberly, when the "war members" gathered in reflective groups to bare their scars and wonder at their own survival.

In honor of another battle burned into the memory of the Savannahians and as a result of the efforts of the Ladies Memorial Association, the remains of a hundred soldiers who had fallen at Gettysburg were brought home and reburied in Laurel Grove Cemetery. On August 22, 1871, Sanford accepted the first shipment containing thirty-two friends who had fallen the day he was shot at Little Round Top. A second shipment arrived on September 23, and a final funeral was held for sixty-eight on September 25. Sanford and the survivors of the Oglethorpes escorted the solemn procession to the cemetery, where the dead were buried seven to a grave.[92]

On April 27, 1872, when it was again legal for militia units to organize, Sanford was elected first lieutenant of the Oglethorpes, a rank he would hold for fifteen years. Offered the captaincy, he modestly refused on the grounds that he had never achieved more than a lieutenancy during the war. He found solace with old comrades who had shared the horrors of battle, the few survivors of Co. B, 8th Georgia. He served as commander for several years until Robert Falligant was elected captain.

Hamilton served as captain of the Cadets. The "war members" mustered regularly, sharing an armory with the Oglethorpes and using a hodgepodge of equipment and uniforms. Younger men joined the companies and participated in the drills and fundraisers that the city enthusiastically supported—and eventually the men again wore fine uniforms. The Savannahians looked forward eagerly to the annual drills, and the military fancy dress balls and picnics were high social events.

One of the worst fires in Savannah's history broke out at midnight on April 29, 1872, sweeping part of the commercial district, in the same location that the disastrous fire of 1796 had begun. Two buildings owned by Charlotte on the corner of Broughton and West Broad were totally destroyed. Fortunately, they were insured, so $10,000 came into her hands at a time when such a sum meant the difference between struggle and comfort.[93]

From this misfortune, Sanford gained. With a share of the money, he went into partnership with William G. Cooper in the wholesale grocery business. On November 28, 1872, Branch & Cooper Grocery opened its doors at 165 Broughton Street. The business thrived and, on September 14,1874, moved into a larger building at 146 Broughton and Whitaker.[94]

Still working for his father-in-law, Hamilton rose to become head stevedore at the Central Railroad Wharf.[95] Hamilton, Jr., their only son, was born to Hamilton and Marie on January 27, 1876.

Charlotte continued her work with the Needle Woman's Friend Society, eventually becoming a manager. In 1879 it became a branch of the Industrial Home and opened an agency at the corner of Drayton & Charleton streets for cutting, making and mending, employing women who needed jobs.

The Branch family had found its footing in a postwar world.

Savannah was slowly allowed to govern her own affairs, and Reconstruction eased by the early 1870s. As the carpetbagger government became less influential, citizens became more involved in civic affairs. A softening of the attitude towards Confederate soldiers tolerated the formation of a committee to erect a monument to the men of Savannah who had given their lives in the bloody war. Sanford served on the committee to select a site and raise funds, and a monument of red sandstone was dedicated on March 25, 1875, in the Park Extension, the parade ground used by the Oglethorpes before the war.

The statue atop the monument was deemed not heroic enough, and in 1878 George Wymberly Jones DeRenne, a prominent citizen of Savannah, offered to replace it with a likeness of a Confederate soldier. The Ladies Memorial Association agreed to help with the funding, and DeRenne hired Welsh sculptor David Richards to execute the figure.[96]

DeRenne was not pleased with the original pose of the figure and discussed it with Hamilton, who suggested the soldier be at parade rest, with his hat thrown back on his head "that winds might cool the heated brow." DeRenne liked the suggestion. He also was not satisfied with the proposed model, Alfred S. Bacon, a veteran of the Oglethorpes. "I want a Confederate soldier, not a dude," he wrote to Hamilton, and suggested that Hamilton pose for photographs. Wearing his old frock coat from the Atlanta campaign and a battered slouch hat that had been issued as part of the Oglethorpe uniform, he went down to the photographer's and stood at parade rest with his hat thrown back while two poses were taken.

These were given to Richards to use as the sculpture model, and the finished likeness to Hammie was astounding. Even the hole in Hammie's trousers, made by the bullet that wounded him, was incorporated into the finished piece.[97] The new memorial was placed in a dedication ceremony in 1879.

Savannah once again boomed with the Gilded Age at the end of the 19th century. Her population grew to nearly 100,000 by the turn of the century. When Capt. Henry J. Dickerson died June 25, 1883, Marie Branch inherited his entire estate—her brother was dead and her sister had become estranged from the family. Hammie sold the captain's business interests except for the Central Railroad and Ocean Steamship Company, which he continued to oversee.

Sanford bought out William Cooper's share of their business, and it became S.W. Branch Grocery. In 1887, at age forty-seven, he resigned his rank of first lieutenant of the Oglethorpes, stepping down to let a younger generation take command. Boys who were not even born when he was wounded at Gettysburg became the keepers of the glory bought with the blood of the first Oglethorpes. He continued to march in their ranks on special occasions, a living symbol of the company's history.

Sanford remained a bachelor, apparently uninterested in romance since losing the affections of several girls during the war, particularly Sally Davis. It must have been a painful reminder to live around the corner from Sally and her husband, George Freeman, when Sanford moved from his quarters in Hamilton's house to 79 Gordon Street after 1885. There he lived with his mother in the last home he would know.

The new year of 1891 found Sanford enjoying much personal success and public respect. Despite a rift between him and his old partner that had resulted in an unsettled court case concerning $5,000, Sanford's business assets totalled nearly $40,000. He had invested well in stocks and ran his store shrewdly. He was a director of the Chatham Bank and an incorporator for the Homeseeker's Mutual Loan Association. While at the store on January 21, he became ill with a headache and went home. The pain became increasingly worse and a doctor was called, but nothing could be done. Sanford had suffered a brain hemorrhage at age fifty. He slipped into a coma and died at home on January 29 in the tender care of his mother, surrounded by a loving family.[98]

Sanford had many friends in Savannah, and he was remembered as a quiet, reticent citizen, loved by all. He was best known for his participation in the Oglethorpe Light Infantry, and his funeral was attended by the corps of both the Oglethorpes and the Savannah Cadets, as well as by members of the many organizations of which he was a member. He was buried beside John, the brother he had watched die, to the sound of "Lights Out."

Charlotte had outlived two sons and a husband. She moved to 126 South Broad, where she boarded. On October 19, 1894, she attended Thursday afternoon prayer services at Independent Presbyterian. Later that evening she stumbled and fell in her room. At eighty years, her age was against her, and she died on October 21. A driving force in the commemoration of Confederate Soldiers and Decoration Day was gone. The Oglethorpe Light Infantry, whose history had been so intertwined with that of Charlotte Branch, attended her funeral and stood at attention as she was laid to rest between her husband and their eldest son.[99]

The adage that tragedy comes in threes more than applied to the Branch family in the 1890s. On December 16, 1896, Hamilton lost his only grandchild, Marie McDevit, age eighteen months, to consumption. His daughter Charlotte, the little girl's mother, died less than six months later. Hamilton himself suffered a slight stroke in 1898 but recovered.

On the evening of February 23, 1899, Hamilton left home to visit friends on Habersham Street. At about 11:00 P.M., while on his way home, he collapsed on the sidewalk, the victim of a massive stroke. A passerby noticed him, and an ambulance was immediately sent for. Hamilton was taken home, where he died about two hours later. Everyone in Savannah was grieved to hear the news. "This announcement will bring sorrow to many hearts," the paper stated. "It is a great shock to his family as it will be to hundreds of friends throughout the city and elsewhere."[100]

Hundreds attended his funeral. "Such a general testimonial to the memory of a man who occupied no public position and was never before the public prominently, except as a worker in the cause dear to him, has seldom been seen in Savannah."[101] The last Branch brother who had marched away to war was gone. They left the world in the same order that they had been born into it, and all three died far too young.

Hamilton's daughter Margaret, called Meta, married James Sexton and moved to Athens, and Marie moved there with her. Hamilton, Jr., attended Yale University, then returned to Savannah to live. He founded the Francis S. Bartow Camp, Sons of Confederate Veterans in 1897, and continued the family tradition of preserving the memory and deeds of Savannah's Confederate soldiers, his uncles and father among them. He later moved to Charlotte, North Carolina, where he started another Sons of Confederate Veterans camp. On a return visit to Savannah, he stopped in Athens to stay with his sister. While there, he contracted typhoid fever and died, tragically, at age twenty-eight.

Meta was the last survivor of the direct Branch line. Through the early years of the 20th century, Margaret Sexton was energetically involved in the United Daughters of the Confederacy and the Children of the Confederacy, carrying on the love for the past that had been so solidly instilled in her by example. In 1905, when she heard of the Society of the Immortal Six Hundred, she knew her uncle Sanford would have been proud to join. She contacted the society, which was composed of survivors of that group of prisoners and had issued special medals for those who had endured the trial together. Margaret bought a posthumous medal for Sanford and had his name engraved on the back.

She was approaching her ninety-second birthday as the centennial of First Manassas was greeted by celebration and commemoration, and Margaret knew that her time was almost up in this life. There was no son or daughter to carry on as the guardian of the family's past, and she was determined to find a suitable repository for the physical remnants of the Confederacy that she had inherited.

Through her conscientious efforts to find a permanent home for the Branch heirlooms, they may be seen today on display at the Atlanta History Center—the personal belongings that went to war and were lovingly kept as cherished reminders of one family's tragedy.

The Branch story ends at the grave in Bonaventure and Laurel Grove cemeteries. Surrounded by the plants native to the Georgia coast, live oaks and palmettos draped in Spanish moss, lie Charlotte, her husband and sons. Lt. John L. Branch's stone tells of his service to his country, followed by a poetic epitaph signed "Lula."

> Son, brother, patriot, friend. Sweet be thy rest,
> In thee Death claimed our bravest and our best.
> Content to fall, thy sole regret was this,
> To die without thy much loved Mother's kiss.
> Thy latest charge was "brothers . . . bid her weep
> No tears for me" then praying, "fell asleep."

Lula herself died in Atlanta on December 30, 1912, at age 76. She is buried in Westview Cemetery there, with two of her children. There was no further correspondence from Lula to the Branch family after her ill-fated marriage to William Pelham.

The Savannah of 1996, with a population of more than 150,000, is much changed from the city familiar to the Branch boys and their generation. But evidence of their lives can still be found. On Broughton Street, the S.W. Branch Grocery is now a catering service and pizzeria, but its exterior has been restored to its proper 19th century appearance. The millinery shop and dwelling, where the family lived in the 1850s and where most of the letters were written to and from, is now the office for the Historic Savannah Foundation. The inside has been converted to office space, but its exterior probably appears much the same as it did when the Branches lived there. The houses at 83 and 81 York Street, where Hammie and Marie married, reared their children, and spent their lives together, remain unchanged. Azaleas and magnolias thrive beneath the sheltering live oaks, replacing the cactus planted there by Hammie in 1880.

Several blocks south of York Street is Forsyth Park, the former parade ground of the O.L.I. One end of the large rectangle of green hosts evening soccer games, picnics and baseball practice. At the other end is the 1858 Fountain with statuary figures, a facsimile of one in the Place de la Concorde in Paris. Between them children play on swings beneath the protecting limbs of live oak trees.

[Author's Note] I visited the park for the first time on a late October day in 1994. As I followed a worn brick path from the beautiful whiteness of the lighted fountain, the tall, red Canadian sandstone base of the Confederate Monument appeared through the trees ahead. There, atop the impressive monolith, stood a soldier at parade rest, guarding the realm that was, and still is, his Savannah. I felt satisfaction in knowing that Hamilton Branch still looks out over the city he knew and loved, the streets he walked and the houses he visited, keeping a watchful eye over the past. —M.P.J.

BIOGRAPHICAL SKETCHES

Adams, John. B. 7/1/25, Nashville, Tenn., of Irish parents. Graduated West Point 1846. Mexican War; breveted capt. for gallantry at Santa Cruz de Rosales. Killed at Franklin 11/30/64 while trying to jump his horse over federal breastworks; at age 50, the oldest gen. and only professional soldier among the six gen. officers killed in that battle. Removed to the McGavock house; later buried at Pulaski, Tenn. *Warner, Generals in Gray*, 2.

Anderson, George "Tige" Led Anderson's Brigade, Hood's Division, Army of Northern Virginia. B. 2/3/24, Covington, Ga. Served in Mexican War as lt. in cavalry. Resigned U.S. Army in 1858 as capt. of the 1st Cavalry. Col. of 11th Ga. Inf. 1861; served as brig. gen. after Bartow's death; officially appointed brig. gen. 11/1/62. Paroled at Appomattox C.H., Va., 4/9/65. Postwar: freight agent for Ga. Railroad in Atlanta; later chief of police in Atlanta. Chief of police and tax collector in Anniston, Ala. Died there 4/4/01; buried Edgemont Cemetery. *Warner, Generals in Gray*, 7.

Anderson, Robert H. B. 10/1/35, Savannah. Enlisted as 1st lt. Confederate artillery 3/16/61. Major, asst. adj. gen. 9/61. Maj. 1st Battalion Ga. Sharpshooters 6/20/62. Col. 5th Ga. Cavalry 1/20/63. Brig. gen. P.A.C.S. 7/26/64. Died 2/8/88. *Warner, Generals in Gray*, 9-10.

Axson, Isaac Stockton Keith. B. 10/3/13, Charleston, S.C. Graduated College of Charleston 1831; Columbia Theological Seminary 1834. Married Rebecca Longstreet Randolph 10/28/34. Pastor of Midway Church, Liberty County, Ga., 1836-53. Resigned due to ill health, then served as president of Greensboro Female College in Greensboro, Ga. Became pastor of the Independent Presbyterian Church, Savannah, Ga., 12/57. His son, Rev. Samuel Edward Axson was father of Ellen Louise Axson, wife of future U.S. president Woodrow Wilson. Dr. Axson presided over the marriage of Ellen and Woodrow in the manse of Independent Presbyterian Church on 6/24/85. Died in Savannah 3/31/9. *Children of Pride, 1456.*

Bailey, Charles F. B. 1839. Appointed 2nd cpl. of Chisholm's Co., Ga. State Troops 5/17/61; mustered out 5/62. Appointed 4th sgt. Co. F, 54th Ga. Inf. 5/13/62; 3rd sgt. 9/22/63. Captured at Marietta, Ga. 6/18/64. Released from Camp Morton Military Prison, Ind. 5/18/65. *Henderson, Roster, 5:677.*

Baker, George. Son of Charles Baker, nephew of Melissa Baker who lived at Athol near Baltimore,

Md. Later attended Washington College in Lexington, Va., when Robert E. Lee was president.

Baker, William. B. c.1771, Baltimore, Md. Father of Melissa Baker. His own father was the only survivor of an Indian massacre in Reading, Pa., and was brought to Baltimore as a young orphan boy.

Baldy, Samuel Hamilton. Joined Co. B, 8th Ga., as pvt. 5/21/61. Wounded at 2nd Manassas 8/30/62. Died at hospital in Warrenton, Va. 9/7/62. *Henderson, Roster, 1:925.*

Barnwell, Stephen. B. 1843, Beaufort District, S.C. Son of planter; military student. Died of wounds at Martinsburg, W.Va., 10/21/62; buried in Old Norbourne Cemetery, Martinsburg.

Bartow, Francis Stebbins. B. 9/6/16, Savannah, Ga. Graduated Franklin College, Athens, (later Univ. of Ga.) with first honor in 1835. Read law with two prominent attorneys in Savannah; attended Yale Law School, no degree. Returned to Savannah in 1837, was admitted to the bar and rose to prominence in local and state politics; several times member of state house and senate. Prominent in the proceedings of the Ga. secession convention; member of Provisional Confederate Congress. Left for Va. on 5/21/61 as captain of Co. A, OLI (later to become Co. B, 8th Ga. Inf.). Elected col. 6/21/61; later promoted to brig. gen. Killed 7/21/61 at 1st Manassas while gallantly leading his command. Survived by wife, Louisa Greene Berrien, daughter of his law mentor. In December 1861 Cass County, Ga., was renamed Bartow County in his honor. *Myers, Children of Pride, 1461-62.*

Bedell, John K. Enlisted as 2d lt. 5/12/62, Co. H., 54th Ga. Inf. Stationed at Beaulieu 8/62 12/62. Elected 1lt. 12/15/63. Sick in Mercer's Brigade Hospital 7/64-8/25/64. *Henderson, Roster, 5:699; Compiled Service Record, Ga. Archives.*

Belvin, John A. Pvt. Co. B, 8th Ga. Inf. 5/21/61. Severely wounded through hips at 1st Manassas 7/21/61. Discharged on account of wounds 9/16/61. *Henderson, Roster, 1:925.*

Berrien, John MacPherson. B. 1843. Clerk in a Savannah commission house; lived with his brother-in-law, Francis S. Bartow. *1860 Chatham Census.*

Bevill, Francis Bartow. B. 1845. Lived with Col. Francis Bartow in 1860. Enlisted in Co. H, 8th Ga. (at age 16) as pvt. 5/20/61. Wounded at 1st Manassas 7/21/61. Discharged with disability in Richmond 9/17/61. Enlisted in Co. B, 8th Ga. Inf., discharged January 1862. Appointed midshipman in Confederate Navy. *1860 Census; Henderson, Roster, 1:973.*

Binford, James W. B. 1811. Farmer from Henrico County, Va., living with wife, Eliza, age 34, and two teenage daughters. *1860 Va. Census.*

Bliss, Alfred. B.1836. Fred's elder brother. Pvt. in Co. G, 1st (Olmstead's) Ga. Infantry. Died of typhoid fever in a Savannah hospital 10/9/63. *Compiled Service Records, Ga. Archives.*

Bliss, Frederick. B. 1840. Son of Emma M. Bliss, widowed, who ran a boardinghouse in Savannah. Joined OLI in 1856. Clerk at a commission house in 1860. 2nd sgt. 5/21/61; elected 2nd lt. 9/1/61; 1st lt. 12/1/61. Serving as capt. 1863. Wounded in the thigh 2nd day of Gettysburg; leg amputated 7/3/63. Died in Hood's Division Hospital at the Plank Farm that night; buried there. Body removed to Laurel Grove Cemetery in Savannah 2/9/86. *1860 Census, Chatham County. Henderson, Roster, 1:923-931; Savannah Morning News, Feb. 10, 1866.*

Bogart, Jane H. Wife of William S. Bogart of Mercer County, N.J., the principal and piano teacher at Chatham Academy, Savannah. Ga. *1860 Chatham Co. census; Henderson, Roster, v. 1:925.*

Bogart, John H. Son of Jane and William Bogart. Member of OLI, enlisted in 8th Ga. Inf. 5/21/61. Reported sick in General Hospital, Richmond 12/31/62. *1860 Chatham Co. Census; Henderson, Roster.*

Boler, O. Enlisted as pvt. Co. B, 8th Ga. Inf. 3/6/62. Captured at Gettysburg 7/2/63; released at Ft. Delaware, De., 5/5/65.

Borchert, Charles F. B.1836. Brother of William. Machinist from Savannah. Father was a baker from Mecklenburg, Germany. Original member of OLI. 1st cpl. 5/21/61. Survived the war; living in Miss. in 1891. *Rockwell, History of the O.L.I.*

Borchert, William. B.1841. Brother of Charles. Appointed 3rd cpl. 9/3/61 in Co. H, 1st (Olmstead's) Ga. Inf. Captured at Fort Pulaski; exchanged. Died at Petersburg, Va. 1862.

Bourquin, Francis Edward. B.1839. Elected jr. 2nd lt. Co. C, 1st Regt., 1st Brigade, Ga. State Troops 9/18/61; mustered out 3/18/62. Elected jr. 2nd lt. Co. I, 54th Ga. Inf. 5/6/62. 2nd lt. 2/27/63. Killed in camp accident 12/20/64. Buried Conf. section of Rose Hill Cemetery, Columbia, Tenn., Grave #114. *Henderson, Roster, 5:709; also per Mr. Tim Burgess, White House, Tenn.*

Bradley, William H. B.1839. Enlisted as pvt. 5/13/62 in Co. F, 54th Ga. Inf. Deserted 12/18/64. Took oath of allegiance to U.S. at Nashville, Tenn. 1/14/65. *Henderson, Roster, 5:679.*

Breedlove, Lt. John Penn. B. 8/1/40, Tuskegee, Ala. Single, working as clerk, living at home in 1860. Enlisted as 4th sgt. Co. B, 4th Ala. Inf. 4/28/61. Promoted to 3rd lt. 4/21/62. Wounded at Fredericksburg 12/12-13/62. Wounded in abdomen and permanently disabled at Little Round Top, Gettysburg. Admitted to Letterman Hospital 7/4/63. One of Immortal Six Hundred placed under fire on Morris Island, S.C., 9-10/64. Postwar: merchant in Tuskegee; tax assessor and state representative. Died 3/14/01; buried Tuskegee Cemetery. *Joslyn, Biographical Roster, 48.*

Breen, John. B. 1820, County Tyrone, Ireland. Enlisted in Co. F, 54th Ga. Inf. 2/12/63. Captured at Egypt Station, Miss. 12/28/64. Paroled from Alton Prison, Ill., to James River, Va., for exchange 2/65. Received by provost marshal's office; Confederate deserter at Savannah, Ga. 3/65. Took oath of allegiance to U.S. 3/30/65. *Henderson, Roster, 5:679.*

Brewer, Thomas A. Enlisted as pvt. in Co. I, 54th Ga. Inf. 9/1/62. Surrendered at Greensboro, N.C. 4/26/65. *Henderson, Roster, 5:711.*

Brewer, Williamson T. Enlisted as pvt. in Co. C, 1st Regt., 1st Brigade, Ga. State Troops 9/18/61; mustered out 3/18/62. Appointed 1st cpl. of Co. I, 54th Ga. Inf. 5/16/62. 5th sgt. 3/27/63. Surrendered at Greensboro, N.C. 4/26/65. *Henderson, Roster, 5:711.*

Brown, John Calvin. B. 1/6/27, Giles County, Tenn. Graduated Jackson College, Columbia, Tenn., 1846. Lawyer. Enlisted as pvt. in 1861; appointed col. of 3rd Tenn. Inf. 5/61. Promoted to brig. gen. 8/30/62; maj. gen. 8/4/64. Severely wounded at Franklin 11/30/64. Rejoined army in N.C. 4/2/65. Paroled at Greensboro, N.C., at end of war. President of Texas & Pacific Railroad. Died 8/17/89 at Red Boiling Springs, Tenn.; buried Pulaski, Tenn. *Warner, Generals in Gray, 35.*

Brown, Joseph E. B. B. 1821, Pickens County, S.C. Brought as infant to Union County, Ga. Attended Yale Law School for one year (1846). Elected governor of Ga. 1857. Forbade OLI to leave state with their guns, which were state property; sent troops to Augusta to intercept Bartow, who left Ga. through Charleston instead. *Hendrick, Statesmen of The Lost Cause, 337-342.*

Brownell, George W. Enlisted as pvt. in Chisholm's Co. Ga. State Troops 5/17/61; mustered out 5/62. Enlisted as a pvt. in Co. F, 54th Ga. Inf. 5/13/62. Paroled at Augusta, Ga. 5/18/65. *Henderson, Roster, 5:680.*

Buist, Henry. B. 12/25/39, Charleston, S.C. Single, working as attorney in 1860. Enlisted as pvt. but promoted to lt. in "Iron Battery" of Palmetto Guard, which fired upon Ft. Sumter in 1861. Resigned to form Co. G, 27th S.C. Inf.; served as capt. Captured at Petersburg, Va. 6/24/64. One of the Immortal Six Hundred; received special exchange from Morris Island, S.C. 10/3/64. Postwar: resumed law practice; elected state senator 1865. Died 6/9/87. Buried in Magnolia Cemetery, Charleston. *Joslyn, Biographical Roster.*

Butler, Alexander F. B. 1838, Savannah. Son of Gilbert Butler of Columbia, N.Y., who came to Savannah c.1815. A master carpenter, Gilbert built many of the fine buildings in Savannah, among them Christ Episcopal Church on Bull Street. In 1860 Alex was employed as clerk for Savannah and Ga. Central Railroad. 2nd lt. 5/21/61. Wounded 1st Manassas 7/61. Elected capt. 12/17/61. Seriously wounded during Seven Days' Battles 6/28-7/1/62; absent 1/63 at Oglethorpe Barracks Hospital in Savannah; returned to duty 5/63. Wounded and captured at Gettysburg 7/2/63. Paroled at Johnson's Island, Ohio; sent to City Point Prison, Va., for exchange 2/24/65. *Lane, Architecture of the Old South, 74, 147; Compiled Service Record for Alexander Butler, Ga. Archives.*

Butler, George. Brother of Alexander F. Butler. Killed at 1st Manassas. *Henderson, Roster, 1:925.*

Butler, Robert M. B. 1840. Son of Worthington C. Butler, who owned boot and shoe store in Savannah, Ga. Appointed 3rd sgt. of Chisholm's Co., Ga. State Troops 5/18/61. Mustered out 5/62; joined Co. F, 54th Ga. Inf. as 2nd sgt. 5/13/62; 1st sgt. 9/22/63; elected lt. Surrendered at Greensboro, N.C. 4/26/65. *1860 census; Henderson, Roster, 5:676.*

Carpenter, Andrew J. B. 1828. Hotel bookkeeper from Oneida, N.Y. Enlisted as pvt. in Co. B, 8th Ga. 3/6/62; present 10/31/64. No further record. *Henderson, Roster, 1:926.*

Carrolan, James E. Pvt. 5/21/61. Killed at Thoroughfare Gap, Va. 8/28/62. *Henderson, Roster, 1:926.*

Carter, Cyrus B. B. 1832. Bank officer in Savannah. Enlisted as capt. in A.C. Davenport's Independent Co., Ga. Volunteer Cavalry, as 2nd sgt. 1/3/61. Elected 2lt. Co. G, 1st (Olmstead's) Ga. Inf. 4/29/62. Killed between Marietta, Ga., and Atlanta in skirmish 6/16/64. *Henderson, Roster, 1:175, 183.*

Carter, James H. Druggist in Savannah, whose store was two doors down from Charlotte's shop and residence. Sanford Branch worked as clerk there before the war. *1860 Chatham census; 1860 Savannah City Directory.*

Carter, John Carpenter. B.12/19/37, Waynesboro, Ga. Univ. of Va. 1854–56. Graduated law school Cumberland Univ., Lebanon, Tenn., and taught there. Practicing law in Memphis 1861. Enlisted as capt. of 38th Tenn. Inf.; promoted brig. gen. 7/7/64. Wounded at Franklin 11/30/64; died of wounds at home of William Harrison on 12/10/64, the last and youngest (age 27) Conf. gen. lost in that battle; buried Rose Hill Cemetery, Columbia, Tenn. *Warner, Generals in Gray, 45.*

Chandler, Daniel Gill. B. 1812, Columbia County, Ga. Became capt. Co. A, 2nd Ga. Inf. 4/20/61. Resigned with disability 4/20/62. Made application as Post QM 6/25/63. Died at Gainesville, Ga. 10/14/87. *Henderson, Roster, 1:375.*

Chisholm, John B. B. 1841. Clerk in 1860. Pvt. in Co. B, 8th Ga. Inf. 5/21/61. Paroled at Burkeville, Va. 4/14-17/65. *1860 Chatham County census; Henderson, Roster, 1:926.*

Chisholm, Walter S. B. 1837. Attorney from Muscogee County, Ga. Joined OLI 1857. Elected capt. of Chisholm's Co. of Ga. State Troops 5/17/61. Capt. of Co. F., 54th Ga. Inf. 5/13/62. Resigned on account of ill health. Accepted appointment as Savannah city court judge 9/22/63. *1860 Census; Henderson, Roster, 5:676.*

Cleburne, Patrick R. B. 3/17/28, County Cork, Ireland. Served three years in HRM 41st Regt. of Foot before purchasing discharge. Emigrated to U.S.; settled in Helena, Ark. His was an American success story. First a druggist's clerk, he studied law in his spare time, was admitted to the bar in Ark. in 1855, and established successful practice. Elected col. 15th Ark. Inf. 1861; brig. gen. 3/4/62; maj. gen. 12/13/62. Wrote manifesto 12/63 that suggested offering slaves freedom for enlisting in Confederate army, a step taken by the Confederate Congress in 1865 but implemented too late to win the war. Died at battle of Franklin, Tenn. 11/30/64. Engaged to be married at time of his death to Susan Tarleton, age 24, of Mobile, Ala., whom he had met at the wedding of Gen. William J. Hardee, a mutual friend. First buried in Ashwood Cemetery, Spring Hill, Tenn.; remains moved to Helena, Ark. 1870. *Purdue, Pat Cleburne, Confederate General.*

Cole, Benjamin Theodore. B. 1839. A blacksmith's apprentice in 1860. 2nd lt. Co. H, 1st (Olmstead's) Ga. Inf. Also served as 2nd lt, Davenport's Independent Cavalry Co., Ga. State Troops. *Compiled Service Records, Ga. Archives.*

Cole, Hollie. Brother of Benjamin. OLI, 8th Ga. Inf. Served with Hamilton Branch.

Coleman, William T. Enlisted Co. C, 54th Ga. Inf. as pvt. 5/6/62. Transferred to Co. F 1/1/63. Captured at Marietta, Ga. 6/18/64; paroled at Camp Morton, Ind. Forwarded to Point Lookout, Md., for exchange 3/10/65. Died 3/65 on way to Richmond, of dysentery contracted in prison; buried at sea. *Henderson, Roster, 5:649, 681.*

Coombs, William D. Pvt. 4/16/61. Wounded at Garnett's Farm in Peninsula Campaign 6/27/62. Died of wounds at 1st Ga. Hospital in Richmond 7/20/62.

Conrad, Holmes and Tucker, brothers. Pvts. Co. D, 2nd Va. Cavalry. Holmes was 22-year-old student at seminary in Alexandria, Va., when war began; promoted to 5th sgt. Both killed by same shell at 1st Manassas and buried in a common grave in Norbourne Cemetery, Martinsburg, W.Va.

Coon, David A. B. 4/34, N.C. Music teacher in Lincolnton, N.C. 1860. Enlisted as pvt. 4/25/61 in Co. K, 1st N.C. Inf.; 1st lt. 2/12/62 in Co. I, 11th N.C. Wounded in right foot and both thighs at Gettysburg 7/3/63 and captured. One of the Immortal Six Hundred; released from Ft. Delaware Prison 6/12/65. Returned to Lincoln County, N.C. Postwar: served on district school committee and county board of education. Died after 1914. *Joslyn, Biographical Roster, 76.*

Cooper, Thomas L. B. 1832. Attorney from Fulton County Ga. Married with three children, one an infant, when he became capt. of Co. F, 8th Ga. Inf. 5/22/61. Appointed lt. col. 7/21/61. Died 12/24/61 from injuries resulting from fall from horse. *Henderson, Roster, 1:955.*

Cowper, John C. B. 1842, Gates County, N.C. Single teacher living with parents in Gatesville, N.C. 1860. Enlisted in Co. E, 33rd N.C. Inf. as sgt. 10/5/61; appt. 2nd lt. 5/4/63. Wounded in left lung and captured at Gettysburg 7/3/63. At Seminary Hospital until transferred to West's Building Hospital, Baltimore 10/6/63. One of the Immortal Six Hundred. Died on Morris Island, S.C. 10/7/64; buried there. *Joslyn, Biographical Roster, 79.*

Crane, William H. B. 1840. Son of Heman A. and Julia R. Crane of Conn. Clerk in commission house 1860. 3rd cpl. 5/21/61. Shot in head and killed at 1st Manassas 7/21/61. *1860 Census, Henderson, Roster. Undated letter in Margaret Branch Sexton Collection, University of Ga., Athens; 1860 Chatham Co. Census.*

Davis, Alfred. Brother of Edward. Enlisted first in OLI, then as pvt. in Co. B, 8th Ga. Inf. 5/21/61. Captured at Antietam; paroled at Shepherdstown, Md. 9/29/62. Still with company 10/31/64. Surrendered at Appomattox, Va. 4/9/665. *Henderson, Roster, 1:926.*

Davis, Charles. Brother of Parish. Enlisted as pvt. in Co. F, 54th Ga. Inf. 4/29/63. Killed at Atlanta 7/64. *Henderson, Roster, 5:681.*

Davis, Edward. Brother of Alfred. B. 1/8/38. Clerk in commission house at time of enlistment in 8th Ga. Inf. 5/21/61. Appointed capt. and asst. QM 10/19/63. Wounded. Surrendered Tallahassee, Fla. 5/10/65; paroled Thomasville, Ga. 5/20/65. Died 9/22/75; buried Laurel Grove Cemetery, Savannah. *1860 Chatham Co, census; Henderson, Roster, 1:926.*

Davis, Henry. Brother of Joseph. Co. B., 8th Ga. Died in Liberty County, Ga., 1892. *Rockwell, The Oglethorpe Light Infantry.*

Davis, Joseph O. B. 1839. Clerk at commission house in Savannah 1860. Appointed 4th cpl. in Co. B. 8th Ga. 8/19/61. Wounded at 1st Manassas 7/21/61. Appointed 4th sgt. 12/17/61. Wounded at Ft. Harrison, Va., 9/29/64. Surrendered at Appomattox 4/9/65. *Rockwell, The Oglethorpe Light Infantry.*

Davis, Parish. Brother of Charles. Co. A, 18th Batt. Ga. Inf. Enlisted as pvt. 6/6/62. Employed on extra duty at Savannah as signal man and telegraph operator. Stationed at Turners Rock battery near Savannah as telegraph operator. *Compiled Service Records, Ga. Archives.*

Davis, Sarah E. "Sallie." B. 1842. Daughter of William H. Davis, a butcher in Savannah. Sanford was in love with her. Married George C. Freeman 12/16/62 at Independent Presbyterian Church, Savannah. *1860 Chatham Co. Census; Chatham Co. Marriages.*

Dell, George W. Enlisted pvt., Co. B, 8th Ga. 8/12/61. Disability discharge 1/3/62. *Henderson, Roster, 1:926.*

Dennard, James Elkin. Enlisted as pvt. in Co. F, 54th Ga. Inf. 8/1/63; disabled. Joined Co. B, 2nd Battalion Troops & Defenses, Macon, Ga. *Henderson, Roster, 5:681.*

Dickerson, George Washington. B. 1841. Engineer apprentice in 1860. OLI. Pvt., 8th Ga. Inf. 5/21/61. Elected 2nd lt. of Co. F 2/6/62. Wounded in head at Ft. Jackson in Savannah; resigned with disability 1/6/63. Died from effects of wound 2/14/69. Hamilton Branch's brother-in-law.

Dickerson, Henry J. Father of George W. Organized Emmett Rifles, which became Co. F, 22nd Battalion Ga. Heavy Artillery. Hamilton Branch's father-in-law.

Dillon, Gertrude. B. 1841. Her mother was a widow, born in Ireland and listed in 1860 census as a lady of leisure.

Dowse, Samuel. Enlisted as pvt. in Co. F, 54th Ga. Inf. 3/17/63. Surrendered at Greensboro, N.C. 4/26/65. *Henderson, Roster, 5:682.*

Drummond, Edward W. B. 1834 in Maine. Bookkeeper in commission house in Savannah and member of Chatham Siege Artillery 1860. Enlisted as pvt., 1st Ga. Inf. 8/1/61; appointed commissary sgt. 9/1/61. Captured at Ft. Pulaski 4/11/62; exchanged. Appointed commissary sgt. in 1st (Olmstead's) Ga. Inf. 10/24/62. Recommended for appointment as maj. and commissary sgt. by Gen. Mercer 5/2/64. *Henderson, Roster, 1:114.*

Eastmead, Lewis Leander. B. 1838, Beaufort, S.C. Mason by trade. Pvt., 8th Ga. Inf. 5/21/61. Wounded at 1st Manassas. Paroled at Lynchburg 4/14/65. *1860 Census; Henderson, Roster, 1:927.*

Elkins, Harmon. Brother of Paul. B. 1830. Clerk at Central Railroad 1860. Co. H, 1st (Olmstead's) Ga. Inf.; appointed 5th sgt. 9/3/61; 1st lt. 1863. *1860 Census; Henderson, Roster, 1:193.*

Elkins, Harrison Clay. B. 1837. Enlisted as pvt. Co. C, 1st Ga. Brigade State Troops, 9/18/61; mustered out 3/18/62. Appointed 1st sgt. Co. I, 54th Ga. Inf. 5/16/62. *Effingham Co. Census.*

Elkins, Paul. Brother of Harmon. B.1838. Clerk in shoe store 1860. Pvt. in Ga. State Troops 5/30/61; mustered out 1/62. Enlisted Pvt. Co. C, 1st (Olmstead's) Ga. Inf. 2/28/62; 4th cpl.; 2nd sgt.; jr. 2nd lt. 1/6/63; 2nd lt. 5/24/63. *1860 Census; Henderson, Roster, 1:142.*

Elliott, Stephen. B.8/31/06, Beaufort, S.C. Graduated Harvard 1824, established law practice in Beaufort and Charleston 1827-33. Ordained priest in Protestant Episcopal Church, elected first bishop of Diocese of Ga. 1840. Rector of St. John's Church, Savannah 1840-45, president of Montpelier Female Institute 1845-53, and rector of Christ Church in Savannah 1853-66. Together with Rt. Rev. James Hervey Otey and Rt. Rev. Leonidas Polk, founded Univ. of the South in Sewanee, Tenn., 1860. Died suddenly in Savannah 12/21/66; buried in Laurel Grove Cemetery. *Myers, Children of Pride, 1514.*

Elliott, Stephen, Jr. Brig. gen. in Confederate army. Died 3/21/66 from wounds received at Petersburg in 1864. *Myers, Children of Pride, 1514.*

Ellsworth, Elmer E. 11th N.Y. Volunteer Inf. Entered Marshal House in Alexandria, Va., 5/24/61, and climbed onto roof to remove Confederate flag placed there. Refused to leave and was shot dead by the proprietor. *Davis, Battle at Bull Run, 9.*

Ettinger, Henry. Enlisted as pvt. in Co. F, 54th Ga. Inf. 1/23/63. Sick in General Hospital No. 1 in Savannah, Ga. 12/63. Deserted 6/14/64. Captured at Golgotha, Ga. 6/15/64 and enlisted in U.S.

Navy at Rock Island, Ill. 7/6/64. *Henderson, Roster,* 5:682.

Eubanks, John J. Enlisted as pvt. 6/16/61 in Co. G, 8th Ga. Inf.; appointed 3rd sgt. Wounded at Wilderness, Va. 5/6/64. Appointed regimental ensign 8/26/64. No further record. *Henderson, Roster, 1:915, 966.*

Falligant, Phillip R. B. 1840. With Walter Chisholm on original committee to organize Savannah Cadets 5/61; founding member. Appointed 1st sgt. of Chisholm's Co., Ga. State Troops 5/17/61; mustered out 5/62. Appointed 1st sgt. Co. F, 54th Ga.Inf. 5/13/62; elected 2nd lt. 9/22/63. *Rockwell, History of the O.L.I.*

Fendell, Philip R. B. 1796, Va. Lawyer in Washington, D.C., who apparently acted as negotiator on behalf of prisoners confined at Old Capitol Prison.

Fields, James. Enlisted Co. C, 8th Ga. Inf.; appointed capt. 7/2/63. Wounded at Knoxville, Tenn. 11/29/63; captured in hospital 12/4/63. Paroled at Ft. Delaware3/7/65. *Henderson, Roster,* 1:893.

Finley, J.J. Col. of 6th Fla. Inf. 4/14/62. Brig. gen P.A.C.S. 11/16/3. His brigade comprised the 1st, 3rd, 4th, 6th, 7th Fla. Inf. and the 1st Florida Cavalry.

Force, Charles. B. 1830. Physician from Washington, D.C. His father was Peter Force, an editor with real and personal property value of $150,000 in 1860. *1860 Census.*

Foy, Edward E. Appt. 4th sgt. Co. C, 1st Regt., 1st Brigade Ga. State Troops 9/18/61; mustered out 3/18/62. Appointed 4th sgt. Co. I, 54th Ga. Inf. 5/16/62; 3rd sgt. 3/27/63. In Atlanta, Ga. hospital 7/22/64. Sent to Fort Valley hospital **(where?)** at close of war. *Henderson, Roster,* 5:710.

Fraser, John Couper. B. 1830, St. Simons, Ga. Enlisted as 1st lt. in Read's Battery, 5/21/61; appt. capt. 3/2/62. Wounded in thigh by shell fragment at Gettysburg; died 7/11/63 at Crawford's Farm. Body was removed to Savannah with Gettysburg dead in 1872; buried in Laurel Grove Cemetery, Lot #97. *Price, Beauty from Ashes.*

Freeman, Henry C. B. 1820. Bookkeeper from Nashville, Tenn. His brother George was Sanford Branch's rival for the affections of Miss Sallie Davis.

Garrett, James L. Enlisted as pvt., 8th Ga. Inf. 5/21/61. Wounded and captured at Gettysburg 7/4/63. Cared for Sanford from 7/2/63 when both were wounded. Died of smallpox at Marine General Hospital, Baltimore, Md. 1/8/64. *Henderson, Roster, 1:927.*

Gist, States Rights. B. 9/3/31, Union District, S.C. Graduated Harvard Law School 1854. Served in S.C. militia as brig. gen. 1859. Volunteer aide to Gen. Barnard Bee at 1st Manassas; succeeded Bee after his death. Killed 11/30/64 while leading brigade on foot at Franklin; bullet pierced heart. Buried on battlefield by his body servant, Wiley Howard, who had accompanied him from home; remains were removed to Columbia, S.C. after the war. *Warner, Generals in Gray, 106-107.*

Gnann, Joseph H. B. 1832. Lumber measurer in Savannah prior to war. Originally in OLI. Enlisted as pvt. 5/21/61 in Co. B, 8th Ga. Inf. Appointed 3rd sgt. Co. I, 54th Ga. Inf. 5/6/62. Elected jr. 2nd lt.3/27/63; acting adj. for post 12/31/63. Killed at Atlanta 7/22/64. *Henderson, Roster,* 5:710.

Godfrey, Charles W. B. 1835. Mariner before war. Enlisted as pvt., Co. B, 8th Ga. Inf. 5/21/61; discharged with disability 8/14/61. Appointed 2nd lt. 4/20/63 and ordered to 1st. (Olmstead's) Ga. Inf. 4/30/63. Paroled at Albany, Ga. 5/15/65. *Henderson, Roster, 1:927.*

Goldsborough, William Worth. B. 10/6/31, Frederick County, Md. Enlisted as pvt., Co. C, 1st Md. Inf. 5/17/61. Commanded 48th Va. Inf. at 2nd Manassas; badly wounded at the railroad cut. Promoted to capt. of 2nd Md. Inf. 12/24/62; maj. 1/26/63. Wounded in chest, captured at Gettysburg 7/3/63. One of the Immortal Six Hundred; released from Ft. Delaware 6/13/65. Postwar: newspaperman and publisher. Died 12/25/01 in Philadelphia; buried Loudon Park Cemetery, Baltimore. *Joslyn, Biographical Roster, 117.*

Goodwin, Sidney P. Pvt. 5/21/61. Enlisted as lt. in 5th Regt. Ga. Cavalry. *Rockwell, The Oglethorpe*

Light Inf. of Savannah in Peace and War, 34.

Gordon, George A. B. 1827. Attorney from Savannah. Appointed capt. of Gordon's Co., 1st (Olmstead's) Ga. Inf. 5/30/61. Elected maj. of 13th Battn. Ga. Inf. 5/26/62; promoted to col. 12/23/62. Transferred to Field and Staff of 63rd Ga. Inf. *1860 Census; Henderson, Roster, 6:369.*

Gordon, George Washington. B. 10/5/36, Giles County, Tenn. Graduate of Western Milit. Inst., Nashville, Tenn. 1859. Surveyor. Entered Confederate service as drillmaster, 11th Tenn. Inf.; promoted to col. of regiment 12/62; brig. gen. 8/15/64. Wounded 11/30/64 at Franklin, Tenn., one of few Confederate gens. who survived battle; surrendered with his men. Released from Ft. Warren Prison 7/65. Elected to U.S. Congress 1906; served three terms, becoming last Confederate gen. to serve in that body. Died 8/9/11 in Memphis, Tenn.; buried in Elmwood Cemetery, Memphis. *Warner, Generals in Gray, 109-110.*

Goulding, Charles H. B. 1833. Nephew of Edwin Ross Goulding. Clerk at Chatham County Courthouse before the war. *1860 Census.*

Goulding, Edwin Ross. Confederate col. Died of disease 4/4/62.

Graham, James A. B. 1825. Presbyterian clergyman in Winchester, Va.; originally from N.Y. He and his wife Fannie had three small children. *1860 census, Frederick County, Va.*

Granbury, Hiram Bronson. B. 3/1/31, Copiah County, Miss. Educated at Oakland College, Rodney, Miss. Moved to Texas in 1850s, practiced law in Waco. Recruited Waco Guards 1861. Elected maj., 7th Texas Inf. 10/61. Captured at Ft. Donelson; exchanged. Elected col. of 7th before Vicksburg; promoted to brig. gen. 2/29/64. Struck by rifle ball just under right eye and killed at Franklin, Tenn. 11/30/64, the first Confederate gen. to die that day. Buried nearby; remains moved to Granbury, Tex. 1893, a town named in his honor. *Warner, Generals in Gray, 114.*

Grant, James B. B. 1844. Brother of Robert. OLI. Enlisted as pvt. in Co. B, 8th Ga. Inf. 5/21/61; appointed 1st lt. and aide-de-camp and ordered to report to Gen. Gardner 6/16/63. *Henderson, Roster, 1:927.*

Grant, Robert. B. 1838. Attorney from Glen County practicing in Savannah 1860. Enlisted as pvt. in Co. B, 8th Ga. Inf. 5/21/61; appointed color-bearer 1861; acting asst. adj. gen. 1861; 2nd lt. 9/18/61. Assigned to duty with Read's Battery, Ga. Light Artillery 7/25/62; capt. and asst. adj. gen. 8/15/63. Surrendered Greensboro, N.C. 4/26/65. *1860 census; Henderson, Roster, 1:928.*

Graybill, Charles. Pvt., Co. B, 8th Ga. Inf. 5/21/61. Discharged for disability 12/28/61 at Richmond; appointed 2nd lt. and drillmaster. Resigned after being elected 1st lt. of Dillard Greys 6/11/63. Elected capt. Co. A, 27th Battn. Ga. Inf. 12/18/63. *Henderson, Roster, 1:928.*

Gregory, William H. Enlisted in 7th Ga. Inf. as private 8/4/62. Died in hospital at Gordonsville, Va. 11/6/82. *Henderson, Roster, 1:877.*

Griffin, James H. B. 4/29/29. Enlisted in Co. E, 54th Ga. Inf. as 2nd lt. 5/6/62; elected 1st lt. 10/29/63. Recovered from wound (when/where?) and surrendered at Greensboro, N.C. 4/26/65. Died 12/10/96. *Henderson, Roster, 5:667.*

Griffin, John J. B. 1838, Kerry, Ireland. Clerk at Central Railroad in Savannah. Enlisted as pvt. 5/21/61 in Co. B, 8th Ga. Wounded. Absent wounded 10/31/64. No further record. *1860 census; Henderson, Roster, 1:928.*

Habersham, Joseph Clay. Brother of William N. Jr. B. 1841, Savannah. Son of planter and commission merchant in Savannah. Medical student in 1860, living at home. Elected jr. 2nd lt., Co. A, 18th Battn. Ga. Inf. 2/25/61. Appointed asst. surgeon, C.S.A., and ordered to report to Gen. A.R. Lawton for duty 7/19/61. Appointed surgeon of 25th Ga. Inf. 9/21/61. Surgeon of 1st (Olmstead's) Ga. Inf. 9/30/61. Enlisted as pvt., Co. B, 18th Battn. Ga. Inf. 4/1/62; transferred to Brig. Gen. W.D. Smith's staff as ADC. Served as lt. to Gen. Hugh Mercer, then to Brig. Gen.

States Rights Gist. Killed at Decatur, Ga. 7/22/64. *Compiled Service Record, Ga. Archives.*

Habersham, William Neyle, Jr. Brother of Joseph. B. 1844. Enlisted as pvt. Co. D, 2nd Battn. Ga. Cav. 12/9/61; discharged, furnished W.T. Hannan as substitute 8/13/62. Enlisted as pvt., Co. F, 54th Ga. Inf. Killed at Atlanta 7/64. *1860 Census; Henderson, Roster, 5:683.*

Hall, Samuel H.M. B. 1825. Wharf clerk from Buffalo, N.Y. Co. B, 8th Ga. Inf. 5/21/61; appointed QM; reduced to ranks and returned to Co. B 7/8/64. Deserted 8/6/64. *1860 Chatham Census; Henderson, Roster, 1:928.*

Hansell, Andrew Jackson. Brother of Tallulah Hansell and state adj. gen. of Ga. during war. Postwar: served as state senator.

Hansell, Tallulah. Friend of John Branch's from his Ga. Milit. Inst. days in Marietta, Ga. Distraught at John's death, Lula corresponded with the Branch family, particularly Charlotte, until her marriage to William Pelham in 1868.

Hardee, William J. B. 10/12/15, Camden County, Ga. Graduated West Point 1838. Twice breveted for gallantry in Mexican War; served as commandant of cadets at West Point. Wrote textbook *Rifle and Light Inf. Tactics* which was standard use manual of arms for Confederate army. Resigned as lt. col. in U.S. Army when Ga. seceded. Appointed brig. gen. 6/17/61; maj. gen. 10/7/61 in C.S.A.; lt. gen. 10/10/62. Surrendered 4/65 in N.C. Postwar: planter in Selma, Ala. Died 11/6/73; buried at Selma. *Warner, Generals in Gray, 124.*

Hardwick, Charles C. B. 1838, Ga. Merchant and factor from Hancock County, Ga. 1860. Original member of OLI. Enlisted as pvt. 5/21/61 in Co. B, 8th Ga. Inf. Elected jr. 2nd lt.12/17/61. Wounded. Appointed capt. in adj. gen.'s dept. reporting to Gen. George T. Anderson, Anderson's Brigade, 11/8/62. Appointed asst. adj. gen. 11/4/64. Surrendered at Appomattox, Va.11/9/65. *Henderson, Roster, 1:928.*

Harper, Charles M. B. 1839. Clerk in Rome, Ga. 1860. Pvt., Co. E., 8th Ga. Inf. 5/14/61; elected 2nd lt. 10/14/61. Wounded at Gettysburg 7/2/63. Appointed adj. 10/15/64. Surrendered at Appomattox 11/9/65. *Henderson, Roster, 1:951.*

Harris, William A. Enlisted as capt. 7/9/61. Appt. maj. 12/9/61. Leg broken by fall from horse at Seven Pines, Va. 5/31/62. Elected lt. col. 10/23/62. Resigned 11/8/62. Elected capt. Co. F, 5th Reg. Ga. Militia 4/64. Resigned due to disability 5/10/64. *Henderson, Roster, 2:86, 339, 380.*

Harrison, Harris Kollock. B. 2/13/27, Montieth plantation near Savannah. Enlisted as capt. 5/13/62 in Co. B, 21st Battn. Ga. Cav., which became Co. E, 7th Ga. Cav. Captured at Trevillian Station, Va. 6/11/64. One of the Immortal Six Hundred. Returned to Savannah to find plantation in ruins; moved with family to Texas, where they worked rice farm for two years. Died in Bell Co., Tex. 1872. *Joslyn, Biographical Roster, 130.*

Harrison, Peyton R. B. 1832. Attorney in Martinsburg, Va. Enlisted at Harpers Ferry 5/11/61 as lt., Co. D, 2nd Va. Inf. Killed at 1st Manassas 7/21/61; his cousins, the Conrad brothers, were killed by same shell. Widow was paid $56, his pay from Confederate govt. Buried Norbourne Cemetery, Martinsburg, W.Va. *Evans, History of Berkeley County, 116.*

Hartridge, Julian A. B. 9/9/29, Beaufort, S.C. Attended Harvard Law School; admitted to bar in Savannah 1851. Served as lt. in Chatham Artillery until elected to the Confederate Congress. One of best speakers in House; followed his conscience, rarely catering to local pressures. *Warner and Yearns, Biographical Register of the Confederate Congress, 112.*

Hassett, William B. B. 1841. Enlisted as pvt. in Chisholm's Co., Ga. State Troops 5/17/61; mustered out 5/62. Enlisted as pvt. in Co. F, 54th Ga. Inf. 5/13/62. Detailed clerk to brigade surgeon 4/24/63. *Henderson, Roster, 5:684.*

Heidt, Jesse C. Enlisted as pvt. in Co. B, 8th Ga. Inf. 6/2/61. Accompanied brother's body home

12/24/61. In Confederate hospital at Charlottesville, Va. 2/62, detailed as nurse. In Chimborazo Hospital in Richmond 5/14/62 with typhoid. Captured at Gettysburg, paroled 8/1/63. Returned to regiment; with the 8th when paroled at Lynchburg, Va. 4/14/65. *Henderson, Roster, 1:928.*

Herrmann, Henry. Lt., Co. B, 1st Battn. Ga. Sharpshooters. Enlisted 6/7/61 in Savanna; 1st lt. 11/3/63. Killed at Jonesboro, Ga. 8/31/64. *Compiled Service Record, Ga. Archives.*

Hinely, Thomas H. Enlisted as pvt., Co. C., 1st Ga. Brigade State Troops 9/18/61; mustered out 3/18/62. Enlisted Co. F, 54th Ga. Inf. 5/6/62; appointed 4th cpl. 1863. Shot in face, legs and back in 6/18/64 action; admitted to 1st Miss. C.S.A. hospital at Jackson, Miss. 8/20/64. Returned to duty 9/18/64. Admitted to Ocmulgee Hospital, Macon, Ga. 10/23/64. Died at Rincon, Ga. 12/1/11. *Henderson, Roster, 5:685.*

Holcomb, Josiah Law. B. 1834. Original member of OLI. Enlisted as 1st. sgt. in Co. B, 8th Ga. 5/21/61; 2d lt. 8/14/61; resigned 12/1/61. Elected 1st. lt., Co. C, 1st Battn. Ga. Sharpshooters 7/13/62. Appointed A.A.A. Gen. to Brig. Gen. C.H. Stevens. Mortally wounded at Jonesboro, Ga. 8/31/64. *1860 Census; Henderson, Roster, 1:923.*

Hopkins, Matthew H. B. 1836. Clerk, boarding in Savannah 1860. 2nd lt. Co. B, 18th Battn. Ga. Inf. 2/26/61; 2nd lt. of Co. A 5/31/61. Appointed adj. of 1st (Olmstead's) Ga. Inf. 1/18/62. Captured at Ft. Pulaski; exchanged. Elected capt. Co. G, 1st Ga. Inf. Surrendered at Greensboro, N.C. c 4/26/65. *Henderson, Roster, 1:114.*

Hull, Eleanor C. B. 1830, Mass. Resident of Sewanee Co., Fla, with husband Noble A. Hull (B. 1827), a merchant from Ga. *1860 Sewanee Co. Census.*

Hull, Fred. Sgt. maj. 10/16/62, 1st. (Olmstead's) Ga. Inf.; appointed capt. and QM 12/7/63. Recommended for Smith's Brigade, Cheatham's Corps, C.S.A. 1/22/65. *Henderson, Roster, 1:115.*

Hunt, Albert R. B. 1848. Living in Bethesda Orphans Home, Savannah, 1860. Enlisted as pvt. in Co. F, 54th Ga. Inf. 4/29/63. Captured at Macon, Ga. 4/20/65. *1860 Chatham Co. Census; Henderson, Roster, 5:685.*

Hunter, Charles C. B. 1838. Clerk at Central Railroad in Savannah before war. Enlisted as pvt. in Co. B, 8th Ga. Inf. 5/21/61. Discharged 1/1/62. Elected jr. 2nd lt., Co. F, 54th Ga. Inf. 5/13/62; 2nd lt. 9/22/63. Surrendered with Johnston's army at Greensboro, N.C. 4/26/65. *Henderson, Roster, 5:676.*

Hunter, James, Jr. Enlisted as pvt. May 21, 1861 in Co. B, 8th Ga. Inf. Severely wounded in neck at 1st Manassas 7/21/61. Appointed 2d lt. of Inf., Regular Confederate States Army 12/20/61. Assigned acting asst. adj. gen., Gen. Military District of Ga. 4/26/64. Recommended for promotion while on duty as A.A.A. Savannah 10/27/64. *Henderson, Roster, 1:929.*

Ivey, William H. B. 1848, Savannah. Clerk when war began. Original member of OLI. Enlisted as pvt., 8th Ga. Inf. 5/21/61. Wounded at 1st Manassas 7/21/61; died of wounds. *1860 Chatham Census; Rockwell, Oglethorpe Light Inf.,*

Jackson, Daniel. B. 1836. Carpenter's apprentice in Savannah. Enlisted 5/18/61 as pvt. in Fraser's Battery of Light Artillery. Attached to Read's Co. L, 1st Regt. Va. Artillery 3/62. Captured at Gettysburg 7/5/63; served as nurse for wounded Confederate prisoners. Sent to Point Lookout, date unknown. *1860 Chatham Co. Census; Compiled Service Records, Ga. Archives.*

Jackson, Henry Rootes. B. 6/24/20, Athens, Ga. Graduated Yale 1839. Newspaper editor, superior court judge and U.S. minister to Austria. Appointed brig. gen. in Confederate army 6/4/61; resigned from service in Va. to accept command of division of Ga. state troops with rank of maj. gen. After his troops mustered into Confederate service he served as aide on staff of Gen. W.H.T. Walker. Commissioned brig. in Confederate Service 9/23/63. Captured at Nashville, Tenn. 12/64; released from Ft. Warren Prison 7/65. Returned to Ga. Practiced law until appointed minister to

Mexico under President Cleveland 1885. President of Ga. Historical Society in Savannah. Died there 5/23/98; buried in Bonaventure Cemetery. *Warner, Generals in Gray, 149.*

Jackson, Thomas G. Capt., staff officer of Anderson's Brigade. One of fifty officers destined to be placed under fire at Hilton Head, S.C. ,who spent three weeks on a boat before being exchanged in Charleston.

Jones, Charles A. Pvt. 5/13/61, Co. F, 8th Ga. Inf.; 2nd lt. 9/15/61; 1st lt. 1/21/62; resigned 9/20/62. *Henderson, Roster,* 1:959, 976.

Jones, David R. B. 4/5/25, Orangeburg District, S.C. Graduated West Point 1846. Appointed brig. gen. in Provisional Confederate Army 6/17/61; maj. gen. 3/10/62. Died 1/15/63. *Warner, Generals in Gray,* 163-64.

Keane, James J. Enlisted as pvt., Co. F, 54th Ga. Inf. 5/13/62. Captured at Kingston, Ga. 5/18/64; Rock Island Prison, Ill. Took oath of allegiance to U.S. and enlisted in U.S. Navy 6/10/64. *Henderson, Roster,* 5:685.

Kesler, James A. B. 8/9/43, Effingham County, Ga. Enlisted as pvt., Co. C, 1st Ga. Brigade State Troops 9/18/61; mustered out 3/18/62. Enlisted Co. I, 54th Ga. Inf. 5/6/62; 4th cpl. 11/12/63; discharged with disability 1865. *Henderson, Roster,* 5:715.

King, Mallory P. B. 1836. Son of Thomas Butler King of Frederica, Glynn County, Ga. Apparently at Ga. Military with John Branch, but name does not appear on surviving rolls. *1860 Census.*

King, Robert. B. 1835. Son of Roswell King. Clerk in his father's company in 1860. May have been subject of Tallulah Hansell's letters of 1859, to which she refers in a letter to Charlotte 8/1/61.

King, Roswell. Prominent businessman in Cobb County, Ga.; built Barrington Hall in Roswell. President of Roswell Manufacturing Co.

Krenson, Frederick. B. 1812. Shipwright and sparmaker who came to Savannah from Prussia, Germany. *1860 Chatham Co. Census.*

Krenson, John Frederick. B. 1843. Member of OLI. *1860 Chatham County Census; Henderson, Roster* 1:929

Kreuger, Paul. Enlisted as musician 5/2/61. Transferred to Co. B., 8th Ga. Inf. Captured at Cashtown, Pa. 7/5/63; confined at Point Lookout, Md. Took oath and enlisted in U.S. Army 2/2/64. *Henderson, Roster,* 1:915, 929.

Lachlison, James J. B. 1833. Member of Co. B, O.L.I., which became Co. H, 1st (Olmstead's).Ga. Inf.; jr. 2nd lt. 9/3/61; elected 1st lt. Captured at Ft. Pulaski 4/11/62; exchanged at Aiken's Landing, Va. 11/10/62. Elected capt. 6/2/63. *Henderson, Roster,* 1:193.

Lamar, Lucius M. B. 1835. Bibb County planter with four children under age six in 1860. Appointed capt. Co. C, 8th Ga. Inf. 4/15/61; elected maj. 9/12/61; lt. col. 12/24/61; col. 1/28/62. Wounded and captured at Savage Station, Va. 6/28/62. Resigned 12/62. *1860 Bibb Co. Census; Henderson, Roster,* 1:912, 913.

Law, Ebenezer Starke. B. 1836, Ga. Prewar civil engineer; his father was attorney in Savannah. Enlisted in Co. B, 8th Ga. Inf. 5/21/61; elected 2nd lt. 2/7/63. Wounded at Gettysburg. In command of company at its surrender at Appomattox, Va. 4/9/65. *Henderson, Roster* 1:929.

Lawrence, S.W. Lt., Co. D, 1st Battn. Ga. Sharpshooters; appointed 1st lt. 7/14/62. Killed at Jonesboro, Ga. 8/31/64. *Compiled Service Record, Ga. Archives.*

Lawton, Alexander Robert. B. 11/4/18, Beaufort District, S.C. Graduated West Point 1839. Resigned commission in U.S. Army 1/41 to enter Dane Law School at Harvard; graduated 1842. Moved to Savannah 1843; practiced law. Married Sarah Gilbert Alexander 11/5/45. Prewar president of Augusta & Savannah Railroad, member of state legislature and state senate. Commissioned brig. gen. in Confederate army 4/13/61, and placed in command of military district of Ga., especially the defense of Savannah and the coast, where many were dissatisfied with his capability. Went to Va. 6/62 and fought in Seven Days' Battles. Wounded at Sharpsburg 9/17/62. QM gen. of C.S.A. 5/63. Resumed law practice in Savannah after war. Member Independent Presbyterian Church. Buried Laurel Grove Cemetery. *Myers, Children of Pride, 1592.*

Ledyard, William N. B. 1844, Clarke County, Ala. Living in Mobile, Ala., in 1860. Enlisted in 3rd Ala. Inf. as pvt. on 4/23/61. Wounded at Boonsboro, Md., 9/14/62. Promoted to 1st lt. 10/11/62. Wounded and captured at Gettysburg 7/1/63; left leg amputated at Letterman Hospital 8/10/63. Sent to Ft. Delaware Prison; one of the Immortal Six Hundred. Paroled in Charleston Harbor, S.C. 12/15/64. Listed as exchanged and furloughed in Mobile, Ala. 1/5/65 with permanent disability. *Joslyn, Biographical Roster.*

Lentz, Francis. B. 1838 in Switzerland. Grocery clerk, boarding in Savannah in 1860. Enlisted as pvt. in Co. B, 8th Ga. Inf. 5/21/61. Wounded and discharged at Centreville, Va. 1/1/62. Enlisted in C.S. Navy; serving as ship's steward at Savannah Station 4-5/62. No further record. *Henderson, Roster, 1:929.*

Lewis, Robert Henry. B.1833. Clerk in commission house in Savannah before war. Enlisted as 1st sgt. in Co. C, 1st Ga. Inf. 5/30/61; appointed sgt. maj. 7/25/61. Captured at Ft. Pulaski 4/10/62; exchanged 8/8/62. Elected jr. 2nd lt., Co. D, 10/13/62. Wounded Smyrna, Ga. 7/2/64. Appointed adj. of post, Wilmington Island. *Henderson, Roster, 5:632; Minute Book of Savannah Cadets.*

Lufburrow, Laura. B. 1831. Wife of **Orlando H. Lufburrow**, who owned brass and iron foundry in Augusta. Orlando manufactured cannon during war for Confederate army. His father, Matthew, was born in Middleton, N.J. in 1787. Master mason who came to Savannah sometime before 1818, his fine work is noted today in Savannah's First Baptist Church built in 1832 and many of the houses on E. Oglethorpe Ave. built in the 1820s. Reference to Lufburrows as relations is only a term of affection. Information provided to author from Mr. Albert Lufburrow of Savannah.

Magruder, E.J. B. 1838. Clerk from Floyd Co., Ga. Capt. of Co. A, 8th Ga. Inf. 5/18/61; elected maj. 1/28/62; lt. col. 12/16/62. Wounded 6/21/64. *Henderson, Roster, 1:916.*

Mann, J.T. Enlisted as pvt. in 1st Co. E, 6th Regt. Va. Cav. 9/17/61. Transferred to Jeff Davis' Legion Miss. Cav., Co. F. Elected 2nd lt., Co. K, 54th Ga. Inf. 7/27/62; 1st lt. 4/25/63. Killed at Vining Station 4/4/64. *Henderson, Roster, 5:417, 720.*

Mann, William H. Elected capt., Co. A, 1st Regt., 1st Brigade, Ga. State Troops 10/3/61; mustered out 4/62. Elected maj. 54th Ga. Inf. 5/16/62. Killed at Atlanta 7/22/64. *Henderson, Roster, 3:633, 5:620.*

Marshall, William J. B. 1828. Bookkeeper in Savannah before war. Joined Tattnall Guards, 3rd Brigade Ga. State Troops as 4th sgt. 1/3/61, for 60-day term of service. Appointed 4th cpl. of Co. A, 18th Battn. Ga. Inf. 5/31/61. 1st sgt., Co. G., 1st (Olmstead's) Ga. Inf. 4/29/62. Captured 12/64 on retreat from Nashville. *Henderson, Roster, 1:175, 183.*

Mastin, Edmund Irby. B. 1841, Huntsville, Ala. Listed as merchant in 1860 census. Adj. of 8th Ark. Inf. 3/26/63, on Gen. Kelly's staff. Captured at Charleston, Tenn. 12/28/64. Sent to Ft. Delaware; traded his gold watch for chance to be one of the Immortal Six Hundred. Requested but was denied special exchange. Remained in prison until his release 6/12/65. Returned to Huntsville; engaged in grocery business, brick manufacturing and construction. Elected mayor 1883. Died 4/14/94; buried in Maple Hill Cemetery, Huntsville. *Joslyn, Biographical Roster, 52.*

May, William F. Enlisted in Co. F, 54th Ga. Inf. as pvt. 1/21/63. Captured and paroled at Macon, Ga., probably as wounded in hospital, 4/20/65. *Henderson, Roster, 5:686.*

McCallum, James R. B. 1/25/39, Knox County, Tenn. Enlisted as 1st. lt., Co. D, 63 Tenn. Inf. at

Jonesboro 4/19/62; promoted to capt. 5/2/64. Captured at Petersburg 6/17/64; sent to Ft. Delaware; one of the Immortal Six Hundred; released 6/17/65. Returned to Knoxville; postwar building contractor. Died 6/24/05; buried Old Gray Cemetery, Knoxville. *Joslyn, Biographical Roster, 182.*

McDonald, Samuel J. B. 7/12/30, Ga. Pvt., 8th Ga. Inf. 5/21/61. Severely wounded at 1st Manassas; disability discharge at Centreville, Va. 11/25/61. *Henderson, Roster, 5:696.*

McFarland, John T. B. 1837. Physician in Savannah 1860. Elected 1st lt. of 2nd Republican Blues, who became Co. C, 1st (Olmstead's) Ga. Inf. 5/31/61. Appointed asst. surgeon of 8th Ga. Inf. 6/5/61; resigned 10/28/61. Appointed asst. surgeon C.S.A. and ordered to report to 1st Battn. Ga. Sharpshooters 2/17/62. Appointed asst. surgeon 5th Ga. Cav. 1/20/63; surgeon 1/1/64. On detached duty at Columbus, Ga. hospital 9/19/64. *1860 Chatham Co. Census; Henderson, Roster, 1:132,914.*

McIntosh, Thomas Spalding. B. 1837, McIntosh County, Ga. Attorney in Savannah in 1860; classmate of John Branch's at Ga. Military Inst. Member of OLI from 1857. Appointed 1st lt., Co. F, 1st Ga. 2/1/61. Capt. and A.A.G. on staff of Gen. Lafayette McLaws 10/19/61. Appointed maj. in adj. gen.'s office 7/16/62. Killed at Sharpsburg, Md. 9/17/62. *1860 Census; Henderson, Roster, 1:339.*

Mell, William B. B. 1842. Clerk in saddlery in Savannah; joined OLI 8/1/61. Appointed 3rd sgt. **(Co. B, 8th Ga. Inf?)** 8/16/61. Served four years; surrendered at Appomattox, Va. 4//9/65 with remnants of OLI. *Compiled Service Records, Ga. Archives.*

Mercer, George Anderson. B 2/9/35, Savannah, son of Brig. Gen. Hugh Mercer. Graduated Princeton Univ.; admitted to Savannah bar 1859. Cpl. in Republican Blues Militia. With occupation troops at Ft. Pulaski 1/3/61. 4th lt., Co. C, 1st Ga Inf.; capt. and A.A.G. on Gen. Mercer's staff 1861. *Evans, Confederate Military History, 7:846-47.*

Mercer, Hugh Weedon. B. 1810, Fredericksburg, Va. Planter's Bank officer in Savannah before war. Graduate West Point 7/28. Brevet 2nd lt. artillery 7/1/28; 1st lt. artillery 10/10/35. Col. of 1st Ga. Inf. 5/27/61; brig. gen. 10/29/61. Brigade sent to Atlanta and attached to Maj. Gen. W.T.H. Walker's Division, then Maj. Gen. Patrick R. Cleburne's Division. After Jonesboro, accompanied Hardee to Savannah; saw no further action. Paroled at Macon, Ga. 5/13/65. Died Baden-Baden, Germany 6/9/77. *Warner, Generals in Gray, 216-17.*

Mickler, W.J. Possibly John, B. 1831. First mate on steamer before war. Killed while on special assignment at Trevillian Station. *Compiled Service Records, Ga. Archives.*

Miller, Benton H. B. 8/26/33. Merchant in Mayfield, Hancock County, Ga. Appointed 2nd sgt. of Capt. Horatio N. Hollifield's Battery, Light Artillery, Ga. State Troops 2/22/62, in Sandersville, Ga.; mustered out at Savannah, Ga. 5/62. Elected 1st lt., Co. D, 59th Ga. Inf. 5/8/62; capt. 12/19/62. Wounded left thigh, permanently disabled by compound fracture and captured at Gettysburg; sent to dead house at the Plank farm, but one of his company persuaded doctor to set the leg. Survived and was paroled at Point Lookout, Md. 3/3/64. Died 2/8/08; buried Linton, Ga. *Henderson, Roster, 6:35*

Mock, George H. Enlisted as pvt. 5/21/61. Surrendered at Appomattox, Va. 4/9/65. *Henderson, Roster, 5:38.*

Montmullin, J. S. Pvt. Co. B., 8th Ga. Inf. 5/21/61. Transferred to Co. I, 5th Ga. Cav. Paroled at Hillsboro, N.C. 4/26/65. *Henderson, Roster, 1:930.*

Morrell, Bryan M. Enlisted as pvt. Co. B, 8th Ga. Inf. 5/21/61. Member of OLI. Shot through the body and killed at 1st Manassas 7/21/61. Buried Laurel Grove Cemetery, Savannah. *Undated letter in Margaret Branch Sexton Collection, Univ. of Ga.*

Nesbitt, Robert Taylor. B. 4/2/40, Savannah, Ga. Son of Hugh O'Keefe Nesbitt and Martha Delony Berrien of St. Mary's in Camden Co. Enlisted as lt., Co. A, 51st Ga. Inf. 3/4/62; resigned 8/14/62. Married Rebecca Lanier Saffold 5/4/65. *Collections of Early County Historical Society, Vol. 2.*

Newell, Tomlinson F. B. 1/31/38. Law student at Oglethorpe College, Milledgeville, Ga. His father Isaac was born in Conn. 1st lt., Co. G, 45th Ga. Inf. 3/4/62. Wounded at Cedar Run, Va. 8/9/62. Wounded in foot at Gettysburg 7/3/63, necessitating amputation. Elected capt. 6/22/64. Discharged with disability near end of war. Returned to Milledgeville after war and became prominent citizen; served as mayor. *Henderson, Roster, 4:891.*

O'Brien, Mary H. B. 1802. Lived with daughter and son-in-law Henry Brigham, a commission merchant from Middlesex Co., N.Y. O'Briens originated from Staten Island, N.Y. *1860 Chatham Co. Census.*

Olmstead, Charles. H. B. 1837, Savannah, Ga. Graduated Ga. Military Inst. 1858. Cashier at commission house when war began. Enlisted as maj. 5/27/61 in 1st Ga. Regt. of Volunteer Inf.; elected col. 12/16/61. In command of Ft. Pulaski when it fell 4/62. Exchanged from prison 11/10/62 and resumed command of 1st Ga. Vol. Inf.; regiment became part of Mercer's Brigade, Army of Tenn. under Gen. Joseph E. Johnston in 1864. Surrendered at Greensboro, N.C. 4/26/65. *1860 Chatham Co. Census; Henderson, Roster, 1:113.*

O'Neill, Henry T. Enlisted as 3rd sgt., Read's Independent Co., Ga. Inf.; mustered out 1/25/62. Enlisted as pvt. in Co. E, 1st (Olmstead's) Ga. Inf. 2/11/62; elected jr. 2nd lt. 12/9/62. *Henderson, Roster, 1:161, 163.*

Orr, James Lawrence. B. 1822. Served in U.S. Congress 1848-59. Signed Ordinance of Secession for S.C. One of three S.C. commissioners to treat for possession of forts in Charleston Harbor. Confederate senator. *Warner and Yearns, Biographical Register of the Confederate Congress, 188.*

Padelford, George. B. 1837. Physician. Son of Edward Padelford, a commission merchant and factor in Savannah from Bristol, Mass. *1860 Chatham Co. Census.*

Patten, George T. B. 1836. Brother of William C. Bookkeeper in Savannah. Enlisted as pvt. 10/13/63, Co. I, 54th Ga. Inf.; appointed adjutant's clerk. *Henderson, Roster, 5:716.*

Patten, William C. B. 1836. Brother of George T. Pvt. Co. I, 54th Ga. Inf. *1860 Census. Henderson, Roster, 5:716.*

Payne, Ira. Enlisted in Co. F, 54th Ga. Inf. as pvt. 7/28/62. Captured at Marietta, Ga. 6/18/64; sent to Camp Morton, Ind., where he died of measles 7/20/64. *Henderson, Roster, 5:688.*

Pelham, William. B. 9/14/36, N.C. Elder brother of Maj. John Pelham of Stuart's Horse Artillery. Enlisted Co. A, 2 Ala. Inf. 5/7/61 at Ft. Morgan; regt. disbanded 3/62. Enlisted Co. A, 51st Ala. Partisan Rangers; breveted 2nd lt. 9/2/62. Captured Shelbyville, Tenn. 6/27/63; sent to prison at Louisville, Ky. 7/3/63; sent to Johnson's Island 7/6/63; transferred to City Point, Va,. for exchange 2/24/65. Married Tallulah Hansell 1/29/68. Killed in shootout with police in Anniston, Ala. 7/9/89. *Compiled Service Records, National Archives, Record Group 109; information provided to author by Mr. Dan Sullivan.*

Pendergrast, Nicholas. Pvt. 9/20/61 in Co. E, 1st. (Olmstead's) Ga. Inf.; appointed cpl. Roll for 4/30/64 shows him present; no further record. *Compiled Service Records, Ga. Archives.*

Philbrick, Ellen H. B. 1842. Her mother, Elvira Philbrick, was from Mass. *1860 Chatham County Census.*

Picquett, Lewis A. B. 1832. Merchant's clerk in Richmond County, Ga. 1860. His father, Benjamin, was born in France. Appointed 1st cpl., Co. D, 1st (Ramsey's) Ga. Inf. 3/18/61; elected jr. 2nd lt. 2/1/62; mustered out at Augusta, Ga. 3/18/62. Elected 2nd lt., 1st Co. A, 12th Battn. Ga. Light Artillery 4/10/62. Transferred to Co. A, 63rd Ga. Inf. 10/62; elected 1st lt. 4/3/63; capt. 7/6/63.

Wounded in leg, necessitating amputation, at New Hope Church, Ga. 5/28/64. Applied for artificial leg at Augusta, Ga. hospital 9/26/64. *Henderson, Roster, 6:372.*

Purse, Thomas, Jr. B. 1842, Savannah. His father was U.S. appraiser in 1860 and the wartime mayor of Savannah (1862). Pvt. in Co. B, 8th Ga. Inf. 5/21/61. *Henderson, Roster, 1:931.*

Rawls, Morgan. Elected capt., Co. C, 1st Regt., 1st Brigade Ga. State Troops 9/18/61; mustered out 3/18/62. Elected capt., Co. I, 54th Ga. Inf. 5/6/62; lt. col. 5/16/62. Granted leave of absence from 10/30/63 to attend session of Ga. legislature, to which he had been elected to represent Effingham Co. Wounded at Atlanta 7/22/64. *Henderson, Roster, 5:620, 709.*

Raymur, Alexander J. B. 1845. Enlisted as pvt., Co. F, 54th Ga. Inf. 2/21/63. Captured in Macon, Ga. 4/20-21/65. *Henderson, Roster, 5:688.*

Read, John P.W. B. 1829. Single planter, living in Savannah in 1861. **(Formed?)** Read's Battery, Ga. Light Artillery. Appointed **(what rank?)** 6/18/61; promoted to maj. 4/4/63. Battery transferred to Co. I, 1st Regiment Va. Artillery 3/27/62. *Compiled Service Records, Record Group 109, Ga. Archives.*

Reddick, William E. B. 1839. Blacksmith from Chatham County, Ga. Enlisted in Phoenix Riflemen, who became Co. B, 63rd Ga. Inf. Wounded at Battery Wagner, S.C. 7/18/63. *Henderson, Roster, 6:394; 1860 Census.*

Richardson, John, Jr. B. 1844, St. Luke Parish, S.C. Enlisted 5/21/61 in Co. B, 8th Ga. Inf.; discharged at Richmond 1862. Enlisted in Chatham Siege Artillery; discharged 7/26/62. *Henderson, Roster, 1:905.*

Rockwell, William S, Jr. B. 1810. Attorney from Albany, N.Y. Lt. col. **(Of what?)** 5/31/61. Last records show him present 2/64. *Henderson, Roster, 1:113.*

Ross, William H. Co. C, 1st Ga. Sharpshooters. Appointed cpl. 6/22/62; promoted capt. Assigned asst. adj. insp. gen. to Hardee's headquarters 8/27/64. *Compiled Service Records, Ga. Archives.*

Sandiford, Ralph B. B. 1838. Clerk in boot & shoe store in Savannah; joined OLI as pvt. 5/21/61. Living in **(which?)** Butler household when war started. *1860 Chatham census. Henderson, Roster, 1:931.*

Saussy, George N. Joined Republican Blues in Savannah 6/31/61; term of service 30 days. Enlisted in 1st Co., 6th Regt. Va. Cav. 9/17/61. Transferred to Jeff Davis's Legion, Miss. Cav. Captured at Madison C.H., Va. 9/22/63; paroled at Elmira, N.Y. 3/65. *1860 Census; Henderson, Roster, 1:136.*

Schaaf, Arthur. B. 1832, Georgetown, D.C. Enlisted 6/55; served in U.S. Army as 2nd lt., 4th U.S. Inf. Resigned while in Calif. 3/16/61; returned to Va. with Albert Sidney Johnston. Enlisted in Confederate service as 1st lt.; served in Sibley's Brigade in New Mexico Campaign until 10/61. Assigned to advanced batteries on Savannah River under command of Lt. Col. Edward C. Anderson 6/62; transferred to Maj. R.H. Anderson's command 7/18/62. Assigned to 1st Ga. Battn. Sharpshooters, Brig. Gen. C.H. Stevens's Brigade, as capt. 8/62; promoted maj. 1/20/63. Assigned to staff of Gen. William Bate 9/19/64. Died in Savannah 7/8/74; buried Laurel Grove Cemetery, Savannah, Ga. *Compiled Service Record, Ga. Archives.*

Scott, Thomas Moore. B. 1829, Ga. Moved to New Orleans and engaged in farming in Claiborne Parish, La. Enlisted in 12th La. Inf. 8/13/61; elected col. His command accompanied Gen. Leonidas Polk to Dalton, Ga., when Atlanta Campaign began. Promoted brig. gen. 5/10/64. Severely wounded at Franklin by shell explosion 11/30/64. Apparently saw no further service. Died in New Orleans 4/21/76. *Warner, Generals in Gray, 270.*

Scriven, Ada. B. 1831, in Savannah. Daughter of Thomas P. Scriven, a physician. *1860 Chatham Co. Census.*

Sessions, Lewis A. Enlisted as pvt. in 8th Ga. Inf. 8/1/61; discharged 1/4/62 with disability. One year ahead of John Branch at Ga. Milit. Inst. Original member of OLI. *Henderson, Roster, 1:932.*

Shaw, William A. B. 1841. Appointed 5th sgt. of Chisholm's Co., Ga. State Troops 5/17/61; mustered out 5/62. Appointed 3rd sgt., Co. F, 54th Ga. Inf. 5/13/62; 2nd sgt. 9/22/63. Captured at Ft. Tyler, West Point, Ga.4/16/65. *Henderson, Roster, 5:677; 6:805.*

Shell, Alexander N. Joined OLI as pvt. 5/21/61. Surrendered at Appomattox, Va. 4/9/65. *Henderson, Roster, 1:932.*

Shellman, William Faye. B. 11/23/40, Springfield, Ga. Railroad clerk in 1860. His father, Joseph, was language teacher in Richmond, Co., Ga. Member of OLI from 1856. Enlisted as 4th sgt., Co. B, 8th Ga. Inf. 5/21/61. Wounded at 1st Manassas 7/21/61. Elected 2nd lt. 12/17/61; 1st lt. and adj. 4/30/62. Wounded at Gettysburg 7/3/63. Wounded in arm at Cold Harbor 6/1/64; arm amputated. Retired on account of wounds 10/15/64. Elected maj. of Shellman's Local Battn. in Savannah. Surrendered at Tallahassee, Fla. 5/10/65. Postwar: employed by Central Railroad. Died 2/7/98; buried Laurel Grove Cemetery, Savannah. *Information from Mr. Reese Shellman, Savannah, Ga.*

Shinholser, James N. Enlisted as lt. 5/3/62 at Savannah in brother John W. Shinholser's Co. K, 57th Ga. Inf. Captured and paroled at Vicksburg, Miss., 7/4/63. In Macon hospital 7/22/64 through 8/64. Paroled at Greensboro, N.C. 5/65. *Compiled Service Records, Ga. Archives.*

Smith, Gustavus Woodson. B. 11/30/21, Georgetown, Ky. Graduated West Point 1842; taught there. Resigned 1854 to become civil engineer. Street commissioner of N.Y. City when war began. Maj. gen. in Confederate army 9/19/61. Secretary of War *ad interim* 11/62. Appointed maj. gen. of Ga. militia by Gov. Joseph Brown. Surrendered at Macon, Ga. 4/20/65. Died 6/24/96 in N.Y. *Warner, Generals in Gray, 280-81.*

Smith, Julia A. B. 1842. Her father, William H. Smith, was cotton merchant from Elizabethtown, N.J., who came to Savannah and married. *1860 Chatham Co. Census.*

Snider, George. B. 1834. Merchant in Savannah before war. Enlisted as pvt. in 8th Ga. Inf. on 5/21/61. On detail duty as surgeon clerk 12/20/62. *Henderson, Roster, 1: 929, 932; 1860 Chatham Co. Census.*

Sorrell, Francis. B. 1795, West Indies. Wealthy merchant. His son, Moxley Sorrel, became well known as aide-de-camp to Gen. Longstreet. *1860 Chatham Co. Census.*

Spear, James Samuel. Enlisted in Co. H. 54th Ga. Inf. as pvt. 5/12/62; transferred to Co. F 1/1/63. Captured at Kennesaw Mountain 6/18/64; released at Camp Morton, Ind. 5/22/65. *Henderson, Roster, 5:689.*

Spencer, William W. B. 1838, Liberty County, Ga. Son of Mary Spencer, widow. Graduated Oglethorpe College, Milledgeville, Ga. 1858. (Attended with William Pelham.) Elected jr. 2nd lt., Co.B, 29th Ga. Inf. 7/27/61. On post of Sapelo Island Battery, Ga. 10/61. Elected capt. 5/10/62; absent on sick furlough 12/62. Sick in Savannah spring 1863. Killed at Franklin, Tenn.11/30/64; buried there in Ga. section of McGavock Confederate Cemetery, Section 80, Grave 48. *Compiled Service Records, Ga. Archives; Student file at Oglethorpe University, Atlanta; McGavock Cemetery marker, Franklin, Tenn.*

Stevens, Clement Hoffman. B. 8/14/21, Norwich, Conn. Family moved to Pendleton, S.C. Planned and constructed what was perhaps the first armored fortification, a battery on Morris Island in Charleston Harbor. Wounded at 1st Manassas while serving as aide to his brother-in-law, Gen. Barnard Bee, who was killed. Elected col. of 24th S.C.; attached to Gist's Brigade at Vicksburg. Transferred to Army of Tenn. Wounded at Chickamauga 1863. Promoted to brig. gen. 1/20/64; assigned to W.H.T. Walker's Division. Wounded at Peachtree Creek 7/20/64; died in Atlanta 7/25/64. *Warner, Generals in Gray, 291-92.*

Stevens, George Whitfield. B. 1837. Clerk in his father Thomas F.'s livery stable. Enlisted as pvt., Co. B, 8th Ga. Inf. 5/21/61. Died 11/14/61. *1860 Chatham Co. Census. Henderson, Roster, 1: 932.*

Stiles, B. Edward. B. 1834. Planter before war. Capt., Co. E., 16th Ga. 7/24/61. Severely wounded at Malvern Hill, Va., 7/1/62. Elected maj. 5/18/63; lt. col. 11/29/63. Killed at Deep Bottom, near Front Royal, Va. 8/16/64. *Henderson, Roster, 2:480, 516.*

Strahl, Otho F. B. 6/3/31, McConnelsville, Oh. Studied law and admitted to bar in Somerville, Tenn. 1858. Entered Confederate service as capt. of 4th Tenn. Vol. Inf. 5/61; promoted lt. col. 1863; col. 1/63. Attained brig. gen. and fought at Chickamauga 7/28/63. Killed at Franklin, Tenn. 11/30/64. Although mortally wounded, continued to hand guns up to his riflemen, enabling them to fire down into Union works. When he fell, one soldier asked him what they should do, to which he replied, "Keep on firing." Those were his last words. *Warner, Generals in Gray, 296.*

Strickland, Bayard J. Pvt., Co. B, 8th Ga. Inf. 5/21/61. Died in camp at Winchester **(when?)**. Buried in Ga. section of Stonewall Cemetery in Winchester, Va. *Henderson, Roster, 932; Cemetery list of Confederate Soldiers buried in Stonewall Cemetery.*

Sturdevant, William B. Original member of OLI. Wounded in shoulder at Little Round Top 7/3/63. Sent to U.S. Hospital at Chester, Pa. Exchanged and returned to service 7/17/64. *Henderson, Roster, 1:932.*

Sweat, James E. B. 1837. Machinist in Savannah 1860. Son of Baptist minister Rev. Farley Sweat. Enlisted as pvt. 5/30/61 in 1st (Olmstead's) Ga. Inf. Transferred to Co. B, 8th Ga. Inf. 8/19/61. Wounded at Gettysburg 7/3/63; taken prisoner. Received at City Point, Va., for exchange 8/30/63. Absent wounded 10/31/64. *Henderson, Roster, 1:148, 931.*

Sydney, Ann L. Staples. B. 1808. Widow who lived in Ward 2, Richmond, Va. *1860 Va. Census, Henrico County.*

Tarver, Fannie. B. 1845. Her father was John V. Tarver, a commission merchant in Savannah. *1860 Chatham census; 1860 City Directory.*

Thomas, Grigsby E., Sr. Enlisted as 2nd lt., Co. G, 54th Ga. Inf. 5/12/62. Wounded at Resaca, Ga. 5/16/64 and again in Atlanta 7/22/64. Elected capt. for gallantry at Bentonville, N.C. 3/18/65. Surrendered at Greensboro, N.C. 4/26/65. *Henderson, Roster, .5:691.*

Thomasson, Eugenia. B. 1795, Kingston, Jamaica. The Blois family lived with the Thomassons. *1860 census, Chatham, County, Ga.*

Thompson, R.B. Enlisted in 8th Ga. Inf. 5/21/61. Wounded and absent 10/31/64. No further service record. *Henderson, Roster, 1:932.*

Tilton, Nathaniel O. B. 1833, Charleston, S.C. Superintendent at rice mill in Savannah before war. Appointed QM, 25th Ga. Inf. 11/16/61. Appointed maj. 5/2/63. Serving as maj. and Acting Chief Inspector of Field Transportation at Augusta, Ga. 3/14/65. *Henderson, Roster, 3:90.*

Tinsley, Addison R. B. 1838, Baldwin County, Ga. Bookkeeper at commission house in Savannah 1860. Pvt. in 8th Ga. Inf. 5/21/61. Wounded. Surrendered at Appomattox, Va. 4/9/65. *Henderson, Roster, 1:932.*

Towers, John R. From Floyd County, Ga. Capt. Co. E, 8th Ga. Inf. 5/14/61. Elected lt. col. 11/16/61; col. 12/16/62. Surrendered at Appomattox, Va. 4/9/65. *Henderson, Roster, 1:912, 913, 947.*

Tucker, Elizabeth. B. 1827. Married to physician in Berryville, Va. Husband was listed as 34-year-old farmer in 1860. *1860 Clarke Co. Va. Census.*

Turner, John Screven. B. 1837. Farmer in Chatham Co. 1st lt., Co. F, 1st (Olmstead's) Ga. Inf. 8/1/61; elected capt. 6/62. Killed 1862. *1860 Census; Henderson, Roster, 1:170.*

Twyman, Horace D. B. 1839, Madison, Va. Resigned from West Point 4/61 as 3rd classman.

Appointed 2nd lt. in Va. state forces 5/4/61; adj. 6/15/61. Assigned to 1st Ga. Battn. Sharpshooters 8/1/61; 1st lt. 10/61; ordnance officer of the command 6/62 while on duty at advanced batteries on Savannah River under command of Lt. Col. Edward C. Anderson. Appointed capt. 11/3/63. Detached as inspector gen. on Walker's staff 11-12/63. Wounded in Atlanta Campaign; sent to Charity Hospital, Gordonsville, Va. 12/7/64. As capt. of Co. E, paroled at Greensboro, N.C. 5/1/65. *Compiled Service Records, Ga. Archives.*

Tyler, Robert Charles. B. 1832. Enlisted as capt. (What unit?) 4/61. Promoted to maj. 1861. Col. 15th Tenn. Inf. 1863. Brig. gen. P.A.C.S. 2/23/64. Military commander at Ft. Tyler, near West Point, Ga.; killed 4/16/65. His command comprised the 37th Ga. Inf., the 10th, 15th, 20th, 30th and 37th Tenn., and 4th Battn. Ga. Sharpshooters. *Warner, Generals in Gray, 313.*

Waddell, Hugh Waddell, Jr. Enlisted as pvt. in Co. F, 54th Ga. Inf. 9/18/63; detailed in Signal Corps in Savannah on same date. Married Ann A. Dickerson 4/13/64. Became Hamilton Branch's brother-in-law when Hamilton married Ann's sister Marie in 1867. Dispute over Marie and Ann's father's estate later estranged the families. Court eventually awarded Hamilton and Marie Branch total value of the estate. *Henderson, Roster, 5:690. Savannah Morning News, June 8, 1884.*

Waring, Joseph F. B. 1832. Planter in Savannah; became capt. of own company in Ga. Hussars. Enlisted 9/17/61; assigned to Co. E, 6th Va. Cav. upon arriving in Va. Later assigned as Co. F, Jeff Davis Legion 12/7/61. *Compiled Service Records, Ga. Archives.*

Way, Charleton H. B. 10/5/34, Liberty County, Ga. Prewar commission merchant and cotton factor. In John Branch's class at Ga. Milit. Inst. Original member of OLI from 1856. Elected capt. of Way's Independent Co. Ga. Inf. (Forrest City Rangers) 7/18/61; mustered out 11/1/61. Original officer in Savannah Cadets, having been elected col. 5/16/62. Given command of 54th Ga. Inf. 9/20/64, of which Hamilton Branch's company became Co. F. *Henderson, Roster, 5:620; 1860 Chatham Co. Census.*

Webb, John. B. 1825. Prewar ice dealer in Savannah. Joined Co. B., 8th Ga. Inf. 5/21/61; appointed 1st sgt. Captured at Gettysburg 7/2/63. Died at Point Lookout Prison, 3/12/64. *1860 Census; Henderson, Roster, 1:993, 994.*

Wellford, Dr. John S. B. 1825. Prominent citizen of Spotsylvania County, Va., with personal and real property holdings of over $54,000. Married. *1860 Spotsylvania Co. Census.*

West, Joseph J. B. 1832. Physician from Liberty County, Ga.; married with three-year-old daughter. Enlisted as 1st lt., 8th Ga. Inf. 5/21/61; elected capt. 7/3/61; resigned 8/1/61. Appointed surgeon C.S.A. *1860 Chatham Co. Census; Henderson, Roster, 1:881, 923.*

White, William E. B. 1841, Morris Co., N.J. Original member of OLI. Enlisted as pvt. 5/21/61, Co. B, 8th Ga. Inf.; 1st cpl., 8/19/61. Wounded 1st Manassas 7/21/61. Captured Deep Bottom, near Front Royal, Va. 8/14/64. Paroled Point Lookout, Md. 3/65; exchanged at Aiken's Landing, Va. 3/19/65. Paroled Albany, Ga. 5/25/65. *1860 Chatham Co. Census; Henderson, Roster, 1:137, 924.*

Wilcox, Edward A. B. 1820. Cotton broker from Bibb County. Appointed jr. 2nd lt. 4/15/61 in Co. C, 8th Ga. Inf.; elected capt. 9/12/61. Appointed asst. QM 10/5/61. Surrendered at Appomattox, Va. 4/9/65. *Henderson, Roster, 1:934.*

Williamson, James Potter. B. 1833. Enlisted as pvt. in Co. B, 8th Ga. Inf. 5/21/65. Temporarily attached to Co. A, 2nd Battn. N.C. Local Defense Troops 5/62. On detached duty at Ordnance Dept., Richmond 6/15-12/30/62. Enlisted as pvt. in Co. F, 54th Ga. Inf. 4/29/63. Appointed asst. ordnance sgt., then ordnance sgt. Captured at Columbia, Tenn. 12/22/64; sent to Camp Chase Prison, Ohio. Took oath of allegiance to U.S.; released 3/11/65. *Henderson, Roster, 1:933; 5:690.*

Willis, Edward. B. 1840, Washington, Ga. Would have graduated from West Point in 1861, but resigned 1/61 to join Confederate army. Mortally wounded at the Wilderness 5/30/64. Died the next day before his commission as brig. gen. arrived, making him the youngest brigadier in the army. Engaged to Gen. Moxley Sorrel's sister. Buried in Sorrel family vault, Laurel Grove Cemetery, Savannah. *Civil War News, August 1995, 49.*

Wilson, Alexander K. B. 1838. Carriage trimmer in Savannah; enlisted as 4th cpl., Co. H, 20th Ga. Inf. 6/6/61. Hospital steward 11/14/64. Exchanged; surrendered at Appomattox, Va. 4/9/65. *1860 Chatham Co. Census; Henderson, Roster, 2:768, 818.*

Wilson, William T. Commissary 5/31/61. Col. 2/13/62. Killed at 2nd Manassas 8/30/62. *Henderson, Roster, 1:833.*

Winder, Charles Sidney. B. 10/18/29, Talbot County, Md. Graduated West Point 1850. Resigned as capt. in U.S. Army 4/1/61. Maj. of artillery in regular Confederate army to rank from 3/16/61. Col. 6th S.C. 7/8/61; brig. gen. 3/1/62. Commanded what would become known as "Stonewall Brigade" of Jackson's Division. Died 8/9/62 from wound received at Cedar Mountain, Va. *Warner, Generals in Gray, 339-40.*

Wragg, Thomas L. B. 1846. Son of Savannah physician. Enlisted as pvt. 5/21/61, Co. B, 8th Ga. Inf. (at age 15). Appointed midshipman in Confederate navy 1863. Appointed master, not in line of promotion, in Provisional Navy 6/2/63; served on CSS *Georgia* until detached and ordered to CSS *Atlanta.* Captured by USS *Weehawken* 6/17/63. *1860 Chatham Co. Census; Henderson, Roster, 1:933.*

Wright, John H. B. 1843. Clerk in commission house in Savannah. Pvt. 5/21/61. Wounded. Appointed 2nd cpl. Surrendered at Appomattox, Va. 4/9/65. *1860 census, Henderson, Roster, 1:933.*

NOTES

1. William Harden, *A History of Savannah and South Georgia*, 18-20 (Hereafter Harden).
2. *Sojourn in Savannah: An Official Guidebook and Map of Historic Savannah and the Surrounding Countryside.*
3. Harden, 66-69.
4. Ibid.
5. James David Griffin, "Savannah, Georgia, During the Civil War," 19-21 (Hereafter Griffin).
6. Joseph Bancroft, *Census of the City of Savannah.*
7. Griffin, 19-21.
8. Margaret Branch Sexton Collection, Univ. of Georgia Archives (Hereafter Sexton Collection).
9. Ibid., Box 1, Folder 1.
10. Ibid.
11. *Savannah Morning News*, 11 February 1900.
12. Oglethorpe Light Infantry Papers, Georgia Historical Society, mss. 837 (Hereafter O.L.I. Papers).
13. Savannah City Directory.
14. Ibid.
15. Griffin, 51.
16. Ibid., 53.
17. Ibid., 54.
18. Undated letters, Sexton Collection, mss. 25, Box 2, Folder 2.
19. Lindsey P. Henderson, Jr., *The Oglethorpe Light Infantry: A Military History*, 34 (Hereafter Henderson); Savannah Morning News, 22 May 1861.
20. Henderson, 4-6.
21. Ibid., 14.
22. Branch Family History, transcript, Sexton Collection.
23. Henderson, 6-7; William Banard Dasher, "Reminiscences of 8th Georgia," Georgia State Univ. Archives, microfilm, Drawer 283, Roll 22 (Hereafter Dasher); *Savannah Morning News*, 22 May 1861.
24. Dasher.
25. *Savannah Morning News*, 22 May 1861.
26. William S. Smedlund, *Campfires of Georgia's Troopers 1861-1865* , 153 (Hereafter Smedlund).
27. William C. Davis, *Battle at Bull Run*, 9 (Hereafter Davis).
28. William Best Hesseltine, *Civil War Prisons: A Study in War Psychology* (New York: 1978), 77.
29. Griffin, 107-9.
30. O.R., Series I, Vol. 2, 285.

31. Davis, 103-7.
32. Ibid., 176.
33. Branch Family History, transcript, Sexton Collection.
34. Clarence C. Buell and Robert U. Johnson, eds., *Battles and Leaders of the Civil War*, Vol. I , 195 (Hereafter *Battles and Leaders*); Henderson, 20.
35. Memorium to John Branch, Sexton Collection.
36. Henderson, 36-37.
37. Smedlund, 434.
38. Eileen Conklin, *Women at Gettysburg* (Hereafter Conklin).
39. 1860 Chatham County census; 1860 Savannah City Directory.
40. Worthington C. Butler to Hamilton Branch, 27 July 1861, Sexton Collection.
41. *Savannah Morning News*, 3 February 1861.
42. O.R., Series I, Vol. 11, 365.
43. Ibid., 400-11; Richard M. McMurry, *Footprints of a Regiment*, 31-35 (Hereafter McMurry); O.R., Series I, Vol. 11, 400-11.
44. McMurry.
45. O.R., Series I, Vol. 11, 408-9.
46. *Encyclopedia of American Forts*, 232-34.
47. *Battles and Leaders*, Vol. III, 80-84.
48. Ibid.
49. Ibid.
50. Benjamin La Bree, *The Confederate Soldier in the Civil War*, 168-74.
51. Ibid.
52. *Gettysburg* Magazine, January 1996: 64-67.
53. John W. Busey and David W. Martin, *Regimental Strengths and Losses at Gettysburg*, 135, 2; 298, 3.
54. Conklin, 348.
55. Gregory A. Coco, *A Vast Sea of Misery*, 170.
56. Ibid., 171.
57. Henry Elliott Shepherd, *Narrative of Prison Life at Baltimore and Johnson's Island, Ohio*, 6-7.
58. *Southern Historical Society Papers*, Vol. 1, October 1876: 82-85.
59. Mauriel P. Joslyn, *Immortal Captives: The Story of 600 Confederate Officers and the U.S. Prisoner of War Policy*, 67-70 (Hereafter Joslyn).
60. J. Thomas Scharf, *History of Baltimore City and County from the Earliest Period to the Present Day*, 144, 147 (Hereafter Scharf).
61. Joslyn, 67-70.
62. Scharf, 460.
63. Joslyn, 59-62.
64. Ibid., 81-84.
65. Ibid.
66. Ibid., 154-55.
67. Henry Clay Dickinson, *Diary of Capt. Henry Clay Dickinson, C.S.A.*, 134.
68. Parole of Sanford W. Branch.
69. Savannah Cadets Minute Book, Georgia Historical Society, mss. 681 (Hereafter Minute Book).
70. Jim Miles, *Fields of Glory: A History and Tour Guide of Sherman's March*, 38-44.
71. Minute Book, papers.
72. Albert Castel, *Decision in the West*.
73. Ibid.
74. Glenna R. Schroeder-Lein, *Confederate Hospitals on the Move: Samuel H. Stout and the Army of Tennessee*, 120-25.
75. Minute Book.
76. *Battles and Leaders*, Vol. IV, 253.

77. Wiley Sword, *The Confederacy's Last Hurrah: Spring Hill, Franklin, and Nashville*. Reprint of *Embrace an Angry Wind*, 34 (Hereafter Sword).
78. Minute Book.
79. Ibid.
80. Sword, 65.
81. Griffin, 275-83.
82. Savannah *Daily News Herald*, 15 February, 31 March 1865; O.R., Series I, Vol. 44, 804.
83. Savannah *Daily News Herald*, 15 February 1867; Ray A. Billington, *American History Before 1877*, 232-37 (Hereafter Billington).
84. Billington, 236.
85. Harden, 466-67.
86. Henry Elliott Shepherd, *History of Baltimore, Maryland 1729-1898*, 1011-12.
87. Harden, 466-67.
88. William Harden, *Recollections of a Long and Satisfactory Life*, 122-23.
89. Minute Book, Folder 2.
90. Jacksonville *Republican* 13 July 1889; Anniston, Ala., *The Evening News* 9 July 1889.
91. Sexton Collection, Box 2, Folder 8.
92. *Savannah Morning News* 22 August 1871; 23, 25 September 1871.
93. Ibid., 1 May 1872.
94. Ibid., 28 November 1872.
95. Savannah City Directory, 1872.
96. *Savannah Morning News* 29 September 1952; DeRenne letter, Georgia Historical Society, Collection 473.
97. Letter to Savannah Press, 24 October 1924, Sexton Collection, Box 2, Folder 8.
98. *Savannah Morning News*, 30 January 1891.
99. Ibid., 22 October 1894.
100. Ibid., 24 February 1899.
101. Ibid., 27 February 1899.

BIBLIOGRAPHY

Primary Sources

Dickinson, Henry Clay. *Diary of Capt. Henry Clay Dickinson, C.S.A.*

Evans, Clement. "Georgia." *Confederate Military History*, Vol. 7.

Jordan, Thomas and J.P. Pryor. *The Campaigns of Lt. Gen. N.B. Forrest, and of Forrest's Cavalry.* 1867. Reprint. Dayton, Oh.: Morningside, 1977.

Norton, Oliver Wilcox. *The Attack and Defense of Little Round Top, Gettysburg, July 2, 1863.* New York: The Neale Publishing Co., 1913.

Rockwell, William S. *The Oglethorpe Light Infantry of Savannah, in Peace and in War.* Savannah, Ga.: 1894.

Scharf, J. Thomas. *History of Baltimore City and County from the Earliest Period to the Present Day.* Philadelphia: Louis H. Everts, 1881.

Shepherd, Henry Elliott. *History of Baltimore, Maryland 1729-1898.* Baltimore: S.B. Nelson, 1898.

_____. *Narrative of Prison Life at Baltimore and Johnson's Island, Ohio.* Baltimore: Commercial Printing and Stationery Co., 1917.

Zettler, B.M. *War Stories and School-Day Incidents for the Children.* New York: The Neale Publishing Co., 1912.

Manuscripts and Papers

Chatham County, Ga., Probate Records. Wills and Estates. Files 763, 817, 674.

Civil War Miscellaneous Personal Papers. Georgia State Archives, Atlanta, Mss. 283-22.

Dasher, William Banard. "Reminiscences of 8th Georgia," microfilm. Georgia State Univ. Archives, Atlanta, Drawer 283, Roll 22.

Directory for the City of Savannah, 1860. Savannah: John M. Cooper & Co., 1860.

Oglethorpe Light Infantry. Papers. Georgia Historical Society, Savannah, Ga., Mss. 837, 67.

Savannah Cadets Minute Book. Georgia Historical Society, Savannah, Ga., Ms. 681.

Sexton, Margaret Branch. Collection. Hargrett Library, Univ. of Georgia, Athens, Ms.25.

United States Federal Census.

U.S. War Department Collection of Confederate Records. Compiled Service Records of

Confederate Soldiers. National Archives, Washington, D.C., Record Group No. 109.

U.S. War Department. *The War of the Rebellion: A Compilation of the Official Records of the Union and Confederate Armies*. Washington, D.C.: Government Printing Office, 1880-1901.

Waring, Joseph. Papers. Georgia Historical Society, Savannah, Ga.

Newspapers and Periodicals

Confederate Veteran Magazine.

Rodgers, Thomas G. "The 4th Alabama at First Manassas." *America's Civil War*. November 1994.

Savannah Daily News and Herald. 1867.

Savannah Republican

Savannah Morning News

Secondary Sources

Billington, Ray A. *American History Before 1877*.

Buell, Clarence C., and Robert U. Johnson, eds. *Battles and Leaders of the Civil War*. Secaucus, N.J.: 1887.

Busey, John W., and David W. Martin. *Regimental Strengths and Losses at Gettysburg*. Hightstown, N.J.: Longstreet House, 1986.

Castel, Albert. *Decision in the West*. Lawrence, Kans.: Univ. Press of Kansas, 1992.

Coco, Gregory A. *A Vast Sea of Misery*. Gettysburg, Pa.: Thomas Publications, 1988.

Colt, Margaretta Barton. *Defend the Valley: A Shenandoah Family in the Civil War*. New York: Orion Books, 1994.

Conklin, Eileen. *Women at Gettysburg*. Shippensburg, Pa.: White Mane Publishing, 1993.

Davis, William C. *Battle at Bull Run*. New York: Doubleday and Company, 1977.

Griffin, James David. "Savannah, Georgia, During the Civil War." Doctor of Philosophy dissertation, Univ. of Georgia, Athens, Ga., 1963.

Groom, Winston. *Shrouds of Glory*. Atlantic Monthly Press, 1995.

Gwin, Minrose C. *A Woman's Civil War*. Madison, Wis.: Univ. of Wisconsin Press, 1992.

Harden, William. *A History of Savannah and South Georgia*. Chicago and New York: Lewis Publishing Company, 1913.

_____. *Recollections of a Long and Satisfactory Life*. Savannah, Ga.: Press of Review Print Co., c.1934.

Henderson, Lillian. *Roster of the Confederate Soldiers of Georgia 1861-1865*. Hapeville, Ga.: Longino & Porter, Inc., 1960.

Henderson, Lindsey P., Jr. *The Oglethorpe Light Infantry: A Military History*. Savannah, Ga.: The Civil War Centennial Commission of Savannah and Chatham County, 1961.

Hesseltine, William Best. *Civil War Prisons: A Study in War Psychology*. New York: 1978.

Joslyn, Mauriel Phillips. *Immortal Captives: The Story of 600 Confederate Officers and the United States Prisoner of War Policy*. Shippensburg, Pa.: White Mane Publishing, 1995.

La Bree, Benjamin. *The Confederate Soldier in the Civil War*. New York: Fairfax Press, 1977.

Lane, Mills. *Architecture of the Old South: Georgia*. Savannah, Ga.: Beehive Press, 1986.

_____. *Dear Mother, Don't Grieve for Me*. Savannah, Ga.: Beehive Press, 1977.

McMurry, Richard M. *Footprints of a Regiment*. Atlanta: Longstreet Press, 1992.

Miles, Jim. *Fields of Glory: A History and Tour Guide of Sherman's March.* Nashville: Rutledge Hill Press, 1989.

Miller, Francis Trevelyan. "Prisons and Hospitals." *The Photographic History of the Civil War*, Pt. 7. Reprint. New York: Castle Books, 1957.

Myers, Robert Manson. *Children of Pride.* New Haven, Conn.: Yale Univ. Press, 1971.

Purdue, Howell and Elizabeth. *Pat Cleburne, Confederate General.* Tuscaloosa, Ala.: Hill Jr. College Press. 1977.

Quarles, Garland R. *Some Old Homes in Frederick County, Virginia.* Winchester, Va.: Winchester-Frederick County Historical Society, 1990.

Robertson, James I., Jr. *Soldiers Blue and Gray.* Columbia, S.C.: Univ. of South Carolina Press, 1988.

Schroeder-Lein, Glenna R. *Confederate Hospitals on the Move: Samuel H. Stout and the Army of Tennessee.* Columbia, S.C.: Univ. of South Carolina Press, 1994.

Smedlund, William S. *Campfires of Georgia's Troopers, 1861-1865.* Kennesaw, Ga.: Kennesaw Mountain Press, 1994.

Sword, Wiley. *The Confederacy's Last Hurrah: Spring Hill, Franklin, and Nashville.* Reprint of *Embrace an Angry Wind.* New York: Harper Collins Publishers, 1992.

INDEX